ANIMAL RIGHTS

ISSN 1546-6736

ANIMAL RIGHTS

Kim Masters Evans

INFORMATION PLUS® REFERENCE SERIES
Formerly Published by Information Plus, Wylie, Texas

THOMSON

GALE™

Detroit • New York • San Francisco • New Haven, Conn. • Waterville, Maine • London

THOMSON
™
GALE

Animal Rights

Kim Masters Evans
Paula Kepos, Series Editor

Project Editors
Kathleen J. Edgar, John McCoy

Permissions
Edna Hedblad, Jhanay Williams

Composition and Electronic Prepress
Evi Seoud

Manufacturing
Cynde Bishop

ISBN-13: 978-0-7876-5103-9 (set)
ISBN-10: 0-7876-5103-6 (set)
ISBN-13: 978-1-4144-0743-2
ISBN-10: 1-4144-0743-2
ISSN 1546-6736

This title is also available as an e-book.
ISBN-13: 978-1-4144-2948-9 (set), ISBN-10: 1-4144-2948-7 (set)
Contact your Gale Group sales representative for ordering information.

Printed in the United States of America
10 9 8 7 6 5 4 3 2 1

TABLE OF CONTENTS

PREFACE

Animal Rights is part of the *Information Plus Reference Series*. The purpose of each volume of the series is to present the latest facts on a topic of pressing concern in modern American life. These topics include today's most controversial and most studied social issues: abortion, capital punishment, care of senior citizens, the environment, health care, immigration, minorities, national security, social welfare, women, youth, and many more. Although written especially for the high school and undergraduate student, this series is an excellent resource for anyone in need of factual information on current affairs.

By presenting the facts, it is the Gale Group's intention to provide its readers with everything they need to reach an informed opinion on current issues. To that end, there is a particular emphasis in this series on the presentation of scientific studies, surveys, and statistics. These data are generally presented in the form of tables, charts, and other graphics placed within the text of each book. Every graphic is directly referred to and carefully explained in the text. The source of each graphic is presented within the graphic itself. The data used in these graphics are drawn from the most reputable and reliable sources, in particular from the various branches of the U.S. government and from major independent polling organizations. Every effort has been made to secure the most recent information available. The reader should bear in mind that many major studies take years to conduct and that additional years often pass before the data from these studies are made available to the public. Therefore, in many cases the most recent information available in 2007 dated from 2004 or 2005. Older statistics are sometimes presented as well, if they are of particular interest and no more-recent information exists.

Although statistics are a major focus of the *Information Plus Reference Series*, they are by no means its only content. Each book also presents the widely held positions and important ideas that shape how the book's subject is discussed in the United States. These positions are explained in detail and, where possible, in the words of their proponents. Some of the other material to be found in these books includes: historical background; descriptions of major events related to the subject; relevant laws and court cases; and examples of how these issues play out in American life. Some books also feature primary documents or have pro and con debate sections giving the words and opinions of prominent Americans on both sides of a controversial topic. All material is presented in an even-handed and unbiased manner; the reader will never be encouraged to accept one view of an issue over another.

HOW TO USE THIS BOOK

Animals have been important to humans for around two million years as sources of food and other natural products, objects of worship and sport, and beasts of burden. But not until the seventeenth century did animal welfare much concern Western society. What legal and moral rights do animals currently possess in the United States and how does society balance such rights with animals' enormous economic value? How do "abolitionists" and "welfarists" differ on these and other issues? In what ways should governments protect, regulate, and control wildlife? Under what conditions are farm animals raised and slaughtered? Should research animals be used in medical and veterinary investigations, product testing, and science classes? Do horse racing, greyhound racing, sled dog racing, and rodeos cause unwarranted harm to animal participants? How should entertainment animals, service animals, and pets be treated? These and other basic questions are discussed in this volume.

Animal Rights consists of nine chapters and three appendixes. Each of the chapters is devoted to a particular aspect of animal rights in the United States. For a summary of the information covered in each chapter, please see the synopses provided in the Table of Contents at the front of the book. Chapters generally begin with an overview of the basic facts and background information on the chapter's topic, then proceed to examine subtopics of particular interest. For example, Chapter 5, Research Animals, begins with an overview of why and how animals are used for research—including product testing by businesses and dissection labs by students. This is followed by an examination of the history of animal research and its opposition. Next the chapter describes the major U.S. laws that govern animal research and the welfare of research animals. Then the use of animals in different types of research is examined in detail. Trends over time are highlighted. The chapter also features sections on animals and genetic engineering research, the sources of research animals, and efforts to end or limit the use of animals in research. Readers can find their way through a chapter by looking for the section and subsection headings, which are clearly set off from the text. Or, they can refer to the book's extensive Index, if they already know what they are looking for.

Statistical Information

The tables and figures featured throughout *Animal Rights* will be of particular use to the reader in learning about this topic. These tables and figures represent an extensive collection of the most recent and valuable statistics on animal rights, as well as related issues—for example, graphics in the book cover what species are on the federal list of endangered and threatened animals, the number of people who participate in recreational/sport fishing (or angling), what percentage of people believe that buying and wearing clothing made of animal fur is morally acceptable, and what type of animals are pursued by the vast majority of hunters. The Gale Group believes that making this information available to the reader is the most important way in which we fulfill the goal of this book: to help readers understand the issues and controversies surrounding animal rights in the United States and reach their own conclusions.

Each table or figure has a unique identifier appearing above it for ease of identification and reference. Titles for the tables and figures explain their purpose. At the end of each table or figure, the original source of the data is provided.

In order to help readers understand these often complicated statistics, all tables and figures are explained in the text. References in the text direct the reader to the relevant statistics. Furthermore, the contents of all tables and figures are fully indexed. Please see the opening section of the Index at the back of this volume for a description of how to find tables and figures within it.

Appendixes

In addition to the main body text and images, *Animal Rights* has three appendixes. The first is the Important Names and Addresses directory. Here the reader will find contact information for a number of government and private organizations that can provide further information on aspects of animal rights in America. The second appendix is the Resources section, which can also assist the reader in conducting his or her own research. In this section, the author and editors of *Animal Rights* describe some of the sources that were most useful during the compilation of this book. The final appendix is the Index.

ADVISORY BOARD CONTRIBUTIONS

The staff of Information Plus would like to extend its heartfelt appreciation to the Information Plus Advisory Board. This dedicated group of media professionals provides feedback on the series on an ongoing basis. Their comments allow the editorial staff who work on the project to make the series better and more user-friendly. Our top priorities are to produce the highest-quality and most useful books possible, and the Advisory Board's contributions to this process are invaluable.

The members of the Information Plus Advisory Board are:

- Kathleen R. Bonn, Librarian, Newbury Park High School, Newbury Park, California

- Madelyn Garner, Librarian, San Jacinto College— North Campus, Houston, Texas

- Anne Oxenrider, Media Specialist, Dundee High School, Dundee, Michigan

- Charles R. Rodgers, Director of Libraries, Pasco-Hernando Community College, Dade City, Florida

- James N. Zitzelsberger, Library Media Department Chairman, Oshkosh West High School, Oshkosh, Wisconsin

COMMENTS AND SUGGESTIONS

The editors of the *Information Plus Reference Series* welcome your feedback on *Animal Rights*. Please direct all correspondence to:

Editors
Information Plus Reference Series
27500 Drake Rd.
Farmington Hills, MI 48331-3535

CHAPTER 1

THE HISTORY OF HUMAN-ANIMAL INTERACTION

At the heart of the animal rights debate is the issue of how humans and animals should interact with each other. Are animals a natural resource for humans to use as they choose? Or are animals free beings with the right to live their lives without human interference? Is there an acceptable compromise somewhere in between? People answer these questions differently depending on their cultural practices, religious and ethical beliefs, and everyday experiences with animals. To understand how the debate has evolved over the centuries, it is necessary to examine history and see how the human-animal relationship developed and changed over time.

PREHISTORIC TIMES

Evolutionary science holds that humans are animals that have changed and adapted over hundreds of thousands of years to take on their current form. Biologists classify the human animal as a member of the order Primate, along with chimpanzees and gorillas. Some scientists believe that humans and other primates shared a common ancestor millions of years ago and that at some point human animals split off to form their own evolutionary path. Skeletons found throughout parts of Africa show both human and nonhuman characteristics.

Those who believe in the evolution theory think that human primates left the treetops and began walking upright, using their hands to make tools and increase their survivability. Most nonhuman primates basically had a vegetarian diet, but human primates began capturing small animals and scavenging for meat from carcasses left behind by predators such as lions. About two million years ago human primates began using stone tools and weapons. This was the beginning of the Stone Age. The use of stone-tipped spears allowed humans to hunt large game, such as wooly mammoths.

Hunter-Gatherers

In 1995 archaeologists found three wooden spears in a cave near Helmstedt, Germany. The spears were estimated to be about 400,000 years old. Humans at that time survived by hunting and fishing and by foraging for edible vegetation, nuts, and seeds; hence, they are called hunter-gatherers. Most lived as nomads, traveling in small groups from place to place. Once they had exhausted all the animals and plants in an area, they would move to a new location.

The earliest known cave drawings date back thirty thousand years and are located in France. In "Science Shows Cave Art Developed Early" (October 3, 2001, http://news.bbc.co.uk/1/hi/sci/tech/1577421.stm), the British Broadcasting Corporation reports that scientists have analyzed hundreds of prehistoric drawings in the Chauvet Caves of southern France and find them to be between 29,700 and 32,400 years old, making them the oldest known art in the world. Many cave drawings depict rhinoceroses, lions, buffalo, mammoths, and horses. Figure 1.1 shows a cave painting of a horse.

The vast majority of prehistoric cave drawings depict animals, not people. Some scientists believe that humans were in awe of the wild and fierce animals that they hunted. The hunters may have believed that they could exert some kind of magical power over animals by drawing pictures of them. Even though little is known for certain about the religious beliefs of the time, it is thought that prehistoric humans believed in a hidden world inhabited by the spirits of their dead ancestors, animals, and birds. Some spirits were considered good and others bad. People may have offered sacrifices of animals or other food to keep the spirits happy.

A belief system called animism has been traced back to the Paleolithic Age (the earliest period of the Stone Age). Animism is the belief that every object, living or not, contains a soul. Thus, animals, trees, and even rocks had spiritual meaning to prehistoric peoples. Anthropologists theorize that humans may have believed that they could capture the spirits (and thus the fierceness, strength,

FIGURE 1.1

Cave painting of a horse, c. 13,000 BC, Lascaux, France. *Corbis. Reproduced by permission.*

and speed) of wild animals by eating their flesh. Likewise, some wild animals may have been worshipped as gods by early humans.

Changing Climate

Around 15,000–13,000 BC the massive glaciers that had covered much of the northern hemisphere during the Great Ice Age began to subside. The habitats and food supplies for both humans and animals began to change. The hunter-gatherers had increasing difficulty finding the big game they had hunted before. Scientists believe that mammoths and many other large animals were driven to extinction around 10,000 BC because of climate changes, overhunting by humans, or both. Humans turned to hunting smaller animals and began gathering and cultivating plants in centralized locations. This major shift from nomadic life to settled existence had a tremendous effect on the human-animal relationship.

HUMANS DOMESTICATE ANIMALS

Between 13,000 and 2,500 BC humans domesticated dogs, cats, cattle, goats, horses, and sheep from their wild counterparts. Although the terms *taming* and *domestication* are often used interchangeably, they are not the same. Individual wild animals can be tamed to behave in a docile manner around humans. By contrast, domestication is a process that takes place with an entire animal species over many generations.

Characteristics of Domesticated Animals

Domesticated animals are not just tamer than their wild ancestors; they are different genetically. Over the ages, desirable qualities, such as size and disposition, were engrained by breeding only those animals that displayed them. This explains some of the physical differences between wild and domesticated animals. For example, most domesticated species are smaller and fatter and have smaller teeth and brains than their wild ancestors. (See Figure 1.2.)

Domestication of Dogs and Cats

The dog is thought to have been the first animal to be domesticated by humans, sometime around 13,000–10,000 BC, from its wolflike ancestor *Canis lupus*. Scientists believe that humans either adopted cubs and raised them or just began to accept into their groups some of the less fierce wolves that hung around their camps scrounging for leftovers. In either event, humans soon found dogs to be a welcome addition. The arrangement benefited both sides, as domesticated wolves helped humans with hunting and guarding duties and shared the food that was obtained.

Although cat remains have been found in settlements that date back to 8,000 BC, it is not clear if these were domesticated cats or small wild cats that were tolerated by or even encouraged to live near the people living there. Cat bones mixed with human and rat bones found on the island of Cyprus date back to around 5,000 BC. Because wild cats are not native to the island, cats must have been transported there by humans on purpose, probably to control the rat population.

The ancient Egyptians are usually credited with domesticating wild cats (*Felis silvestris libyca*, originating in Africa and southwestern Asia) around 4,000 BC. The Egyptians most likely raised cats from small kittens to protect their grain stores from rats and mice. Cat domestication is strongly associated with the establishment of permanent settlements and the growing and storage of grains. Cats became important to agricultural societies, just as dogs had been important to hunting cultures.

Domestication of Livestock

The domestication of livestock—chiefly pigs, cows, sheep, horses, and goats—is thought to have occurred between 9,000 and 5,000 BC as agriculture became more of a factor in human societies scattered across Asia and Europe.

History shows that the most suitable animals for domestication (and use by humans) are those that naturally live in groups with a hierarchical social structure. This allows humans to assume a dominant role in the hierarchy and exert control over the animals' behavior. Of the animals that have been domesticated, only cats and ferrets are considered to exhibit solitary lifestyles rather than herd/group behavior. In fact, scientists are not convinced that all species of cats and ferrets are completely domesticated in the classic sense.

FIGURE 1.2

Domestic farm animals and their ancestors

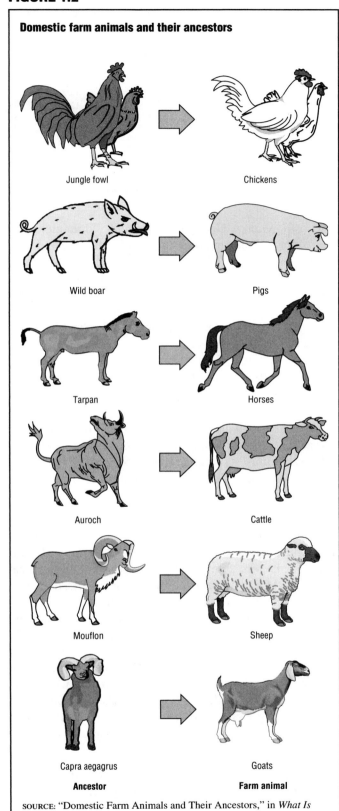

Jungle fowl → Chickens

Wild boar → Pigs

Tarpan → Horses

Auroch → Cattle

Mouflon → Sheep

Capra aegagrus → Goats

Ancestor → **Farm animal**

SOURCE: "Domestic Farm Animals and Their Ancestors," in *What Is Animal Domestication?* University of Saskatchewan, College of Agriculture and Bioresources, http://ag2.usask.ca/in_the_community/displays/what/animdom.html (accessed January 3, 2007)

The ability to keep and control groups of meat-supplying animals allowed humans to give up their previously nomadic lives and produce excess food. This freed people to build cities and roads, invent new things, and cultivate the arts.

ANCIENT CULTURES AND RELIGIONS

The peoples of most ancient civilizations were polytheistic (meaning that they believed in more than one god). Many ancient peoples worshipped animals as gods, used animals to represent their gods, or thought that their gods could assume animal form when they wished. At various times, ancient Egyptians held different animals as sacred and as representations of their gods and goddesses. Some animals may have been worshipped as deities, but others were most likely used to present deities in a recognizable form.

Some early civilizations also worshipped heavenly bodies, such as the sun and moon. These cultures believed that the stars and planets had magical influences over earthly events. They tracked the positions and aspects of the heavenly bodies closely and believed that such information could be used to foresee the future. Astrology and the zodiac evolved from these beliefs and were adopted by people in many different cultures, including the Babylonians, Egyptians, Hindus, and early Chinese. (See Table 1.1.) Most ancient zodiacs used animals to represent some or all the constellations. In fact, the word *zodiac* comes from the Greek term *zodion kuklos*, meaning "circle of little animals."

Although ancient Indians had varied spiritual beliefs, many of these beliefs were blended together into the practice of Hinduism around 3,000 BC. In general, Hindus believe that animals and people experience rebirths after they die. In other words, a human can be reincarnated as an animal, or vice versa. This means that all life forms are to be respected. Because Hindus consider virtually everything to be divine, they worship many animal gods and believe that their gods can take many forms, including human-animal forms.

Buddhism was founded during the sixth century by Siddhartha Gautama, an Indian philosopher who came to be called Buddha. Buddha believed that animals were important spiritually and were evolving toward a higher consciousness, just as humans were. Therefore, Buddhists consider it wrong to cause any harm to an animal or any other living being.

Jainism also originated in India and is similar in many respects to Buddhism, although it is perhaps much older. The Jains are so adamantly opposed to killing any life form that they allow themselves to be bitten by gnats and mosquitoes rather than swatting them. They often carry brooms so they can brush worms out of their path

TABLE 1.1

Chinese zodiac

Rat	Ox	Tiger	Rabbit	Dragon	Snake	Horse	Sheep	Monkey	Rooster	Dog	Boar
1912	1913	1914	1915	1916	1917	1918	1919	1920	1921	1922	1923
1924	1925	1926	1927	1928	1929	1930	1931	1932	1933	1934	1935
1936	1937	1938	1939	1940	1941	1942	1943	1944	1945	1946	1947
1948	1949	1950	1951	1952	1953	1954	1955	1956	1957	1958	1959
1960	1961	1962	1963	1964	1965	1966	1967	1968	1969	1970	1971
1972	1973	1974	1975	1976	1977	1978	1979	1980	1981	1982	1983
1984	1985	1986	1987	1988	1989	1990	1991	1992	1993	1994	1995
1996	1997	1998	1999	2000	2001	2002	2003	2004	2005	2006	2007
2008	2009	2010	2011	2012	2013	2014	2015	2016	2017	2018	2019

SOURCE: Created by Kim Masters Evans for Thomson Gale

to avoid stepping on them. The Jains strongly condemn the eating of any meat. They became well known in later centuries for their animal hospitals.

Archaeological evidence indicates that farming and animal husbandry were practiced in ancient China and that horse-drawn chariots were in use. (Animal husbandry is defined by the eleventh edition of *Merriam-Webster's Collegiate Dictionary* as "a branch of agriculture concerned with the production and care of domestic animals.") A Chinese emperor of the first century BC established the Garden of Intelligence, one of the largest zoos in the world. Confucianism is based on the teachings of Confucius, a Chinese philosopher who became famous for his sayings about how to live a happy and responsible life. In general, Confucius encouraged respect for animals, but not reverence. In other words, animals were not to be treated as deities. Killing animals for food was allowable, but killing them for sport was not.

Taoism is a spiritual philosophy that developed in China during the fifth and fourth centuries BC. Taoists believe that there is a power that envelops and flows through all living and nonliving things and that all life should be respected.

Hebrew Tribes and Judaism

The origins of Judaism lie with Hebrew tribes that populated the Mesopotamian region of the Middle East. Although the Hebrews followed various worship practices, including animism, they eventually developed a central religion known as Judaism. The followers of Judaism came to be called Jews. Judaism was unique among the many religions of the time because it is monotheistic. The Jews worship only one god instead of many gods. The Hebrew Bible—which is also called the Old Testament and comprises part of what later became the sacred text of Christianity—says that humans were created in the image of God. Therefore, the Hebrew God is anthropomorphic, or humanlike.

According to the first book (Genesis) of the Hebrew Bible, God created the earth and populated it with all kinds of creatures. God granted humans "dominion over the fish of the sea, and over the birds of the air, and over all the wild animals of the earth, and over every creeping thing that creeps upon the earth." This idea of dominion was to have a profound effect on Western civilization for centuries to come. However, the Old Testament also states that "the righteous person regards the life of his animals."

Arabic Cultures and Islam

The first kingdom appeared in the Arabian desert around 1,000 BC. Before that time the region was inhabited by scattered families and clans, many of whom were nomadic, called Bedouins, who raised camels. The Bedouins were animists who believed that spirits lived within all natural things. They also worshipped their ancestors and heavenly bodies.

Over the next few centuries society became more centralized, and the worship of many gods became common in temples and cults throughout the Arabian Peninsula. Islam was founded by the prophet Muhammad (570–632 AD), who believed in only one god. The Koran is the Islamic sacred text and includes many references to animals, particularly camels. Falcons, pigeons, cats, and horses were also considered important in early Islamic cultures. Legend has it that Muhammad was so fond of cats that he once cut a hole in his robe to keep from disturbing a cat that had fallen asleep on his sleeve. Muhammad also spoke highly of horses and considered their breeding to be an honorable task. The Arabs bred fine and fast horses that were used in warfare, transportation, and sporting events.

Although the Koran does not specifically mention animal souls, it does teach respect for all living creatures.

Classical Greece

Even though Greece was associated with a variety of cultures, the classical Greek period from 500 to 323 BC was the most influential for future ideas about animals. The classical Greeks did not have one central philosophy but followed the teachings of various schools established by wise men and philosophers. Some of the most famous were Socrates, Plato, and Aristotle.

In general, animals were widely used for food, clothing, and work in Greek society. These uses were not questioned on moral or philosophical grounds because the people believed that everything in nature had a purpose. In other words, plants existed for animals and both plants and animals existed for the welfare and enjoyment of humans. However, the philosopher and mathematician Pythagoras and his followers did not eat meat because they believed that animals had souls. Many other Greeks, including Plato, recommended a vegetarian diet for ethical or practical reasons. Plato believed that a vegetarian diet made good economic sense because it required less land than animal husbandry to produce food.

Plato's student Aristotle is considered the father of zoology in Western history. He wrote extensively about animal anatomy, behavior, and reproduction in *History of Animals* and *On the Parts of Animals*. Aristotle believed that there was a natural hierarchy in which humans, animals, plants, and inanimate objects were arranged by their level of perfection. This arrangement came to be called the *scala naturae* or "ladder of nature." Later philosophers called it "The Great Chain of Being."

The top rungs of Aristotle's ladder were occupied by humans, because Aristotle believed that they alone had rational souls that were capable of belief, reason, and thought. Below the humans were animals; Aristotle believed that animals had limited souls that allowed them to feel, but not to reason. Plants had the lowest forms of souls and ranked the lowest on the ladder. Among humans, Aristotle believed that there was a natural hierarchy, with free men ranked above slaves, women, and children. Aristotle's ideas about the rank of humans and animals in society would influence thinking in Western cultures for centuries.

Christianity

Christianity began as a sect of Judaism during the first century AD. Its followers believe that God had come among them in the form of a human named Jesus Christ. They set down their beliefs in scriptures that came to be known as the New Testament of the Bible.

Christ's followers considered Jesus's death to be a human sacrifice, similar to the animal sacrifices that were common in Jewish religious practice. This symbolism played an important role in the new religion. The New Testament mentions many animals, but mostly in the context of everyday life and as food sources. Christians did maintain the belief from the Hebrew Bible that humans had dominion over animals. The importance of the human soul was central to Christian theology. Many Christian philosophers of later centuries, such as Saint Augustine, argued that only humans (not animals) had rational minds and souls.

Roman Empire

The Roman Empire actually began as a single city, the city of Rome, which became a republic in 510 BC. The Romans had a warrior mentality and built their empire by conquering other peoples and cultures. The rulers of the Roman Empire delighted in brutal competitions and sports and invented many "games" to entertain their citizens. The Coliseum of Rome was a massive arena that featured events in which wild animals fought to the death with each other or with humans. Ancient texts describe the deaths of bulls, lions, tigers, elephants, and other animals. Often, the animals were chained together or tormented with burning irons and darts to make the fighting fiercer.

Historical evidence shows that the Romans were fond of horses. Their economy, troops, and postal service were dependent on the work done by horses. The Romans also practiced animal husbandry with cattle, pigs, sheep, goats, and chickens and kept cats and dogs as pets or working animals. Christianity became the official religion of the Roman Empire in AD 325. This put an end to the killing of humans in the Coliseum, because the human soul is sacred to Christianity. There is no evidence that animal games ceased, however, until the empire became too poor to acquire exotic and wild animals for them.

MEDIEVAL PERIOD

In general, Europe's medieval period, also called the Middle Ages, is considered the era from the fall of the Roman Empire in the late fifth century through the sixteenth century. The early centuries of the period are called the Dark Ages, because few known scientific and cultural achievements were made by Western societies during this time. Once the Roman emperors were gone, the authorities of the Christian church began to hold great power over the peoples of Europe.

Saint Francis of Assisi is arguably the most famous animal lover of the medieval period in Europe. The Franciscan friar was said to preach to birds and animals and release captured animals from traps. There are many legends about the saint, the most famous being that he once convinced a wolf to stop terrorizing a town and eating the livestock. Saint Francis was said to have "the gift of sympathy" for animals and in modern Catholicism is the patron saint of animals and ecology.

One of the most influential philosophers of the Middle Ages was Saint Thomas Aquinas. In 1264 he published *Of God and His Creatures*, in which he included a section titled "That the Souls of Dumb Animals Are Not Immortal." Aquinas argued that animals can neither understand nor reason and that their actions are driven entirely by natural instincts rather than by "art" or self-consciousness. Because animals can comprehend only the present and not the future, Aquinas believed that their souls are not immortal like human souls.

Crusades

During the medieval period the Christian church worked to stamp out paganism, cults, animal worship, and all other non-Christian beliefs. Many Crusades, or holy wars, were launched between 1095 and 1291 to try to conquer the Muslims, who had taken over Jerusalem. Many people (and horses) on both sides were killed in these wars.

Domestic crusades were also launched against groups and individuals throughout Europe who were considered dangerous to the church or its teachings. Medieval people became obsessed with the devil and believed that he and his servants assumed human and animal forms. Although different animals were suspected of being agents of the devil at different times and places, the cat was by far the most closely associated with evil. During the Middle Ages roughly a million cats were burned at the stake, along with their owners, on suspicion of being witches. By the beginning of the fourteenth century, Europe's cat population had been severely depleted. Only semiwild cats survived in many areas.

In 1347 the bubonic plague swept across Europe. Called the Black Death, it killed twenty-five million people (nearly a third of Europe's population) in only three years. The disease was spread to humans by fleas on infected rodents. Centuries of cat slaughter had allowed the rodent population to surge out of control. The persecution of cats during the Middle Ages seems to have been unique to Europe. In Asia and the Middle East during the same period, cats retained their prestige as protectors of grains and other food supplies.

AGE OF ENLIGHTENMENT AND THE USE OF VIVISECTION

The centuries immediately following the Middle Ages are called the Age of Enlightenment because waves of intellectual and scientific advancement swept across Europe. Many superstitions and customs disappeared as societies became more urban and less rural. Church authorities began to lose much of their power over people's lives. Medical researchers gained permission to perform autopsies (mostly on executed prisoners) to learn about human anatomy. Autopsies had been forbidden by the church for centuries, and little medical progress had been made in the field of anatomy since the second century, when the Roman doctor Galen practiced dissection on gladiators and animals. Animal experimentation was to become a major research tool of modern medicine.

In 1543 the Belgian doctor Andreas Vesalius published "Some Observations on the Dissection of Living Animals" in *De Humani Corporis Fabrica*. Vesalius hoped to convince other doctors that the study of anatomy was essential to improving medical care. He advocated cutting open living animals to teach students about blood circulation.

During the 1600s the French philosopher and mathematician René Descartes published some influential essays in which he argued that animals could not think at all. Descartes said that only humans had eternal souls; thus, only humans could reason. He described the human gift of language as proof that humans were philosophically different from animals. Descartes was fascinated with the field of mechanics and extended its ideas to nonhuman animals. He wrote that animals were mechanical things like clocks and therefore could not feel pain. This helped make it socially acceptable to cut open animals while they were still alive for medical and scientific purposes. The process became known as vivisection and was widespread in Europe in the seventeenth and eighteenth centuries.

Literature from this time describes live dogs being nailed to tables in classrooms and dissected to learn about their anatomy. Writers dismissed the cries of the dogs as being similar to the screeching sounds that a piece of machinery makes when it is forcibly taken apart.

BLOOD SPORTS

As the Middle Ages drew to a close, sports in which animals were pitted against each other became popular in England. These "blood sports" included bull- and bear-baiting with dogs, cockfighting, and dog fighting.

Baiting began as more of a practical matter than a sport. Medieval people believed that an animal that was whipped immediately before slaughter would provide more tender meat. Whippings administered by butchers eventually evolved into events where teams of dogs were allowed to set upon bulls and bite and tear at their flesh. Such baitings soon became popular entertainment and were expanded to include other animals, such as bears. Baiting events were generally held in a ring or arena or in a field near a town's shops.

Most church authorities considered animal blood sports to be harmless pastimes, but this was not true of the Puritans. The Puritans were a Christian group that wanted to change the Church of England. In 1583 Puritan social reformer Philip Stubbes published *The Anatomie of Abuses* in which he asked, "What Christian heart can take pleasure to see one poor beast rend, tear, and kill another?" The Puritans took power over the British Parliament in the mid-1600s and outlawed baiting and other blood sports for a short time. When the Puritans were thrown out of power, blood sports returned and became even more popular.

MOVE TO AMERICA

During the seventeenth century many Puritans fled England for the New World—North America. The Puritans brought their unique perspective on animals with them. In 1641 the Massachusetts Bay Colony enacted a Body of Liberties that set out the fundamental rights of the colonists. Included in these rights was Article 92, which stated, "No man shall exercise any Tirranny or Crueltie towards any Bruite creature which are usuallie kept for man's use." This is generally considered the first modern law against animal cruelty; however, it did not have a major effect on American laws or customs regarding animals.

Livestock was vitally important to the new colonies because of its economic value. Thus, laws were passed making it a capital crime to kill a farm animal without the owner's permission.

EUROPEAN PHILOSOPHERS ARGUE AGAINST CRUELTY TO ANIMALS

Meanwhile, in Europe new social and philosophical movements were to have far-reaching effects on the welfare of animals. During the seventeenth and eighteenth centuries several notable philosophers and writers spoke out against the mistreatment of animals. John Locke of England wrote that children should be taught from an early age that torturing and killing any living thing was despicable. In 1713 the poet Alexander Pope wrote the article "Against Barbarity to Animals" for London's *Guardian* newspaper.

David Hume of Scotland advocated "gentle usage" of animals for the sake of humanity. The German philosopher Immanuel Kant argued that cruelty to animals easily escalated to cruelty to humans and should therefore be stopped. Stopping animal cruelty for the sake of humans became a rather popular idea and was embraced more easily than the idea of preventing cruelty just for animals' sake.

In 1751 the British artist William Hogarth released a series of etchings and engravings called *The Four Stages of Cruelty*. The graphic images depicted the life of a fictional boy named Tom Nero who graduates from harming animals as a child to harming people as an adult. In the first scene the boy, in a white cap, tortures a dog with an arrow. Although one boy tries to stop him, the boys are surrounded by other children also torturing animals. In the second scene Tom Nero is shown as a young man beating a horse on the street, while other acts of animal cruelty take place around him. The third scene shows fully grown Tom Nero immediately after he has

murdered his girlfriend. In the fourth scene Tom Nero has been hanged for his crime, and his body is being dissected at a medical school.

Hogarth's intention was to illustrate some of the horrors of animal cruelty, but the connection between cruelty to animals and cruelty to humans was what captured people's attention. Even those who did not care about animal issues could see the dangers to civilized society of ignoring animal cruelty.

In 1764 the "mechanical animal" theory advocated by Descartes during the previous century was attacked by the French philosopher François-Marie Arouet de Voltaire in *Dictionnaire Philosophique Portatif*. Voltaire argued that the scientists who dissected live animals found "organs of feeling" within them similar to those of humans, thus proving that animals could indeed feel pain.

In 1776 the Anglican clergyman Humphrey Primatt published *A Dissertation on the Duty of Mercy and the Sin of Cruelty to Brute Animals*. Primatt wrote, "Pain is pain, whether it is inflicted on man or on beast." He equated cruelty to animals with sin and even atheism, and complained that legal authorities were doing little to stop it. Primatt argued that eliminating barbaric practices against animals might cut down on the number of "shocking murders" that were occurring.

One of the most poignant pleas for animals was made by the British philosopher and political scientist Jeremy Bentham. In 1789 he published *An Introduction to the Principles of Morals and Legislation*, in which he advocated making cruelty to animals punishable by law. Bentham wrote, "The question is not, Can they reason? Nor, Can they talk? but, Can they suffer?" Toward the end of the eighteenth century a few court cases were successfully tried against people who had abused animals, but only because the animals did not belong to the guilty parties.

BRITISH LAW TAKES HOLD

Modern legal protections for animals date back to nineteenth-century England. In 1822 Richard Martin, a member of the Parliament, sponsored a bill prohibiting cruelty to cattle, horses, and sheep. It became the first anticruelty law of its kind.

"Humanity Martin," as he came to be called, soon learned that having a law in effect and getting it enforced were two different things. The authorities were not interested in spending time gathering evidence and prosecuting animal abuse cases. Martin conducted his own investigations and managed to get a conviction and fine levied against a man for beating horses. He was helped in his efforts by a group of people led by the Reverend Arthur Broome. In 1824 this group became the Society for the

Prevention of Cruelty to Animals (SPCA). Although people had tried to form such societies before, most notably in 1808 in Liverpool, this was the first time that a group fighting against animal abuse had legal backup for its endeavors. The SPCA managed to win 149 convictions against abusers during its first year of operation.

In 1835 Martin's original act was expanded to protect dogs and bulls. In addition, cockfighting and the practice of baiting were outlawed. In 1840 the SPCA was recognized by Queen Victoria and became the Royal Society for the Prevention of Cruelty to Animals (RSPCA). The RSPCA appointed inspectors to patrol the markets and slaughterhouses of London and other large cities looking for abuses. The group continued to push for new and tougher legislation against animal cruelty, and the Cruelty to Animals Act was passed in 1849 (and amended in 1854). This act made many common abuses against animals illegal, including cropping (shortening by cutting) a dog's ears. It also spelled out rules for the proper treatment of animals during their impoundment and transport to slaughter. The act was amended again in 1876 to restrict the use of animals in research.

Many people involved in furthering animal welfare in England were also involved in other humanitarian movements of the time, including child welfare and anti-slavery causes. They believed that these issues were all related by common problems: abuse of power and the domination of the strong over the weak using cruel measures. There was also a growing moral belief that permitting cruelty to animals would lead to violence against humans and weaken society in general. It was also during the mid-1800s that the keeping of pets became popular among the middle classes.

U.S. LAW

Early U.S. law was patterned after British common law, which viewed animals as pieces of property. However, the reform movements that swept England during the nineteenth century also reached the United States. The Animal Legal and Historical Center (2007, http://www.animallaw.info/historical/statutes/sthusny1829.htm) notes that in 1828 the state of New York passed the first law against animal cruelty, which read: "Every person who shall maliciously kill, maim or wound any horse, ox or other cattle, or any sheep, belonging to another, or shall maliciously and cruelly beat or torture any such animal, whether belonging to himself or another, shall, upon conviction, be adjudged guilty of a misdemeanor."

Within the next decade similar laws were passed in states throughout the Northeast and Midwest. Some state laws covered only livestock, whereas others included all domestic animals. Some laws applied only if the animal belonged to someone other than the abuser.

In 1866 Henry Burgh founded the American Society for the Prevention of Cruelty to Animals (ASPCA). Fashioned after the RSPCA, the ASPCA received permission from the New York Legislature to enforce anticruelty laws in the state. This meant that ASPCA officers could arrest and seek convictions of animal abusers. Burgh was elected the first ASPCA president and held that post for twenty-two years. Similar societies soon formed in other major cities, including Philadelphia and Boston.

Vivisection, practiced at Europe's medical schools for some time, had also been incorporated into U.S. medical training. In 1871 Harvard University established one of the first vivisection laboratories in the country. The Massachusetts SPCA launched an aggressive media campaign to educate the public about the cruelties of vivisection and turn public support against the university. Antivivisection societies were also started in Illinois and New England, but their attempts to outlaw the practice failed.

The first federal law in the United States dealing with animal cruelty was the Twenty-Eight Hour Law of 1873. This law required that livestock being transported across state lines be rested and watered at least once every twenty-eight hours during the journey.

MODERN TIMES

By the early twentieth century American society was becoming increasingly urban and industrial. Working animals, such as horses, were gradually replaced with machinery on farms and city streets. The growing middle class had more time and money for leisure activities, many of which involved animals—hunting, fishing, keeping pets, and visiting wildlife refuges, circuses, zoos, and animal parks. Horseracing and greyhound racing both became popular sports in the 1930s as many states legalized this type of gambling.

In 1938 the Food, Drug, and Cosmetics Act was passed. This legislation required animal testing of certain chemicals and drugs to ensure their safety for human use. It was to have a profound effect on the human-animal relationship and later debates on the topic of animal rights. Following World War II (1939–45), the use of animals in medical and scientific research exploded. The demand for dogs and cats in the laboratory led to animal procurement laws in many states, allowing scientists to obtain test subjects from dog pounds and animal shelters.

By this time, the country's animal protection organizations had largely turned their attention from farm animals to pets. Some people within these groups were deeply opposed to the use of animals in research, whereas others saw it as a regrettable necessity. Differences in opinion led to splintering and the formation of new

TABLE 1.2

Animal protection organizations founded, selected years 1951–91

Organizations founded	
1951	Animal Welfare Institute
1954	Humane Society of the U.S.
1955	Society for Animal Protective Legislation
1957	Friends of Animals
1959	Catholic Society for Animal Welfare (now ISAR)
	Beauty Without Cruelty
1967	Fund for Animals
	United Action for Animals
1968	Animal Protection Institute
	Canadian Council on Animal Care
1969	International Fund for Animal Welfare
1971	Greenpeace
1973	International Primate Protection League (IPPL)
1974	North American Vegetarian Society (NAVS)
1976	Animal Rights International (ARI)
	Committee to Abolish Sport Hunting (CASH)
1977	Sea Shepherd Conservation Society
	Scientists Center for Animal Welfare
	American Fund for Alternatives to Animal Research
1978	Animal Legal Defense Fund (ALDF)
	Medical Research Modernization Committee
1979	Committee to End Animal Suffering in Experiments (CEASE)
1980	People for the Ethical Treatment of Animals (PETA)
	Psychologists for the Ethical Treatment of Animals (PsyETA)
	Student Action Corps for Animals (SACA)
1981	Farm Animal Reform Movement (FARM)
	Trans-Species Unlimited (TSU)
	Mobilization for Animals (MfA)
	Association of Veterinarians for Animal Rights (AVAR)
1981	Johns Hopkins Center for Alternatives to Animal Testing (CAAT)
	Primarily Primates Sanctuary
1982	Food Animal Concerns Trust (FACT)
	Vegetarian Resource Group (VRG)
	National Alliance for Animal Legislation (NAA)
	Feminists for Animal Rights (FAR)
1983	In Defense of Animals (IDA)
1984	Humane Farming Association (HFA)
	Performing Animal Welfare Society (PAWS)
1985	Physicians Committee for Responsible Medicine (PCRM)
	Last Chance for Animals (LCA)
	Culture and Animals Foundation (CAF)
	Tufts Center for Animals and Public Policy
1986	Farm Sanctuary
	Animal Welfare Information Center (AWIC)
1988	Doris Day Animal League (DDAL)
1990	United Poultry Concerns
1991	Ark Trust

SOURCE: Adapted from Deborah J. Salem and Andrew N. Rowan, "Milestones in Postwar Animal Protection," in *The State of the Animals: 2001*, Humane Society of the United States, 2001

organizations. The Animal Welfare Institute and the Humane Society of the United States (HSUS) were both founded in the early 1950s. Table 1.2 lists other organizations devoted to animal welfare that were founded between 1951 and 1991.

Animal protection groups began to develop separate identities and missions. Some retained a local focus, whereas others focused on national issues. They gained an ally in Senator Hubert Humphrey, a Democrat from Minnesota, who championed animal causes as well as civil rights and other social movements. Humphrey was instrumental in the passage of the Humane Methods of Slaughter Act of 1958. The law required the use of humane slaughter methods at slaughterhouses subject to federal inspection. It was the first piece of federal animal protection legislation in eighty-five years.

The next year Congress passed the Wild Horses Act to outlaw the use of motorized vehicles and the poisoning of watering holes "for the purpose of trapping, killing, wounding, or maiming" wild horses on federal lands.

In the 1960s another animal issue, this time dog-related, achieved national prominence because of the efforts of a handful of people. Pepper was a family pet that disappeared from her backyard in Pennsylvania in 1965 and wound up dead in a New York City laboratory. Pepper's family diligently tracked down what had happened to her and helped expose a network of shady animal dealers and pet thieves selling animals by the pound to research laboratories. The public demanded action. In 1966 Congress passed the Laboratory Animal Welfare Act, which required the licensing of animal dealers and the regulation of laboratory animals. It is still the primary federal law that covers the welfare of animals used in research and public exhibitions and that regulates aspects of the handling, transport, care, and commerce related to covered animals. The major provisions of the act and its four amendments are shown in Table 1.3.

Several other federal laws were passed in the 1960s and 1970s designed to protect wild animals, including eagles, seals, and endangered species. Some animal protection issues were intertwined with causes devoted to conservation, ecology, and the environment. "Save the Whales" became a popular slogan.

Animal Rights Becomes an Issue

In 1975 a new twist developed in an old movement. The Australian philosopher Peter Singer published the book *Animal Liberation: A New Ethics for Our Treatment of Animals*, which calls for a fundamental change in the human-animal relationship. Singer argues that animals are victimized by humans on a massive scale because of a social evil called speciesism, a term he uses for the widespread belief that the human species is superior to all others. Singer equates humans' mistreatment of animals throughout history with racism and sexism and blamed speciesism for the systematic abuse of animals in agriculture, research, and other human activities. The year after Singer's book was published, Animal Rights International was founded by social reformer Henry Spira.

Some people working for animal causes embraced the idea that animals are not resources to be protected by benevolent humans but individual beings with their own interests and rights. This meant that humans could not use animals for any purpose (food, clothing, sport, entertainment, and so on) because it was morally and ethically wrong to do so. This opened a new agenda in the animal welfare movement that went beyond calls for kind treatment and humane methods of slaughter. Adherence to the

TABLE 1.3

The Animal Welfare Act and its amendments

Laboratory Animal Welfare Act Public Law 89-544 (August 24, 1966)

Authorizes the Secretary of Agriculture to regulate transport, sale, and
   handling of dogs, cats, nonhuman primates, guinea pigs, hamsters, and rabbits
   intended to be used in research or "for other purposes."
Requires licensing and inspection of dog and cat dealers and humane
   handling at auction sales.

Animal Welfare Act of 1970 Public Law 91-579 (December 24, 1970)

Expands the list of animals covered by the act.
Incorporates exhibitors into the act and defines research facilities.
Exempts retail pet stores, state and county fairs, rodeos, purebred dog and
   cat shows, and agricultural exhibition.
Directs development of regulations regarding recordkeeping and humane care
   and treatment of animals in or during commerce, exhibition, experimentation,
   and transport.
Establishes inspections, and appropriate anesthetics, analgesics, and tranquilizers.
   Includes regulations on dog and cat commerce.

Animal Welfare Act Amendments of 1976 Public Law 94-279 (April 22, 1976)

Primarily refines previous regulations on animal transport and commerce.
Licenses, method of payment, and penalties for violations are discussed.
Introduces and defines "animal fighting ventures."
Exempts animals used in hunting waterfowl, foxes, etc.
Makes it illegal to exhibit or transport via interstate or foreign commerce
   animals used in fighting ventures such as dogs or roosters.

**Food Security Act of 1985, Subtitle F-Animal Welfare also called "The Improved
Standards for Laboratory Animals Act" Public Law 99-198 (December 23, 1985)**

Clarifies and specifies "humane care" specifics such as sanitation, housing,
   and ventilation.
Directs development of regulations to provide exercise for dogs and an
   adequate physical environment to promote the psychological well-being of
   nonhuman primates.
Specifies that pain and distress must be minimized in experimental procedures
   and that alternatives to such procedures be considered by the principal
   investigator.
Defines practices that are considered to be painful.
Stipulates that no animal can be used in more than one major operative experiment
   with recovery (exceptions are listed).
Establishes the Institutional Animal Care and Use Committee (IACUC).
Forms an information service at the National Agricultural Library to assist those
   regulated by the act.
Explains the penalties for release of trade secrets by regulators and the regulated
   community.

**Food, Agriculture, Conservation, and Trade Act of 1990, Section 2503-Protection
of Pets Public Law 101-624 (November 28, 1990)**

Establishes a holding period for dogs and cats at shelters and other holding
   facilities before sale to dealers.
Requires dealers to provide written certification regarding each animal's
   background to the recipient.

SOURCE: Adapted from "Animal Welfare Act and Regulations," in *Animal
Care: Animal Welfare Act and Regulations*, U.S. Department of Agriculture,
Agricultural Research Service, National Agricultural Library, Animal
Welfare Information Center, 2006, http://www.nal.usda.gov/awic/legislat/
usdaleg1.htm (accessed January 8, 2007)

most radical animal rights theory meant that eating meat
and killing vermin were wrong. So were zoos and circuses, hunting and fishing, and experimenting on animals
to find cures for human diseases, no matter how
humanely any of these activities were carried out.

This philosophical leap was too much for many people, and the idea that animals had rights like humans was
not generally embraced. The public supported anticruelty
laws and animal protection measures (within reason) but
did not go so far as to say that animals have a moral
standing in society that makes it inherently wrong to eat

or use them. Opponents of animal rights argued that to do
so would go against centuries of tradition and beliefs,
disrupt many accepted systems for feeding and entertain-
ing people, have crippling economic consequences, hurt
millions of people who earned their living through animals, and impede scientific progress. Because of such
arguments, most Americans of the 1970s rejected the
idea of animal rights. So did most of the traditional
animal protection organizations, though they continued
their work to educate and reform.

However, the idea did not go away. More books
examining this issue were published, and new organizations formed, including People for the Ethical Treatment
of Animals (PETA) in 1980. Many others followed.
These animal rights groups were much bolder than traditional animal welfare organizations. They held protest
marches and publicly condemned companies and
research institutions using animals for various purposes.
The radical group Animal Liberation Front raided laboratories and farms to "free" animals and destroy property. The first such raid happened in 1979 at the New
York University Medical Center.

Some animal rights groups worked through the legal
system to achieve change, filing lawsuits and working
with prosecutors to strengthen animal protection laws.
The more traditional animal protection groups supported
these efforts. Legal reform was one area in which the
entire animal movement found some common ground.
The traditional groups increased their political power
during the 1980s through swelling membership rolls,
and animal issues gained momentum in society, particularly among pet owners.

LINK BETWEEN ANIMAL ABUSE
AND VIOLENCE AGAINST PEOPLE

As illustrated in Hogarth's artwork, there has long been
a belief that cruelty toward animals and cruelty toward
humans are related. In more recent times this belief has
been reinforced by scientific and anecdotal evidence. Many
notorious serial killers and mass murderers—including Jeffrey Dahmer, Ted Bundy, David Berkowitz ("Son of
Sam"), and Albert de Salvo ("the Boston Strangler")—
are known to have tortured and killed animals. Many of the
children who have carried out school shootings since the
1990s (notably Eric Harris and Dylan Klebold, who killed
twelve fellow students, one teacher, and themselves at
Columbine High School in Littleton, Colorado, in April
1999) had a history of cruelty to animals before they began
committing violent acts against humans.

The fourth edition of the American Psychiatric Association's *Diagnostic and Statistical Manual of Mental
Disorders* (1994) includes cruelty to animals in the broad
category of "conduct disorder." According to Frank
R. Ascione, Claudia V. Webber, and David S. Wood in

"The Abuse of Animals and Domestic Violence: A National Survey for Shelters of Women Who Are Battered" (*Society and Animals: Journal of Human-Animal Studies*, 1997), conduct disorder is "a pattern of antisocial behavior that can persist into adulthood." The American Academy of Child and Adolescent Psychiatry (July 2004, http://www.aacap.org/publications/factsfam/conduct.htm) also lists cruelty to animals as a typical behavior exhibited in conduct disorder.

Many animal welfare activists, sociologists, psychologists, and law enforcement officials agree that a person who has abused animals will likely become involved in further antisocial and/or criminal behavior at some point. In "A Social Sentinel: Acts of Animal Cruelty Can Point to an Offender's Potential for Violence against Humans" (October 5, 2005, http://www.arkonline.com/violence .html), Eleanor Shelburne notes that studies find that as many as 75% of incarcerated criminals in the United States have a history of torturing or killing animals. The National Crime Prevention Council reports in "Strategy: Screening Animal Cruelty Cases for Domestic Violence" (2005, http://www.ncpc.org/topics/Personal_Safety/Strategy _Screening_Animal_Cruelty_Cases_for_Domestic_Violence .php), a U.S. study of battered women who had sought the help of shelters, that 54% reported that their abuser had also tortured or killed animals in the home, versus 3% of women surveyed overall.

Given these data, animal abuse is increasingly recognized as a serious crime in itself, with more states bringing felony charges against offenders. Additionally, successful programs have been created across the United States that join animal welfare organizations, local law enforcement, animal control officers, and child protective services so that all parties can be trained to look for signs of both animal abuse and domestic violence.

RECENT RECORD OF THE ANIMAL MOVEMENT

By the 1990s the major animal welfare organizations were starting to achieve sufficient financial support and political clout to successfully pursue their efforts for change in two main areas: the courts and the ballot box. As of the beginning of 2007 the HSUS Animal Protection Litigation Section (http://www.hsus.org/in_the_courts/) employed ten full-time lawyers and was engaged in more than forty lawsuits pertaining to animal issues around the country. In many of the cases the HSUS was partnered with one or more other animal welfare or conservation organizations, such as the ASPCA or Defenders of Wildlife. Targets of the litigation included various corporate entities involved in animal-related businesses and government agencies in charge of implementing laws and regulations that pertain to animals.

Table 1.4 lists the major pieces of animal-related federal legislation that were passed or amended between

TABLE 1.4

Federal animal protection legislation passed or amended, selected years 1958–2003

Year	Federal legislation passed/amended
1958	Humane Methods of Slaughter Act
1959	Wild Horses Act
1962	Bald and Golden Eagle Act
1966	Endangered Species Act
	Laboratory Animal Welfare Act
1970	Animal Welfare Act (amendments to Laboratory Animal Welfare Act)
1971	Wild Free-Roaming Horse and Burro Act
1972	Marine Mammal Protection Act
1973	Endangered Species Act amendments
	CITES
1976	Animal Welfare Act amendments
	Horse Protection Act
	Fur Seal Act
1978	Humane Methods of Slaughter Act amendments
1985	Animal Welfare Act amendments (focus on alternatives and pain and distress)
	PHS Policy on animals in research revised
1990	Animal Welfare Act amendments
1992	Wild Bird Conservation Act
1993	International Dolphin Conservation Act
	Driftnet Fishery Conservation Act
	NIH Revitalization [Reauthorization] Act mandates development of research methods using no animals
1995	USDA ends face branding
1999	Ban on the interstate shipment of "crush videos"
2000	Chimpanzee Health Improvement, Maintenance, and Protection Act
2002	Dog and Cat Protection Act
	Interagency Coordinating Committee on the Validation of Alternative Methods (ICCVAM) Authorization Act
	Safe Air Travel for Animals Act
	Ban on interstate transportation of birds and dogs for fighting purposes
2003	Captive Exotic Animal Protection Act

SOURCE: Andrew N. Rowan and Beth Rosen, "Table 1. Federal Legislative Summary, 1958–2003," in *The State of the Animals III: 2005*, Humane Society of the United States, December 31, 2005, http://www.hsus.org/web-files/PDF/hsp/SOA_3-2005_Chap7.pdf (accessed November 28, 2006). Data from B. Unti and A.N. Rowan, "A Social History of Postwar Animal Protection," in *The State of the Animals: 2001*, Humane Society of the United States, 2001.

1958 and 2003. Table 1.5 highlights major accomplishments of the animal movement at the federal level from 1979 to 1983 and between 1999 and 2003. Both tables are from the HSUS report *The State of the Animals III* (December 31, 2005, http://www.hsus.org/web-files/PDF/hsp/SOA_3-2005_Chap7.pdf). The report notes that the animal movement rose "from political oblivion in the first half of the twentieth century to a position where lawmakers would listen if the context and the proposal were timely and supported by the societal and political mood."

One of the major issues at the federal level is funding for the Animal Welfare Act (AWA). Figure 1.3 shows federal monies appropriated (assigned) to enforcement of the AWA between 1970 and 2005 as reported by the HSUS. More than $16 million was appropriated to the AWA in 2005. Animal advocates believe that this amount is far too small to adequately ensure that the AWA is properly enforced by the U.S. Department of Agriculture

TABLE 1.5

Federal legislation benefiting the animal care and protection movement, selected years 1979–2003

	1979–1983	1999–2003
Animal Welfare Act	• Provision on marine mammal care care standards added	• USDA AWA* enforcement budget boosted by ca. 50 percent
Companion animals		• Interstate commerce in birds and dogs used in animal fighting prohibited
Cruelty issues		• Banned dog and cat fur products
Farm animals		• Banned "crush videos" (where small animals are tortured/crushed to death)
		• Obtained additional $6 million for enforcement of Humane Slaughter Act
		• Banned the use of downer cattle for human consumption
		• Obtained $703,000 for hoop barns for pig raising
Animals in research		• Passed legislation authorizing the Interagency Coordinating Committee for the Validation of Alternative Methods (ICCVAM)
		• Passed legislation authorizing a national sanctuary system for retired laboratory chimpanzees
Wildlife	• Passed Alaska Lands bill—designating more than 100 million acres in Alaska as parks or wildlife refuges	• Banned commerce in big cats for the pet trade
	• Added Marine Mammal Protection Act regulations	• Banned practice of cutting fins off sharks and discarding their bodies at sea while still alive
	• National Park Service published final regulations banning trapping on some lands	

*United States Department of Agriculture Animal Welfare Act.

SOURCE: Adapted from Andrew N. Rowan and Beth Rosen, "Table 3. Comparative Analysis of Federal Accomplishments," in *The State of the Animals III: 2005*, Humane Society of the United States, December 31, 2005, http://www.hsus.org/web-files/PDF/hsp/SOA_3-2005_Chap7.pdf (accessed November 28, 2006)

FIGURE 1.3

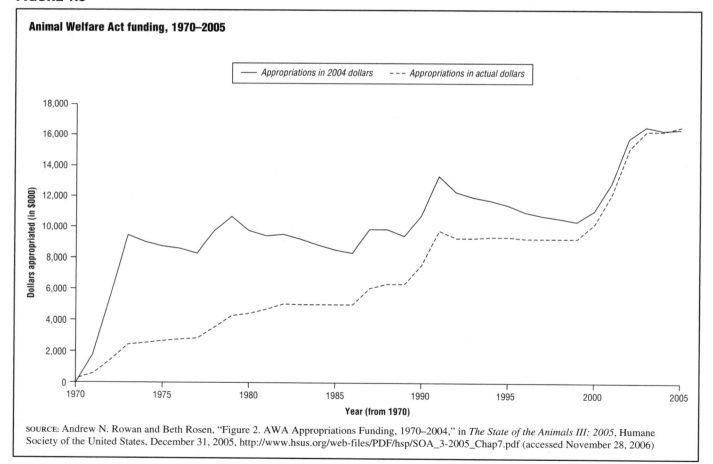

Animal Welfare Act funding, 1970–2005

SOURCE: Andrew N. Rowan and Beth Rosen, "Figure 2. AWA Appropriations Funding, 1970–2004," in *The State of the Animals III: 2005*, Humane Society of the United States, December 31, 2005, http://www.hsus.org/web-files/PDF/hsp/SOA_3-2005_Chap7.pdf (accessed November 28, 2006)

(USDA). USDA records shown in Table 1.6 list the number of AWA inspections conducted during fiscal year 2004—the most recent data available. More than eleven thousand compliance inspections were completed at the eighty-three hundred facilities covered by the AWA during that year. In addition, just over two thousand non-compliance (prelicensing) inspections were also conducted.

TABLE 1.6

Animal Welfare Act inspections, by facility type and inspection category, fiscal year 2004

	Total number of facilities	Number of inspections by category
Inspections for compliance		
Dealers	4,571	6,001
Research facilities	1,079	1,693
Exhibitors	2,284	3,577
Handlers	242	149
Carriers[a]	124	463
Attempted inspections[b]		976
Total	**8,300**	**11,883**
Non-compliance Inspections		
Prelicensing inspections		2,003
Total of inspections for compliance and non-compliance inspections		**13,886**

[a]Carriers is a category representing commercial airlines.
[b]Attempted inspections could not be performed because facility personnel were not available.
Note: Compliance and prelicensing inspections are unannounced.

SOURCE: "FY 2004 AWA Inspections," in *Animal Care Reports: Annual Reports of Enforcement by Fiscal Year: 2004*, U.S. Department of Agriculture, Animal and Plant Health Inspection Service, 2004, http://www.aphis.usda.gov/ac/awreports/awreport2004.pdf (accessed November 28, 2006)

In 2004 the HSUS launched a new arm called the Humane Society Legislative Fund (HSLF). According to the HSLF (2006, http://www.fund.org/about_us/), the organization "works to pass animal protection laws at the state and federal level, to educate the public about animal protection issues, and to support humane candidates for office." One of the goals of the HSLF is to convince voters at election time to support candidates it considers animal-friendly on the issues. It does this through targeted media campaigns and mass mailings to potential voters. The HSLF also compiles a Humane Scorecard for each session of Congress that grades every legislator on his or her voting and bill-sponsorship record as it relates to animal issues. Humane Scorecards for the 106th session (1999–2000) through the 109th session (2005–06) are available on the organization's Web site.

Many animal protection groups have actively pursued stricter state laws dealing with animal cruelty and neglect. According to the HSUS, only seven states had felony anticruelty laws at the end of the 1980s. As shown in Table 1.7, this number had grown to forty-four states as of April 2006. The six states lacking such statutes were Alaska, Arkansas, Hawaii, Idaho, North Dakota, and Utah. However, states vary widely in how the felony classification is applied to crimes against animals. For example, some states consider a first offense or convic-

tion for anticruelty to be a misdemeanor and subsequent offenses or convictions to be felonies. The species of the animal victims are also a factor in some state laws. Alabama law designates cruelty against dogs and cats as a felony, whereas other animals fall under the misdemeanor statute. The HSUS (2007, http://www.hsus.org/legislation_laws/citizen_lobbyist_center/animal_cruelty_laws_where_does_your_state_stand.html) urges its members to push for felony state anticruelty laws that meet all the following criteria:

- Apply to all species of animals
- Apply to first offenders
- Include large fines and long prison sentences as penalties
- Do not include exemptions
- Include counseling provisions for convicted abusers
- Prevent convicted abusers from owning or living with animals in the future

One of the ways in which animal organizations achieve change at the state level is through initiative petitions. These are petitions dealing with specific issues that receive enough signatures from the public to spur the inclusion of proposed measures on ballots during state elections. According to the *State of the Animals III*, initiative petition drives coordinated by animal protection groups were largely unsuccessful until 1990, when a new approach was undertaken. The HSUS and the Fund for Animals began selectively targeting specific animal issues in states where research indicated a good chance for collection of the signatures and the money needed to put particular measures on the ballot and win support for them on election day. Table 1.8 shows twenty-six animal protection initiatives and referendums passed by voters in various states between 1990 and 2002. Table 1.9 lists thirteen animal initiatives and referendums considered, but rejected, by voters between 1992 and 2002.

The midterm elections of November 2006 were hailed as a great victory for animals by the major animal protection groups in the country. According to the HSLF (November 8, 2006, http://www.fund.org/feature/2006_key_race_summary.html), 86% of the candidates for the U.S. Senate and 91% of the candidates for the U.S. House of Representatives it had endorsed were victorious. In addition, several statewide ballot measures were passed that animal welfare groups had championed—chiefly a ban on the use of confining cages for pigs and veal calves in Arizona and a defeat of a proposed mourning dove hunt in Michigan.

TABLE 1.7

Animal anti-cruelty laws, by state, April 2006

State	Statute number of cruelty law	Felony	Classification of crime/ maximum level of penalty	Maximum fine	Maximum jail time	Psychological counseling	Year enacted into a felony
Alabama	§13A-11-241	Yes	Class C felony on the first offense (cruelty in the first degree)	$5,000	10 years		2000
	§13A-11-14	No	Class B misdemeanor				
Alaska	11.61.140	No	Class A misdemeanor	$5,000	1 year		
Arizona	13-2910	Yes	Class 6 felony on the first offense	$150,000	1 year		1999
Arkansas	5-62-101	No	Class A misdemeanor	$1,000	1 year	May order (2001)	
California	597	Yes	Felony can apply on first conviction.	$20,000	1–3 years	Mandatory	1988
Colorado	18-9-202	Yes	Aggravated cruelty is a class 6 felony and any subsequent offense would be a class 5 felony.	Minimum $1,000 maximum $100,000	Class 6: min. 1 year, max. 18 mo.; class 5: min. 1 year, max. 3 years.	May order an evaluation or anger management treatment on the 1st offense. Shall order on the 2nd offense.	2002
Connecticut	53-247	Yes		$5,000	5 years	May order animal cruelty prevention or counseling & education program.	1996
Delaware	1325	Yes	Class F felony	$5,000	3 years		1994
District of Columbia	D.C. Code 22-1001	Yes	Felony	$25,000	5 years		2001
Florida	828.12	Yes	Felony of the third degree	$10,000	5 years	Psychological counseling/ anger management treatment is mandatory for acts of intentional torture/torment.	1989
Georgia	16-12-4 (b) (c)		First offense–misdemeanor. Second offense–misdemeanor for unjustifiable pain/suffering. Second offense of causing death is a high aggravated misdemeanor.	$1,000 (up to) $5,000 (up to) $10,000 (up to)	Up to 1 year Up to 1 year 3 months to 1 year.	Sentencing judge may require psychological evaluation and shall consider the entire criminal record of the offender.	2000
		Yes	First offense Second offense	$15,000 $100,000	1–5 years.		
Hawaii	711-1109	No	Misdemeanor	$2,000			1999
Idaho	25-304 Penalties 25-3520A definitions: 25-3502	No	3 stages of misdemeanor	$5,000– $9,000	6 months to 1 year.		
Illinois	510 §3.02 & 510 70/4.01& 70/16	Yes	Class 3 felony for torture on 1st offense. Class 4 felony for aggravated cruelty.	$50,000	3–5 years 1–3 years	May order	1999
Indiana	35-46-3-12	Yes	Class D felony on the first conviction of torture or mutilation.	$10,000	3 years	Mandatory evaluation and treatment.	1998 In 2002 felony on the first.
Iowa	717B.3A- Animal torture 717B.1 717B.2	Yes	Second offense committed is a Class D felony.	$7,500	5 years	Shall order	2000
Kansas	21-4310	Yes	First offense is a non-person misdemeanor.	$500–$5000	30 days to 1 year	Evaluation is mandated.	2006
Kentucky	525.135 525.130 class A mis.	Yes	First offense of torture is a Class A misdemeanor. Subsequent offenses are a Class D felony.	$1000–$10,000 $500–for misdemeanor	1–5 years for felony 1 year–for misdemeanor		2003
Louisiana	La. R.S.14: 102.1 (2004)	Yes		$25,000	10 years		1995

TABLE 1.7

Animal anti-cruelty laws, by state, April 2006 [CONTINUED]

State	Statute number of cruelty law	Felony	Classification of crime/ maximum level of penalty	Maximum fine	Maximum jail time	Psychological counseling	Year enacted into a felony
Maine	§7-4011 Civil	No	If two or more convictions of civil or criminal animal cruelty charges, a felony or max fine is charged.	$5,000	Not ordered in civil prosecution	Shall order if JV May order for all others	2001
	§17-1031 Criminal	Yes	Felony penalty for the first violation of aggravated animal cruelty.	$10,000	5 years		
Maryland	Criminal Law, § 10–606	Yes	First conviction of aggravated cruelty is a felony.	$5,000	3 years	May order	2001
Massachusetts	272 §77 and 266§112	Yes	First conviction is a felony.	$2,500	5 years in a the state prison or $2\frac{1}{2}$ in the house of correction		1804 increased penalties in 2004
Michigan	750 §50b	Yes	Felony	$5,000	4 years	May order	1931
Minnesota	343.21	Yes	Felony	10,000	2 years	May order	2001
Mississippi	97-41-16	No		$1,000	6 months		
	97-41-1	No		$1,000	6 months		
	97-41-15	Yes–for livestock only	Special felony for livestock (does not include companion animals or wildlife)	$1500–$10,000 $500	12 months–5 years		
Missouri	578.012	Yes	Class D felony (first offense of torture or mutilation)	$5,000	5 years		1994
Montana	45-8-217	Yes	First offense of aggravated cruelty is a felony.	Up to $2,500	2 years (Dept. of corrections).		1993
Nebraska	28-1009	Yes	The first conviction of torture, beating or mutilation is a IV degree felony.	$10,000	5 years	5 years	2002— 2nd offense, 2003— 1st offense
Nevada	574.100	Yes	The third offense committed is a felony.	$10,000	5 years	Mandatory for juveniles	1999
New Hampshire	RSA 644:8	Yes	First offense of beating or torturing	$4,000	7 years		1994
New Jersey	4:22-17	Yes	Crime of the fourth degree on the first offense (felony equivalent)	$15,000	3–5 years	Shall order juveniles for certain animal cruelty offenses	2001
New Mexico	30-18-1	Yes	"Extreme cruelty to animals" is a felony in the first offense. Fourth offense committed of "cruelty to animals" is a felony.	$5,000	18 months	May order Shall order for JV's.	1999
New York	353-a 55.10 penal law	Yes	Aggravated cruelty to a companion animal is a Class E felony.	$5,000 (§80)	4 years (§70)		1999
North Carolina	14-360	Yes	First offense of cruelly beating, mutilating, torturing, poisoning of killing any animal is a Class I felony.	$1,000	6 months		1998
North Dakota	36-21.1-02	No	Class A misdemeanor	$2,000	1 year		
Ohio	959.13	Yes	Second offense committed is a 5th degree felony.	$2,000	1 year	May order	2002
	959.02	No	1st degree misdemeanor	$1,000	180 days		
Oklahoma	21-1685	Yes	Felony on first offense committed	$5,000	5 years in state jail, 1 year in a county jail		1887
Oregon	167.322	Yes	Class C felony on the first offense	$100,000	5 years	May order	1995
Pennsylvania	18-5511	Yes	The second offense committed on a dog or cat is a felony of the 3rd degree. First offense committed on a zoo animal is a felony of the 3rd degree.	$15,000	7 years	May order (the court may order a presentence mental evaluation)	1995

TABLE 1.7

Animal anti-cruelty laws, by state, April 2006 [CONTINUED]

State	Statute number of cruelty law	Felony	Classification of crime/ maximum level of penalty	Maximum fine	Maximum jail time	Psychological counseling	Year enacted into a felony
Rhode Island	4-1-3		First offense committed is a felony.	$1,000	2 years	§4–1-36—May order an evaluation	1896
	4-1-4	Yes		$1,000			
South Carolina	47-1-40	Yes	First offense is a felony.	$5,000	5 years		2000
South Dakota	40-1-21 & 40-1-27	No No Yes for bestiality only	Class 1 misdemeanor	$1,000	1 year		
Tennessee	39-14-202 39-14-212	Yes	First offense of aggravated cruelty is a felony.		9 month minimum (mandatory) no suspended sentence or probation until 9 months are served.	Shall order	2001 2002 Felony on the 1st offense was passed in 2004
Texas	Sec. 42.09 Sec. 12.21 Sec. 12.35	Yes	Felony of the 3rd degree if the person has been convicted two times prior. The first offense is a lesser felony.	$10,000	2 years	Mandatory for juveniles	1997
Utah	76-9-301	No	Class A misdemeanor	$5,000	1 year	Mandatory for juveniles	
Vermont	352	Yes	First act of cruelty committed is a felony.	$7,500	5 years	May order	1998 improved 2004
Virginia	3.1-796.122	Yes	First offense committed is a felony.	$2,500	5 years	May order	1999– felony Upgraded in 2002.
Washington	16.52.205	Yes	First offense committed is a class C felony.	$10,000	5 years	May order	1994
West Virginia	61-8-19	Yes	First offense committed is a felony.	$1,000–$5,000	5 years	Shall order an evaluation	2003
	For livestock §61-3-27	Yes	Felony only applies to animals with "value" over $100.				
Wisconsin	§951.18 (2004) §951.02 -mistreating	Yes	Felony	$10,000	5 years		1986
Wyoming	§6-3-203	Yes	Felony	$5,000	2 years		2003
Puerto Rico	Law 439 Amends 67		Grave offense in the 4th degree				2004
Virgin Islands	§181	Yes	Felony	$2,000–$5,000	2 years		2005

SOURCE: Adapted from "State Animal Anti-Cruelty Law Provisions," in *State Anti-Cruelty Laws: Fact Sheet*, Humane Society of the United States, April 2006, http://www.hsus.org/web-files/PDF/state_cruelty_chart.pdf (accessed January 1, 2007)

TABLE 1.8

Successful animal protection initiatives and referendums, by state, selected years 1990–2002

Year	State	Wins	Percentage voting yes	Percentage voting no
1990	CA	Proposition 117: Prohibits sport hunting of mountain lions	52	48
1992	CO	Amendment 10: Prohibits spring, bait, and hound hunting of black bears	70	30
1994	AZ	Proposition 201: Prohibits steel-jawed traps and other body-gripping traps	58	42
	OR	Measure 18: Bans bear baiting and hound hunting of mountain lions	52	48
1996	AK	Measure 3: Bans same-day airborne hunting of wolves and foxes	58	42
	CA	*Proposition 197 *: Allows trophy hunting of mountain lions*	42	58
	CO	Amendment 14: Bans leghold traps and other body-gripping traps	52	48
	MA	Question 1: Restricts steel-jawed traps and other body-gripping traps, bans hound hunting of bears and bobcats, and eliminates quota for hunters on Fisheries and Wildlife Board	64	36
	OR	*Measure 34 *: Repeals ban on bear baiting and hound hunting of bears and cougars*	42	58
	WA	Initiative 655: Bans bear baiting and hound hunting of bears, cougars, bobcats, and lynx	63	37
1998	AZ	Proposition 201: Prohibits cockfighting	68	32
	CA	Proposition 4: Bans the use of cruel and indiscriminate traps and poisons	57	43
	CA	Proposition 6: Prohibits slaughter of horses and sale of horse meat for human consumption	59	41
	CO	Amendment 13: Provides uniform regulations of livestock	39	61
	CO	Amendment 14: Regulates commercial hog factories	62	38
	MO	Proposition A: Prohibits cockfighting	63	37
2000	AK	*Measure 1*: Bans wildlife issues from ballot*	36	64
	AK	Measure 6: Bans land-and-shoot wolf hunting	53	47
	AZ	*Proposition 102 *: Require two-thirds majority for wildlife issues*	38	62
	MT	Initiative 143: Prohibits new game farm licenses	52	48
	WA	Initiative 713: Restricts steel-jawed traps and certain poisons	55	45
2002	AZ	Proposition 201: Expands gambling at greyhound tracks	20	80
	FL	Amendment 10: Bans gestation crates for pigs	55	45
	GA	Measure 6*: Specialty license plate for spay/neuter	71	29
	OK	State question 687: Bans cockfighting	56	44
	OK	*State question 698 *: Increases signature requirement for animal issues*	46	54

Note: Italics indicate bad measures that were defeated.
*Referendum (referred to ballot by state legislature).

SOURCE: Andrew N. Rowan and Beth Rosen, "Table 7a. Animal Protection Initiatives and Referendums—Wins," in *The State of the Animals III: 2005*, Humane Society of the United States, December 31, 2005, http://www.hsus.org/web-files/PDF/hsp/SOA_3-2005_Chap7.pdf (accessed November 28, 2006)

TABLE 1.9

Defeated animal protection initiatives and referendums, by state, selected years 1992–2002

Year	State	Losses	Percentage voting yes	Percentage voting no
1992	AZ	Proposition 200: Bans steel-jawed traps and other body-gripping traps	38	62
1996	ID	Proposition 2: Bans spring bait, and hound hunting of black bears	40	60
	MI	Proposal D: Bans baiting and hounding of black bears	38	62
	MI	Proposal G*: Exclusive authority over wildlife to National Resources Committee in Michigan	64	36
1998	AK	Proposition 9: Bans wolf snare trapping	36	64
	MN	Amendment 2: Constitutional recognition of hunting	77	23
	OH	Issue 1: Restores ban on mourning dove hunting	40	60
	UT	Proposition 5*: Requires two-thirds majority for wildlife ballot issues	56	44
	MA	Question 3: Bans greyhound racing	49	51
2000	ND	Question 1: Constitutional recognition of hunting	77	23
	OR	Measure 97: Restricts steel-jawed traps and certain poisons	59	41
	VA	Question 2*: Constitutional recognition of hunting	60	40
2002	AR	Initiated Act 1: Increases penalties for animal cruelty	38	62

*Referendum (referred to ballot by state legislature).

SOURCE: Andrew N. Rowan and Beth Rosen, "Table 7b. Animal Protection Initiatives and Referendums—Losses," in *The State of the Animals III: 2005*, Humane Society of the United States, December 31, 2005, http://www.hsus.org/web-files/PDF/hsp/SOA_3-2005_Chap7.pdf (accessed November 28, 2006)

CHAPTER 2
THE ANIMAL RIGHTS DEBATE

According to the eleventh edition of *Merriam-Webster's Collegiate Dictionary* (2003), a right is a "power or privilege to which one is justly entitled." In *The Animal Rights Crusade: The Growth of a Moral Protest* (1992), the sociologists James M. Jasper and Dorothy Nelkin define a right as "a moral trump card that cannot be disputed." The phrase "human rights" came into usage during the late 1700s to refer to generally recognized privileges (or freedoms) that every person should enjoy.

RIGHTS AND SOCIETY

The United Nations has the Universal Declaration of Human Rights (1998, http://www.un.org/rights/50/decla .htm), which states, "Everyone has the right to life, liberty and security of person." The declaration specifies dozens of particular human rights, including the right to be free from slavery, torture, and cruel or degrading treatment. Other rights involve equal protection under the law, fair and public trials, freedom of movement, marriage and raising families, ownership of property, worship and religion, peaceful assembly, expression of opinions, access to public services, social security, working conditions, rest and leisure, education, culture, and standard of living.

The U.S. Declaration of Independence, written in 1776, states, "We hold these truths to be self-evident, that all men are created equal, that they are endowed by their Creator with certain unalienable Rights, that among these are Life, Liberty and the pursuit of Happiness." Although the United States' founding fathers considered these rights to be inherent, they did note that people form governments to "secure these rights." Thus, while rights have a moral basis, they are upheld through the law.

Since the 1970s a debate has arisen about whether animals have moral rights that should be recognized and protected by human society. This is largely a philosophical question, but the answer has many practical consequences. For example, if animals have a right to life, then

it is wrong to kill them. If animals have a right to liberty, then it is wrong to hold them in captivity. If animals have a right to pursue happiness and enjoy security, then it is wrong to interfere in their natural lives.

Societies and governments make decisions about who should be granted rights and how those rights should be secured. In general, an individual's legal right to life and liberty ends if that person infringes on someone else's right to life and liberty. In some states a person who kills another person can be executed by the government. At the very least, the government can restrict the killer's liberty. People debate the moral issues involved in such affairs, but the legal issues are generally spelled out clearly in U.S. law.

Sometimes it is not considered morally or legally wrong for one person to kill another—for example, in the case of self-defense or in defense of others. The same holds true for a person killing an animal. There is general moral and legal agreement that killing an attacking tiger or rabid dog is reasonable and right behavior. In human society the moral and legal arguments that protect a person acting in self-defense begin to melt away as the threat level descends. Killing an unarmed burglar or trespasser may or may not be perceived as justified under the law. Killing a loud, annoying neighbor crosses over the line.

This line is set much lower when it comes to killing animals. People can sometimes kill animals that burgle or trespass, make too much noise, or become a nuisance, without moral or legal condemnation. The same holds true for animals that taste good, have attractive skin or pelts, or are useful laboratory subjects. Why is it acceptable to kill an animal for these reasons, but not a human?

People answer this question in different ways depending on their belief systems and moral and social influences, including religion, philosophy, and education. The following are some of the most common reasons people give for denying animals rights:

- Animals do not have souls.
- God gave humans dominion over the animals.
- Humans are intellectually superior to animals.
- Animals do not reason, think, or feel pain like humans do.
- Animals are a natural resource to be used as humans see fit.
- Animals kill each other.

Animal Rights Activists and Welfarists

Some people believe it is not acceptable to use animals for any human purpose at all. They believe that animals have moral rights to life, liberty, and other privileges that should be upheld by society and the rule of law. These are hardcore believers in animal rights, the fundamentalists of the animal rights movement. When they speak out, write, march, or otherwise publicize their beliefs, they are called animal rights activists. An activist is someone who takes direct and vigorous action to further a cause (especially a controversial cause).

Other people believe that some animals have (or should have) some moral and/or legal rights under certain circumstances. They may rescue abandoned pets, lobby for legislation against animal abuse, feed pigeons in the park, or do any number of other things on behalf of animals. These people are broadly categorized as animal welfarists. Their adherence to the idea of animal rights generally depends on the circumstances. For example, a welfarist might defend the rights of pet dogs and cats but eat chicken for dinner.

This is unacceptable to animal rights fundamentalists. They argue that all animals (not just the lovable or attractive ones) have rights that apply all the time (not just when it is convenient). Such fundamentalists face opposition from a variety of sources. Some of this opposition is driven by moral and philosophical differences of opinion. Some is also driven by economics.

Many animals (alive or dead) have financial value to humans. Livestock farmers, ranchers, pharmaceutical companies, zookeepers, circus trainers, jockeys, and breeders are among the many people who have a financial interest in the animal trade. If humans were to stop using animals, these people would be out of work. Many others would be deprived of their favorite sport and leisure activities. Given such economic arguments and the moral and philosophical arguments noted previously, those opposed to the idea of animal rights feel as strongly about the topic as those who support it.

HISTORY OF THE ANIMAL RIGHTS DEBATE

Early Arguments for Animal Rights

Most historians note that the modern animal rights movement began during the 1970s. However, the roots of the movement date back much further, to a handful of philosophers and thinkers. Celsus was a second-century Greek writer who argued against the Jewish/Christian belief that humans are morally superior to animals. Celsus points out that animals might actually be more favored by God because they do not have to sow seeds or plow fields to live, whereas people do. He does not believe that humans must be superior to animals because they are able to capture and eat animals. He notes that humans have to use weapons, traps, and hunting dogs to capture animals, whereas animals are naturally equipped with the tools they need to capture humans.

Over time, other writers and thinkers questioned society's attitudes toward animals. Their arguments were usually based on philosophical or ethical ideals. The Italian artist Leonardo da Vinci refused to eat meat. At one point, he wrote in his notebook, "The time will come when men such as I will look upon the murder of animals as they now look upon the murder of men."

Legal protection was extended to some animals during the 1800s in the form of antiabuse laws. These laws were often passed based on the theory that animal abuse was bad for society in general—they did not protect animals for the animals' sake but for humanity's sake. In 1894 the humanitarian Henry S. Salt wrote *Animals' Rights, Considered in Relation to Social Progress*, in which he asks, "Why should the law refuse its protection to any sensitive being? The time will come when humanity will extend its mantle over everything which breathes."

Modern Animal Rights Movement

Despite periodic calls throughout history for greater sensitivity toward animals, it was not until the 1970s that the question of their rights became a major social issue. In 1970 the British psychologist Richard Ryder coined the word "speciesism" to describe prejudice and discrimination practiced by humans against animals. Ryder's ideas received little publicity, but they were embraced by the Australian philosopher Peter Singer. In 1975 Singer published the influential book *Animal Liberation: A New Ethics for Our Treatment of Animals*, which describes in vivid detail the ways in which animals are subjected to pain and suffering on farms, in slaughterhouses, and in laboratory experiments. Singer publicizes the notion of speciesism and calls for an end to it. He argues that speciesism is similar to racism and sexism, in that they all deny moral and legal rights to one group in favor of another.

Henry Spira formed Animal Rights International after attending one of Singer's lectures. Spira was a social reformer who had worked in the civil rights and women's liberation movements. Barnaby J. Feder notes in Spira's obituary (*New York Times*, September 15, 1998) that Spira turned his attention to the animal rights movement after he "began to wonder why we cuddle some animals and put a fork in others." Spira was instrumental in bringing various animal groups together to work for common causes. Many people credit him with pressuring cosmetics companies to seek alternatives to animal testing for their products during the late 1980s.

By 1980 the animal rights movement had become prominent enough to attract the attention of critics. In *Interests and Rights: The Case against Animals* (1980), the philosopher Raymond G. Frey of Bowling Green State University argues that animals do not have moral rights. He insists that animal lives do not have the same moral value as human lives because animals cannot and do not undergo the same emotional and intellectual experiences as humans.

In 1979 the organization Attorneys for Animal Rights was founded by the lawyer Joyce Tischler. The group held the first national conference on animal rights law in 1980. The next year it successfully sued the U.S. Navy and prevented the killing of five thousand burros at a weapons-testing center in California. In 1984 the group adopted a new name: the Animal Legal Defense Fund (ALDF). One of ALDF's goals is to end the belief that animals are merely property. The group's anticruelty division also works with state prosecutors and law enforcement agencies to draft felony anticruelty laws and stiffen penalties for violations. The American Prosecutors Research Institute indicates in *Animal Cruelty Prosecution: Opportunities for Early Response to Crime and Interpersonal Violence* (July 2006, http://www.ndaa.org/pdf/animal_cruelty_06.pdf) that in 2006 forty-one states, the District of Columbia, and the Virgin Islands had felony animal abuse provisions.

The British philosopher Mary Midgley joined the debate when she published *Beast and Man: The Roots of Human Nature* (1978) and *Animals and Why They Matter* (1983). Midgley argues that Charles Darwin's *On the Origin of Species by Means of Natural Selection* (1859) was the catalyst for ending the moral separation that humans felt toward animals because it proved that humans were in fact animals. Midgley compares speciesism to other social problems, such as racism, sexism, and age discrimination.

It was during the 1970s and 1980s that some animal rights advocates began using high-profile tactics, such as sit-ins at buildings and protest marches on the streets, to attract public attention to their cause. These are examples of civil disobedience (refusing in a nonviolent way to obey government regulations or social standards). A radical element of the movement went even further by breaking into laboratories and fur farms to release animals and damaging buildings and equipment. Some people who used these methods referred to themselves as part of the Animal Liberation Front (ALF). ALF followers became known as the "domestic terrorists" of the animal movement.

Many in the scientific community were disturbed by this new wave of moral and social opposition to the use of animals in research. In 1981 the Foundation for Biomedical Research was founded to defend such usage and promote greater understanding of its medical and scientific benefits among the general public. The foundation began tracking and reporting on the activities of criminal animal activists who broke into laboratories to release animals and/or destroy property.

People for the Ethical Treatment of Animals (PETA) was founded in 1980 and quickly came to prominence. One of the group's cofounders infiltrated a research laboratory and obtained photographs of the primates being held there. The incident attracted national media attention and greatly helped Spira's efforts to reduce animal use in cosmetic testing. Animal issues also became important to a larger number of Americans in the 1980s.

In 1981 the Association of Veterinarians for Animal Rights (2007, http://www.avar.org/about.asp) was founded by two veterinarians who were concerned that animals "were routinely being used and abused by society, sometimes for the most trivial of reasons." The association's goal is to educate the public and people within the veterinary profession about these practices and to change social policy toward animals. Furthermore, its philosophy echoes that of many other animal rights groups in that it believes "all nonhuman animals have value and interests independent of the values and interests of other animals, including human beings."

In 1983 Tom Regan, a professor of philosophy at North Carolina State University, published *The Case for Animal Rights*. Regan argues that animal pain and suffering are consequences of a bigger problem: the idea that animals are a resource for people. Regan presents detailed philosophical arguments outlining why he believes animals have moral rights as "subjects-of-a-life." Regan states that acknowledging the rights of animals requires people to cease using them for any purpose, not just those associated with pain and suffering.

Frey responded to the growing pro-vegetarian movement in 1983 with his book *Rights, Killing, and Suffering: Moral Vegetarianism and Applied Ethics*. The idea of moral vegetarianism (adhering to a vegetarian diet for moral reasons, rather than for physical reasons) dates back centuries. It was advocated by the Indian leader Mahatma Gandhi in the early 1930s as a moral duty of humans toward animals and gained new life during the animal movement of the 1970s. Frey, however, argues that a widespread adherence to a vegetarian lifestyle would result in the collapse of animal agriculture and other animal-based industries and massive social disruption.

In 1984 the philosopher Ernest Partridge attacked Singer's speciesism philosophy and Regan's animal rights view in the article "Three Wrong Leads in a Search for an Environmental Ethic: Tom Regan on Animal Rights, Inherent Values, and Deep Ecology" (*Ethics and Animals*). Partridge maintains that both Singer and Regan miss a crucial point about the nature of rights: that rights have no biological basis, only a moral basis. In other words, it does not matter how humans and animals are alike or dissimilar in biology. What really matters is that no animals exhibit the capacities of "personhood," such as rationality and self-consciousness. Partridge contends that lack of personhood effectively disqualifies animals from being rights holders.

Carl Cohen, a professor of philosophy at the University of Michigan, also attacked Singer's and Regan's views in his article "The Case for the Use of Animals in Biomedical Research" (*New England Journal of Medicine*, October 2, 1986). Cohen acknowledges that speciesism exists, but denies that it is similar to racism or sexism. He argues that racism and sexism are unacceptable because there is no moral difference between races or between sexes. However, he writes that there is a moral difference between humans and animals that denies rights to animals and allows animals to be used by humans.

Animals as Property

In 1988 researchers at Harvard University obtained a patent for the OncoMouse—a mouse that had been genetically engineered to be susceptible to cancer. This was the first patent ever issued for an animal. Animal rights groups, led by the ALDF, challenged the issuance of the patent in court, but the case was dismissed because the court found that the ALDF had no legal standing in the matter. Since that time, several other animals have been patented, including pigs, sheep, goats, and cattle. Regan states in the *Case for Animal Rights* that patents can be issued for "nonnaturally occurring nonhuman multicellular living organisms, including animals" as long as they are given "a new form, quality, properties or combination not present in the original article existing in nature."

In 1995 Gary L. Francione published *Animals, Property, and the Law*, in which he argues that there is an enormous contradiction between public sentiment and legal treatment when it comes to animals. Francione notes that most of the public agrees that animals should be treated humanely and not subjected to unnecessary suffering, but he claims that the legal system does not uphold these moral principles because it regards animals as property.

Francione compares the situation to that which existed in slave states before the Civil War (1861–65). Although there were laws that supposedly protected slaves from the abuse of slave owners, they were seldom enforced. Slaves, like animals, were considered property, and the law protects the right of people to own and use property as they see fit. Property rights date back to English common law. According to Francione, the law has always relied on the assumption that property owners will treat their property appropriately to protect its economic value. Under this reasoning, the courts of the nineteenth century refused to recognize that a badly beaten slave was "abused," as defined by the law.

Francione believes that this same logic gives legal support to common practices in which animals are mistreated—for example, in the farming industry or in laboratory testing. He explains that humans are granted "respect-based" rights by the law and that animals are only considered in terms of their utility and economic value. Francione points out that animals are treated by the legal system as "means to ends and never as ends in themselves." In other words, existing animal laws protect animals because animals have value to people, not because animals have inherent value as living beings.

PHILOSOPHICAL ARGUMENTS

At the base of the animal rights debate is philosophy. Philosophical discussions involve abstract ideas and theories about questions of ethics and morality. These can be difficult subjects to comprehend and apply to real-life situations, but philosophy is important because it explains people's motivations and why people feel the way they do about a particular issue. Philosophical arguments are commonly used to either justify or condemn certain actions toward animals.

Not all people involved in the "animal movement" believe in animal rights. Many are motivated to work for animal causes for other reasons. Historically, the most common motivator has been concern for animal welfare, or welfarism.

Welfarism

Welfarism is defined as the beliefs associated with the social system known as the welfare state. The term *welfare state* was first used during the 1940s to refer to a society in which the government has the primary responsibility for the individual and social welfare of its citizens. When applied to animals, welfarism assumes that humans have the primary responsibility for the welfare of animals. Welfarists acknowledge that society uses animals for various purposes. Their goal is to reduce the amount of pain and suffering that animals endure. Welfarism centers on compassionate and humane care and treatment.

The best-known welfarist organization in the United States is the American Society for the Prevention of Cruelty to Animals (ASPCA), which was founded in 1866. Its mission is "to provide effective means for the prevention of cruelty to animals throughout the United States" (2007, http://www.aspca.org/site/PageServer?pagename=pp_pc _mission). The ASPCA defines itself not as an animal rights organization but as an animal welfare or animal protection organization. Its main programs include sheltering and providing medical and behavioral care to stray animals; placing stray and unwanted animals in adoptive homes; raising funds to care for animals affected by natural and human disasters, such as the flooding that followed Hurricane Katrina in 2005; tracking and investigating cruelty cases through its Humane Law Enforcement Division, which works in conjunction with the New York Police Department; and offering affordable spay/neuter and vaccination services to low-income pet owners, as well as public services such as education on humane issues. Even though the ASPCA does advocate for stronger anticruelty laws, it does not actively promote issues such as vegetarianism or banning the use of animals in medical research.

The Humane Society of the United States (HSUS) was founded in 1954. It is an animal organization that fits into the welfarist category, but its agenda is more sweeping than that of the ASPCA, encompassing protection of wild and marine animals as well as companion animals. Although it defines itself as an animal protection organization, critics charge that the HSUS quietly supports an animal rights agenda because it is openly against the use of animals in research, inhumane farming practices, and the fur industry.

Animal welfarists believe that humans have a responsibility to ensure the well-being of animals and reduce their suffering. This responsibility is upheld by society in the form of anticruelty laws. However, these laws do not prevent farm animals from being slaughtered for food or laboratory animals from being experimented on, usually without anesthetic to numb their pain. In these situations, welfarists work for humane slaughtering methods and prevention of "unnecessary" or excessive suffering during experimentation.

Utilitarianism

Utilitarianism is a philosophy popularized by English social reformer Jeremy Bentham in his book *Introduction to the Principles of Morals and Legislation* (1789). The basic premise of utilitarianism is that right actions are those that maximize utility. Bentham defines utility as either the presence of positive consequences—"benefit, advantage, pleasure, good, or happiness"—or the absence of negative consequences—"mischief, pain, evil, or unhappiness." In other words, right actions are those that maximize the best consequences or minimize the worst consequences. An important aspect of utilitarianism is that the interests of all parties involved in a particular situation must be considered. Likewise, the consequences to all parties involved must be taken into account. This is a difficult enough task when only humans are involved; it becomes much more complicated when animals are taken into consideration.

Singer uses a form of utilitarian logic in *Animal Liberation*. He argues that the suffering endured by animals on farms and during slaughtering far outweighs the pleasure and nutrition that the meat gives to humans. Likewise, he contends that laboratory animals suffer so much that this outweighs their usefulness to humans as test subjects. Singer concludes that the moral consequences of these practices (and other practices in which animals suffer) are so severe that they must be abolished. As a result, advocates of Singer's theory are often called liberationists or abolitionists. Even though his book is frequently called the bible of the animal rights movement, Singer does not specifically call for animal rights in the book. He has stated, however, that he believes that the term is politically useful for drawing attention to animal suffering.

Many philosophers reject the notion that utilitarianism can be applied to human-animal situations because, historically, animals have not been considered to have interests at all, or their interests have not been considered equal to human interests. In 1992 the philosopher Peter Carruthers wrote *The Animals Issue: Moral Theory in Practice*, in which he argues that utilitarianism is not an acceptable moral theory for examining animal issues because it equates animal lives and suffering with human lives and suffering, an idea Carruthers calls "intuitively abhorrent" and a violation of "common-sense beliefs." In *Interests and Rights*, Frey also discounts the utilitarian theory as a model of morality for dealing with animals, saying that animals do not have interests because they do not experience wants, desires, expectations, or remembrances.

Contractarianism

Contractarianism is another philosophy that is used to examine morality. According to this theory, society establishes right actions (or moral norms) through an arrangement in which individuals (called agents) voluntarily agree to abide by certain rules of morality. Following these rules is beneficial to both individuals and society in general. Although there are many different models of contractarianism, the most common are based on the writings of Immanuel Kant and the contemporary philosopher John Rawls. Kant believes that the moral code arising out of contractarianism reflects what rational agents would choose under ideal circumstances. Rawls expands this view by saying that the right actions are those that rational agents would choose if they were unaware of their own personal ambitions or prejudices.

When contractarianism is used to discuss human society, the rational agents are assumed to have direct duties. In other words, the rational agents know they are bound by a moral contract and are responsible for acting accordingly. The rational agents also have direct rights under the contract and have duties to those that lack the rationality to enter into the contract, such as babies, small children, and the mentally challenged.

Some philosophers use the contractarian model to explain the moral relationship between humans and animals. In *Animals Issue*, Carruthers argues that contractarianism is the best moral model for describing the human-animal relationship, but he concludes that animals do not have moral standing under the contract because they do not qualify as rational agents. He notes that humans have only indirect duties toward animals, one of which is to treat them humanely out of respect for the feelings of the rational agents (other humans) that care about them. Carruthers does, however, extend direct rights to human beings who are not rational agents (such as babies), noting that this is necessary to maintain social stability.

In the contractarian model, humans are moral agents, meaning that they make decisions and take actions based on morality. Many philosophers believe that animals are amoral—neither moral nor immoral. For example, a lion that kills a baby zebra to feed her cubs is acting out of instinct. The action is neither morally good nor morally bad. Some opponents of animal rights argue that because animals do not make decisions based on morality, they are not part of the moral contract and do not have moral rights. The philosopher Tibor R. Machan is an outspoken critic of the notion of animal rights. In *Putting Humans First: Why We Are Nature's Favorite* (2004), he argues that animals cannot have rights because they are not capable of making moral decisions.

In practice, the moral code of contractarianism seems to provide some protections for selected species of animals. For example, in American society there is widespread moral repugnance to the idea of eating dogs and cats or killing animals with sentimental or patriotic significance (such as bald eagles). These views might be argued to be rooted in their moral and philosophical impact on humans and could therefore be extensions of the contractarian model.

Rights View

The rights view is defined and defended by Regan in the *Case for Animal Rights* and in many subsequent books. He maintains that all beings who are "subjects-of-a-life with an experiential welfare" have inherent value that qualifies them to be treated with respect and gives them a right to that treatment. In other words, living beings with conscious awareness and self-identity deserve moral rights. Regan does not define exactly which animals fall into this category, but higher species, such as vertebrates (animals with a spinal cord), fit his criteria.

This philosophy is fundamentally different from welfarism and utilitarianism. The rights view holds that animals have moral rights to certain privileges and freedoms, just as humans do. It does not mean that animals have exactly the same rights as humans. Most animal rights advocates believe that animals at least have the right to life and the right to freedom from bodily interference.

The philosopher best known for criticizing the animal rights view is Carl Cohen. In 2001 Cohen and Regan coauthored *The Animal Rights Debate*, which presents a point-counterpoint examination of the issue. Cohen sums up his argument against animal rights: "Animals cannot be the bearers of rights, because the concept of rights is *essentially human*; it is rooted in the human moral world and has force and applicability only within that world." He admits that animals are sentient (conscious of sensory impressions), feel pain, and can experience suffering, but insists that sharing these traits with humans does not make animals morally equal to humans.

Cohen writes that some people confuse rights with obligations and assume that because humans have obligations to animals, it means that animals have rights. This assumption is called symmetrical reciprocity, and he believes it is based on false logic. The difference, Cohen explains, is that an obligation is what "we ought to do," whereas a right is "what others can justly demand that we do."

Cohen states that humans are moral agents who are restrained by moral principles from treating animals inhumanely. This means that humans should not inflict "gratuitous" pain and suffering on animals. However, it does not mean that humans must stop every activity that could or does harm animals in some way. Medical research on animals is an example. He believes that scientists have moral obligations to humanity to use animals in their experiments if that is the best way for them to achieve their goals. According to Cohen, "our duties to human subjects are of a different moral order from our duties to the rodents we use."

Cohen's overall conclusion—that rights do not apply to animals because rights are essentially human—is a point commonly made by those who oppose the animal rights movement. Many of them find it ludicrous to even debate the issue. Adrian R. Morrison is a scientist engaged in animal research and a vocal critic of the animal rights movement. In "Understanding the Effect of Animal-Rights Activism on Biomedical Research"

(January 27, 2002, http://www.rau.edu.uy/universidad/medicina/actas8/morrison.pdf), he notes that few philosophers besides Cohen and almost no scientists bother to dispute in detail the philosophy behind the animal rights view. Morrison suggests that most scientists and philosophers "think the subject to be too far from reality to be worth the trouble."

PRACTICAL IMPLICATIONS

Assuming that animals have rights would have massive consequences to society. If animals have moral rights to life and freedom from bodily interference, then they cannot be purposely killed, harmed, or kept in captivity by humans. Billions of domesticated animals would be spared from slaughter and would have to be released from cages and pens.

PETA (2007, http://www.peta.org/) states that it "believes that animals have rights and deserve to have their best interests taken into consideration, regardless of whether they are useful to humans. Like you, they are capable of suffering and have an interest in leading their own lives; therefore, they are not ours to use—for food, clothing, entertainment, experimentation, or any other reason." Implementation of this belief would mean the elimination of all commercial animal operations—livestock and fur farms, animal research facilities, circuses, zoos, animal parks and aquariums, game ranches, hunting lodges, animal breeding facilities, pet stores, dog and horse racetracks, and so on. All the people working in these businesses would be put out of work. The economic consequences would be enormous. Animal rights advocates point out that dismantling the slave trade after the Civil War was costly as well, but it was done anyway because it was the right thing to do.

Besides an economic cost, there would be a scientific cost. Medical and scientific research has relied on animal test subjects for centuries. Some research and development would have to stop until alternatives could be found. Students in schools and universities would have to learn anatomy and biology without dissecting animals. Doctors, surgeons, and veterinarians in training would have to practice on something besides animals. Cloning, twinning, and other genetic manipulation of animals would have to stop. Eliminating the use of animals would disrupt the entire scientific community. Animal rights activists believe the move is overdue because it would force scientists to think about their research in new ways. Many school districts have already implemented alternatives to animal dissection, including computer models that accurately mimic animal bodies.

There are also implications to private individuals in terms of dining, fashion, sport, recreation, and leisure. None of these activities could include personal use of animals. Hunting, fishing, eating meat, wearing leather, and keeping pets would come to a stop. The activity that would affect the most Americans would be the elimination of meat and animal products (milk, eggs, cheese, and so on) from their diet. According to a *Time*/CNN poll (July 15, 2002, http://www.time.com/time/covers/1101020715/poll/), 4% of the respondents consider themselves vegetarians. Of those, 5% were vegans (people who eat no animal products). In other words, less than 1% of those surveyed avoided all animal products in their diet. Most animal rights advocates and liberationists are vegetarians or vegans. They believe that a vegetarian diet would not only help animals but also would be healthier for humans and better for the environment.

Opponents of animal rights are always eager to point out that keeping pets would be forbidden if animals had rights. Ingrid Newkirk, a PETA cofounder, has been quoted as saying that pets are a symbol of the human manipulation of animals, and the notion of pets should be phased out. This idea is controversial even within the animal rights community because it is so radical. Many people involved in both the animal rights and animal welfare movements refer to pets as "companion animals" and to owners as "animal guardians" or "animal caretakers." These terms are intended to downplay the ownership element between humans and animals.

Legally, most animals are considered property. In fact, the word *cattle* was derived from a Latin word meaning "property." This raises difficulties for pet owners who wish to ensure that their pets will be properly cared for in the event the owners die or become incapacitated. In "What Is a Pet Trust" (October 2006, http://www.pet-trust.net/what-is-a-pet-trust.html), the attorney Rachel Hirschfeld notes that pets cannot inherit money through wills, because pets are legally considered to be property. Pet owners can designate a caretaker in their wills and leave money to that person intended for pet care, but the arrangement is not legally enforceable by the courts. Hirschfeld recommends another option, called a trust, to pet owners. A trust is a legally enforceable arrangement that allows a person to leave money to another person (called a trustee) for management of certain assets, such as property. Pet trusts have become extremely popular as a means for pet owners to ensure that their pets will be cared for after the owners' death. According to the ASPCA, thirty states and the District of Columbia had laws in place specifically allowing for pet trusts as of 2006. (See Table 2.1.)

Cynthia Hubert, in "What If Your Pet Outlives You? A New Endeavor at the UC Davis Veterinary School Ensures That It Will Be Loved for a Lifetime" (*Sacramento Bee*, November 18, 2006), reports that between 12% and 27% of American pet owners have made provisions for their pets in their estate planning.

In 2000 Tennessee became the first state in the country to allow owners to sue for loss of love and affection if

TABLE 2.1

State laws regarding pet trusts, 2006

State	Code section	Date of enactment
Alaska	Alaska Stat. § 13.12.907	1996
Arizona	A.R.S. § 14-2907	1995
Arkansas	S.B. 336	2005
California	Cal Prob Code § 15212	1991
Colorado	C.R.S. 15-11-901	1995
District of Columbia	§ 19-1304.08	2003
Florida	2002 Fl. ALS 82, Fla. Stat. § 737.116	2002
Hawaii	H.B. 1453	2005
Illinois	760 I.L.C.S. 5/15/.2	2005
Indiana	H.B. 1153	2005
Iowa	Iowa Code § 633.2105	2000
Kansas	KSA § 58a-408	2003
Maine	Me. Rev. Stat. Ann. Tit. 18-B, 408	1995
Michigan	MCLS § 700.2722	2000
Missouri	Mo. Ann. Stat. § 456.4-408	2004
Montana	Mont. Code Anno., § 72-2-1017	1993
Nebraska	Neb. Rev. Stat. § 30-3834	2005
Nevada	Nev. Rev. Stat Ann § 163.0075	2001
New Hampshire	N.H. Rev. Stat. Ann. § 564-B:4-408	2004
New Jersey	N.J. Stat. § 3B:11-38	2001
New Mexico	N.M. Stat. Ann. § 45-2-907	1995
New York	NY CLS EPTL § 7-8.1	1996
North Carolina	N.C. Gen. Stat. § 36A-147	1995
Oregon	ORS § 128.308	2001
South Carolina	S.B. 422; H.B. 3487	2005
Tennessee	Tenn. Code Ann. § 35-15-408	2004
Texas	SB 1157	2005
Utah	Utah Code Ann. § 75-2-1001	1998
Washington	Wash. Rev. Code § 11.118.005-.110	2001
Wisconsin	Wis. Stat. § 701.11	1969
Wyoming	W.S. 1977 § 4-10-409	2003

SOURCE: Adapted from "Pet Trusts: State Laws," in *Planned Giving*, American Society for the Prevention of Cruelty to Animals, 2006, http://www.aspca.org/site/PageServer?pagename=donate_planned_pettrustslaws (accessed December 29, 2006). Copyright © 2007 The American Society for the Prevention of Cruelty to Animals (ASPCA®). Reprinted with permission of the ASPCA. All rights reserved.

a pet is wrongfully killed. The ALDF helped the legislature draft the bill that was passed. It allows damages of up to $4,000 for the death of a pet, assuming certain conditions are met—for example, if the person causing the death was negligent. Although many lawsuits are filed around the country seeking recovery of emotional distress damages for loss or injury of a companion animal, most are thrown out because of the legal precedent that animals are property.

Still, lawyers report many more cases involving animal law today than in the past. Some state bar associations have formed animal law sections to deal with the increase. Carolyn B. Matlack, in "Sentient Property: Unleashing Legal Respect for Our Companion Animals" (*Animal Law Section*, Summer 2003), describes the spectrum of animal law cases the Washington State Bar Association's animal law section handles: "Legal disputes over pets arise in actions involving dissolution of property or custody agreements, nuisance actions, assistance animal privileges, cruelty allegations, landlord-tenant contracts, police or dog warden brutality, airline negligence, veterinary malpractice and in the area of wills, trusts and estates."

Matlack suggests that companion animals receive a new property classification under the law: sentient property (feeling property). She argues that courts could determine the best interests of sentient property based on the testimony of experts, as is done for young children and the mentally disabled.

Even wild animals are categorized by ownership. Private landowners assume power of ownership over wild animals on their land. As long as the animals are not protected by specific legislation, property owners may kill them as they please. Wild animals inhabiting government lands are considered public property and are treated as such. The mission of the U.S. Fish and Wildlife Service (December 29, 2006, http://www.fws.gov/help/mission.cfm) is "to conserve, protect and enhance fish, wildlife, and plants and their habitats for the continuing benefit of the American people."

Public and private landowners exhibit implied animal ownership when they grant hunters permission to hunt on lands under their control. If these animals are assumed to have moral rights, then they can no longer be considered property.

Many animal welfarists are uneasy with the animal rights movement. They worry that it draws attention away from goals that are more easily obtainable for animals in the near future. They also worry that the radical statements and actions of some animal rights activists will turn the public against the entire animal movement. Radical animal rights activists have been known to demonstrate in the nude, splash paint on people wearing fur coats, and destroy and vandalize property. Many have spent time in prison for their actions.

Although welfarists and liberationists/abolitionists sometimes work together to achieve change, there is a philosophical gulf between them. This was made clear by the animal rights advocate Joan Dunayer in *Speciesism* (2004). Dunayer supports the idea that humans and animals should have "absolute moral equality." She accuses animal rights groups of compromising their beliefs by campaigning for welfarist reforms in animal treatment, rather than complete liberation. Dunayer compares the plight of animals to that of prisoners in Nazi concentration camps during World War II, arguing that the prisoners would have begged their supporters on the outside to work for liberation rather than more humane living conditions or kinder slaughtering techniques.

Abolitionists ask welfarists to give up meat and leather; close down all circuses, zoos, animal parks, aquariums, and racetracks; and stop laboratories from using animals. Most welfarists are not willing to go so far, preferring to focus on finding practical solutions to problems such as pet overpopulation and cruelty to domestic animals.

At the other end of the spectrum is the radical element of the animal movement. This element does not debate philosophy but takes direct action—sometimes illegally—to free animals from farms and laboratories. The ALF is not really a group, as it has no leadership structure, but is instead a set of guidelines. The ALF (January 2007, http://www.animalliberationfront.com/ALFront/alf_credo.htm) states that "the . . . short-term aim is to save as many animals as possible and directly disrupt the practice of animal abuse. [The] long term aim is to end all animal suffering by forcing animal abuse companies out of business." The ALF also states that any vegans or vegetarians who carry out actions according to ALF guidelines can regard themselves as part of the ALF. These actions include liberating animals from "places of abuse" and inflicting "economic damage" on the people involved. ALF followers are urged to take precautions to prevent harming humans and animals. The ALF receives funding from the ALF Supporters Group, which is made up of people who believe in the ALF guidelines but do not want to be involved in criminal activities.

PUBLIC OPINION

In May 2003 the Gallup Organization conducted a poll to determine Americans' opinions regarding animal rights issues. The results are based on telephone interviews with 1,005 adults aged eighteen and up.

As shown in Figure 2.1, 25% of those asked believed that animals deserve the same rights as people. A large majority (72%) said that animals deserve some protection but can still be used to benefit people. Only a tiny percentage (3%) felt that animals do not need much protection from harm and exploitation. The Gallup reporter David W. Moore notes that support for animal rights was much higher among women (33%) than among men (17%).

The respondents were also asked whether they supported or opposed four specific proposals concerning the treatment of animals. (See Figure 2.2.) More than 60% favored passing strict laws regarding the treatment of farm animals. Nearly 40% favored a ban on all product testing performed on laboratory animals. Around one-third favored a similar ban on medical research testing. Support was far lower (22%) for a total ban on hunting.

Moore notes that examination of these results by gender, age, and political affiliation reveals far more support for these proposals among women than among

FIGURE 2.1

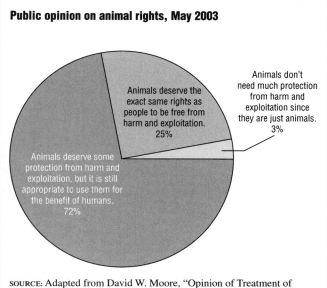

Public opinion on animal rights, May 2003

Animals deserve the exact same rights as people to be free from harm and exploitation. 25%

Animals don't need much protection from harm and exploitation since they are just animals. 3%

Animals deserve some protection from harm and exploitation, but it is still appropriate to use them for the benefit of humans. 72%

SOURCE: Adapted from David W. Moore, "Opinion of Treatment of Animals," in *Public Lukewarm on Animal Rights*, The Gallup Organization, May 21, 2003, http://www.galluppoll.com/content/?CI=8461 (accessed January 3, 2007). Copyright © 2003 by The Gallup Organization. Reproduced by permission of The Gallup Organization.

men. Support was also significantly higher from Democrats and Independents than from Republicans. No significant differences were found between age groups.

Degrees of adherence to the animal rights philosophy varied. Some of the people who said they supported animal rights did not want to eliminate all the practices in which animals are killed or harmed. (See Figure 2.3.) More than half of those who supported animal rights were opposed to banning hunting. About 43% of them did not want to ban medical research on laboratory animals. Roughly 39% did not want to ban product testing on animals, and more than 20% of them opposed passing strict laws concerning the treatment of farm animals.

These answers are somewhat puzzling. Moore suggests that the people indicating support for animal rights had pets in mind when they answered that question. Later, when asked about the specific proposals (hunting, research, product testing, and farm animals), these same people may have envisioned different animals. It is also possible that people do not have a clear idea of the concept of animal rights or what the philosophy means in practice.

FIGURE 2.2

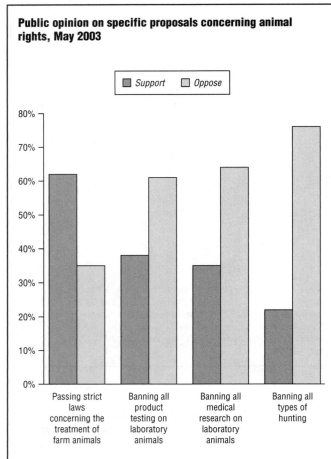

Public opinion on specific proposals concerning animal rights, May 2003

SOURCE: Adapted from David W. Moore, "Summary Table: Animal Rights Issues," in *Public Lukewarm on Animal Rights*, The Gallup Organization, May 21, 2003, http://www.galluppoll.com/content/?CI= 8461 (accessed January 3, 2007). Copyright © 2003 by The Gallup Organization. Reproduced by permission of The Gallup Organization.

FIGURE 2.3

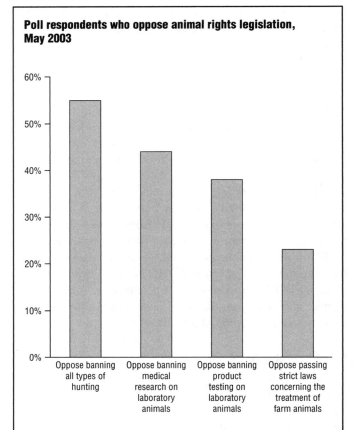

Poll respondents who oppose animal rights legislation, May 2003

SOURCE: Adapted from David W. Moore, "Support for Animal Rights Proposals," in *Public Lukewarm on Animal Rights*, The Gallup Organization, May 21, 2003, http://www.galluppoll.com/content/?CI= 8461 (accessed January 3, 2007). Copyright © 2003 by The Gallup Organization. Reproduced by permission of The Gallup Organization.

CHAPTER 3
WILDLIFE

Wildlife are animals that have not been domesticated by humans. This does not mean that wild animals live without human interference. Humans control, manage, manipulate, use, and kill wildlife for various reasons. Humans tend to think of wild animals in terms of the threat they pose to people or the value they hold for them.

Some wildlife threaten human safety, health, property, and/or quality of life. This is true of large carnivores (such as lions, tigers, and alligators), poisonous snakes and spiders, disease-carrying animals, and animals that endanger moving vehicles. In addition, there are carnivores (such as coyotes and bobcats) that prey on livestock and pets, herbivores that eat crops and lawns, beavers that dam up streams, and wild animals that invade or damage human spaces. Many rodents, skunks, rabbits, deer, and birds are considered nuisance animals.

However, many wild animals, even dangerous ones, have value to humans. This value might be economic, educational, or emotional in nature. Valuable wildlife fall into the following categories:

- Wild animals that produce products people want to eat, wear, or use. This category includes deer, buffalo, elk, wildfowl, fur-bearing creatures, many fish and marine mammals, and animals such as tigers and bears with bones and organs that are used in traditional medicines.

- Wild animals that humans kill for sport through hunting or fishing. In the United States people primarily hunt native game, such as deer, bears, rabbits, squirrels, and waterfowl. Exotic (foreign) animals are imported and killed at some hunting ranches (called canned hunts because the hunters pay to participate and are guaranteed to kill the animals). African lions, giraffes, antelopes, gazelles, Cape buffaloes, Corsican sheep, and Angora goats are some of the most popular. Sport fish include a variety of freshwater and saltwater species.

- Wild animals that can be manipulated to do labor or entertain people. For example, elephants are used as beasts of burden in many Asian countries. They also perform in circuses and shows, along with bears, primates, birds, lions, tigers, dolphins, seals, whales, and other trainable animals. Some wild animals even have military uses, particularly dolphins, whales, and sea lions.

- Wild animals that humans enjoy watching, hearing, feeding, or photographing. This category is very diverse and ranges from songbirds in the backyard to whales in the open sea. (See Figure 3.1.) It includes a variety of animals that humans can encounter in the wild and at refuges, sanctuaries, zoos, parks, and entertainment venues.

- Wild animals that are useful in scientific and medical research. These include primates and some strains of rats, mice, and rabbits.

- Wild animals kept as pets. This includes a wide variety of species, some of which are dangerous to humans. Keeping wild animals as pets is highly controversial and, in many states, illegal.

Most animal rights advocates believe that wild animals should not be used at all—not for food, clothing, entertainment, companionship, or any other purpose. They consider wild animals not commodities but free beings with the right to live undisturbed in their natural habitats. Animal welfarists are concerned that wild animals are exploited and mistreated because of human greed and ignorance. They work to publicize the fate of animals in captivity and to save them from mistreatment.

Most people consider wildlife a valuable natural resource, such as water or coal. They may disagree about how wild animals should be used, but they generally agree that humans have the right to use them, especially if the supply is plentiful. Wild species threatened by

FIGURE 3.1

Boaters observe a humpback whale off the coast of Massachusetts. *AP/Wide World Photos.*

extinction are a different matter, however, as many people rally to conserve them. Successful conservation ensures that the species will continue to thrive in the future.

Every aspect of wildlife-human interaction raises questions in the animal rights debate. For example:

• The American bison was nearly extinct in the nineteenth century. Thanks to conservationists, the species was saved and is even thriving. By the year 2000, bison burgers were being sold at trendy restaurants. Is it acceptable to save an endangered species and then eat it?

• The government allows people to kill deer to keep the population down. Otherwise, lack of food could lead to starvation among the deer population. Is hunting deer more humane than letting them starve?

• Many people enjoy experiencing wildlife up close for its entertainment and educational value. Should wild animals be kept in captivity to satisfy this desire?

These are just some of the major questions in the animal rights debate.

HISTORY

Prehistoric humans constantly struggled with wildlife. Both sides were sometimes predators and sometimes prey, but humans quickly tipped the balance in their favor with two big advantages: superior intellect and weapons. As humans gained more control over nature, they began using wild animals not just as a food source but as a source of labor and entertainment. Elephants became beasts of burden. Mongooses and birds of prey were trained to be hunting assistants. Some lions, tigers, and bears were kept in cages to entertain or educate humans. Dangerous animals that could not be contained were often eliminated.

Eventually, governments declared their authority over wild animal populations. Some ancient rulers enacted game laws to allow species to multiply. The explorer Marco Polo described a law of the Chinese ruler Kublai Khan that prohibited the killing of deer, rabbits, and large waterfowl during certain months to allow the species time to replenish.

Other rulers restricted the hunting of the most desirable animals to the upper social classes. Under English law, wildlife was the property of royalty. Members of the lower classes were permitted to hunt only low-value animals such as rabbits. Big game were reserved for the upper classes. English royalty had exclusive hunting rights until 1215, when the Magna Carta was signed.

Wildlife in the United States

Problems with wildlife management plagued the first European colonists in North America. Historical records show that the colonists fought off animal predators, including wolves, coyotes, cougars, bears, and mountain lions. They also lost domesticated animals to wild predators. Livestock, particularly hogs, sometimes wandered away and lived in the wild. Their offspring were feral animals (animals born and living in the wild that are descendants of domesticated animals). The colonists killed wild and feral animals whenever they could because they were a threat to livestock and crops. The colonists found wolves to be particularly bothersome. Early governing bodies established wolf bounty acts that paid people for killing wolves. Virginia had a wolf bounty act as early as 1632. It paid colonists and Native Americans for every wolf head they presented.

By the early 1700s official hunting seasons for certain species were established in some colonies. Over the next century, state governments set up fish and game departments and enacted hunting restrictions, requiring licenses and setting limits on the number of some species that could be killed during each hunting season.

Colonization severely depleted the ranks of some native wild species through a combination of overhunting and disease. The introduction of livestock brought new animal diseases that were devastating to some native species. Passenger pigeons and heath hens died out altogether. Bison, elk, and beaver stocks were severely diminished, though they did not become extinct.

DEVELOPMENT OF THE CONSERVATION MOVEMENT. Late in the nineteenth century people began to become aware of the value of natural resources, such as land, water, and wildlife, and worked to conserve wilderness spaces and protect them from development. Some of the most important representatives of the conservation movement include:

- John Muir (see Figure 3.2), who established the Sierra Club in 1892 and worked toward the creation of Yosemite National Park
- President Theodore Roosevelt, who set aside millions of acres of land under federal government control for national refuges, forests, and parks

FIGURE 3.2

John Muir, founder of the Sierra Club. *The Library of Congress.*

- Gifford Pinchot, who was a firm believer in conservation and a key adviser to Theodore Roosevelt
- Aldo Leopold, who wrote *Game Management* in 1933, the first known publication on the science of wildlife management
- Ding Darling, who advocated the restoration of wetlands and waterfowl habitats and was the driving force behind many wildlife protection programs and laws

Early conservationists initiated programs that helped wild animals by preserving natural habitats, but they were not always motivated by the same concerns that drove people involved in the animal welfare movement. Many prominent conservationists were avid hunters. For example, President Roosevelt enjoyed hunting big game. Leopold also hunted and said that it gave him a deep appreciation and respect for wild animals. Many welfarists were (and are) opposed to hunting for sport. The ethical battle over hunting that began between conservationists and welfarists in the nineteenth century continues today.

GOVERNMENT ENACTS REGULATION LAWS. In the twentieth century dozens of federal laws were enacted that regulated wildlife. Table 3.1 lists the most notable

TABLE 3.1

Major federal laws impacting wildlife, 1900–92

Major federal laws impacting wildlife	Year enacted
Lacey Act	1900
Game and Bird Preserves Act	1905
Weeks-McLean Act	1912
National Park Service Act	1916
Migratory Bird Treaty Act	1918
Migratory Bird Conservation Act	1920s
Tariff Act (Enhanced Lacey Act)	1930
Animal Damage Control Act	1931
Fish and Wildlife Coordination Act	1934
Migratory Bird Hunting and Conservation Stamp Act (Duck Stamp Act)	1934
Taylor Grazing Act	1934
Federal Aid in Wildlife Restoration Act (Pittman-Robertson Act)	1937
Bald Eagle Protection Act	1940
Federal Aid in Sport Fish Restoration Act (Dingell-Johnson Act)	1950
Whaling Convention Act	1950
Tuna Conventions Act	1950
Fisherman's Protective Act	1954
Fish and Wildlife Act	1956
Great Lakes Fishery Act	1956
Multiple Use Act	1960
Surplus Grain for Wildlife Act	1961
Refuge Recreation Act	1962
Wilderness Act	1964
Refuge Revenue Sharing Act	1964
Land and Water Conservation Fund Act	1965
Anadromous Fish Conservation Act	1965
National Wildlife Refuge System Administration Act	1966
Endangered Species Preservation Act	1966
Fur Seal Act	1966
National Environmental Policy Act	1969
Endangered Species Conservation Act	1969
Federal Wild and Free Roaming Horses and Burros Act	1971
Marine Mammal Protection Act	1972
Endangered Species Act	1973
Alaska National Interest Lands Conservation Act	1980
Fish and Wildlife Conservation Act	1980
National Aquaculture Act	1980
Salmon and Steelhead Conservation and Enhancement Act	1980
Atlantic Salmon Convention Act	1982
Northern Pacific Halibut Act	1982
Atlantic Striped Bass Conservation Act	1984
Pacific Salmon Treaty Act	1985
The North American Wetlands Conservation Act	1986
South Pacific Tuna Act	1988
The African Elephant Conservation Act	1988
Dolphin Protection Consumer Information Act	1990
Non-Indigenous Aquatic Nuisance Prevention and Control Act	1990
Wild Bird Conservation Act	1992
Alien Species Prevention and Enforcement Act	1992
Rhinoceros and Tiger Conservation Act	1994
National Wildlife Refuge System Improvement Act	1997

SOURCE: Created by Kim Masters Evans for Thomson Gale

ones. The first federal wildlife law was the Lacey Act of 1900, which banned the transportation of illegally taken wildlife across state lines. It also established regulations regarding the importation of wildlife into the country. Many laws were designed to fund conservation efforts through hunting fees. For example, the Migratory Bird Hunting and Conservation Stamp Act of 1934 required people to purchase a stamp before they could hunt waterfowl. The Federal Aid in Wildlife Restoration Act of 1937 added a special tax on guns and ammunition.

By the early twenty-first century wildlife in the United States was extensively regulated. In "Digest of

Federal Resource Laws" (2006, http://www.fws.gov/laws/laws_digest/resource_laws.htm), the U.S. Fish and Wildlife Service (USFWS) lists 164 federal laws that have been passed dealing with the control, preservation, eradication, and management of wildlife. Some laws pertain directly to particular species, whereas others address preservation of habitat and use of federal lands.

GOVERNMENT AGENCIES THAT CONTROL WILDLIFE

Wildlife issues in the United States are overseen by various federal and state agencies. At the federal level, the USFWS is the primary agency. Originally called the U.S. Commission on Fish and Fisheries, the USFWS was formed in 1871 to examine problems with declining food-fish stocks and recommend remedies. In 1903 the agency was given oversight of the first national wildlife refuge, Pelican Island, a three-acre bird sanctuary in Sebastian, Florida.

In "Wild Places, Wild Things" (2006, http://www.fws.gov/midwest/Horicon/documents/WildPlacesWildThings.pdf), the USFWS states that it manages 95 million acres in 545 refuges in the National Wildlife Refuge System. It also manages migratory bird conservation, oversees thousands of wetlands and other management areas, and operates dozens of national fish hatcheries, fishery resources offices, and ecological services field stations. The USFWS administers and enforces many federal wildlife laws and issues import and export permits under those laws.

The USFWS works with the U.S. Customs and Border Protection and the U.S. Department of Agriculture to monitor wildlife trade and stop illegal shipments of protected plants and animals. The USFWS also enforces the country's participation in the Convention on International Trade in Endangered Species of Wild Fauna and Flora (CITES). This international agreement regulates the importing and exporting of thousands of species. Other federal agencies involved in controlling wild populations include the Wildlife Services (WS) of the U.S. Department of Agriculture (USDA), the Bureau of Reclamation, and the National Park Service. The WS is the primary federal agency in charge of controlling wildlife that can damage agriculture, property, and natural resources or threaten public health and safety. It operates the National Wildlife Research Center in Fort Collins, Colorado.

GOALS OF GOVERNMENT WILDLIFE REGULATION

Historically, wildlife control efforts in the United States have focused on protecting human interests and preserving endangered species. Human interests include health, safety, property, and resources—livestock, crops, trees, lawns, structures, water, food supplies, vehicles, pets, and so forth. Wild animals that threaten any of these are subject to removal or elimination. In the past, control was left up to private citizens, who could kill any wild animals they considered a threat. Today, most control efforts are led or managed by government agencies. For example, hunting requires a license and payment of fees. However, private citizens may legally kill some wildlife that are considered pests (such as rodents) in and around their homes or businesses.

Protecting Health and Safety

Violent confrontations between wild animals and people are relatively rare in contemporary times. Of greater concern is the danger from zoonotic diseases—diseases that can be passed from animals to people. Zoonotic diseases associated with wild animals include rabies, West Nile virus, Lyme disease, bovine tuberculosis (a respiratory disease associated with buffalo, bison, and deer), chlamydiosis (a respiratory disease most commonly found in tropical birds, such as parrots), histoplasmosis (a lung disease transmitted through bird and bat droppings), salmonellosis (an intestinal illness transmitted through contaminated feces, particularly from infected reptiles), and granulocytic ehrlichiosis (a tick-borne disease similar to Lyme disease).

One of the most feared zoonotic diseases is rabies. Rabies killed an average of a hundred people annually in the early twentieth century, but a combination of control methods greatly reduced its threat. By the end of the century, only one or two people died each year from the disease. The Centers for Disease Control and Prevention (CDC) conducts rabies epidemiology (the study of the distribution and causes of disease in populations). In *Rabies: Epidemiology* (December 1, 2003, http://www .cdc.gov/ncidod/dvrd/rabies/Epidemiology/Epidemiology .htm), the latest report available, the CDC reports that there were 7,437 confirmed cases of animal rabies in the United States in 2001. Wild animals, primarily raccoons, skunks, and bats, accounted for 93% of those cases. Figure 3.3 shows the areas of the country most associated with terrestrial (land-dwelling) wild animals that can carry rabies.

The number of rabies cases reported in wild animals greatly increased between the mid-1970s and 2001. This was because of an epidemic of rabies in raccoons in the mid-Atlantic states. This type of epidemic that affects many of the same species of animals is called an epizootic. According to the CDC, in *Rabies: Prevention and Control* (December 1, 2003, http://www.cdc.gov/ncidod/ dvrd/rabies/prevention&control/ovalvacc.htm), the rabies epizootic in raccoons began in 1977 along the border between Virginia and West Virginia. It spread quickly to neighboring states and reached Canada in 1999. State and federal wildlife officials began using baits laden with oral rabies vaccine (ORV) in the early 1990s. More than 12.3 million ORV doses were distributed during 2006 alone, as shown in Table 3.2. Wildlife authorities hope to create a barrier to prevent the epizootic from spreading westward.

Besides diseases, humans face dangers posed by collisions between moving vehicles and wild animals and birds. In *Wildlife Services Program: Information on Activities to Manage Wildlife Damage* (November 2001, http://www.aphis.usda.gov/ws/GAOreports.pdf), the U.S. General Accounting Office (GAO; now the Government Accountability Office), reports that more than one million collisions between deer and automobiles occur each year, injuring approximately twenty-nine thousand people and killing two hundred. Bradley F. Blackwell and Glen E. Bernhardt state in "Efficacy of Aircraft Landing Lights in Stimulating Avoidance Behavior in Birds" (*Journal of Wildlife Management*, July 2004) that 46,514 collisions between wildlife and civil aircraft were reported to the Federal Aviation Administration from 1990 through 2002. These collisions had associated costs of approximately $489 million annually. Birds were involved in 97% of the collisions. Although multiple species of birds can be involved in a single incident, aircraft collisions were most commonly associated with waterfowl and raptors. Wildlife and aircraft collisions caused 140 human deaths between 1990 and 2000.

Protecting Property and Pleasure

According to the USDA's Animal and Plant Health Inspection Service (APHIS), in *Managing Wildlife Conflicts: The Mission of the APHIS Wildlife Services Program* (October 2005, http://www.aphis.usda.gov/publications/wildlife_damage/content/printable_version/Manage WildlifeDamage2005.pdf), wildlife causes $600 million to $1.6 billion worth of damage annually to agriculture. Each year, farmers and ranchers lose thousands of calves and lambs, worth more than $71 million, to wild predators such as coyotes, wolves, and mountain lions. The GAO estimates in *Wildlife Services Program* that 273,000 sheep and lambs, 147,000 cattle and calves, and 61,000 goats and kids were lost to wild predators in 1999. Coyotes are blamed for most of the losses. Wild predators are primarily a problem in western states where ranchers graze their livestock on open rangelands. Furthermore, APHIS reports in *Wildlife Services: The Facts about Wildlife Damage Management* (2004, http://www .aphis.usda.gov/ws/ca/usda_fact_sheets/usda_fact_ sheet _wildlife_damage_management.pdf) that wildlife damages more than $50 million worth of corn, sunflowers, and blueberries annually.

The GAO *Wildlife Services Program* report involved an extensive investigation into wildlife damage across the country. Table 3.3 lists wildlife problems reported by each state. Birds, especially Canada geese, are a problem in thirty-nine states. Coyotes are mentioned as an issue in twenty states. Beavers are considered a problem in eighteen states.

FIGURE 3.3

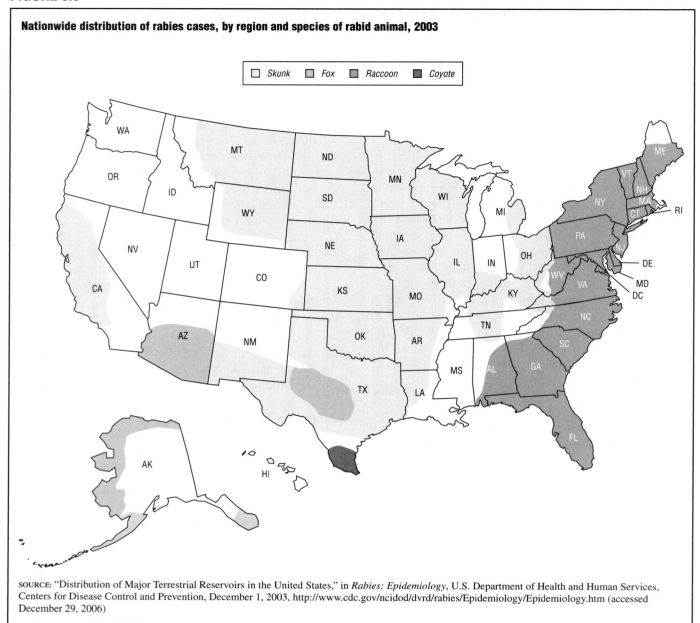

Nationwide distribution of rabies cases, by region and species of rabid animal, 2003

☐ Skunk   ▢ Fox   ▢ Raccoon   ◼ Coyote

SOURCE: "Distribution of Major Terrestrial Reservoirs in the United States," in *Rabies: Epidemiology*, U.S. Department of Health and Human Services, Centers for Disease Control and Prevention, December 1, 2003, http://www.cdc.gov/ncidod/dvrd/rabies/Epidemiology/Epidemiology.htm (accessed December 29, 2006)

Federal and state wildlife agencies use a variety of direct control methods to deal with so-called nuisance wildlife, including relocation, poisons, sharpshooters, contraceptives, and repellents. The agency dispersed nearly 18.9 million animals during fiscal year (FY) 2004, primarily by chemical methods (http://www.aphis .usda.gov/ws/ tables/PDR6,%20FY%202004.pdf). More than 2.7 million animals were killed by the WS during FY 2004. (See Table 3.4.) Birds made up the vast majority of the animals eliminated, accounting for nearly 92% of the total. Among terrestrial species the largest numbers of animals killed by the WS were coyotes (75,674), beavers (32,085), and feral (wild) hogs (11,484). Nearly 34,000 northern pikeminnow, a fish species, were also eliminated.

Government agencies also indirectly control wildlife by issuing hunting permits and allowing recreational hunts to take place. Lethal control methods employed by wildlife agencies are described in government publications as "depopulating" or "harvesting" surplus animals.

Controversies over Government Control of Wildlife

Animal rights and welfare groups maintain that government wildlife agencies rely far too much on killing as a control method. The WS denies this. According to the GAO *Wildlife Services Program* report, approximately 75% of the program's budget in FY 2000 was devoted to research and development of nonlethal control methods. One example is called the Electronic Guard. This

TABLE 3.2

Oral rabies vaccine distribution, by state, number of baits, and areas covered, 2006

State	Baits	Area (km²)
Alabama	1,063,350	16,273.2
Arizona	3,626	100.6
Florida	903,264	8,413.6
Georgia	96,528	1,448.8
Maine	49,680	747.3
Maryland	99,645	765.8
Massachusetts	101,893	776.4
New Hampshire	29,473	529.7
New Jersey	45,600	480.3
New York	1,474,067	17,907.6
North Carolina	184,932	2,888.5
Ohio	1,110,046	15,148.4
Pennsylvania	1,359,812	20,580.0
Tennessee	770,618	11,508.8
Texas	2,807,763	91,313.3
Vermont	383,179	7,182.8
Virginia	320,617	5,024.3
West Virginia	1,503,365	22,533.9
Total	**12,307,458**	**223,623.3**

SOURCE: "Oral Rabies Vaccine (ORV): 2006 Summary by State," in *Wildlife Services National Rabies Management Program: 2006 U.S. ORV Distribution Summary*, U.S. Department of Agriculture, Animal and Plant Health Inspection Service, 2006, http://www.aphis.usda.gov/ws/rabies/orv/dist/2006/us2006.html (accessed December 29, 2006)

device uses sirens and strobe lights to frighten coyotes away from sheep and lamb herds. The GAO notes that the WS uses lethal methods when nonlethal methods have proven ineffective and that WS "officials strive to select the method that will kill the bird or mammal quickly, effectively, and humanely."

Critics say that overuse of lethal methods actually aggravates problems because predators naturally respond by producing more offspring. The WS counters this argument in *Wildlife Services: The Facts about Wildlife Damage Management*, in which it cites Robert Crabtree's study, *Carnivores in Ecosystems: The Yellowstone Experience* (1999), which finds that coyote litter size "appears largely unaffected by levels of human exploitation." Furthermore, the WS states that habitat conditions and abundance of food are the determining factors in predator litter sizes.

PROBLEM HORSES. Wild horse and burro populations on public lands are managed by the Bureau of Land Management (BLM). As Table 3.5 shows, in FY 2006 there were more than thirty-one thousand of these animals scattered across the western states. They were maintained on approximately eighty-eight million acres. Table 3.5 also lists the appropriate management level (AML) established by the federal government as the maximum number of wild horses or burros appropriate for a particular area. In 2006 populations in Arizona, California, Colorado, Montana, Nevada, Utah, and Wyoming exceeded their AMLs.

The BLM states in "BLM Strategy to Manage Horses Upheld in Federal Court" (September 24, 2004, http://www.blm.gov/nhp/news/releases/pages/2004/pr040924_whb.htm) that its policy is to remove wild horses and burros from overpopulated areas to "prevent damage to the rangelands and threats to watershed health." The animals are gathered and held in holding pens. Some are adopted out to private citizens or organizations.

In 2000 the groups Fund for Animals (FFA) and Animal Legal Defense Fund filed a lawsuit against the BLM challenging the agency's wild horse management policy. The lawsuit claimed that the policy violated the Wild Free-Roaming Horse and Burro Act, the Administrative Procedure Act, and the National Environmental Policy Act. In September 2004 a federal court dismissed the lawsuit, saying that the groups had no standing in the case.

In December 2004 Congress passed the FY 2005 Omnibus Appropriations Bill, which included an amendment allowing some "excess" wild horses and burros to be sold at auction "without limitation." The bill applies to animals greater than ten years old and those that have unsuccessfully been offered for adoption at least three times. The amendment was added by then Montana senator Conrad Burns, who argued that the animals damage valuable grazing land and that maintaining them in holding pens is too expensive for the federal government. Critics explain that the phrase "without limitation" means that the animals can be slaughtered for horse meat. The amendment was condemned by animal protection groups and even drew criticism from mainline media sources not ordinarily sympathetic to animal causes. For example, the editorial "Save the Wild Horses" (*Washington Times*, December 6, 2004) was harshly critical of the amendment. It argued that wild horses have symbolic prestige in U.S. history and that the federal government should not allow their slaughter as a population control method. The editorial questioned the validity of claims that wild horses damage grazing land, citing a federal government study that found that overgrazing of cattle is a much more serious threat.

According to a BLM fact sheet (January 3, 2007, http://www.blm.gov/nhp/spotlight/whb_authority/fact_sheet.htm), there were approximately eighty-four hundred wild horses eligible for sale at the time of passage of the Burns amendment. In March 2005 the BLM conducted the first of several sales of wild horses under the new law. The following month the agency learned that some horses sold to a private individual had been resold to a horse slaughter plant. A BLM spokesperson noted that the agency was "extremely disappointed" but had no control over what happened to the horses once they were sold. Animal protection groups were outraged by the news.

TABLE 3.3

Examples of and concerns connected with resources damaged by wildlife, by state and type of injurious wildlife, 2001

State	Injurious wildlife	Resource damaged (annual damage estimate, if available)	Emerging concerns
Alabama	Fish-eating birds (e.g., cormorants, pelicans, herons, egrets)	Catfish ($4 million)	Wildlife diseases pose greater threats to humans, livestock, and pets; populations of fish-eating birds continue to increase; and diminished sport trapping is adding to the increase in beaver populations.
	Beavers	Timber ($19 million), transportation infrastructure	
Alaska	Arctic foxes	Aleutian Canada goose (threatened), nesting seabirds	Increased air travel throughout the state, coupled with immense populations of migratory birds and other wildlife, has created an urgent need for state and federal management of wildlife threats. Also, farmers and ranchers need assistance with damage from birds and predators.
Arizona	Coyotes, black bears, mountain lions	Livestock	Increased human populations and increased recreational use of public lands emphasize the need to deal with risks of wildlife disease transmission.
	Blackbirds	Dairy cattle, feedlot cattle (disease risk from contaminated feed and water)	
Arkansas	Blackbirds	Rice crops ($3.5 million)	The growing rice and aqua cultures industries require additional protection from the increasing populations of fish-eating birds.
	Fish-eating birds	Catfish ($2.3 million)	
California	Coyotes, black bears, mountain lions	Livestock (nearly $2 million)	Increased airline traffic and population growth of many bird species has created a greater need for wildlife control at airports; the recent surge in the number of direct attacks on humans creates an increased need to protect humans from large predators such as coyotes, black bears, and mountain lions.
	Birds, rodents	Row crops, fruit and nut crops, vineyards	
	Feral cats, red foxes, raccoons, coyotes, striped skunks, raptors	Threatened or endangered species (e.g., California red-legged frog, salt marsh harvest mouse, Sierra Nevada big horn sheep, Monterey Bay western snowy plover)	
Colorado	Coyotes	Sheep and lambs ($1.5 million), black-footed ferrets (endangered)	Human population growth, especially in rural and semi-rural areas, creates an increased potential for human-wildlife conflicts.
Connecticut	Starlings, blackbirds	Dairy cattle (salmonella risk from contaminated feed and water)	Preventing wildlife-borne diseases from affecting humans and livestock has become a growing concern with the recent out breaks of rabies, West Nile virus, salmonella, and E. coli; increased air travel and growing bird populations also call for increased wildlife control at airports.
	Canada geese, blackbirds, mute swans	Vegetable crops, cranberries	
	Birds, bats, squirrels, monk parakeets, ospreys	Buildings, landscaping, utilities	
Delaware	Snow geese	Coastal salt marsh habitat	West Nile virus is a major health concern. In fiscal year 2000, Delaware reported that four horses tested positive for the virus. Growth in air travel, coupled with growth in deer and bird populations, has created a greater need for wildlife control at airports.
	Canada geese	Grain crops, golf courses ($75,000)	
Florida	Raccoons, red foxes, coyotes, feral hogs, ghost crabs, armadillos	Threatened or endangered sea turtles (e.g., leatherback, hawksbill, loggerhead turtles)	Wildlife continue to threaten the safety of air travelers at many airports, but resource constraints have prevented Wildlife Services from resolving the hazards; livestock producers suffer losses from coyote and vulture predation, and direct assistance from Wildlife Services, rather than advice, would help reduce these losses.
	Foxes, coyotes, black rats, skunks, raccoons, snakes, armadillos, dogs	Endangered beach mice (e.g., Perdido Key, Anastasia Island, Choctawhatchee beach mice)	
	Red foxes, rats, coyotes, raccoons, feral cats	Threatened or endangered birds (e.g., roseate tern, least tern, Puerto Rican parrot)	
	Beavers	Flooded timber lands, croplands, roadways ($620,000)	
Georgia	Armadillos, raccoons, coyotes	Ground-nesting birds (e.g., bobwhite quail)	Increased habitat loss, human population growth, and the adaptability of many wildlife species to human environments increase the need for professional resolution of wildlife problems. Of concern are deer, geese, beavers, vultures, cormorants, pigeons, feral hogs, and raccoons.
	Beavers	Landscapes, pastures, timber, sanitation lines, culverts, highways, wells ($152,000)	
	Resident Canada geese, while-tailed deer	Crops, property, neighborhood landscapes and gardens	
Hawaii	Feral goats, sheep, pigs, deer	Endangered waterbirds, plants	The state is concerned about the time and expense involved in complying with the National Environmental Policy Act (conducting environmental analyses of Wildlife Services' actions performed for nonfederal cooperators), and the associated administrative requirements.
	Tree frogs	Horticulture, parrots, Axis deer	
	Rats	Agricultural products, native plants, seabirds, turtles	

TABLE 3.3

Examples of and concerns connected with resources damaged by wildlife, by state and type of injurious wildlife, 2001 [CONTINUED]

State	Injurious wildlife	Resource damaged (annual damage estimate, if available)	Emerging concerns
Idaho	Coyotes, black bears, mountain lions, wolves, red foxes	Sheep, lambs ($1.5 million)	Efforts to control crop damage by the sandhill crane have been limited by the lack of resources. Populations of ravens and red foxes have increased, to the detriment of the sage grouse.
	Ravens, coyotes, badgers, red foxes	Sage grouse, endangered northern Idaho ground squirrels	
Illinois	Canada geese, white-tailed deer	Private and municipal property	Bird predation at fish production facilities—an emerging agricultural industry in Illinois—is a concern, as is the transmission of wildlife-borne diseases such as West Nile virus.
	European starlings	Private and industrial property, risk of disease (histoplasmosis)	
Indiana	Canada geese	Private and industrial property ($169,000 in property damage reported in fiscal year 2000)	Over 12,000 people used Indiana's toll-free wildlife conflicts hotline during its first 2 years of service, preventing an estimated $100,000 in wildlife damage; now an additional person is needed to respond to calls.
	Starlings	Property damage (e.g., buildings and equipment), risk of disease (histoplasmosis)	
Iowa	Coyotes	Sheep, cattle, hogs ($20,000 in confirmed losses to coyotes)	Requests for assistance continue to increase, especially in regard to livestock predators (especially coyotes) and beavers.
	Beavers	Roads, crops, bridges	
Kansas	Blackbirds (grackles, starlings, cowbirds)	Livestock feed (more than $660,000 in damage at three feedlots during a recent winter)	Wildlife Services' success in addressing blackbird problems at feedlots has fueled demand for similar services statewide.
Kentucky	Starlings, Canada geese	Agriculture, residential and industrial property, aquaculture, golf courses, parks, utility structures	Increased urbanization and expansion into formerly rural areas, coupled with escalating wildlife populations, have led to a rise in wildlife-human conflicts.
Louisiana	Blackbirds, cowbirds, egrets, cormorants, white pelicans, herons	Sprouting rice ($5 million to $10 million a year in damage), strawberries, pecans, crawfish, catfish	Increased damage by birds is becoming more difficult to control, despite the more than $17 million spent annually by aquaculture facilities throughout the state. Beavers are another source of increasing wildlife damage in the state.
	Beavers	Threatened Louisiana pearlshell (a mussel), timber, roadways, bridges, public utilities. Nearly $5 million in beaver-caused losses was reported between 1998 and 2000.	
Maine	Birds, deer, moose, raccoons, skunks, black bears	Blueberries, strawberries, vegetable crops, beehives, campsites, summer homes, fences	Increasing predation from a rising cormorant population is harming the commercial, pen-raised Atlantic salmon industry and is thought to be the primary cause of the dwindling wild Atlantic salmon population.
	Beavers	Commercial timberlands, municipal roads, highways	
Maryland	Canada geese, vultures	Crops, waterfront properties	The state has an increased need to protect humans, their pets, and livestock from wildlife-borne diseases. Rabies and West Nile virus are two major health concerns on the East Coast.
Massachusetts	Canada geese, blackbirds	Cranberries, vegetables, dairy feed	Preventing the spread of wildlife-borne diseases to humans and livestock is a growing concern, given the recent outbreaks of rabies, West Nile virus, salmonella, giardia, and E. coli.
	Eider ducks, swans, cormorants, gulls	Trout hatcheries, shellfish	
Michigan	Starlings	Dairies, feedlots	Wolf populations will likely increase and expand from the Upper to the Lower Peninsula, causing increased demand for prompt and professional response in wolf management services. Also, demand for help in reducing damage by congregating starlings has grown significantly.
	Gray wolves (endangered)	Livestock	
	Deer	Bovine tuberculosis in cattle (projected impact to the state's producers is $121 million over 10 years)	
Minnesota	Gray wolves	Cattle, horses, sheep, poultry, dogs	As the wolf population continues to expand, the need for Wildlife Services' professional assistance is expected to increase. Nuisance bear complaints are also increasing.
	Beavers	Private property, roads, timber, fish habitat	
Mississippi	Double-crested cormorants, American white pelicans	Aquaculture (about $5 million)	Feral hogs are causing more crop damage and posing a disease threat (pseudorabies) for the domestic hog industry. Canada geese and black bears are becoming a growing concern for property owners.
	Beavers	Roads, bridges, drainage structures, agricultural fields, private property, timber (several million dollars a year in damage)	
	Black bears	Beehives, crops, private property	
Missouri	Beavers, muskrats	Crops, roads, levees	The state's resident Canada goose population has quadrupled since 1993, causing increased damage; the feral hog population is also increasing, and the state needs Wildlife Services' help with this problem.
	Blackbirds, herons	Rice crops, aquaculture	
	Canada geese	Crops, lawns, golf courses (more than $122,000 in turf and crop damage in fiscal year 2000)	
Montana	Grizzly bears, Rocky Mountain gray wolves (threatened or endangered)	Livestock (predators caused a $1.1 million loss to state's sheep industry in 2000)	With the successful reintroduction and recovery of Rocky Mountain gray wolves in nearby states, Montana Wildlife Services expects a growing demand for its expertise in handling wolf-related livestock predation issues.

TABLE 3.3

Examples of and concerns connected with resources damaged by wildlife, by state and type of injurious wildlife, 2001 [CONTINUED]

State	Injurious wildlife	Resource damaged (annual damage estimate, if available)	Emerging concerns
Nebraska	Coyotes, foxes, mountain lions, bobcats	Livestock	Areas requiring increased attention include wildlife management at airports, livestock predation, and public protection from wildlife-borne diseases. Increased public awareness of Wildlife Services' professional role in these issues has increased the demand for its services.
	Prairie dogs	Rangeland	
	Blackbirds	Feedlots	
Nevada	Rodents	Public health risk of sylvatic plague (wild form of bubonic plague)	Aviation safety is a growing concern. Population growth and city development around Nevada's major airports has created an ideal habitat for migratory birds such as Canada geese, mallard ducks, and American coots.
	Coyotes, mountain lions	Livestock; humans and pets in urban areas	
New Hampshire	Black bears	Apiaries, row crops, livestock	Controlling the spread of West Nile virus is an emerging concern, along with rabies, Lyme disease, salmonella, and chronic wasting disease. Also, the 10-year trend of increasing conflicts associated with bears and bird feeding activities needs to be addressed.
	Deer	Apples, fruit crops, ornamental shrubbery	
	Woodchucks	Earthen dams and levees, wild lupine (essential to the endangered Karner blue butterfly)	
	Gulls	Roseate and common tern recolonization efforts	
New Jersey	Canada geese	Human health effects of goose feces, human safety threats from aggressive geese, crops, turf	The state's large population of resident Canada geese will pose increasing challenges for the protection of human health and safety, as well as property, at schools, hospitals, airports, and urban and suburban areas. The spread of West Nile virus is another concern.
	Deer, blackbirds	Crops, fruit trees, vegetables	
	Red foxes, raccoons, opossums	Threatened and endangered shorebirds (e.g., piping plovers, least terns, black skimmers)	
New Mexico	Coyotes, cougars, bobcats, black bears	Livestock (losses in excess of $1.6 million in 1999)	Coyotes are becoming an increasing problem in urban and suburban areas, killing pets and other domestic animals and posing safety risks to humans. Wildlife Services' assistance will be needed to resolve conflicts between humans and the black-tailed prairie dog, a candidate threatened species.
	Prairie dogs, pocket gophers, ground squirrels	Agricultural crops, pasture land, turf, human health and safety (nearly $500,000 in rodent damage in fiscal year 2000)	
	Sandhill cranes, snow geese	Crops (e.g., alfalfa, chile, wheat)	
New York	Cormorants, gulls	Catfish, bait fish, crawfish, sport fish	Bat and raccoon rabies remain a health concern, and urban winter crow roosts are emerging as a unique problem to city residents, resulting in conflicts over droppings, noise, odor, and fear associated with zoonotic disease.
	Canada geese	Property, crops	
North Carolina	Beavers	Timber, crops, roads, drainage systems, landscapes. In fiscal year 2000, Wildlife Services prevented about $8.5 million in damage to such resources: nearly $9 saved for every $1 spent.	Threats to public safety, not only by wildlife at airports, but also by the rapidly growing beaver population, must be addressed. A rabid beaver's recent attack on a human has increased public awareness of this issue.
North Dakota/ South Dakota	Coyotes, foxes	Cattle, sheep, poultry	More work at airports is needed, and the threat of rabies transferring from skunks to humans or domestic animals continues to be a concern.
	Blackbirds	Sunflowers and other grain crops (over $5 million in losses annually in the upper Great Plains), feedlots	
	Canada geese and other waterfowl	Grain crops (damage increased by 80 percent in 2000, resulting in $162,000 in losses)	
Ohio	Coyotes, vultures	Cattle, sheep, poultry	Increasing populations of gulls, vultures, and starlings are causing significant human health and safety issues and crop and property damage.
	Raccoons	Human health and safety	
	Rooftop nesting gulls	Property	
	Blackbirds, Canada geese	Crops, property	
Oklahoma	Beavers	Dams, timber, crops, roads, private property	Feral hogs cause many problems (livestock predation, crop destruction); Canada geese are growing in number and are damaging crops.
	Coyotes	Cattle, sheep, goats, poultry	
	Canada geese	Crops (especially winter wheat)	
Oregon	Canada geese	Turf grass seed, other crops	Successful wolf reintroduction in Idaho means future wolf coflicts with livestock in Oregon. Wolves will hamper present predator control efforts because control tools and methods will be restricted around wolves.
	Cougars	Human safety (Wildlife Services addressed 386 cougar complaints in 2000; 118 involved threats to humans)	
	Black bears, beavers	Timber	

TABLE 3.3

Examples of and concerns connected with resources damaged by wildlife, by state and type of injurious wildlife, 2001 [CONTINUED]

State	Injurious wildlife	Resource damaged (annual damage estimate, if available)	Emerging concerns
Pennsylvania	Deer	Human safety (automobile collisions)	The state's large population of resident Canada geese will pose increasing challenges over time, as will increasing populations of deer, vultures, and gulls. Emerging public health issues (e.g., West Nile virus) will also be a challenge.
	Canada geese	Landscape, crops (program annually assists over 300 residents with goose-related problems)	
	Starlings	Livestock facilities	
Rhode Island	Canada geese, gulls, crows, turkey vultures	Property, turf, vegetable crops	The needs of some citizens are currently unmet. Increasingly, the program is able to respond to requests for assistance only from entities that can fully fund it. Preventing wildlife-borne diseases is a growing concern.
	Mute swans	Pond water quality	
	Monk parakeets, ospreys	Landscaping, utilities	
South Carolina	Beavers	Timber, crops, roads, levees, dams	The demand for beaver management has overwhelmed the program, yet some counties cannot afford to share the costs. At the same time, the vulture population and related complaints have increased.
	White-tailed deer	Landscaping, human safety (automobile collisions), human health (tick-borne diseases)	
Tennessee	Canada geese	Turf (at golf courses, parks, etc.)	The growing number and variety of wildlife-human conflicts pose a challenge to the program, especially in terms of wildlife control at airports and urban damage by large birds.
	Beavers	Roads, bridges, timber, wildlife management areas	
	Vultures	Municipal utility structures, residential property	
Texas	Coyotes, foxes	Human health (rabies)	The feral hog population in the state exceeds 1 million. Hogs damage many crops (e.g., corn, rice, peanuts, hay), and they prey on lambs, kids, fawns, and ground nesting birds. Also, damage by migratory birds (e.g., cattle egrets, vultures, cormorants) has increased, taxing the program's response abilities.
	Coyotes	Sheep and goats	
	Beavers	Dams, dikes, railroad track beds, timber, roads, pastures, crops	
	Blackbirds	Citrus crops, rice, feedlot operations	
	Feral hogs	Agricultural crops, livestock	
Utah	Coyotes, mountain lions, black bears	Sheep and lambs (nearly $2 million in losses in 1999, even with controls in place), endangered black-footed ferrets, sage grouse, mule deer fawns	Demands for wildlife damage management are increasing, yet the program already has more requests than it can address. Protection of native wildlife continues to be of importance.
	Skunks, raccoons, feral and urban waterfowl, pigeons	Human health and safety (threat of rabies, raccoon roundworm, salmonella, plague)	
Vermont	Raccoons	Human health (rabies), threatened Eastern spiney softshell turtle	Wildlife diseases like West Nile virus, Lyme disease, salmonella, and chronic wasting syndrome continue to emerge and need to be addressed.
	Starlings	Cattle feed at dairies	
Virginia	Coyotes, black vultures	Livestock	Challenges include finding a way to provide damage management services to low- and middle-income people and protecting Virginia's rare natural resources (e.g., the threatened piping plover and Wilson's plover).
	Beavers	Roads, railroads	
	Canada geese, crows, vultures, starlings, muskrats	Urban and suburban property, water quality, human health and safety. (Canada geese are involved in 26 percent of all requests for program assistance in Virginia.)	
Washington	Northern pikeminnows, gulls	Threatened and endangered salmon and steelhead	Increasing problems are caused by urban Canada geese and by predators (damage to livestock, agriculture, and forestry resources), but program resources are already strained.
	Starlings, feral pigeons, Canada geese, gulls	Bridges, buildings (bird feces are corrosive to paint and metal), fruit crops, public and private property, human health (over $6 million a year in damage to the fruit industry)	
	Coyotes	Livestock, endangered Columbian white-tailed deer, pygmy rabbits	
West Virginia	Coyotes, vultures	Sheep, cattle, goats	With its limited resources, the program concentrates on the highest priorities (human health and safety). As a result, though, program staff cannot make much-needed on-site evaluations of wildlife damage to property; rather, they make recommendations based on telephone interviews. Also, problems caused by starlings and roosting birds need attention.
	Raccoons	Human health (rabies)	
	Muskrats, beavers	Levees and dams	

TABLE 3.3

Examples of and concerns connected with resources damaged by wildlife, by state and type of injurious wildlife, 2001 [CONTINUED]

State	Injurious wildlife	Resource damaged (annual damage estimate, if available)	Emerging concerns
Wisconsin	Deer	Crops (over $1 million a year in damage)	The endangered gray wolf population has grown from 34 wolves in 1990 to about 250 in 2000, and the wolf's recovery is considered a success. But problems, such as depredation on livestock and pets, have come with the wolf's recovery. Also problematic is the damage done by the burgeoning population of resident Canada geese, which now numbers over 70,000.
	Black bears	Crops, property, human safety	
	Beavers	Trout streams	
	Gray wolves	Livestock, pets	
	Canada geese	Municipal and private property	
Wyoming	Coyotes, black bears, red foxes, mountain lions, grizzly bears, wolves	Livestock (losses of over $5.6 million to predators in 2000)	As wolf and grizzly bear populations expand, new or different control methods will be needed to prevent unnecessary conflicts with them. Also, skunk rabies seems to be spreading westward across the state, and a program is needed to contain it.
	Skunks	Human health (rabies risk)	
	Coyotes	Black-footed ferrets	
Guam	Brown tree snakes	Power transmission lines, poultry and small animals, endangered species (e.g., Vanikoro swiftlets, Mariana crows, Guam fruit bats, Guam rails, Micronesian kingfishers), human health and safety	The magnitude and complexity of the work to control the brown tree snake pose significant challenges, and the administrative burden is increasing.
U.S. Virgin Islands	Black rats	Endangered sea turtles, migratory birds, native vegetation	Invasive species' impacts on native plants and animals is a major and growing problem.
	Roosting birds	Human health concerns	

SOURCE: "Table 6. Examples of Resources Damaged by Injurious Wildlife, and Related Emerging Concerns, by State," in *Wildlife Services Program: Information on Activities to Manage Wildlife Damage*, U.S. General Accounting Office, November 2001

In May 2005 the Ford Motor Company established the Save the Mustangs fund to build public awareness and raise contributions to save wild horses. In January 2007 Ford reported that more than $200,000 had been raised for the fund and that the funds would be distributed to carefully screened horse rescue groups that agree to purchase the horses (http://www.ford.com/en/goodWorks/environment/natureAndWildlife/saveTheMustangs/default .htm).

The BLM fact sheet reports that nearly twenty-two hundred wild horses and burros had been sold through the Burns amendment program as of December 2006. The agency denies that it sells the animals to slaughterhouses or "killer buyers." The BLM spent $36.8 million during FY 2006 on the wild horse and burro program. More than half of the money ($19.6 million) was devoted to short- and long-term holding facilities for the animals.

Protecting Endangered and Threatened Species

The Endangered Species Act was passed in 1973. It built on protection measures first laid out in the 1966 Endangered Species Preservation Act. The purpose of the Endangered Species Act is to conserve the ecosystems on which endangered and threatened species depend and to conserve and recover listed species. An endangered species is in danger of extinction throughout all or a significant portion of its range. A threatened species is considered likely to become endangered in the future. Some species are listed as endangered in some areas of the country and only threatened in other areas.

As of January 1, 2007, there were 567 native species on the federal list of endangered and threatened animals—412 endangered species and 155 threatened species. (See Table 3.6.) Another 565 foreign animal species were listed as endangered or threatened. Animals are placed on the list based on their biological status and the threats to their existence. Some species are put on the list because they closely resemble endangered or threatened species.

The USFWS and the National Marine Fisheries Service (NMFS) share responsibility for administering the Endangered Species Act. They work in partnership with state agencies to enforce the act and develop and maintain conservation programs. The USFWS operates fifty-nine national wildlife refuges around the country that were established specifically to protect endangered species. (See Table 3.7.)

The Endangered Species Act prohibits any person from taking a listed species. Taking includes actions that "harass, harm, pursue, hunt, shoot, wound, kill, trap, capture, or collect" listed species or attempt to do so. Harm is defined as an action that kills or injures the animal and includes actions that significantly modify or degrade habitats or significantly impair essential behavior patterns such as breeding, feeding, and sheltering.

TABLE 3.4

Animals killed by Wildlife Services, by species, 2004

Alligators, American	11
Armadillos, nine-banded	317
Badgers	445
Bats (all)	9
Bears, black	397
Beavers	32,085
Bobcats	1,918
Cats, feral/free ranging	1,099
Cattle, feral	2
Chipmunks (all)	6
Coyotes	75,674
Deer	2,923
Dogs, feral/free ranging & hybrids	519
Elk, wapiti (wild)	1
Fish (other)	54
Foxes	3,907
Frogs/toads	147
Goats, feral	26
Gophers, pocket (all)	201
Hares	1,405
Hogs, feral	11,484
Lions, mountain (cougar)	359
Lizards, monitor	7
Mammals, exotic	164
Marmots/woodchucks (all)	3,296
Mice/rats	4,987
Minks	12
Moles (all)	6
Mongooses, Indian	1,329
Moose	1
Muskrats	1,722
Nutrias	6,335
Opossums, Virginia	3,236
Otters, river	496
Peccaries, collared (javelina)	140
Pikeminnow, northern	33,972
Porcupines	192
Prairie dogs	2,190
Pronghorn (antelope)	2
Rabbits	274
Raccoons	10,518
Reptiles, exotic	205
Sheep, feral/free-ranging/exotic	16
Skunks	6,791
Snakes	9,797
Squirrels	5,574
Turtles (all)	648
Voles (all)	135
Weasels (all)	9
Wolves	191
Sub total	**225,234**
Birds & poultry	
Starlings, European	2,320,086
Pigeons, feral (rock dove)	59,784
Dove, zebra	15,205
Cowbirds, brown-headed	14,473
Other	132,370
Sub total	**2,541,918**
Grand total	**2,767,152**

SOURCE: Adapted from "PDR 10. Number of Animals Killed and Methods Used by the WS Program, FY 2004," in *Wildlife Services' 2004 Annual Tables*, U.S. Department of Agriculture, Animal and Plant Health Inspection Service, August 31, 2005, http://www.aphis.usda.gov/ws/tables/TABLE%2010Killed,%20FY%202004.pdf (accessed December 28, 2006)

These measures are designed to allow endangered and threatened species to repopulate. However, once a species does repopulate, it can be delisted (removed from the list of endangered species), and the taking prohibition no longer applies. Table 3.8 shows the delisting status for specific wildlife species that have been delisted or are expected to be delisted by 2015.

In addition, endangered species that pose a threat to humans and livestock can be killed under certain circumstances. In 1967 gray and red wolves were listed as endangered, because centuries of extermination had severely depleted their numbers. (See Figure 3.4.) In the 1990s wolves were reintroduced to certain areas of the western United States and designated "nonessential experimental populations." This designation allowed government agencies and private citizens flexibility in controlling wolf populations. For example, wolves could be killed, moved, or harassed to protect domestic livestock. By 2002 wolf populations in some western states had reached the government's recovery goals. However, before the species can be delisted the USFWS requires that state and tribal governments have approved wolf management plans in place that will protect both the wolves and human interests.

INTERESTS OF HUMANS VERSUS THOSE OF ENDANGERED SPECIES. Protecting endangered and threatened species becomes extremely controversial when it threatens human economic interests. One example is the northern spotted owl. Its primary habitat is among old-growth trees (greater than one hundred years old) in the coniferous forests of the Pacific Northwest, which were heavily logged in the 1960s. John Weier reports in "Spotting the Spotted Owl" (June 15, 1999, http://earthobservatory.nasa.gov/Study/SpottedOwls/) that in 1972 researchers at Oregon State University estimated that 85% to 90% of the owl's suitable habitat had already been eliminated. The researchers assessed the future harvest plans of major logging companies and learned that most of the remaining old-growth trees in these forests were also to be cut down. The resulting publicity caused a major showdown between environmental conservation groups and the logging industry.

Environmental activists chained themselves to trees and damaged logging equipment to protest removal of the old-growth forests. Protest marches captured national headlines. There was tremendous political pressure to protect the owl's remaining habitat, particularly because approximately half of it was on federal lands. Since the mid-1980s the U.S. Forest Service (USFS) has tried to develop plans for managing federal forests in the Pacific Northwest that balance timber harvesting with habitat protection. Neither side has been happy with the proposals. The timber industry complains that protecting owls puts loggers out of work. Environmentalists believe that all old-growth forests can be saved. In 1990 the USFWS added the northern spotted owl to the federal list of threatened species. The decision followed years of study and lawsuits filed by environmental groups and representatives of the timber industry.

TABLE 3.5

Wild horse and burro herd statistics, fiscal year 2006

	Herd area			Herd management area			Acres transferred from BLM	Populations			Total AML
	BLM acres	Other acres	Total acres	BLM acres	Other acres	Total acres		Horses	Burros	Total	
AZ	2,019,932	1,617,998	3,637,930	1,756,086	1,327,777	3,083,863	0	230	1,542	1,772	1,570
CA	5,112,778	1,851,661	6,964,439	1,946,590	471,855	2,418,445	1,477,076	3,166	889	4,055	2,199
CO	658,119	76,572	734,691	366,098	38,656	404,754	0	884	0	884	812
ID	428,421	49,235	477,656	377,907	40,287	418,194	0	594	0	594	617
MT	104,361	119,242	223,603	28,282	8,865	37,147	0	159	0	159	105
NV	19,593,299	3,088,027	22,681,326	15,778,284	1,695,925	17,474,209	444,112	13,384	834	14,218	13,535
NM	88,653	37,874	126,527	24,505	4,107	28,612	0	62	0	62	83
OR	3,559,935	785,250	4,345,185	2,703,409	259,726	2,963,135	0	2,113	15	2,128	2,715
UT	3,236,178	689,176	3,925,354	2,462,726	374,614	2,837,340	79,120	2,545	169	2,714	2,151
WY	7,297,778	3,030,010	10,327,788	3,638,330	1,137,121	4,775,451	0	4,615	0	4,615	3,725
Total	**42,099,454**	**11,345,045**	**53,444,499**	**29,082,217**	**5,358,933**	**34,441,150**	**2,000,308**	**27,752**	**3,449**	**31,201**	**27,512**

Notes:
Herd area statistics are a reflection of each state's current population information as of February 28, 2006.
Populations do not reflect any changes after February 2006 (i.e. foal crops or gathers).
Bureau of Land Management (BLM) policy is to establish appropriate management level (AML) as a range with upper and lower levels; the numbers displayed represents the upper limit.
Acres have been calculated using current digitized (GIS) maps.
Acreage transferred from BLM to another agency is not deducted from the herd area.

SOURCE: "Herd Area Statistics, 2006," in *Wild Horse and Burro Herd Area Statistics—FY 2006*, U.S. Department of the Interior, Bureau of Land Management, 2006, http://www.wildhorseandburro.blm.gov/statistics/2006/HA_Acreages.pdf (accessed November 28, 2006)

TABLE 3.6

Endangered and threatened species as of January 1, 2007

Group	United States			Foreign			Total listings (US and foreign)
	Endangered	Threatened	Total listings	Endangered	Threatened	Total listings	
Mammals	69	13	82	255	20	275	357
Birds	76	15	91	175	6	181	272
Reptiles	14	23	37	65	16	81	118
Amphibians	13	10	23	8	1	9	32
Fishes	75	62	137	11	1	2	149
Clams	62	8	70	2	0	2	72
Snails	25	11	36	1	0	1	37
Insects	47	10	57	4	0	4	61
Arachnids	12	0	12	0	0	0	12
Crustaceans	19	3	22	0	0	0	22
Total	**412**	**155**	**567**	**521**	**44**	**565**	**1,132**

Notes: 34 animal species (17 in the U.S. and 17 foreign) are counted more than once in the above table, primarily because these animals have distinct population segments (each with its own individual listing status). One listing represents an entire genus or family that includes several different species.

SOURCE: Adapted from "Summary of Listed Species, Species and Recovery Plans as of 01/01/2007," in *Threatened and Endangered Species System (TESS) Summary of Listed Species as of 01/01/07*, U.S. Department of the Interior, U.S. Fish and Wildlife Service, January 1, 2007, http://ecos.fws.gov/tess_public/TESSBoxscore (accessed January 1, 2007)

The legal battles continued throughout the 1990s. In 1994 the administration of President Bill Clinton formulated the Northwest Forest Plan as an attempt to satisfy both sides. The plan requires completion of biological surveys on dozens of plants and animals before logging is allowed on federal timberlands in the Northwest. It also includes other measures designed to protect owl habitat. Critics contend that this protection has a high human cost. According to Hal Bernton, in "Forest Service Halts Timber Sales in Northwest Spotted Owl Regions" (*Oregonian*, August 12, 1999), more than ten thousand jobs in the forest products industry were lost in Oregon and Washington between 1991 and 1998, as mills dependent on federal timber closed down.

In 2002 the Western Council of Industrial Workers and the American Resource Forest Council sued the USFWS over its spotted owl management policy. The groups claimed that the agency had undercounted the number of spotted owls in old-growth forests and that limits on timber harvesting in these areas were not needed. In response, the USFWS agreed to conduct a listing status review. All studies performed since 1990 on spotted owl habitats and populations were reviewed

TABLE 3.7

National Wildlife Refuges (NWR) established for endangered species, by state, acreage, and species of concern, 2005

State	Unit name	Species of concern	Unit acreage
Alabama	Sauta Cave NWR	Indiana Bat, Gray Bat	264
	Fern Cave NWR	Indiana Bat, Gray Bat	199
	Key Cave NWR	Alabama Cavefish, Gray Bat	1,060
	Watercress Darter NWR	Watercress Darter	7
Arkansas	Logan Cave NWR	Cave Crayfish, Gray Bat, Indiana Bat, Ozark Cavefish	124
Arizona	Buenos Aires NWR	Masked Bobwhite Quail	116,585
	Leslie Canyon	Gila Topminnow, Yaqui Chub, Peregrine Falcon	2,765
	San Bernardino NWR	Gila Topminnow, Yaqui Chub, Yaqui Catfish, Beautiful Shiner, Huachuca Water Umbel	2,369
California	Antioch Dunes NWR	Lange's Metalmark Butterfly, Antioch Dunes Evening-primrose, Contra Costa Wallflower	55
	Bitter Creek NWR	California Condor	14,054
	Blue Ridge NWR	California Condor	897
	Castle Rock NWR	Aleutian Canada Goose	14
	Coachella Valley NWR	Coachello Valley Fringe-toed Lizard	3,592
	Don Edwards San Francisco Bay NWR	California Clapper Rail, California Least Tern, Salt Marsh Harvest Mouse	21,524
	Ellicott Slough NWR	Santa Cruz Long-toed Salamander	139
	Hopper Mountain NWR	California Condor	2,471
	Sacramento River NWR	Valley Elderberry Longhorn Beetle, Bald Eagle, Least Bell's Vireo	7,884
	San Diego NWR	San Diego Fairy Shrimp, San Diego Mesa Mint, Otay Mesa Mint, California Orcutt Grass, San Diego Button-celery	1,840
	San Joaquin River NWR	Aleutian Canada Goose	1,638
	Seal Beach NWR	Light-footed Clapper Rail, California Least Tern	911
	Sweetwater Marsh NWR	Light-footed Clapper Rail	316
	Tijuana Slough NWR	Light-footed Clapper Rail	1,023
Florida	Archie Carr NWR	Loggerhead Sea Turtle, Green Sea Turtle	29
	Crocodile Lake NWR	American Crocodile	6,686
	Crystal River NWR	West Indian Manatee	80
	Florida Panther NWR	Florida Panther	23,379
	Hobe Sound NWR	Loggerhead Sea Turtle, Green Sea Turtle	980
	Lake Wales Ridge NWR	Florida Scrub Jay, Snakeroot, Scrub Blazing Star, Carter's Mustard, Papery Whitlow-wort, Florida Bonamia, Scrub Lupine, Highlands Scrub Hyopericum, Garett's Mint, Scrub Mint, Pygmy Gringe-tree, Wireweed, Florida Ziziphus, Scrub Plum, Eastern Indigo Snake, Bluetail Mole Skink, Sand Skink	659
	National Key Deer Refuge	Key Deer	8,542
	St. Johns NWR	Dusky Seaside Sparrow	6,255
Hawaii	Hakalau Forest NWR	Akepa, Akiapolaau, 'O'u, Hawaiian Hawk, Hawaiian Creeper	32,730
	Hanalei NWR	Hawaiian Stilt, Hawaiian Coot, Hawaiian Moorhen, Hawaiian Duck	917
	Huleia NWR	Hawaiian Stilt, Hawaiian Coot, Hawaiian Moorhen, Hawaiian Duck	241
	James C. Campbell NWR	Hawaiian Stilt, Hawaiian Coot, Hawaiian Moorhen, Hawaiian Duck	164
	Kakahaia NWR	Hawaiian Stilt, Hawaiian Coot	45
	Kealia Pond NWR	Hawaiian Stilt, Hawaiian Coot	691
	Pearl Harbor NWR	Hawaiian Stilt	61
Iowa	Driftless Area NWR	Iowa Pleistocene Snail	521
Massachusetts	Massasoit NWR	Plymouth Red-bellied Turtle	184
Michigan	Kirtland's Warbler WMA	Kirtland's Warbler	6,535
Mississippi	Mississippi Sandhill Crane NWR	Mississippi Sandhill Crane	19,713
Missouri	Ozark Cavefish NWR	Ozark Cavefish	42
	Pilot Knob NWR	Indiana Bat	90
Nebraska	Karl E. Mundt NWR	Bald Eagle	19
Nevada	Ash Meadows NWR	Devil's Hole Pupfish, Warm Springs Pupfish, Ash Meadows Amargosa Pupfish, Ash Meadows Speckled Dace, Ash Meadows Naucorid, Ash Meadows Blazing Star, Amargosa Niterwort, Ash Meadows Milk-Vetch, Ash Meadows Sunray, Spring-loving Centaury, Ash Meadows Gumplant, Ash Meadows Invesia	13,268
	Moapa Valley NWR	Moapa Dace	32
Oklahoma	Ozark Plateau NWR	Ozark Big-eared Bat, Gray Bat	2,208
Oregon	Bear Valley NWR	Bald Eagle	4,200
	Julia Butler Hansen Refuge for Columbian White-tail Deer	Columbian White-tailed Deer	2,750
	Nestucca Bay NWR	Aleutian Canada Goose	457
South Dakota	Karl E. Mundt NWR	Bald Eagle	1,044
Texas	Attwater Prairie Chicken NWR	Attwater's Greater Prairie Chicken	8,007
	Balcones Canyonlands NWR	Black-capped Vireo, Golden-cheeked Warbler	14,144
Virgin Islands	Green Cay NWR	St. Croix Ground Lizard	14
	Sandy Point NWR	Leatherback Sea Turtle	327
Virginia	James River NWR	Bald Eagle	4,147
	Mason Neck NWR	Bald Eagle	2,276
Washington	Julia Butler Hansen Refuge for Columbian White-tail Deer	Columbian White-tailed Deer	2,777
Wyoming	Mortenson Lake NWR	Wyoming Toad	1,776

SOURCE: ÒNational Wildlife Refuges Established for Endangered Species,Ó in *AmericaÕs National Wildlife Refuge System*, U.S. Department of the Interior, U.S. Fish and Wildlife Service, 2005, http://refuges.fws.gov/habitats/endSpRefuges.html (accessed January 03, 2007)

TABLE 3.8

Selected endangered species and their delisting status, 2006

Species name	Year species was listed and target delisting time frame[a, b]	Primary threat that has been, or is being, mitigated
Bald eagle	Listed: 1967/1978[c] Proposed for delisting: 1999 and 2006 Anticipated to be delisted: by 2010	The insecticide DDT causes reproductive failure in bald eagles. This threat was mitigated when the Environmental Protection Agency banned DDT in 1972. Habitat protections and guidance to avoid disturbing nesting sites have also helped. FWS proposed delisting the eagle in 1999; however, action was delayed because of legal concerns. FWS reinitiated the process to delist the bald eagle in February 2006.
Borax Lake chub (fish)	Listed: 1980 Anticipated to be delisted: by 2015	The primary threats were geothermal development, and shoreline alteration due to grazing. Legislation prevented geothermal development and land acquisition is protecting shoreline.
Columbian white-tailed deer —Douglas County DPS[d]	Listed: 1967 Delisted: 2003	Habitat protection via land acquisition and hunting restrictions were critical to the deer's recovery and subsequent delisting in July 2003.
Gray wolf—western Great Lakes recovery population	Listed: 1967 Proposed for delisting: 2006 Anticipated to be delisted: by 2010	Human predation was the primary threat facing the gray wolf; for instance, wolves were frequently killed by farmers to protect their livestock from predation. Programs that removed livestock-killing wolves, and compensated farmers who lost livestock to wolves, helped reduce this practice. Delisting has been delayed due to legal questions about how to delist this population, since all gray wolves are currently listed as a single entity rather than as distinct population segments.
Papery whitlow-wort—central Florida subspecies (plant)	Listed: 1987 Anticipated to be delisted: by 2010	Habitat has been protected and restored through land acquisition and management activities.
Steller sea lion—eastern DPS[d]	Listed: 1990 Anticipated to be delisted: by 2010	The killing of steller sea lions by humans (for example, to protect fishing gear or to reduce population numbers) was a major threat that has been prohibited.
Magazine Mountain shagreen (land snail)	Listed: 1989 Anticipated to be delisted: by 2010	Two planned actions that could have affected the species' habitat were withdrawn or mitigated.
Virginia round-leaf birch (tree)	Listed: 1978 Anticipated to be delisted: by 2015	Helping propagation of seedlings in the wild and protecting them until they could withstand herbivory helped ensure the species' survival. Additionally, distributing seedlings to the public helped reduce illegal collecting.

[a]Target time frames for delisting assume that remaining recovery actions are taken. However, many factors, including availability of funding, cooperation with partners, acquisition of land, and responsiveness of the species, may render these time frames unattainable or obsolete. We present estimates in 5-year increments.
[b]Species with a listing date before 1973, the year the Endangered Species Act was enacted, were originally listed under provisions of the Endangered Species Preservation Act of 1966 or the Endangered Species Conservation Act of 1969, and "grandfathered" onto the list of threatened and endangered species under the 1973 act.
[c]The bald eagle was first listed in 1967, but the listing only applied to bald eagles in southern states. Fish and Wildlife Service (FWS) later determined that there was no morphological or geographical basis to distinguish northern and southern eagles and extended protection to all bald eagles in the 48 conterminous states in 1978.
[d]ADPS is a subdivision of a vertebrate species that, for purposes of listing, is treated as a species under the Endangered Species Act.

SOURCE: "Table 1. Species Facing a Primary Threat That Has Been, or Is Being, Mitigated," in *Endangered Species: Many Factors Affect the Length of Time to Recover Select Species*, U.S. Government Accountability Office, September 2006,http://www.gao.gov/new.items/d06730.pdf (accessed December 29, 2006)

again and summarized. In November 2004 the USFWS announced that the status review had reinforced the necessity of keeping the northern spotted owl listed as a threatened species under the Endangered Species Act.

Similar conflicts between conservation and economic interests have raged in the United States over the protection of other animal species. These include the snail darter (a fish inhabiting the Tennessee River valley), Florida's gopher tortoises, and Coho salmon and sucker fish in Oregon's Klamath River Basin.

INTERNATIONAL EFFORTS. On the international front, endangered wild animals are protected by CITES. Under the Endangered Species Act, the United States participates in CITES to prohibit trade in listed species.

CITES includes three lists:

• Appendix I—Species for which no commercial trade is allowed. Noncommercial trade is permitted if it does not jeopardize species survival in the wild. Importers and exporters of Appendix I species must obtain permits.

• Appendix II—Species for which commercial trade is tightly regulated and managed with permits.

• Appendix III—Species that may be negatively impacted by commercial trade. Permits are used to monitor trade in these species.

Listing of any species in Appendix I or Appendix II requires approval by a two-thirds majority of CITES nations. The CITES appendices list thousands of animals from all over the world.

Animals of major concern internationally include Asian and African elephants and primates. In "Catastrophic Ape Decline in Western Equatorial Africa" (*Nature*, April 10, 2003), Peter D. Walsh et al. report that gorillas and chimpanzees in western Africa are on the verge of extinction because of poaching (illegal hunting) and the Ebola virus. Walsh et al. estimate that approximately 80% of all wild gorillas and most wild chimpanzees live in western Africa. Their populations had dropped by more than half since the 1980s and are expected to continue to decrease rapidly unless drastic action is taken.

Logging roads associated with deforestation allow poachers easy access to areas that were previously inaccessible. They supply the growing trade in bushmeat (meat from wild animals such as elephants, primates,

FIGURE 3.4

A gray wolf. *AP/Wide World Photos/National Park Service. Reproduced by permission.*

antelope, and crocodiles). Although ape meat makes up only a tiny percentage of bushmeat, wild chimpanzees are in great danger from the trade. Scientists say that consumption of contaminated bushmeat has passed the Ebola virus from animals to people.

KILLING WILDLIFE

Wildlife all over the world are killed for various reasons, including sport, commerce, and perceived threats to human interests.

Recreational Hunting

Hunting was originally a means of survival for humans. As societies became more dependent on agriculture and livestock, hunting gradually became more an activity of leisure, recreation, and sport than survival (though many hunters do still use the meat they procure to make up varying degrees of their diets). The USFWS conducts a national survey on hunting, fishing, and other wildlife-related activities every five years. The latest survey was conducted in 2001 and published in 2002. According to the survey, more than thirteen million Americans aged sixteen and over hunted wildlife in 2001. The

vast majority of hunters surveyed (nearly eleven million) pursued big game, such as deer, elk, bear, and wild turkey. (See Table 3.9.) Other popular game included rabbits, squirrels, pheasants, quail, grouse, doves, ducks, geese, groundhogs, raccoons, foxes, and coyotes.

Hunters use a variety of implements to kill animals, including rifles, shotguns, handguns, and bows and arrows. Animal welfarists argue about which methods they consider the least cruel and which are associated with the smallest number of nonfatal injuries. In general, they consider firearms more humane than bows and arrows.

In January 2004 the FFA released the report *A Dying Sport: The State of Hunting in America.* The report provides statistics on hunter demographics and expenditures and the number of animals killed by hunting each year. According to the FFA, the number of U.S. hunters declined by 7% between 1991 and 2001, even though expenditures for licenses, permits, and so on increased by 22%. The decline in numbers of hunters is attributed to the decrease in the country's rural population coupled with less availability of land for hunting.

TABLE 3.9

Hunters and days of hunting, by type of game, 2001

[Population 16 years old and older; numbers in thousands]

Type of game	Hunters		Days of hunting		Average days per hunter
	Number	Percent	Number	Percent	
Total, all big game	**10,911**	**100**	**153,191**	**100**	**14**
Deer	10,272	94	133,457	87	13
Elk	910	8	6,402	4	7
Bear	360	3	3,334	2	9
Wild turkey	2,504	23	23,165	15	9
Other big game	527	5	5,010	3	10
Total, all small game	**5,434**	**100**	**60,142**	**100**	**11**
Rabbit, hare	2,099	39	22,768	38	11
Quail	991	18	7,926	13	8
Grouse/prairie chicken	1,010	19	9,169	15	9
Squirrel	2,119	39	22,333	37	11
Pheasant	1,723	32	12,769	21	7
Other small game	505	9	5,200	9	10
Total, all migratory birds	**2,956**	**100**	**29,310**	**100**	**10**
Geese	1,000	34	10,508	36	11
Ducks	1,589	54	18,290	62	12
Doves	1,450	49	9,041	31	6
Other migratory bird	210	7	1,523	5	7
Total, all other animals (fox, raccoon, groundhog, etc.)	**1,047**	**100**	**19,207**	**100**	**18**

Note: Detail does not add to total because of multiple responses.

SOURCE: "Hunters and Days of Hunting," in *Quick Facts from the 2001 National Survey of Fishing, Hunting, and Wildlife-Associated Recreation*, U.S. Department of the Interior, U.S. Fish and Wildlife Service, October 2002, http://www.census.gov/prod/2002pubs/QFBRO.pdf (accessed January 9, 2007)

The FFA also notes that in 2001 the vast majority (91%) of all hunters were male, and 97% were white. Nearly half of all hunters were between the ages of thirty-five and fifty-four. Hunters spent just over $642 million in 2001 on licenses, tags, and other fees required by state wildlife agencies. Total hunting expenditures were around $20.6 billion in 2001. Approximately half of this amount goes toward the cost of hunting equipment.

The FFA estimates that 115 million animals were killed by hunters during the 2002–03 hunting season. Table 3.10 provides a breakdown by species of the most hunted animals during the 2001–02 deer and 2002–03 nondeer hunting season. The animal protection group In Defense of Animals (IDA) claims that hunters injure millions of other animals, damage habitats, and disrupt the eating, migration, hibernation, and mating habits of protected animals. For example, the IDA (June 7, 2006, http://www.idausa.org/facts/hunting.html) estimates that for every animal killed instantly by hunters, at least two wounded animals die slow, painful deaths from hunting injuries. Furthermore, it states that careless hunters also kill and wound domestic animals and people each year.

TROPHY HUNTING AND CANNED HUNTS. Trophy hunting is the hunting of animals, particularly exotic (foreign) species, for collection of the carcasses or parts thereof (such as the head or horns) as trophies, or symbols, of the

TABLE 3.10

Number of animals killed by hunters, 2001–02 deer season and 2002–03 season for nondeer game

Doves	22,702,000
Squirrels	22,650,000
Ducks	12,740,000
Rabbits	10,942,000
Grouse, quail, partridges	10,500,000
Deer*	6,400,000
Pheasants	5,900,000
Geese	3,379,000
Raccoons	3,090,000

*Deer number is from 2001–02 hunting season.

SOURCE: Adapted from "Table 1. National Overview," in *A Dying Sport: The State of Hunting in America*, Fund for Animals, January 2004

hunter's conquest over the animal. As shown in Figure 3.5, just over one third of all animal import permits issued by the USFWS during FY 2003 were for the purpose of trophy hunting.

One type of trophy hunting conducted by commercial enterprises is called canned hunting. This is a type of hunting in which animals are fenced in or otherwise enclosed in a space for the enjoyment of trophy hunters. Canned hunting dates back to at least the seventh century BC, when the Assyrians captured lions and then released them to be hunted to death.

FIGURE 3.5

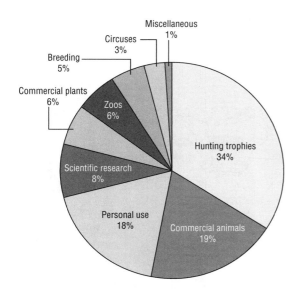

Intended uses of wildlife by U.S. permit applicants, fiscal year 2003

- Miscellaneous 1%
- Circuses 3%
- Breeding 5%
- Commercial plants 6%
- Zoos 6%
- Scientific research 8%
- Personal use 18%
- Commercial animals 19%
- Hunting trophies 34%

SOURCE: "Figure 1. Intended Uses of Wildlife by U.S. Permit Applicants, Fiscal Year 2003," in *Protected Species: International Convention and U.S. Laws Protect Wildlife Differently*, U.S. Government Accountability Office, September 2004, http://www.gao.gov/new.items/d04964.pdf (accessed November 28, 2006)

TABLE 3.11

Sample prices for canned hunts, by type of animal hunted, 2003

Antelope

Addax $1,200–$4,000
Antelope, Sable $3,000–$8,000
Blackbuck $750–$2,500
Blesbok $1,500–$3,000
Eland $1,200–$2,500
Gazelle, Grants $800–$2,000
Gazelle, Dama $800–$3,500
Gazelle, Thompsons $800–$2,400
Gemsbok $800–$3,500
Gnu $1,500–$4,000
Impala $1,000–$2,400
Kudu $3,500–$6,000
Nilgai $1,500
Oryx, horned Scimitar $1,500–$3,500
Oryx, Beisa $1,500–$3,500
Sitatunga $1,000–$2,500
Springbuck $800–$1,600
Waterbuck $1,500–$3,500

Cattle

Buffalo, Cape $4,000–$6,000
Buffalo, Water $3,500

Deer

Barsingha (E) $3,500
Deer, Axis $500–$1,500
Deer, Fallow $500–$1,500
Deer, Red $1,500–$6,000
Deer, Sika $700–$1,500

Goats

Goat, Angora $250–$325
Goat, Catalina $250–$325
Goat, Pygmy $350
Ibex $2,000
Tahr $2,500

Sheep

Aoudad $750–$2,000
Mouflon $400–$1,500
Sheep, Barbados $250–$350
Sheep, Corsican $250–$500
Sheep, Four-Horn $850

Swine

Wild Boar $200–$1,000

Miscellaneous

Rhinoceros (E—all except Southern white subspecies) $10,000–$20,000
Zebra, Grants $800–$2,000

Note: List is a composite based upon actual brochures/price lists from canned hunt operators.
E=Federally listed endangered species.

SOURCE: "Sample Prices for Canned Hunts," in *Canned Hunts: Unfair at Any Price*, Humane Society of the United States, 2003, http://www.hsus.org/wildlife/stop_canned_hunts/sample_prices_for_canned_hunts.html (accessed January 3, 2007)

The Humane Society of the United States (HSUS) estimates that there are hundreds of canned hunt operators in the United States, mostly in Texas. Many offer a "no kill, no pay" policy. The most common animals involved in canned hunting are exotic species of antelope, deer, goats, sheep, cattle, swine, bears, zebra, and big cats. Hunters generally pay a set price for each exotic animal killed. Table 3.11 shows a price list compiled by the HSUS that gives the price range for various animals involved in canned hunts.

In August 2006 the country music singer Troy Lee Gentry was indicted by a federal grand jury for killing a bear named Cubby during a canned hunt in Minnesota and falsifying papers to make it appear that the bear was killed in the wild. According to "Troy Gentry Accused of Killing Tame Bear" (ABCNews.com, August 16, 2006), Gentry paid $4,650 for the bear. The killing was videotaped but edited so it appeared that Gentry killed the bear in a natural hunting situation. The article "Troy Gentry Pleads Guilty to Cubby the Bear Killing" (*USA Today*, November 27, 2006) states that in November 2006 Gentry pleaded guilty to falsifying records on a game animal and testified against the local hunting guide who had arranged the canned hunt. The guide pleaded guilty to two felony charges of violating wildlife laws. Gentry was assessed a $15,000 fine, was banned from hunting in Minnesota for five years, and had to relinquish the bear's hide, which he had kept as a trophy.

In 2005 the first known canned hunt conducted via the Internet took place. According to the HSUS, in "The Latest Fad in Internet Animal Cruelty: Pay-Per-View Hunting" (April 8, 2005, http://www.hsus.org/wildlife/wildlife_news/pay_per_view_slaughter.html), a canned hunting ranch in Texas arranged for Internet users to fire shots at animals on the ranch via computer-controlled hunting rifles. The HSUS calls it "trophy hunting without the fuss and muss of having to hunt at all." Animal welfare and mainstream hunting groups have criticized

FIGURE 3.6

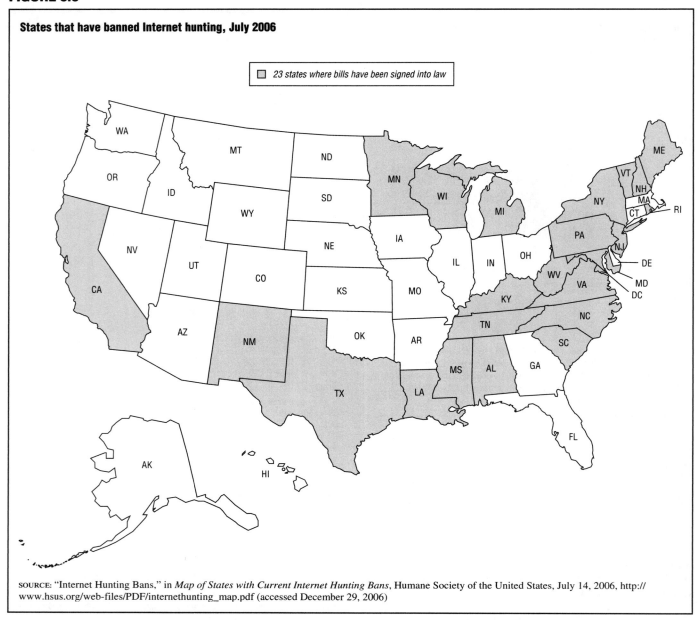

States that have banned Internet hunting, July 2006

☐ 23 states where bills have been signed into law

SOURCE: "Internet Hunting Bans," in *Map of States with Current Internet Hunting Bans*, Humane Society of the United States, July 14, 2006, http://www.hsus.org/web-files/PDF/internethunting_map.pdf (accessed December 29, 2006)

the practice as unsportsmanlike. As of July 2006, twenty-three states had banned Internet hunting. (See Figure 3.6.)

The HSUS and other animal welfare groups are opposed to canned hunting. They consider it unsportsmanlike and cruel. Animal welfare groups believe that many relatively tame animals dumped by zoos, circuses, and exhibitors wind up victims of canned hunts. These animals are not afraid of humans and make easy targets for trophy hunters. There are many surplus exotic animals in the United States because of overbreeding. The HSUS believes that canned hunts provide a financial incentive that aggravates the problem. Unwanted and purposely overbred exotic animals are passed on by breeders and dealers to game and hunting preserves specializing in canned hunts.

According to the press release "Congress Shoots Down Taxidermy Tax Scam" (August 4, 2006, http://www.hsus.org/press_and_publications/press_releases/congress_shoots_down_taxidermy.html), the HSUS spearheaded passage in 2006 of a provision in the Pension Reform Act that will tighten restrictions on trophy hunters that deduct certain hunting expenses from their taxes. A loophole in the tax code had allowed trophy hunters to deduct the costs of hunting excursions if the killed animal was donated to a museum. According to a two-year HSUS investigation, some trophy hunters were donating their kills to phony museums and writing off all costs for the hunting expedition on their taxes. Under the new provision trophy hunters donating their kills to museums can only deduct the amount that it would have cost to buy a comparable trophy on the open market, not

FIGURE 3.7

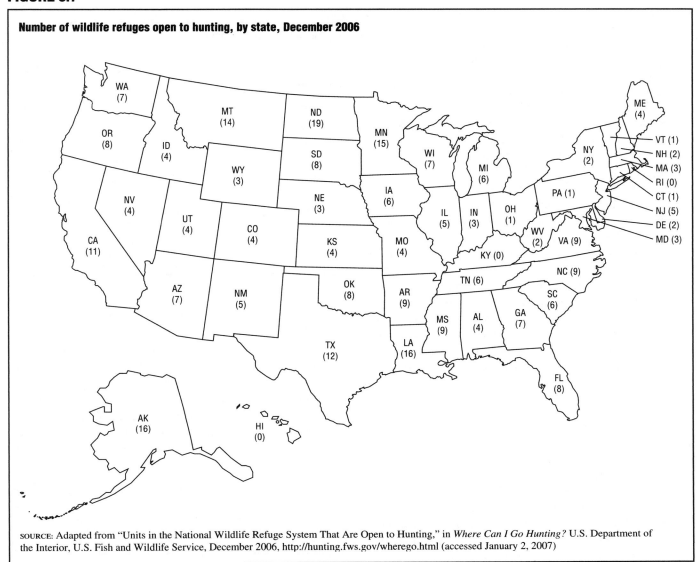

Number of wildlife refuges open to hunting, by state, December 2006

SOURCE: Adapted from "Units in the National Wildlife Refuge System That Are Open to Hunting," in *Where Can I Go Hunting?* U.S. Department of the Interior, U.S. Fish and Wildlife Service, December 2006, http://hunting.fws.gov/wherego.html (accessed January 2, 2007)

the cost of the hunting trip. The law change is expected to save taxpayers nearly $5 million per year.

Wildlife Control

HUNTING AS A WILDLIFE CONTROL METHOD. Killing is often the control method of choice on federal lands, including national parks, forests, wildlife refuges, and other areas overseen by the USFWS, USFS, BLM, and the National Park Service. The USFWS notes in the *2001 National Survey of Fishing, Hunting, and Wildlife-Associated Recreation* (October 2002, http://www.census.gov/prod/2002pubs/FHW01.pdf) that 40% of hunters hunted on public lands in 2001.

Most people assume that national wildlife refuges are truly refuges, where animals are protected from hunting; however, federal law allows the government to permit secondary uses, such as hunting, on wildlife refuges if a

review of the potential effects indicates that protected wildlife will not be adversely affected. Other allowed secondary uses include fishing, wildlife watching, and environmental education programs.

The USFWS notes in "Where Can I Go Hunting?" (December 2006, http://www.fws.gov/hunting/wherego.html) that hunting was permitted on 317 of the nation's 545 national wildlife refuges. Figure 3.7 shows the number of refuges open to hunting in each state. North Dakota has the most units (nineteen), followed by Alaska and Louisiana (sixteen each), Minnesota (fifteen), and Montana (fourteen).

The USFWS insists that hunting is necessary to manage wildlife populations. Animal rights advocates are opposed to all hunting and bitterly criticize the federal government for allowing hunting in national refuges. Welfare groups are openly skeptical that hunting is an effective solution to overpopulation. The IDA points out that hunters seek out not starving animals but large and healthy ones. It argues that hunting is not about conserving species but about human power, status, and collecting wild animal heads and antlers as trophies.

Deer are the animals most often associated with hunts designed to prevent overpopulation. The deer population has exploded in the latter part of the twentieth century for a variety of reasons, including lack of natural predators. The USFWS and state wildlife agencies commonly justify hunting as a humane method of killing deer that would otherwise starve because of overpopulation. They argue that death by hunting is more humane than allowing deer to slowly starve to death. Animal welfare groups believe that hunting actually aggravates population problems, claiming it upsets the natural ratio between bucks (male deer) and does (female deer) and results in higher reproduction rates. The IDA says that deer make up only a small percentage of the animals killed by hunters and claims that the vast majority of hunted wild species are not considered overpopulated. It believes that sport hunting should be banned and that natural predators, such as wolves and mountain lions, should be reintroduced wherever possible to control deer populations.

Hunters just as vigorously defend their sport and their role in conserving wildlife. The U.S. Sportsmen's Alliance (USSA) and the Safari Club International (SCI) are major groups representing the interests of hunters. The USSA operates the Sportsmen's Legal Defense Fund (SLDF). The SLDF and the SCI intervene in lawsuits filed by antihunting groups against government wildlife management and natural resources agencies. The SCI also operates Sportsmen against Hunger, a program that donates wild game meat to hunger-relief agencies.

Hunting proponents note that hunting fees support government conservation programs. According to the "2005–2006 Federal Duck Stamp Fact Sheet" (2006, http:// www.fws.gov/duckstamps/federal/pdf/2005FactSheet .doc), the USFWS notes that the duck stamp has raised more than $700 million since its inception in 1934 and this money has purchased more than 5.2 million acres of land for the wildlife refuge system. Nearly $239 million in federal excise taxes on hunting equipment was collected for FY 2005. (See Table 3.12.) Most of this money (more than $219 million) was earmarked for distribution to individual states to support their wildlife management programs. Figure 3.8 shows the annual distribution of excise tax receipts from 1996 to 2005.

Critics claim that hunting fees account for only a small portion of the money required to operate the country's conservation programs and that the government uses money obtained from hunting fees to set aside more areas for hunting. They want greater focus on activities such as

TABLE 3.12

Disposition of federal excise taxes collected on hunting equipment, fiscal year 2005

Total excise tax receipts available for fiscal year 2005	$238,807,000*
Firearm and bow hunter Education and safety grants	$8,000,000
Multi-state conservation Grant program	$3,000,000
Administration	$8,611,000
Available for state apportionment	**$219,196,000**

*Total excise tax receipts available for fiscal year 2005 were collected in fiscal year 2004. Note: As required by law, deductions from excise tax receipts are for specific programs and funding levels. Data are of undetermined reliability.

SOURCE: "Figure 1. Wildlife Restoration Program Tax Receipts, Deductions, and Apportionment to States for Fiscal Year 2005," in *Fish and Wildlife Service: Federal Assistance Program Is Making Progress Addressing Previously Identified Concerns*, U.S. Government Accountability Office, July 5, 2006, http://www.gao.gov/new.items/d06731r.pdf (accessed December 29, 2006)

wildlife watching and environmental education at wildlife refuges.

The USFWS states in the *2001 National Survey of Fishing, Hunting, and Wildlife-Associated Recreation* that 66.1 million American adults observed, fed, or photographed wildlife in 2001. This is five times the number that hunted wildlife that year. These wildlife recreationists spent $38.4 billion on travel, equipment, and other items. This represents 35% of the total dollars spent on wildlife-related activities in 2001.

WILDLIFE TRAPPING. A killing method that receives much criticism from animal protection groups is the trapping of fur-bearing animals. Welfarists consider traps to be especially cruel because the panicked animals are often trapped for a long period before being discovered and killed; sometimes they chew off their own limbs to escape. Trapping is used as a control method on federal lands, including refuges. It is done by refuge staff, by trappers under contract to the refuges, and by members of the public who obtain special permits.

The Animal Protection Institute (API) examined USFWS data collected in 1997 as part of an investigative study of trapping at wildlife refuges around the country. The API (2007, http://www.bancrueltraps.com/b1_problem .php) claims that many nontarget species were captured in body-gripping traps at refuges, including river otters, feral and domestic cats and dogs, rabbits, geese, alligators, ducks, hawks, owls, eagles, and bears. Some of these animals were killed immediately by the trapping devices or died from injuries sustained during trapping. Others were released unharmed upon their discovery by the trappers.

Table 3.13 lists the states and cities around the country that have banned certain types of traps and snares, particularly old-fashioned leghold traps that use steel jaws to clamp down on the legs of trapped animals.

FIGURE 3.8

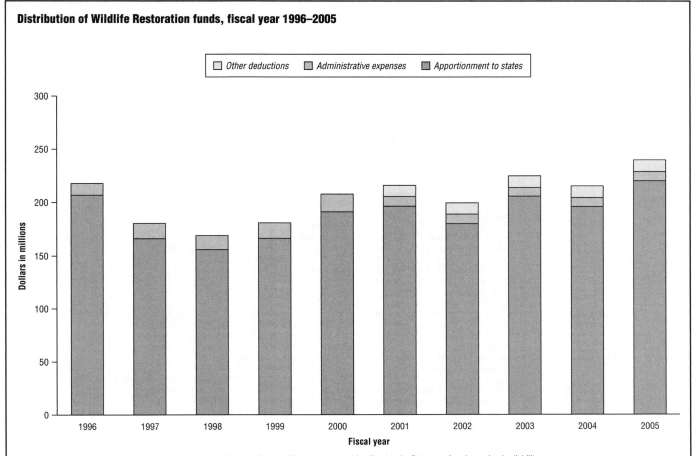

Distribution of Wildlife Restoration funds, fiscal year 1996–2005

☐ Other deductions ▦ Administrative expenses ▨ Apportionment to states

Dollars in millions

Fiscal year

Note: As required by law, deductions from excise tax receipts are for specific programs and funding levels. Data are of undetermined reliability.

SOURCE: "Figure 2. Wildlife Restoration Program 10-Year Distribution of Funding," in *Fish and Wildlife Service: Federal Assistance Program Is Making Progress Addressing Previously Identified Concerns*, U.S. Government Accountability Office, July 5, 2006, http://www.gao.gov/new.items/d06731r.pdf (accessed December 29, 2006)

Fur and Other Products

Many wild animals are killed purely for their fur or parts. The most common wildlife commodities are:

- Fur from mink, beaver, foxes, rabbits, bears, and seals

- Hides from tigers, leopards, and other big cats

- Rhinoceros horns, reindeer antlers, snake blood, shark fins, various organs, and the penises from seals, tigers, and rhinoceros (these items are believed by some people to act as aphrodisiacs—supplements designed to enhance sexual performance)

- Bones, claws, paws, fangs, brains, eyeballs, tails, and internal organs from tigers (all are used in traditional Asian medicines)

- Bile from wild boars, bears, and snakes (used in aphrodisiacs and traditional Asian medicines)

- Elephant tusks (for ivory)

- Bear paws (considered a delicacy in some Asian countries)

SEALS. Most animals used in the fur trade are bred and raised in cages on farms. Some animals, however, are still trapped or killed in the wild, particularly seals. The killing of seals for fur was a high-profile issue of the animal rights movement during the 1970s. Greenpeace activists traveled to hunting areas to splash dye on seals and draw media attention to their slaughter.

The killing of seals caught public attention because seals—usually babies only a few weeks old—on ice floes were usually clubbed in the head, then dragged with hooks across the ice. Animal welfarists who witnessed seal hunts claimed to have seen seals skinned while still alive and conscious. Seal hunters argued that clubbing was humane and killed the seals quickly. Seals swimming in the water were shot instead of clubbed. Critics claimed that many of these seals were injured and drowned after they sank below the surface.

In 1972 the United States banned all imports of seal products. A decade later the European Union put strict importation limits on seal pelts. As a result, Canada's seal

TABLE 3.13

State and local bans on trapping methods, 2006

States	Year	Ban
Washington	2000 ballot initiative	Citizens voted in favor (55%) of banning the use of leghold traps, other body-gripping traps, and snares for recreation and commerce in fur. In May 2003, the governor vetoed a rollback of the ban.
California	1998 ballot initiative	Voters supported (57%) Proposition 4, which banned the use of leghold traps, other body-gripping traps, and snares for recreation and commerce in fur.
Massachusetts	1996 ballot initiative	Voters passed (64%) The Wildlife Protection Act, banning the use of leghold traps, other body-gripping traps, and snares for capturing fur-bearing animals.
Colorado	1992 ballot initiative	Citizens voted in favor (52%) of a constitutional amendment banning the use of leghold, other body-gripping traps and snares.
Arizona	1992 ballot initiative	Voters (58%) enacted a ban on the use of leghold traps, other body-gripping traps, and snares on public land— which makes up 80% of the state.
New Jersey	1986 legislation	The New Jersey legislature banned both possession and use of leghold traps, making it the most restrictive of the leghold trap bans.
Rhode Island	1977 legislation	Rhode Island legislators banned the use of the leghold trap to capture any animal.
Florida	1974 regulation	The Florida Fish and Game Commission enacted a regulation prohibiting the use of any steel or leghold trap where wildlife might be found.
Cities		
Columbia, Maryland	2003 city ordinance	The city council unanimously voted to ban leghold traps.
Nashua, New Hampshire	1994 city ordinance	The city council passed a ban on the use of leghold traps and other body-gripping traps and snares.
Two Harbors, Minnesota	1990 city ordinance	The city council voted to ban the leghold trap throughout most of the city.
St. Paul, Minnesota	1985 city ordinance	The city council unanimously voted to ban all lethal trapping and the sale of all lethal traps.

SOURCE: "City and State Trapping Bans," in *Fur and Trapping—City and State Trapping Bans*, Humane Society of the United States, 2006, http://www.hsus.org/wildlife/fur_and_trapping/city_and_state_trapping_bans.html (accessed December 29, 2006)

TABLE 3.14

Animal organizations worldwide that support the Protect Seals Network, 2006

- American Society for the Prevention of Cruelty to Animals (ASPCA)
- Anima (Denmark)
- Animal (Portugal)
- Animalia (Finland)
- Animal Alliance of Canada
- Animal Friends Croatia
- Animal Protection Institute (API) (USA)
- Animal Rights Sweden
- Asociacion Nacional Para la Defensa de los Animales (ANDA, Spain)
- Bont Voor Dieren (Fur for Animals, The Netherlands)
- Born Free Foundation (United Kingdom)
- CETA (Life, Ukraine)
- Compassion in World Farming (CIWF, Ireland)
- Dyrevernalliansen (Norwegian Animal Welfare Alliance)
- Earth Island Institute (USA)
- Environment Voters (Canada)
- Eurogroup for Animal Welfare
- The Franz Weber Foundation (Switzerland)
- Fundación Altarriba (Spain)
- Fondation 30 Millions d'Amis (France)
- GAIA (Belgium)
- Global Action Network (Canada)
- Greenpeace
- The Humane Society of the United States (HSUS)
- International Wildlife Coalition (IWC)
- Asian, Australian, and United Kingdom branches of Humane Society International (HSI)
- LAV (Lega Anti Vivisezione, Italy)
- The Marine Mammal Center (USA)
- Massachusetts Society for the Prevention of Cruelty to Animals (USA)
- Marchig Animal Welfare Trust (United Kingdom)
- Nova Scotia Humane Society (Canada)
- Ocean Futures Society (USA)
- One Voice (France)
- Organization International pour la Protection des Animaux (France)
- Respect for Animals (United Kingdom)
- Royal Society for the Prevention of Cruelty to Animals (RSPCA, United Kingdom)
- Sea Shepherd Conservation Society (USA)
- STS/PSA (Schweizer Tierschutz/Protection Suisse des Animaux/Swiss Animal Protection)
- Svoboda Zvirat (Freedom for Animals, Czech Republic)
- Vancouver Humane Society (Canada)
- Vier Pfoten e.V. (Germany)
- VITA (Russia)
- World Society for the Protection of Animals (WSPA)

SOURCE: "The Protect Seals Network," in *Marine Mammals: The Protect Seals Network*, Humane Society of the United States, 2006, http://www.hsus.org/marine_mammals/protect_seals/the_protect_seals_network.html (accessed December 28, 2006)

fur industry was virtually eliminated. However, Clifford Krauss reports in "New Demand Drives Canada's Baby Seal Hunt" (*New York Times*, April 5, 2004) that Canada's seal fur industry became larger than ever because of high demand from eastern Europe and China. Krauss notes that baby seals are still clubbed to death on the ice, but new regulations mean that only seals older than two weeks are subject to the hunt. At this age the seals have lost their pure white fur and developed a gray spotted coat. According to Krauss, the renewed hunt has not aroused widespread public protest because "tougher hunting rules, including stiffer regulations to avert skinning the seals alive, have muted the effort to stop the hunt and eased the consciences of Canadians."

In 2004 many animal welfare and rights groups launched new campaigns against Canadian seal hunting. Dozens of groups, including the American Society for the Prevention of Cruelty to Animals, HSUS, FFA, and Greenpeace, joined together to form the Protect Seals Network. (See Table 3.14.) The network calls for a boycott of Canadian seafood to protest the seal hunt. According to the HSUS, in "A Cruel Hunt That Must Be Stopped" (2007, http://www.hsus.org/protect_seals.html), more than 354,000 seals were killed in the 2006 Canadian seal hunt in the North Atlantic ocean.

BIG CATS. There is a huge market for wild animal parts throughout Asia, particularly in China. Many parts are used in traditional remedies for various illnesses and diseases. In addition, animal penises are sold as aphrodisiacs. The animal most sought after is the tiger. Tiger hides sell for as much $20,000 each, and tiger bones are ground up and used in medicines for rheumatism and arthritis. Tiger penises are used in aphrodisiacs, soups, and various medicines.

Tigers are listed as endangered under the federal Endangered Species Act. Leopards are classified as either endangered or threatened, depending on the location of the wild population. According to the USFWS, many tigers are worth more dead than alive. The animals breed easily in captivity and have been extremely overbred in the United States. Baby tigers are popular at zoos and animal parks, but they grow up quickly and are expensive to care for as adults. Unwanted and overbred tigers from zoos, refuges, and game parks can wind up in the hands of unscrupulous dealers who kill the animals for their valuable parts. Federal law allows the possession of captive-bred tigers, but only if their use enhances the propagation or survival of the species. It is illegal to kill the animals for profit or sell their parts, meat, or hide in interstate commerce. It is not illegal to donate the animals.

ELEPHANTS. Ivory is a hard, creamy white substance found in the tusks of African elephants and some male Asian elephants. Demand for ivory was so high during the twentieth century that hundreds of thousands of elephants were poached (illegally killed) for it. Conservation groups estimate that more than half the population of African elephants was wiped out during the 1980s alone. In 1990 an international ban on ivory trade was established under CITES. Although the ban helped to severely reduce elephant poaching, it did not eliminate the problem. In "Elephant Poaching and Ivory Seizures" (2007, http://www.hsus.org/wildlife/issues_facing_wildlife/wildlife_trade/elephant_trade_fact_sheet/elephant_poaching_and_ivory_seizures/), the HSUS reports that during 2001 and early 2002 at least 965 African elephants and 39 Asian elephants were poached and had their ivory tusks removed. It is believed that hundreds of elephants are still killed illegally each year for their ivory.

In 1997 CITES restrictions were loosened to allow some countries to sell surplus quantities of ivory. Hillary Mayell notes in "Enlist Ivory Carvers to Help Save Elephants?" (*National Geographic News*, June 26, 2003) that approximately two hundred tons of ivory were stockpiled in more than a dozen African and Asian countries by 1998. This ivory accumulated through seizures from poachers and from legitimate sources, such as elephants that died from natural causes or were legally killed by game wardens. Countries with large wild elephant populations are pressing the international community to allow them to sell ivory reserves to finance expensive elephant conservation programs. Animal welfare groups fear that releasing large

amounts of ivory into the market will raise demand for ivory and reinvigorate illegal trade and poaching.

A LARGE PROBLEM. International trade in exotic animals and their parts is a multibillion-dollar industry. TRAFFIC is an organization that monitors worldwide wildlife trade. According to TRAFFIC (2006, http://www.traffic.org/wildlife/wild4.htm), the worldwide trade in wildlife products was worth approximately $160 billion per year during the early 1990s.

Whaling and Fishing

WHALING. Whaling has been an industry in northern seas for hundreds of years. The oil and blubber from whales were popular commodities in many markets. By the beginning of the twentieth century whaling had taken a significant toll on whale populations. The United States banned commercial whaling in 1928. In 1946 the International Whaling Commission (IWC) was founded by twenty-four member countries (including the United States) as a means of self-regulating the industry and limiting the number and type of whales that could be killed. In 1986 all IWC countries agreed to ban commercial whaling after most whale populations were placed under Appendix I of the CITES agreement. Whaling was still allowed for "scientific purposes," however.

Conservation and animal rights groups have complained for years that some IWC countries, particularly Japan, kill many whales under this loophole. Whalers and some scientists say that some whale species are not endangered and should be subjected to controlled hunts.

In 2002 Iceland rejoined the IWC after dropping out in 1991, but with the reservation that it would not support a ban on commercial whaling. This started an internal battle within the IWC about what the commission's role should be. Some countries believe that the IWC's focus should be entirely on conservation. Others would like to see the IWC become more industry-friendly. In "Iceland Begins Commercial Whaling" (BBC News, October 17, 2006), Richard Black reports that in 2006 Iceland announced that it will resume commercial whaling and plans to take nine fin whales (an endangered species) and thirty minke whales annually. As of January 2007, seventy-two countries were members of the IWC.

RECREATIONAL FISHING. In the *2001 National Survey of Fishing, Hunting, and Wildlife-Associated Recreation*, the USFWS reports that the number of U.S. hunters was down considerably in 2001 from historical levels. However, as shown in Figure 3.9, the number of people participating in recreational/sport fishing (or angling) has risen dramatically since 1955, the year in which the first survey was conducted. In the figure, the 1955 participant estimates are set to an arbitrary index value of one hundred. The number of participants in successive surveys

FIGURE 3.9

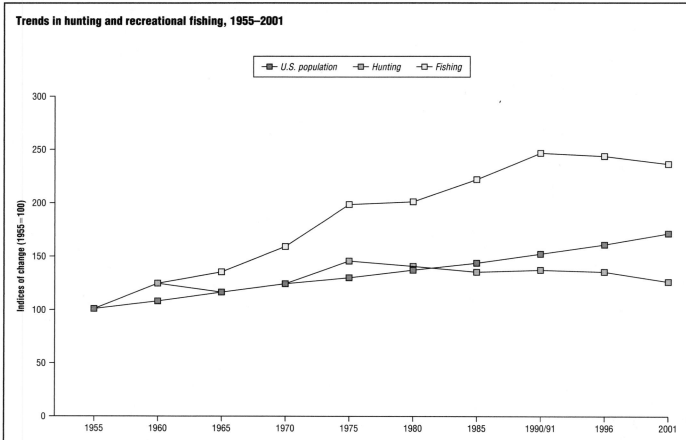

Trends in hunting and recreational fishing, 1955–2001

SOURCE: "Figure 1. 1955–2001 Trend" in *Fishing and Hunting 1991–2001: Avid, Casual, and Intermediate Participation Trends: Addendum to the 2001 National Survey of Fishing, Hunting, and Wildlife-Associated Recreation*, U.S. Department of the Interior, U.S. Fish and Wildlife Service, Sport Fish and Wildlife Restoration, July 2004, http://library.fws.gov/nat_survey2001_trends.pdf (accessed January 8, 2007)

was then calculated relative to the beginning index value. Thus, by 1975 the number of Americans participating in recreational fishing had doubled and continued to climb through the early 1990s, before beginning to decline.

In 1950 the federal government established the Sport Fish Restoration Program following passage of the Federal Aid in Sport Fish Restoration Act. This program funnels excise tax receipts from the sale of certain fishing and boating equipment to various state and federal programs and agencies devoted to furthering sports fishing. As shown in Table 3.15, nearly $461 million was collected for FY 2005. More than half of the money ($273 million) was earmarked for state agency spending on sport fishing programs. Figure 3.10 shows the annual amounts collected through the Sport Fish Restoration Program for FYs 1996 through 2005.

COMMERCIAL FISHING. Commercial fishing of many species is blamed for a host of environmental and conservation problems in the world's oceans. Overfishing and poor management have caused severe declines in some populations. In "Rapid Worldwide Depletion of Predatory Fish Communities" (*Nature*, May 15, 2003), Ransom A.

Myers and Boris Worm report that commercial fishing has decreased the world's population of large predatory ocean fishes by 90%. These fish include blue marlin, cod, tuna, and swordfish. Scientists find that the most sought-after species were quickly diminished by overfishing and then replaced by less desirable species. These replacement species were also depleted quickly. Technological advances such as global positioning systems and sonar have allowed commercial fisherman to better find and follow great schools of fish in previously uncharted waters.

Another criticism of commercial fishing is that it endangers marine mammals and other fish besides those the fisherman want to catch. Experts estimate that thousands of nontarget specimens are killed each year after becoming entangled in fishing nets and devices. According to Earthtrust (August 31, 2005, http://www.earthtrust.org/fsa.html), a nonprofit wildlife conservation organization headquartered in Honolulu, Hawaii, approximately seven million dolphins were killed between 1959 and 1991 because of purse-seining in the eastern tropical Pacific. Purse-seining is a fishing technique in which giant nets are encircled around schools of fish. It is a popular way to capture tuna. Schools of tuna are fre-

TABLE 3.15

Disposition of federal excise taxes collected on fishing equipment, fiscal year 2005

Total excise tax receipts available for fiscal year 2005	$460,752,000*
Boat safety Transfers to Coast Guard	$64,000,000
Army Corps of Engineers Coastal wetlands	$58,054,804
Fish and Wildlife Service wetlands grants	$24,880,630
Fish and Wildlife Service clean vessel grants	$10,000,000
Recreation vessel Access grants	$8,000,000
Fish and Wildlife Service outreach grants	$10,000,000
Multi-state conservation Grant program	$3,000,000
Fishery Commissions and Boating Council	$1,200,000
Administration	$8,611,000
Available for state apportionment	**$273,005,978**

*Total excise tax receipts available for fiscal year 2005 were collected in fiscal year 2004 and include interest income.
Note: As required by law, deductions from excise tax receipts are for specific programs and funding levels. Data are of undetermined reliability.

SOURCE: "Figure 3. Sport Fish Restoration Program Tax Receipts, Deductions, and Apportionment to States for Fiscal Year 2005," in *Fish and Wildlife Service: Federal Assistance Program Is Making Progress Addressing Previously Identified Concerns*, U.S. Government Accountability Office, July 5, 2006, http://www.gao.gov/new.items/d06731r.pdf (accessed December 29, 2006)

FIGURE 3.10

Distribution of Sport Fish Restoration Program funds, fiscal years 1996–2005

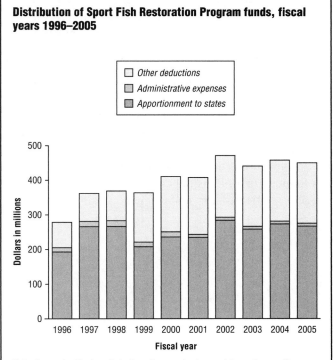

Note: As required by law, deductions from excise tax receipts are for specific programs and funding levels. Data are of undetermined reliability. In commenting on a draft of this report, Fish and Wildlife Service provided new expenditure data for fiscal years 1996 through 2000. We did not incorporate these new data because the source of the new information was unclear. The new data indicate that an additional $174 million was provided as other deductions during these 5 fiscal years.

SOURCE: "Figure 4. Sport Fish Restoration Program 10-Year Distribution of Funding," in *Fish and Wildlife Service: Federal Assistance Program Is Making Progress in Addressing Previously Identified Concerns*, U.S. Government Accountability Office, July 5, 2006, http://www.gao.gov/new.items/d06731r.pdf (accessed December 29, 2006)

quently accompanied by pods of dolphins. In fact, some fishermen chase and set their nets around dolphins to capture the nearby tuna. Because dolphins are mammals, they require air to breathe. The dolphins can get caught and drown in the nets. Negative publicity about the problem during the 1980s led consumers to demand changes in tuna fishing and labeling.

In 1990 the Dolphin Protection Consumer Information Act was passed, establishing an official definition of "dolphin-safe" tuna. Canners must meet certain criteria before they can label their tuna dolphin-safe, and U.S. fishermen modified their fishing techniques to meet the criteria. Purse-seine fishing is still widely practiced by foreign fishing industries, particularly in Mexico and South America.

In 2002 the NMFS (December 31, 2002, http://www.publicaffairs.noaa.gov/releases2002/dec02/noaa02168.html) announced its finding that the tuna purse-seine industry has "no significant adverse impact" on dolphin populations in the eastern tropical Pacific. This finding allows foreign fishermen using the technique to import their fish into the United States as dolphin-safe if an onboard observer certifies that no dolphins were killed or seriously injured during the catch.

Critics claim that purse-seine fishing is inhumane to dolphins even if they are released from the nets alive because it can separate baby dolphins from their mothers. In January 2003 the Earth Island Institute and eight other environmental, conservation, and animal welfare groups (including the HSUS) filed suit against the NMFS in federal court to halt implementation of the ruling. In August 2004 a federal judge ruled that the "dolphin-safe" label could not be used on any tuna products caught by netting dolphins.

RESCUE AND REHABILITATION OF WILDLIFE

A variety of individuals, groups, and agencies are involved in rescue or rehabilitation of wildlife. Most state wildlife and fish and game agencies operate rehabilitation programs and require private individuals and groups rehabilitating and releasing native wildlife to be licensed. In addition, the USFWS requires federal permits for those rehabilitating migratory bird species.

The HSUS operates the five-acre Cape Wildlife Center in West Barnstable, Massachusetts. The center includes a wildlife rehabilitation facility and a veterinary clinic for injured, sick, and orphaned wild animals. Although the center is not open to the public, it operates a hotline to answer questions and offer suggestions about ways in which wildlife and humans can coexist.

The Association of Sanctuaries (TAOS) is a non-profit organization founded in 1992 to accredit sanctuaries that rescue and care for all kinds of animals, including wild animals. The rescued animals are not used for commercial purposes or allowed to breed in captivity. As of January 2007 twenty-two TAOS-accredited sanctuaries in the United States rehabilitated and released or provided sanctuary for wild animals that could not be returned to their natural habitat (http://www.taosanctuaries.org/sanctuaries/atoz.htm). These include unwanted exotic pets and circus and zoo animals. One example is the Elephant Sanctuary near Hohenwald, Tennessee. It was founded in 1995 as the country's first natural habitat refuge specifically for endangered Asian and African elephants. As of January 2007, the 2,700-acre sanctuary housed twenty-three female elephants.

There are hundreds of other rescue and rehabilitation facilities around the country. Many are nonprofit, tax-exempt operations run by individuals or animal groups. The quality of care offered by these facilities depends on the expertise of the staff and the funds available. The HSUS is critical of some of these facilities. In "Neglecting over 90 Tigers, 58 Cubs Found Stuffed into Freezer" (April 22, 2003, http://www.pet-abuse.com/cases/1275/), Wayne Pacelle, the vice president of HSUS, said, "We call them pseudo-sanctuaries. They're primarily engaged in commercial activities while passing themselves off as a nonprofit."

CHAPTER 4
FARM ANIMALS

Farm animals are animals that are kept for agricultural purposes. This includes such domesticated animals as cows and chickens, and wild animals that are raised in confinement, including mink and fish. Animals are farmed for a variety of reasons. Most are raised to be killed. Meat from cattle, hogs, and chickens provides the bulk of protein in the American diet, whereas animals with beautiful fur are killed for their pelts. However, some farm animals are more useful and profitable alive. These animals produce something of value to humans, such as milk, eggs, wool, or honey, or are farmed for their skills, such as horses, mules, and burros. Whatever the reason, the cultivation of farm animals is an enormous business.

Table 4.1 shows the production value for the ten top money-making livestock commodities in 2005. Livestock and their output accounted for nearly $107 billion in value. Figure 4.1 shows a breakdown of value by percentage. Cattle, milk from milk cows, broilers (chickens raised for meat), and swine (hogs and pigs) made up the vast majority of the total in 2005.

The number of animals involved in the agricultural industry is staggering. As shown in Table 4.2, in 2005 U.S. farms included 8.9 billion broilers and nearly 770 million cattle, swine, sheep, turkeys, egg-laying hens, horses, and other farmed animals. Table 4.3 shows slaughter statistics for 2005 for a variety of farmed animals. Over 9.4 billion farm animals were slaughtered in 2005.

In 2005 more farm animals were living in the United States than there were humans on earth. The use and well-being of these animals is of major importance to people concerned with animal rights and welfare. Most animal rights activists abhor the idea that animals are commodities at all. Many believe that animals should not be used for any purpose, especially to feed humans. Welfarists focus their attention on the treatment of

farmed animals—how they are housed, fed, transported, and slaughtered.

People in the U.S. livestock business argue that farm animals are well treated. They point to the high productivity of the industry as proof. In other words, farm animals must be thriving because there are so many of them. The American Meat Institute (AMI; September 20, 2005, http://www.animalhandling.org/), a trade organization that represents the meat and poultry industry, sums up this viewpoint by stating: "Optimal handling is ethically appropriate, creates positive workplaces and ensures higher quality meat products." In the brochure "Animal Welfare in the Meat Industry: A Commitment to Consumers and Livestock" (January 2001), the AMI notes that livestock farmers practice humane animal care because it is ethical and results in calmer animals. In turn, calmer animals help make farms and meat plants safer working environments, resulting in higher-quality meat. The link between humane animal treatment and high production of good-quality products is commonly cited by the livestock industry.

Critics argue that high productivity is an indicator of the efficiency of the overall system, not the welfare of individual animals. They have a long list of complaints about how farm animals are raised and slaughtered in the United States.

Farming animals is an old and respected business. It feeds people and supplies products they want. Forcing farmers to radically change the way they treat animals might jeopardize the relatively cheap and plentiful supply of animal products that Americans enjoy. Would society tolerate this just for the sake of the animals? This is the ultimate question at the center of the farm animal debate. However, animal rights supporters, welfarists, and environmentalists point to evidence that the use of farm animals as a food source is an inefficient and in some ways harmful practice and argue that alternatives to the

TABLE 4.1

Production value for selected agricultural products, 2005

Cattle	$36,739,445,000
Milk from milk cows	$26,903,822,000
Broilers	$20,901,939,000
Swine	$13,643,568,000
Eggs	$4,042,282,000
Turkeys	$3,232,576,000
Catfish and trout	$556,316,000
Sheep, including wool	$482,298,000
Honey	$157,795,000
Miscellaneous poultry	$64,554,000
Total	**$106,724,595,000**

SOURCE: Adapted from "Table A1.2. Value of Production for Selected Agricultural Commodities for 2004 and 2005," and "Table A1.9. Poultry Production in the United States, 2004 and 2005," in *2005 United States Animal Health Report*, U.S. Department of Agriculture, Animal and Plant Health Inspection Service, August 2006, http://www.aphis.usda.gov/publications/animal_health/content/printable_version/AHR_Web_ PDF/J_appendices.pdf (accessed November 28, 2006)

FIGURE 4.1

Production value for selected agricultural products, 2005

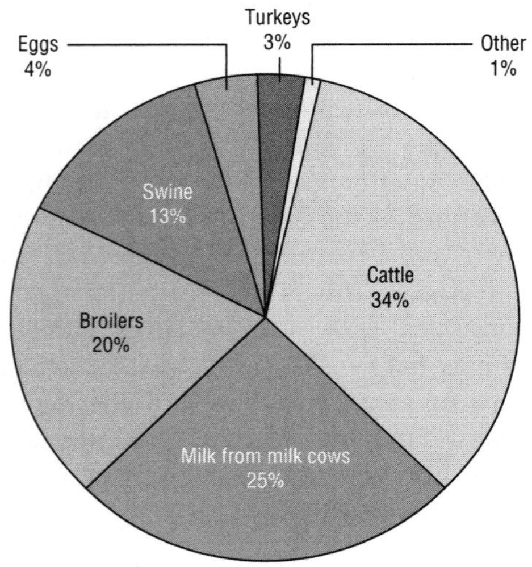

SOURCE: Adapted from "Table A1.2. Value of Production for Selected Agricultural Commodities for 2004 and 2005" and "Table A1.9. Poultry Production in the United States, 2004 and 2005," in *2005 United States Animal Health Report*, U.S. Department of Agriculture, Animal and Plant Health Inspection Service, August 2006, http://www.aphis.usda.gov/publications/animal_health/content/printable_version/AHR_Web_PDF/J_appendices.pdf (accessed November 28, 2006)

TABLE 4.2

Livestock and poultry inventory, by usage type, 2005

Commodity	Inventory (rounded to nearest thousand)	Operations	Value of production ($1,000)
All cattle and calves	97,102,000[a]	982,510	36,739,445
Milk cows	9,058,000[a]	78,295	NA[b]
Beef cows	33,253,000[a]	770,170	NA
Cattle on feed	14,132,000[a]	88,199	NA
Hogs and pigs	61,449,000[c]	67,330	13,643,568
Sheep and lambs (plus wool)	6,230,000[a]	68,280	482,298
Poultry	NA		28,241,351
Annual average number of egg layers	343,501,000		4,042,282
Number of broilers produced	8,870,350,000		20,901,939
Number of turkeys raised	256,270,000		3,232,576
Equine	5,317,000[d]	NA	NA

[a]Inventory as of January 1, 2006.
[b]Not available.
[c]Inventory as of December 1, 2005.
[d]Inventory as of January 1, 1999.

SOURCE: Adapted from "Table 1. Livestock, Poultry, and Aquaculture Statistics for 2005," and "Table A1.9. Poultry Production in the United States, 2004 and 2005," in *2005 United States Animal Health Report*, U.S. Department of Agriculture, Animal and Plant Health Inspection Service, August 2006, http://www.aphis.usda.gov/publications/animal_health/content/printable_version/AHR_Web_PDF/C_chapter_%201.pdf, and http://www.aphis.usda.gov/publications/animal_health/content/printable_version/AHR_Web_PDF/J_appendices.pdf (both accessed January 11, 2007)

turn their focus away from hunting and toward building civilizations. It also changed the fundamental attitudes that humans had about animals. Domesticated animals lost the status that their ancestors had as independent, free-roaming creatures and became pieces of property.

Humans devoted a great deal of energy to maximizing the value of their new property. Control over breeding was particularly important. Certain animals were mated with each other to produce offspring that were even more valuable, whereas animals with undesirable properties were eliminated from the gene pool. Because farm animals were viewed as property, many decisions were based on logic and economics. Society at large benefited from the ready availability of meat and other products from this system.

Livestock Protection Laws

In the 1800s a number of laws were enacted in England and the United States to protect animals from abuse, neglect, and mistreatment by their owners. Some of these laws specifically included livestock, whereas others did not. Many state anticruelty laws excluded what they called "customary agricultural practices." These laws were often interpreted not to apply to animals raised for food.

The Twenty-Eight Hour Law of 1873 was the first federal law dealing with livestock welfare. It required that livestock being transported across state lines be rested and watered at least once every twenty-eight hours during the journey. At the time, livestock transport was

most common modern farming techniques would provide for a more sustainable and humane agricultural system.

HISTORY

Humans have been farming animals for thousands of years, dating back to when animals were first domesticated. The ability to keep and control animals allowed people to

TABLE 4.3

Livestock and poultry slaughter statistics, 2005

	Federally inspected slaughter	Other commercial slaughter	Total commercial slaughter
Calves	718,000	17,000	734,000
Cattle	31,831,000	556,000	32,388,000
Dairy cows	2,252,000	N/A	2,252,000
Other cows	2,523,000	N/A	2,523,000
Hogs and pigs	103,582,000	N/A	103,582,000
Sheep and lambs	2,698,000	N/A	2,698,000
Chickens			9,000,473,000
Turkeys			284,094,000
Ducks			27,890,000

Breakdown of slaughtered cattle

Steers	16,797,000
Heifers	9,761,000
All cows	4,775,000
Bulls & stags	498,000

Breakdown of slaughtered hogs & pigs

Barrows & gilts	99,123,000
Sows	3,116,000
Stags & boars	280,000
Other	1,063,000

Breakdown of slaughtered sheep & lambs

Lambs	2,425,000
Mature sheep	129,000
Other	143,000

SOURCE: Adapted from "Table A1.3. Cattle and Calves Production: 2004 and 2005," "Table A1.4. Milk Cow Production: 2004 and 2005," "Table A1.7. Hog and Pig Production: 2004 and 2005," "Table A1.8. Sheep Production in the United States: 2004 and 2005," and "Table A1.9. Poultry Production in the United States, 2004 and 2005," in *2005 United States Animal Health Report*, U.S. Department of Agriculture, Animal and Plant Health Inspection Service, August 2006,http://www.aphis.usda.gov/publications/animal_health/content/printable_version/AHR_Web_PDF/J_appendices.pdf (accessed November 28, 2006)

done by rail, and for more than 130 years the law was only enforced on railroad transport of livestock. In 2005 the animal group Compassion Over Killing conducted an undercover investigation of a pig transport operation and produced videos documenting the suffering allegedly inflicted on pigs forced to travel by truck for long time periods. The U.S. Department of Agriculture (USDA) launched its own investigation after learning that more than 150 pigs transported by truck for more than twenty-eight hours in the summer heat arrived dead at a livestock facility in Texas. Compassion Over Killing and other animal welfare organizations petitioned the USDA to include truck transport under the provisions of the Twenty-Eight Hour Law. In September 2006 the USDA officially agreed and concluded that "trucks which operate as express carriers or common carriers" for livestock will from now on be covered under the law (http://www.hsus.org/farm/news/ournews/usda_reverses_28_hour_policy.html).

The Animal Welfare Act was enacted in 1966 to provide protection for animals used for certain purposes, but the regulations enforcing the law specifically excluded livestock.

The major legislation of the twentieth century to affect livestock was the Humane Methods of Slaughter Act of 1958. The law required slaughter by humane methods at slaughterhouses subject to federal inspection. This meant that livestock had to be rendered insensitive to pain before being slaughtered. The act excluded chickens and all animals slaughtered using techniques associated with religious rituals. For decades, animal welfare organizations have been contesting the USDA policy that excludes some animals, particularly chickens and turkeys, from coverage under this law. In 2005 the Humane Society of the United States (HSUS) and other plaintiffs filed a lawsuit against the USDA challenging the policy that excludes birds from the act. In September 2006 a federal judge refused a USDA request to dismiss the case and noted that the plaintiffs presented a credible argument in their lawsuit.

Concern Grows

Following the Humane Methods of Slaughter Act of 1958, farm animals received little more attention until a 1964 book by Ruth Harrison was published. *Animal Machines: The New Factory Farming Industry* described the brutality inflicted on livestock in Britain by the modern farming industry. In 1975 Peter Singer published *Animal Liberation: A New Ethics for Our Treatment of Animals*, which detailed similar problems on U.S. factory farms. It was also during the 1960s and 1970s that the vegetarian movement gained momentum.

The plight of farm animals became a major issue with animal rights activists and welfarists. In the 1980s and early 1990s several groups dedicated to livestock concerns formed, among them the Farm Animal Reform Movement, Humane Farming Association, Farm Sanctuary, and United Poultry Concerns. Since 2000 these and other groups began publicizing abuses that occur in the agricultural industry and have achieved new legislation to protect farm animals.

Specific goals include:

- Banning the slaughter of horses for food
- Legislation for poultry to be covered under the Humane Methods of Slaughter Act
- Protecting animals at the slaughterhouse that have been injured during transport and are unable to walk (so-called downed animals)
- Outlawing the keeping of veal calves and pregnant and nursing hogs in small iron crates so that they cannot move
- Publicizing the abuse and mishandling of animals at slaughterhouses

FIGURE 4.2

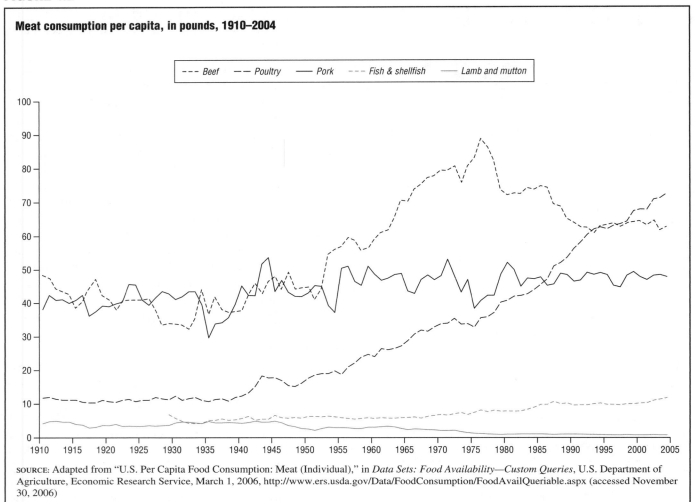

Meat consumption per capita, in pounds, 1910–2004

--- Beef — — Poultry —— Pork --- Fish & shellfish —— Lamb and mutton

SOURCE: Adapted from "U.S. Per Capita Food Consumption: Meat (Individual)," in *Data Sets: Food Availability—Custom Queries*, U.S. Department of Agriculture, Economic Research Service, March 1, 2006, http://www.ers.usda.gov/Data/FoodConsumption/FoodAvailQueriable.aspx (accessed November 30, 2006)

ANIMAL PRODUCTS

Animal products are used in many ways by modern society. People consume them and wear them and buy items every day that contain animal-derived components. According to the Economic Research Service (ERS; 2007, http://www.ers.usda.gov/Data/FoodConsumption/FoodAvailQueriable.aspx), Americans consumed 201.2 pounds of meat per capita (per person) during 2004. From 1909 until the late 1930s the annual meat consumption averaged about 100 pounds per person. After World War II Americans began consuming more meat. The annual per capita consumption climbed steadily throughout the remainder of the century.

For much of the twentieth century, beef and pork accounted for most of the meat consumed in the United States. (See Figure 4.2.) Concerns about the fat and cholesterol content of red meat led to greater demand for chicken and turkey. Figure 4.2 shows that these "white" meats began to make up a larger share of meat consumption. By 2004 beef and pork accounted for 56% of the pounds of meat consumed per year, whereas chicken and

turkey made up 38%. (See Figure 4.3.) Consumption of fish, shellfish, lamb, and mutton was much lower.

Animals killed for meat must be processed immediately. This means that meat animals must arrive alive at the slaughterhouse. They cannot be humanely euthanized with drugs as pets are when put to sleep because humans will be consuming them. Those parts that are not readily edible by humans are rendered into other marketable products. Bones, hooves, beaks, feet, feathers, fat, and inedible organs and tissues are recycled at one of several hundred rendering plants in the United States. The fat is processed for industrial use, and the other byproducts are ground into a powder or boiled to make gelatin. Tallow (rendered fat) is used to make soap, candles, and lubricants.

According to the National Renderers Association (June 29, 2006, http://www.renderers.org/Statistics/index.htm), nearly 8.1 million tons of animal byproducts were produced by the rendering industry in 2005. Approximately one-third was inedible tallow and greases. The remainder included bone meal, edible tallow, lard, poultry fat, inedible feather meal, and miscellaneous products.

FIGURE 4.3

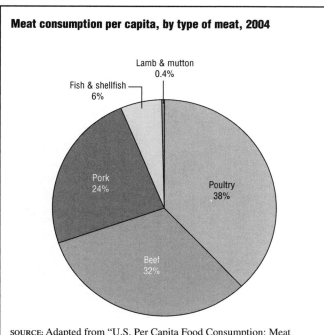

Meat consumption per capita, by type of meat, 2004

Lamb & mutton
0.4%

Fish & shellfish
6%

Pork
24%

Poultry
38%

Beef
32%

SOURCE: Adapted from "U.S. Per Capita Food Consumption: Meat (Individual)," in *Data Sets: Food Availability—Custom Queries*, U.S. Department of Agriculture, Economic Research Service, March 1, 2006, http://www.ers.usda.gov/Data/FoodConsumption/FoodAvailQueriable .aspx (accessed November 30, 2006)

Rendered byproducts are sold to a variety of industries and become ingredients in lubricants, paints, varnishes, waxes, soaps, candles, cement, pharmaceuticals, pet food, toothpaste, and cosmetics (such as lipstick and shampoo). Gelatin is an ingredient in many food products, including some ice cream, yogurt, candy, and marshmallows. Before the 1990s a primary use of rendered byproducts was as a protein supplement (or food source) for livestock. In 1997 the U.S. Food and Drug Administration (FDA) outlawed the use of most mammal-based protein in feed intended for cattle. This is to prevent the spread of disease, particularly mad cow disease, should it appear in the United States. Rendering plants also process whole carcasses of farm animals that die of illness or injury and other dead animals, including euthanized pets.

Table 4.4 lists some of the many products that contain animal-derived ingredients. In addition, animal products are increasingly used for human medical and health purposes.

ROUTINE FARMING PRACTICES

Historically, farm animals have not been covered by animal welfare legislation. As a result, some practices relating to the treatment of farm animals are considered standard by farmers but may be thought of as cruel or

TABLE 4.4

Uses of animal byproducts in our daily lives

Intestines	Fats and fatty acids	Bones, horns, and hooves	From hide and wool
Sausage casings	Explosives	Syringes	Lanolin
Instrument strings	Solvents	Piano keys	Clothing
Surgical sutures	Chewing gum	Marshmallow	Drum heads
Tennis racket strings	Paints	Pet food ingredients	Luggage
	Industrial lubricants	Bandage strips	Yarns
	Cosmetics, shampoo	Bone charcoal products	Artist's brushes
	Dog food	Gelatin	Sports equipment
	Mink oil	Adhesive tape	Fabrics
	Oleo margarine	Phonograph records	Pelt products
	Ceramics	Combs & toothbrushes	Insulation
	Medicines	Buttons	Textiles
	Soaps	Jewelry	Tennis balls
	Creams & lotions	Bone meal	Carpet
	Tires, rubber products	Emery boards & cloth	Footwear
	Paraffin	Ice cream	Woolen goods
	Biodegradable detergents	Horn & bone handles	Baseballs
	Antifreeze	Wallpaper and wallpaper paste	Upholstery
	Crayons	Dog biscuits	Hide glue
	Floor wax	Steel ball bearings	
	Chemicals	Fertilizer	
	Insecticides	Neatsfoot oil	
	Candles	Adhesives	
	Herbicides	Plywood & paneling	
	Shaving cream	Shampoo & conditioner	
		Dice	
		Collagen cold cream	
		Crochet needles	
		Cellophane products	
		Glycerine	
		Photographic film	
		Laminated wood products	

SOURCE: Adapted from "Animal Byproducts in Our Daily Lives," Minnesota Foundation for Responsible Animal Care, 2000, http://www.mnbeef.org/ MnFRAC/byproducts.htm (accessed January 3, 2007)

inhumane by animal activists and other people. Such practices include culling, castration, dehorning, branding, and various forms of physical alteration. Culling means the rejection of inferior or undesirable animals. Because it costs money to feed and care for livestock, unwanted farm animals are usually killed. This is particularly true in the hen-breeding business. Male chicks of laying breeds will never lay eggs and are not suitable meat chickens. Millions of them are routinely killed each year when they are only one day old.

Another ancient farming practice is animal castration (removal of the male sex organs). Humans have used castration to control the reproduction of farm animals for centuries. This is particularly true in cattle and hog farming. Only the males with the most desirable characteristics are allowed to remain intact for breeding purposes. This is believed to be beneficial for herd management, because castration reduces aggressive behavior and physical confrontations between males that might damage their meat. In addition, sexually mature males release hormones that can affect the taste of meat.

The vast majority of cattle are dehorned to make them easier to handle and to prevent them from accidentally or intentionally injuring each other. In grown cattle the fully developed horns are cut off, but a more common practice is to treat the emerging horn buds of baby calves with a caustic salve to prevent horns from developing. According to Todd Duffield, in *How to Dehorn Calves to Minimize Pain* (June 2006, http://www.ansci.cornell.edu/prodairy/manager/2006pdf/june26.pdf), this procedure causes "minimal" pain and the use of a local anesthetic block is unnecessary.

Branding and other forms of identification, such as ear notching, are used to distinguish ownership. Cattle and swine have their tails clipped to prevent them from chewing on each other's tails and to improve cleanliness and reduce disease. Chicken beaks are trimmed to reduce injuries that might result from the animals pecking at each other.

All these procedures are regarded as practical and necessary by farm animal producers and considered inhumane by many animal welfarists. Castration, dehorning, branding, beak trimming, tail clipping, and ear notching are widely conducted in the United States without the use of anesthetics or pain medication. Use of a local anesthetic is recommended (but not required) in Canada and is required by law in most cases in the United Kingdom.

FACTORY FARMING

What Is a Farm?

The farming of livestock has changed dramatically over the past century. Many people think of a farm as a rural collection of barns and fields run by one farming

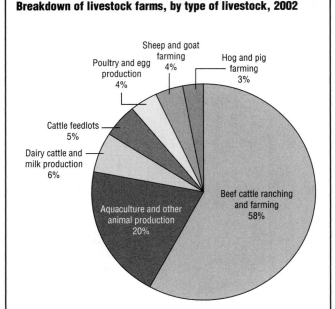

FIGURE 4.4

Breakdown of livestock farms, by type of livestock, 2002

- Sheep and goat farming 4%
- Poultry and egg production 4%
- Hog and pig farming 3%
- Cattle feedlots 5%
- Dairy cattle and milk production 6%
- Aquaculture and other animal production 20%
- Beef cattle ranching and farming 58%

Note: Data were taken from 2002 Agricultural Census and are based on 1,142,357 livestock producing establishments.

SOURCE: Adapted from "Table 59. Summary by North American Industry Classification System: 2002," in *2002 Census of Agriculture*, U.S. Department of Agriculture, National Agricultural Statistics Service, 2004, http://www.nass.usda.gov/census/census02/volume1/us/st99_1_059_059.pdf (accessed January 3, 2007)

family. In reality, some farms are massive industrial-type facilities owned and operated by large corporations. These are called factory farms. Although they make up a small percentage of U.S. farms, they handle a large percentage of the animals killed for food in the United States.

According to the *2002 Census of Agriculture* (June 2004, http://www.nass.usda.gov/Census_of_Agriculture/index.asp), the USDA defines a farm as an establishment that produces or sells $1,000 or more of agricultural products during a year. According to the 2002 census, there were more than 2.1 million farms in the United States, just over half of which produced livestock. The breakdown by animal type is shown in Figure 4.4. Cattle farms, ranches, and feedlots accounted for 63% of the total. Far fewer farms were engaged in raising swine, poultry, sheep, goats, aquatic animals (such as fish), and other animals. The other category includes specialty animals, such as fur-bearing animals, honeybees, bison, llamas, snakes, and worms.

Consolidation of Agricultural Businesses

The USDA reports in *2002 Census of Agriculture* that in 2002, 89.7% of all farms were owned and operated by individuals and families. Only 3.5% were owned by corporations, but many small farms operate under contract to corporations. The farmers may sign away ownership of their animals and be paid to raise them to a contracted age or weight. Then the animals are turned over to the companies for finishing or slaughtering.

Agribusiness has undergone much consolidation since the 1950s. According to Mary Hendrickson and William Heffernan, in "Concentration of Agricultural Markets" (January 2005, http://www.foodcircles.missouri.edu/CRJanuary05.pdf), only four companies controlled 83.5% of the beef packing industry in 2003: Tyson Foods Inc., Cargill Meat Solutions Corp., Swift and Company, and National Beef Packing Company. In the pork industry the top four producers and packers controlled 49% and 64% of the market, respectively. The top four broiler producers controlled 56% of that industry.

Many corporations have vertically integrated their operations. In other words, they not only own facilities that raise animals but they also own the facilities that produce feed for them and the facilities that slaughter and process them. Economies of scale—that is, larger volumes—allow corporations to spend less on each of these steps than small farmers do.

How Factory Farms Work

The most visible symbol of factory farming is the animal feeding operation (AFO) or concentrated animal feeding operation (CAFO). By federal definition, an AFO is a facility that "congregates animals, feed, manure and urine, dead animals, and production operations on a small area of land." The difference between an AFO and a CAFO is based in part on how many animals are involved. Both feature highly concentrated confinement areas with no pasture or grazing land.

In this way, the animals can be housed, fed, medicated, and processed with utmost efficiency. Every aspect of animal life and behavior is controlled to ensure that productivity and profits are maximized. The animals are kept in the smallest space possible and fed the cheapest food that will quickly and effectively fatten them up. Breeding facilities ensure a constant supply of replacements.

Modern technology is employed whenever it is economically feasible. Females are artificially inseminated rather than mated. Pregnancies are spaced close together to increase production. Mothers and offspring are separated quickly to keep the process moving. Antibiotics, hormones, and growth-enhancing drugs are administered to ensure rapid growth and to prevent deadly diseases. Slaughterhouses are run like assembly lines with an emphasis on speed and meat quantity.

Pros and Cons

The overwhelming advantage of the factory farming system to society is economic—satisfaction of the demand for meat at acceptable prices. Factory farming provides the United States with a continuous and rela-

tively inexpensive meat supply. However, animal rights activists blame the factory farming system for many animal abuses. They believe that the industry's emphasis on profits, efficiency, and productivity has contributed greatly to inhumane treatment and sloppy slaughtering of farm animals.

There is no doubt that industrial methods have changed the way in which farmers and animals interact. Traditionally, farmers had a lot of personal interaction with their animals during feeding and handling. Even though this did not change the ultimate usage of the animals, many people believe that it built a bond that led farmers to care more about the welfare of individual animals. Certainly sick or injured animals were more likely to be noticed and cared for in this system. Many small farms, particularly in communities that use traditional methods (such as Amish farms) still achieve this level of human-animal contact.

By contrast, factory farms are almost entirely automated. For example, on most chicken farms the food is dispensed by machines, and the eggs are collected on conveyor belts. The chickens rarely see people until they are gathered by human handlers into crates for their journey to the slaughterhouse. Such automation in modern animal husbandry saves money by reducing labor costs and increasing efficiency.

CATTLE

Cattle are bovines that descend from ancient animals called aurochs. They have complex, four-compartment stomachs called rumens and eat vegetation. In nature, cattle swallow their food whole. Later, the partially digested food, or cud, is regurgitated into their mouths for them to chew. "Chewing the cud" is a well-known cattle trait. The natural lifespan for cattle is twenty to twenty-five years.

There are many different breeds of cattle. Some are specially bred for meat (such as Angus and Hereford), whereas others are bred to produce milk (such as Jerseys). Adult female cattle are called cows. They produce milk for their newborn calves for months. People learned long ago to take calves away from their mothers and collect the milk for human consumption. Young female cows that have not yet given birth are called heifers. Uncastrated adult male cattle are called bulls. They are used only for breeding purposes. Male cattle castrated before they reach sexual maturity are called steers. They are a major source of beef in this country.

As shown in Table 4.2, there were over 97.1 million cattle on U.S. farms in 2005. Figure 4.5 shows that the cattle inventory increased dramatically through the early 1970s and then declined, before leveling off in the mid-1990s.

FIGURE 4.5

Number of cattle and calves on U.S. farms, selected years 1869–2005

SOURCE: "Figure 1C. Cattle and Calves: U.S. Inventory on January 1 for Selected Years, 1869–2005," in *2005 United States Animal Health Report*, U.S. Department of Agriculture, Animal and Plant Health Inspection Service, August 2006, http://www.aphis.usda.gov/publications/animal_health/content/printable_version/AHR_Web_PDF/C_chapter_%201.pdf (accessed November 28, 2006)

Beef Cattle

HISTORY. At the beginning of the twentieth century, the U.S. cattle industry was concentrated in the western states. Cattle were herded by cowboys to markets in large cities with railroad hubs. Cattle were shipped by rail to massive stockyards and slaughtering/processing centers in places such as Chicago and Kansas City. As refrigeration and electricity spread throughout the country, slaughterhouses were able to move away from the big cities and into rural areas.

During the 1950s large meat companies began setting up feedlots for cattle, first in the Great Plains and later further west. (See Figure 4.6.) Before that time cattle mostly ate grass, with some corn and other grains added to fatten them. They were slaughtered when they reached marketable size, around three to four years of age. U.S. farmers began producing a surplus of corn in the mid-1950s, and it became a primary feed for beef cattle. Cattle fed a diet rich in corn got fatter much faster and could be slaughtered much earlier than grass-fed cattle. Corn-fed beef had a rich, fatty taste with a marbled texture and was more tender than grass-fed beef. It was also much cheaper. Heavy marketing by grocery stores led to huge demand for corn-fed beef.

PRESENT CONDITIONS. Table 4.5 shows the number of feedlots and their inventories as of January 1, 2006. At that time there were more than fourteen million cattle on approximately eighty-eight thousand feedlots in the United States. The vast majority of feedlots (97.5%) each contained less than one thousand head of cattle. However, the small number of feedlots that each contained more than thirty-two thousand head of cattle accounted for a large portion (40.4%) of all the cattle on feedlots. More than 5.7 million cattle were on these massive feedlots at that time.

Most beef cattle are slaughtered around the age of fourteen to sixteen months. Calves spend the first six to eight months of their lives with their mothers, drinking milk and grazing on grass at farms and ranches around the country. This is called the cow-calf stage of the business. Following weaning, most calves are moved to large, crowded feedlots—outdoor grassless enclosures—to be "finished" for slaughter. During finishing the cattle receive virtually no exercise to prevent muscle buildup and fat loss. The animals are given various drugs to help them digest the rich corn diet and fend off disease from the crowded and often dirty conditions.

In March 2002 the reporter Michael Pollen purchased an eight-month-old calf from a South Dakota ranch and chronicled the calf's life in "Power Steer" (*New York Times*, March 31, 2002). Following weaning, Pollen's calf spent several months in a backgrounding pen becoming accustomed to a corn diet before being shipped to a feedlot. At the feedlot, crowded with thirty-seven thousand cattle, the calf was fed a diet of corn, fat, protein supplements, and some alfalfa hay and corn silage for

FIGURE 4.6

A cattle feedlot. *Photo Researchers Inc. Reproduced by permission.*

TABLE 4.5

Cattle feedlot breakdown, by number and inventory, January 1, 2006

Feedlot capacity (head)	Number of feedlots	%	January 1, 2006, inventory (1,000 head)	%
<1,000	86,000	97.5	2,328	16.5
1,000–1,999	855	1.0	506	3.6
2,000–3,999	547	0.6	777	5.5
4,000–7,999	350	0.4	1,009	7.1
8,000–15,999	184	0.2	1,363	9.6
16,000–31,999	137	0.2	2,438	17.3
≥32,000	126	0.1	5,711	40.4
All feedlots	88,199	100.0	14,132	100.0

SOURCE: "Table A1.6. Cattle-on-Feed Production," in *2005 United States Animal Health Report*, U.S. Department of Agriculture, Animal and Plant Health Inspection Service, August 2006, http://www.aphis.usda.gov/publications/animal_health/content/printable_version/AHR_Web_PDF/J_appendices.pdf (accessed November 28, 2006)

roughage. The calf was given antibiotics to help it digest this new diet.

Pollen notes that feedlot cattle must be fed antibiotics and antacids to overcome digestive problems from eating corn rather than grass. Corn-fed cattle are prone to severe bloat, indigestion, and other conditions that can weaken

their immune systems and make them susceptible to serious diseases. Thus, many are fed continuous low-level doses of antibiotics to keep them reasonably healthy. The corn diet damages their livers, but this is a trade-off acceptable to the beef industry because cow liver is not in high demand. Pollen's steer also received a hormone injection of synthetic estrogen to help him gain weight, a common and legal practice.

According to Pollen, the cattle on the feedlot lived amid a thick layer of manure during their entire stay, another reason that antibiotics are required for feedlot cattle. Generally, manure is not a concern until slaughtering time, when it is washed off the carcasses during processing. Pollen argues that this practice is not healthy for the people who will eat the beef or for the cattle living in this environment.

Ranchers use the feedlot system because it is much cheaper for them than finishing the cattle at the ranch. The price of beef is so low that profit margins on cattle are slim. Ranchers and farmers must cut costs wherever they can. Many ranchers sell their calves to corporations and companies running feedlots. Others retain ownership and pay rent to the feedlot during the finishing process.

FIGURE 4.7

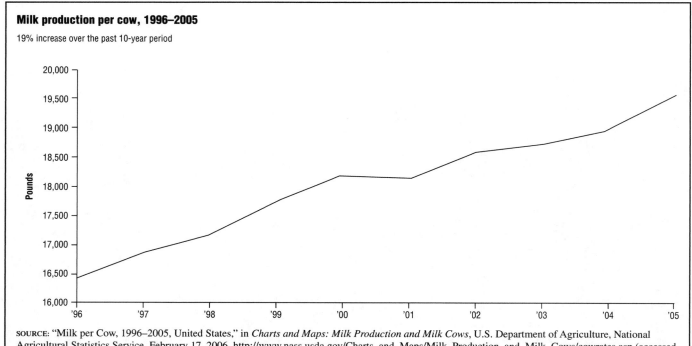

Milk production per cow, 1996–2005

19% increase over the past 10-year period

SOURCE: "Milk per Cow, 1996–2005, United States," in *Charts and Maps: Milk Production and Milk Cows*, U.S. Department of Agriculture, National Agricultural Statistics Service, February 17, 2006, http://www.nass.usda.gov/Charts_and_Maps/Milk_Production_and_Milk_Cows/cowrates.asp (accessed December 28, 2006)

Dairy Cattle

Dairy cattle are a valuable commodity because they produce milk that can be consumed as a drink or used to make other dairy products. According to the ERS, the average per capita consumption in the United States during 2004 was 21.2 gallons of milk, 31.3 pounds of cheese, and 26.4 pounds of frozen dairy products (mostly ice cream).

The USDA's National Agricultural Statistics Service reports in *Charts and Maps: Milk Production and Milk Cows* (February 17, 2006, http://www.nass.usda.gov/Charts_and _Maps/Milk_Production_and_Milk_Cows/milkprod.asp) that dairy cows produced more than 175 trillion pounds of milk during 2005. The combination of factory farming, high-tech breeding, and modern medicine means that the average dairy cow produced three times as much milk in 2005 as did a cow in 1955. Milk production per cow increased by 19% between 1996 and 2005 alone. (See Figure 4.7.)

Even though some people assume that dairy cattle spend leisurely days in rolling fields of grass and are only occasionally milked, the reality is that dairy cows have become milk-producing machines. Most dairy cows live in small indoor stalls or are confined to large dirt pens called dry lots. To produce milk, the cows must have calves. Modern farmers keep dairy cows pregnant almost continuously, often through artificial insemination. They take the calves away from their mothers as soon as possible after birth to prevent the calves from drinking the valuable milk. Male calves and any cows that cease to

produce milk are slaughtered for beef. Common health problems in dairy cows include mastitis (an udder infection) and lameness because of back and leg problems.

Many dairy cattle are given antibiotics and other drugs on a routine basis. One of the most controversial drugs is called bovine growth hormone (BGH). The Animal Protection Institute, in "Get the Facts: The Destructive Dairy Industry" (2007, http://www.api4animals.org/facts?p=373&more=1), indicates that BGH can increase by 25% the amount of milk that a cow can produce. Animal welfarists note that BGH enlarges cows' udders to such a degree that the cows suffer from spine and back problems and have difficulty keeping their udders from dragging in dirt and manure. The International Dairy Foods Association (November 2006, http://www.idfa .org/reg/biotech/rbst_idfa_position.cfm) states that BGH has been used in U.S. dairy herds since 1993 and that Americans have consumed billions of gallons of milk from BGH-supplemented cows. The IDFA reports that the milk has been deemed safe for human consumption "by the FDA, the World Health Organization, the American Medical Association, the National Institutes of Health, the American Dietetic Association, Health Canada, and regulatory agencies in 50 countries." The use of BGH, which is also called bovine somatotropin, is banned in Europe and Canada because of its effects on cow health.

Another criticism of the factory farming of dairy cattle is that the cows spend long periods standing on hard surfaces. This includes concrete floors, metal gratings, and dirt-packed dry lots. Welfarists contend that this contributes to lameness problems in dairy cattle. Lameness is a major reason for cows to be culled (killed) during the raising process. Experts studying downed animals (those that cannot stand and walk because of injury or illness) arriving at slaughterhouses report that a large percentage of downers are dairy cows.

Veal

Veal is meat from young calves that are raised in a way that produces tender, light-colored flesh. This meat is highly prized for its pale color and delicate flavor. According to the American Veal Association (2004, http://www.vealfarm.com/industry-info/facts.asp), veal farmers purchase unwanted calves from the dairy industry (mostly male Holstein calves) and raise them to the desired weight.

The Cattlemen's Beef Board and National Cattlemen's Beef Association (2005, http://www.veal.org/Content/Veal101Veal.aspx) explains that there are three main types of veal:

- Special-fed veal calves are fed a nutritionally complete milk supplement until they reach eighteen to twenty weeks of age and typically weigh from 400 to 450 pounds. The meat is ivory or creamy pink, with a firm, fine, and velvety texture. Approximately 85% of the veal consumed in the United States is special-fed veal. This is the veal industry's premium product.

- Bob veal calves are fed milk. They usually weigh less than 150 pounds and are approximately three weeks old when marketed. The meat has a light-pink color and a soft texture.

- Grain-fed veal calves are initially fed milk and then receive a diet of grain, hay, and nutrition formulas. The meat tends to be darker in color and has additional marbling and often visible fat. Grain-fed veal calves are usually marketed at five to six months of age and weigh from 450 to 600 pounds.

THE CONTROVERSY. Veal production is harshly criticized by both animal rights supporters and welfarists. They view the early separation of calves from their mothers and the extremely confined conditions under which the calves live as inhumane. Some calves are kept in very narrow stalls or boxes that prevent them from turning around and are allowed no exercise that would help them build muscles. Also, critics accuse producers of feeding the calves diets that are extremely low in iron to prevent the flesh from darkening. This results in anemic calves that suffer from health problems and stress brought on by their living conditions. The British government has banned the use of veal crates that do not allow a calf to turn around and requires that calves be fed a diet containing sufficient iron and fiber.

American veal producers defend the use of individual stalls to raise their calves. They point out that this method reduces the spread of disease by preventing interaction among the calves. Each calf receives its own feed and does not have to compete with others for food. Also, each calf can receive individual attention to its nutrition and health needs. The American Veal Association claims that the stalls are designed so that calves "can comfortably lay in a natural position, stand up, groom themselves and interact with their neighbors."

In November 2006 Arizona voters passed a measure banning the use of confining crates for veal calves. It was the first state ban of its kind.

CONSUMPTION OF VEAL. Figure 4.8 shows annual consumption data for veal on a per capita basis. Americans consumed only 0.41 pounds of veal per person during 2004, down from a high of 8.4 pounds per person in 1944.

Cattle Slaughter

Cattle killed at federally inspected slaughterhouses are required by law to be killed humanely. In most plants the preferred method is use of a stun gun. Cattle are directed single-file through chutes that lead to the stunner. As each animal passes by, the stunner shoots a stun bolt into the animal's forehead to render it unconscious.

The animal is then hoisted up by one rear leg to hang from a bleed rail. At that time, its throat is cut so that the blood can drain out. Federal law requires that no animal fall into the blood of other slaughtered animals. This is why bloodletting is performed while the animal is suspended in the air. Following bloodletting, the animal moves down the line to a number of processing stations where the tail and hocks are cut off, the belly is cut open, and the hide is removed.

SPECIALLY DESIGNED METHODS. Temple Grandin is a professor at Colorado State University and a renowned expert on cattle handling and slaughter. She maintains a comprehensive Web site full of useful information on this subject at http://www.grandin.com. Grandin designed the systems in use at most U.S. slaughterhouses and has written many guidance documents for the American Meat Institute.

Grandin suffers from autism and says that this allows her to see the world "in pictures," as animals see it. She has published many books and articles on the proper design of livestock chute systems. For example, chutes must be curved to trick the animals into thinking they are going back to where they came. The chutes must have high walls to keep the animals from seeing what is going on around them. Each animal should only see the rear end of the animal in front of it as it walks toward the stunner.

Grandin's recommendations are designed to keep cattle moving efficiently and peacefully. This has both

FIGURE 4.8

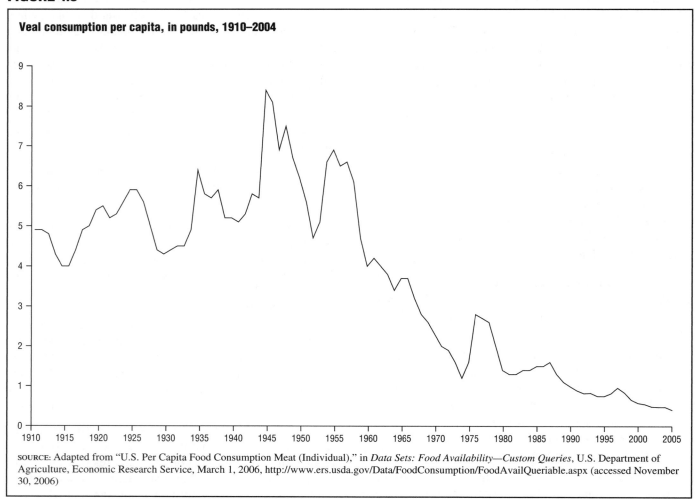

Veal consumption per capita, in pounds, 1910–2004

SOURCE: Adapted from "U.S. Per Capita Food Consumption Meat (Individual)," in *Data Sets: Food Availability—Custom Queries*, U.S. Department of Agriculture, Economic Research Service, March 1, 2006, http://www.ers.usda.gov/Data/FoodConsumption/FoodAvailQueriable.aspx (accessed November 30, 2006)

economic and welfare benefits. Cattle that balk (refuse to move ahead or try to go back down a chute) hold up production. Also, animals that panic are believed to release stress chemicals that taint their meat. Therefore, it is in the best interest of producers that their cattle remain calm in the slaughterhouse. Maintaining quiet and calm also leads to less stress for the animals, which is of importance to animal welfarists.

Grandin says that she is often asked if animals entering the slaughterhouse know they are about to die. She believes that the animals do not suspect their fate, because if they did, they would all balk and panic. She reports that cattle will calmly walk into restraining devices covered with the blood of other cattle, as long as the previous cattle were also calm. However, cattle will refuse to approach a location in which a stressed animal has been killed. Grandin believes that animals that become agitated for several minutes release fear pheromones that other animals can smell.

Grandin (June 2006, http://www.grandin.com/welfare .audit.using.haccp.html) has developed an audit procedure with which slaughterhouses can be graded on how well they meet AMI guidelines. The audit procedure centers on five main performance categories that can be graded numerically:

- Stunning proficiency (the number of cattle stunned correctly on the first try)

- Insensibility on the bleed rail (the number of cattle that are still breathing, moving their eyes or blinking, making sounds, or trying to lift themselves up)

- Electric prod usage (the number of cattle that are prodded to keep them moving and the manner in which the prodding is performed)

- Slipping and falling cattle (the number of cattle that slip and fall while they are being moved through the plant)

- Vocalizing cattle (the number of cattle that moo, bellow, or make some other noise during handling and stunning)

In addition, the auditor assesses how the plant handles nonambulatory animals (downers), the condition of flooring and pens, truck unloading and handling procedures, the presence of drinking water in the pens, problems with overcrowding, and the general health condition of the cattle at the plant.

Grandin reports in "Survey of Stunning and Handling in Federally Inspected Beef, Veal, Pork, and Sheep Slaughter Plants (January 7, 1997, http://www.grandin.com/survey/usdarpt.html), an audit she did for the USDA in 1996 of ten federally inspected slaughterhouses in various states, that only three of the plants were able to stun at least 95% of the cattle with a single shot. She also describes problems with poor equipment maintenance, lack of management supervision, excessive use of electric prods, transport of downed animals with forklifts, and other such practices.

Grandin notes in "Corporations Can Be Agents of Great Improvements in Animal Welfare and Food Safety and the Need for Minimum Decent Standards" (April 4, 2001, http://www.grandin.com/welfare/corporation.agents.html) that in 1999 she was hired by McDonald's Corporation to audit the company's beef and pork suppliers for their compliance with the standards. She states that compliance greatly improved after McDonald's fired a supplier that failed the audit. For example, 90% of the plants audited after that firing were able to stun at least 95% of the cattle with a single shot. In addition, the use of electric prods was reduced or eliminated, and most abusive behavior by employees stopped.

Between 2001 and 2005 Grandin oversaw audits conducted for restaurants at dozens of beef and pork plants. The most recent audit findings are in the "2005 Restaurant Animal Welfare Audits of Federally Inspected Beef and Pork Slaughter Plants" (April 2, 2006, http://www.grandin.com/survey/2005.restaurant.audits.html). She reports that all the beef plants rendered 100% of their cattle insensible before the bleedline. More than half of the plants (55%) stunned 99% to 100% of their cattle on the first shot. The remaining plants stunned 95% to 98% on the first shot. Nearly a third of the beef plants received an "excellent" rating for their ability to move cattle through the plant using electric cattle rods on less than 5% of the cattle. Ten plants received an "acceptable" rating in this category, and one plant had a "very bad 61% electric prod score."

Grandin notes that better stunning technology and equipment maintenance have led to continuous improvements in the audits she has conducted over the years. She warns plants that they must have "zero tolerance" for hoisting, skinning, or cutting any animal showing any obvious signs of sensibility or even partial return to sensibility after stunning.

PROBLEMS WITH THE PROCESS? Stories in the media since the late 1990s have exposed some problems with slaughterhouse procedures. In "'They Die Piece by Piece': In Overtaxed Plants, Humane Treatment of Cattle Is Often a Battle Lost" (*Washington Post*, April 10, 2001), Joby Warrick analyzed USDA records and conducted interviews with current and former slaughterhouse workers and federal inspectors. The workers, who made about $9 an hour, claimed to have seen many conscious cattle moving down the bleed rail.

A worker responsible for cutting off the cattle's hocks reported that dozens of conscious animals reached his station each day. He said the animals were blinking, moving, looking around, and making noises. Other workers also reported having to cut into living cattle. Workers in charge of stunning complained that the line moved so fast that they did not have time to do their job properly.

Warrick notes that the USDA had relaxed its oversight of slaughtering plants since 1998 and did not track the number of humane slaughter violations that occur each year. A records review, however, showed that inspectors found 527 violations in 1996–1997, including incidents in which "live animals were cut, skinned, or scalded."

Warrick reports that footage from hidden cameras at slaughterhouses show blinking cattle hanging from bleed rails. Other cattle twist, turn, and arch their backs as if trying to pull themselves upright. Footage also shows squealing hogs being lowered into the scalding water baths that are designed to soften the hides of dead animals. Industry officials claim that the videotaped incidents were staged by disgruntled employees and that unconscious animals kick and twitch by reflex.

Live animals on the bleed rail are a danger to line workers. According to Warrick, many workers are kicked by the animals and suffer broken bones and teeth. Although the line is supposed to be stopped when a conscious animal is detected, workers said that this does not happen.

Animal welfare activists say that the allegations made by Warrick are not unusual. They blame many of the problems on the extremely fast line speed at slaughterhouses and the use of low-paid workers. According to Warrick, most plants process around four hundred animals per hour. This figure has increased eightfold since the early 1900s.

Another major concern of welfarists relates to the problem of downed animals. Downed animals are primarily dairy cattle that collapse from illness, injury, or other causes. They are often tossed alive onto trash heaps, or dragged by chains or pushed by forklifts around stockyards and slaughterhouses. Animal welfare organizations consider processing of these animals inhumane and have tried unsuccessfully since the 1990s to achieve legislation called the Downed Animal Protection Act, which would require that critically ill or injured farm animals be humanely euthanized at the stockyards. In December

2003 a downer cow in Washington State tested positive for bovine spongiform encephalopathy (BSE), commonly known as mad cow disease. This is an extremely serious disease in cattle. It has been linked to a similar fatal disease in humans believed to have eaten beef contaminated with BSE. The USDA promptly announced a ban on the processing of downer cattle for human consumption. However, the audit report *Animal and Plant Health Inspection Service Bovine Spongiform Encephalopathy (BSE) Surveillance Program* (January 2006, http://www.usda.gov/oig/webdocs/50601-10-KC.pdf) by the USDA inspector general reports that twenty-nine downer cattle were slaughtered at two plants audited during fiscal year 2004.

RITUAL SLAUGHTER. The Humane Methods of Slaughter Act has exceptions for ritual slaughter—that is, slaughter conducted according to religious dictates. Ritual slaughter is practiced by some orthodox Jews and Muslims. Their teachings require that animals killed for food be moving and healthy when they are killed by having their throats slit. This was originally intended to ensure that sick animals were not eaten by humans. Meat from animals killed in this manner is said to be kosher in Jewish tradition and Halal in Muslim tradition. Regarding ritual slaughter, the Humane Methods of Slaughter Act does require "simultaneous and instantaneous" cutting of the throat arteries "with a sharp instrument" to render the animal insensible (unconscious).

Animal welfarists complain that strict interpretation of the directives for ritual slaughter means that cattle are not stunned before being bled out. They may be jerked up to the bleed rail by a hind leg while still fully conscious. The jerking action can break the leg and tear apart joints, causing them severe pain. Their thrashing makes it more difficult for the cutter to cleanly cut their throats, which prolongs the entire process.

There are upright restraining devices that hold animals more humanely while their throats are being cut. The AMI strongly recommends the use of these devices, both for the welfare of the animals and the safety of the plant workers. Grandin and Gary C. Smith report in "Animal Welfare and Humane Slaughter" (November 2004, http://www.grandin.com/references/humane.slaughter.html) that throat cutting must be done precisely with a long, razor-sharp knife to induce "near-immediate collapse." Otherwise, the animal can remain conscious for more than a minute. Animals that struggle against their restraints or become agitated stay conscious the longest.

Singer states in *Animal Liberation* that critics of ritual slaughter are often accused of being racist or anti-Semitic. He points out that parts of ritually killed animals wind up on supermarket shelves and are purchased by people who may not be aware of how the animal was killed. This is because Jewish law requires the removal of the lymph nodes and sciatic nerve from cattle. Singer says that this is difficult to do efficiently on the hindquarters of cattle, so often only the front portion is sold as kosher. The hindquarters are processed and sold in usual commercial markets.

Donald G. McNeil Jr. reports in "Inquiry Finds Lax Federal Inspections at Kosher Meat Plant" (*New York Times*, March 10, 2006) on an animal welfare controversy involving the nation's largest kosher slaughterhouse in Postville, Iowa. In 2004 an undercover investigator for People for the Ethical Treatment of Animals (PETA) captured video of cattle not being rendered unconscious by throat slitting. However, workers immediately used hooks to pull out the trachea and esophagus of each animal. This practice vastly speeds up the bleeding process. The video shows steers thrashing about for up to three minutes before passing out. According to the article the video's release spurred outrage among Jewish organizations around the world—outrage at PETA for allegedly being "anti-Semitic" and at the processing plant for causing animal suffering. The plant has reportedly altered its slaughtering procedures since the issue became public.

A resulting six-month investigation by the USDA found that its inspectors at the plant knew that the practice was going on but ignored it because they assumed the USDA had no say over ritual slaughter techniques. In addition, the inspectors had accepted free gifts of meat from employees at the slaughter plant. In response, the agency suspended one of the inspectors for two weeks and issued warning letters to two other inspectors. McNeil reports that PETA learned about the USDA investigation only after PETA obtained a copy of the USDA inspector general's report under the Freedom of Information Act.

POULTRY

Poultry are domesticated birds cultivated for their eggs or meat. This includes chickens, turkeys, geese, and ducks. Chickens are by far the most common type of poultry raised in the United States. In 2005 there were nearly 8.9 billion broilers produced in the United States, more than 343.5 million egg-laying hens, and over 256.2 million turkeys. (See Table 4.2.)

Chickens

Chickens were originally domesticated from wild Asian jungle fowl. In natural conditions chickens tend to live in small groups composed of one male chicken (called a rooster or cock) and a dozen or more female chickens (called hens). Chickens are known for their hierarchy, or "pecking order." Each member of the group has a particular rank that determines its place in society. The average natural lifespan of a chicken is six to ten years, although they can live to be as old as twenty-five.

FIGURE 4.9

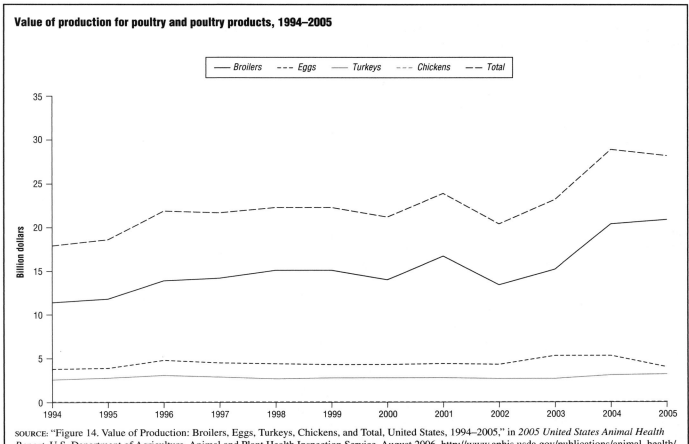

Value of production for poultry and poultry products, 1994–2005

— Broilers --- Eggs —— Turkeys --- Chickens —— Total

SOURCE: "Figure 14. Value of Production: Broilers, Eggs, Turkeys, Chickens, and Total, United States, 1994–2005," in *2005 United States Animal Health Report*, U.S. Department of Agriculture, Animal and Plant Health Inspection Service, August 2006, http://www.aphis.usda.gov/publications/animal_health/content/printable_version/AHR_Web_PDF/C_chapter_%201.pdf (accessed November 28, 2006)

Chickens are omnivores, meaning that they will feed on both vegetable and animal substances. They spend a good part of their day foraging and pecking at the ground for food. They also like to perch, flap their wings, and take dust baths. Hens prefer to lay eggs in a private nest. Young hens above the age of five months produce two hundred to three hundred eggs per year. Unless the hen has recently mated with a rooster, however, the egg is infertile and does not develop into a chick. In the wild the hen would leave infertile eggs to rot or be eaten by predators.

CHICKEN BECOMES BIG BUSINESS. Before the 1920s chicken meat was not common in the American diet. Female chickens were valued on the farm for egg production. Besides being sometimes used for cockfighting, male chickens were considered to have little value at all. They were relatively scrawny and aggressive. This began to change in the 1920s when enterprising farmers started cultivating chickens for meat. Scientific advances led to chicken breeds that were much meatier and grew faster. The use of vitamins, antibiotics, and growth hormones allowed mass production of chickens to become a thriving business. In the 1950s producers began using large CAFOs. This became the preferred method for raising chickens.

In the twenty-first century the vast majority of U.S. chickens are raised by contract farmers and finished in CAFOs. Hendrickson and Heffernan indicate that in 2003 only four producers accounted for 56% of the broiler market: Tyson Foods Inc., Pilgrim's Pride, Gold Kist, and Perdue. The sale of poultry and poultry products was valued at about $28 billion in 2005, with broilers providing the bulk of the value. (See Figure 4.9.)

CHICKEN WELFARE CONCERNS. Chickens raised in crowded conditions are prone to aggression. They peck and claw at each other, which can cause feather loss and injury. Injured chickens may be pecked to death and even eaten by other chickens. It is common practice in factory farming of chickens to debeak a certain percentage of chickens by removing part of the upper and/or lower beak. Toe clipping involves cutting off parts of the chicken claw. Producers say that these practices are for the good of the chickens, to spare them injury. They claim that the chickens do not experience any pain because beaks are similar to human fingernails.

United Poultry Concerns (UPC) is a nonprofit group based in Maryland that advocates for the humane treatment of domestic poultry. The UPC (August 23, 1999, http://www.upc-online.org/debeaking/ota.html) claims that scientific studies show that chicken beaks contain nerves and pain receptors. Thus, the UPC suggests, debeaked chickens suffer pain that is evident through their decreased desire to eat for several weeks following debeaking. The group describes debeaking operations as "haphazard and uncontrollable."

Animal welfarists say that debeaking and toe clipping would not be necessary if chickens were raised in more natural environments. They believe that it is the stress of living in cramped cages in buildings housing tens of thousands of other chickens that drives chickens to demonstrate aggressive behavior. Instead of changing the way in which chickens are raised, welfarists say producers accommodate these brutal systems by mutilating the chickens.

Chicken producers defend these practices as necessary. The National Chicken Council (NCC) is an industry organization for companies that produce, process, and market chickens. The NCC's voluntary *Animal Welfare Guidelines and Audit Checklist* (April 5, 2005, http://www.nationalchickencouncil.com/files/AnimalWelfare2005.pdf) states: "Today's chicken has been purposefully selected to thrive under modern management. We believe current good management practices that avoid destructive behavior, prevent disease, and promote good health and production are consistent with the generally accepted criteria of humane treatment."

BROILERS. Chicken meat is extremely popular in the United States. The annual per capita consumption increased from eleven pounds per person in 1910 to 59.2 pounds per person in 2004. (See Figure 4.2.) Billions of broilers are raised and slaughtered each year to keep up with the demand for chicken meat. As shown in Figure 4.10, broiler production increased dramatically between 1953 and 2005.

Broiler-type chicks are bred to gain weight fast. They start their lives at hatcheries. Day-old chicks are moved into chicken houses that may be hundreds of feet long and contain tens of thousands of chickens. These buildings are windowless and usually have dim lighting, because this is considered more calming. Under the crowded conditions and unused to the presence of humans, the chickens are prone to panic attacks at sudden loud noises. In modern chicken houses nearly everything is automated. Food and water are dispensed by machine. Chicks are vaccinated against common poultry diseases. Broilers are routinely given antibiotics and other drugs to overcome disease and speed up growth.

The NCC specifies in the *Animal Welfare Guidelines and Audit Checklist* that bird density should not exceed

FIGURE 4.10

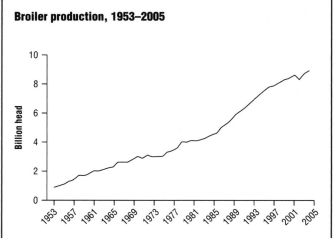

Broiler production, 1953–2005

SOURCE: "Figure 15A. U.S. Broiler Production, 1953–2005," in *2005 United States Animal Health Report*, U.S. Department of Agriculture, Animal and Plant Health Inspection Service, August 2006, http://www.aphis.usda.gov/publications/animal_health/content/printable_version/AHR_Web_PDF/C_chapter_%201.pdf (accessed November 28, 2006)

8.5 pounds per square foot of living space. Because a typical broiler weighs four to five pounds at slaughter weight, two birds of this size would have approximately one square foot of space under this system. The NCC also recommends that broilers not be beak trimmed unless they are used for breeding purposes.

LAYING HENS. Laying hens, or layers, are chickens specifically bred for their egg-laying abilities, rather than for meat production. There were over 343.5 million layers on U.S. farms during 2005. (See Table 4.2.) These chickens produced nearly ninety billion eggs that year. (See Figure 4.11.) This value is up dramatically from the mid-1940s, when less than sixty billion eggs were produced by layers annually. However, as indicated by Figure 4.12, egg consumption per capita in the United States has declined sharply since the 1940s, from a peak of 421.4 eggs per person in 1945 to 256.1 eggs per person in 2004. Processed eggs (pasteurized and packaged nonshell eggs) have been steadily increasing since the 1960s because of demand from food manufacturers and restaurants.

In "'No Battery Eggs' Campaign Exposes the Hard-Boiled Truth about Laying Hens" (2006, http://www.hsus.org/farm/camp/nbe/), the HSUS calls laying hens "the most abused animals in all agribusiness." Animal protection groups are highly critical of three common practices in the factory farming of laying hens: killing male chicks, forced molting, and use of battery cages.

Laying-hen chicks are sorted by gender when they are one day old. Only the females are kept. The males are killed because they have not been bred for meat production and will not grow up to be used as food. According to animal rights groups, millions of culled male chicks are thrown into garbage bags, where they suffocate. The

FIGURE 4.11

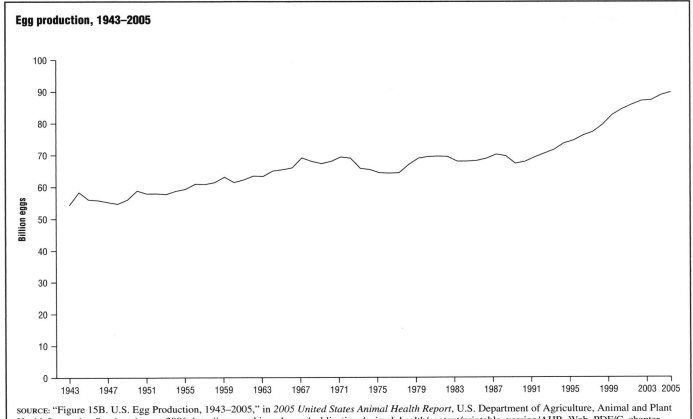

Egg production, 1943–2005

SOURCE: "Figure 15B. U.S. Egg Production, 1943–2005," in *2005 United States Animal Health Report*, U.S. Department of Agriculture, Animal and Plant Health Inspection Service, August 2006, http://www.aphis.usda.gov/publications/animal_health/content/printable_version/AHR_Web_PDF/C_chapter_%201.pdf (accessed November 28, 2006)

poultry industry does not generally discuss its methods of culling male chicks, but it is widely believed that methods including suffocation and maceration (instantaneous death in a high-speed grinder) are commonly used.

Under natural conditions hens can lay eggs for more than a decade, but egg-laying production of hens in factory farms ceases dramatically after the first year. One method used by producers to rejuvenate laying is forced molting, in which all food is withheld from the hens for either a set number of days (usually five to fourteen), or until the hens lose a particular amount of weight. This forced fast mimics the conditions that wild chickens experience in the fall or winter when food is not as plentiful. Lower food intake causes a hen to molt (lose her feathers). Also, her reproductive system temporarily ceases producing eggs. When food is fully restored, the hen is much more productive at making eggs than she was before.

Animal welfarists are extremely critical of forced molting, saying that because all food is withheld from the hens, it is much more brutal than natural molting. They equate the practice to forced starvation and note that food deprivation for the purpose of forced molting is banned in Europe.

The United Egg Producers states in *United Egg Producers Animal Husbandry Guidelines for U.S. Egg Laying Flocks* (2005, http://www.animalcarecertified.com/docs/2005_UEPanimal_welfare_guidelines.pdf) that approximately 98% of all laying hens in the United States are confined to plain wire cages called battery cages. Animal welfarists complain that the cages are so small that the birds cannot spread their wings or engage in nesting, perching, and other natural behaviors. The HSUS reports in "'No Battery Eggs'" that battery cages have been banned in Germany, Switzerland, Sweden, and Austria, and will be phased out throughout the European Union by 2012. Many animal welfare organizations urge consumers to buy eggs only from cage-free chickens. However, the HSUS notes that even cage-free chickens may suffer from welfare problems, including overcrowding within buildings, lack of access to the outdoors, debeaking, and/or forced molting.

CONTROVERSY IN THE CHICKEN INDUSTRY. In early 2002 the egg producer Cypress Foods went out of business, leaving about 1.7 million layers in facilities in Georgia and Florida with no food. Animal rights groups say that twenty thousand to thirty thousand of the hens starved to death after the company declared bankruptcy. Another half million hens had to be euthanized by authorities because they were half-starved and not salvageable. In "Florida Decides Not to File Cruelty Charges against

FIGURE 4.12

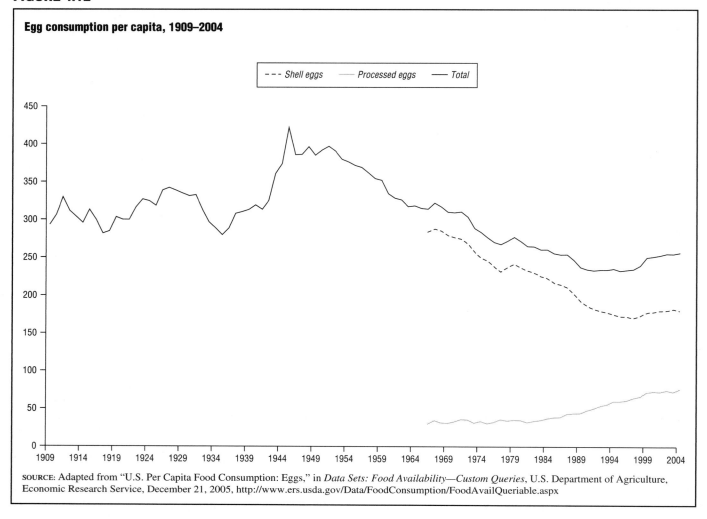

Egg consumption per capita, 1909–2004

--- Shell eggs   —— Processed eggs   —— Total

SOURCE: Adapted from "U.S. Per Capita Food Consumption: Eggs," in *Data Sets: Food Availability—Custom Queries*, U.S. Department of Agriculture, Economic Research Service, December 21, 2005, http://www.ers.usda.gov/Data/FoodConsumption/FoodAvailQueriable.aspx

Cypress Foods" (September 25, 2002, http://www.hsus .org/farm/news/ournews/archive/florida_cypress_foods .html), the HSUS reports that state authorities refused to prosecute the company for animal cruelty, explaining that the deaths were because of economic factors rather than criminal intent. A spokesman for the animal welfare group Farm Sanctuary criticized the decision, saying "running out of money is no defense for animal cruelty."

The U.S. poultry industry had to destroy millions of birds in California, Nevada, and Arizona beginning in 2002 because of exotic Newcastle disease (END). END is a highly contagious and deadly viral disease that affects birds' nervous, respiratory, and digestive systems. Industry and government officials feared that millions of birds would have to be killed as a preventive measure to halt the spread of the disease.

The HSUS notes in "DA Declines to File Charges in California Wood Chipper Case" (April 17, 2003, http:// www.hsus.org/farm/news/ournews/archive/california_wood _chipper_case.html) that in early 2003 there was a mass chicken kill at the Ward Egg Ranch near San Diego, California. Employees reportedly tossed more than thirty thousand live chickens into wood chippers to dispose of them. The chickens were spent hens that were no longer wanted. Ordinarily, they would have been shipped to a slaughterhouse in northern California, but the county had enacted a chicken quarantine because of fears about the spread of END in the state. Local authorities were harshly criticized by animal welfare groups, including the HSUS, for not filing animal cruelty charges in the case. The county district attorney defended the decision, explaining that the ranch owners did not act with criminal intent. Also, the owners insisted that they had consulted with a veterinarian before destroying the animals and were told that use of a wood chipper was acceptable.

CHICKEN SLAUGHTER. When they are ready to go to the slaughterhouse, chickens are gathered by their feet by handlers, who carry them upside down to put into crates. At the slaughterhouse the chickens are shackled upside down by their feet to a conveyor belt. The Humane Methods of Slaughter Act does not apply to poultry, which means that chickens do not have to be stunned unconscious before having their throats slit. Some plants do, however, use a stunning method based on the availability of electricity.

Each live chicken strapped to the conveyor belt has its head dunked into a water bath containing salt. An electric current is passed through the shackles to knock the chicken unconscious. Then the birds pass by an automated cutting blade that slits their throats. After the blood is drained (which takes about ninety seconds), the birds are dipped into scalding water baths to loosen their feathers before moving on to cutting stations.

In January 2003 PETA and the UPC obtained a signed affidavit from a former worker at a chicken slaughterhouse in Arkansas. The man, who worked at the plant from 1997 to 2002, claimed to have witnessed many acts of brutality toward the birds, saying that other workers regularly ran over chickens with forklifts, stomped them to death, and threw snowballs made of dry ice at them for fun. He also claimed that chickens were often not stunned or killed before entering the scalding baths. He described working one night when equipment breakdowns delayed the conveyor belt and allowed stunned chickens to wake up before their throats were slit. The workers did not have time to do the slitting, so they sent the chickens straight to the scalding baths.

Over the following two years similar abuses were reported by undercover investigators at other chicken slaughtering facilities operated by various poultry producers. In response, the HSUS and East Bay Animal Advocates spearheaded a lawsuit against the USDA challenging the exclusion of chickens from the Humane Methods of Slaughter Act. As of January 2007, the suit had not been settled.

During 2005 Grandin oversaw an audit based on NCC standards of nineteen poultry plants. Her findings were reported in "2005 Poultry Welfare Audits: National Chicken Council Animal Welfare Audit for Poultry Has a Scoring System That Is Too Lax and Allows Slaughter Plants with Abusive Practices to Pass" (http://www.grandin.com/survey/2005.poultry.audits.html). Grandin is highly critical of the NCC standards and reports that five of the plants passed the audit even though they had committed "serious abuses." These incidents included four birds that had been scalded while still alive, operators throwing birds during handling, and a live bird found in the trash. Grandin points out that she oversaw a poultry audit at twenty-six plants during 2005 for a client with much higher animal welfare standards and found that none of the plants audited engaged in serious abuses. She concludes, "When plants are required to uphold a higher standard, they are capable of doing it. Unfortunately, there are some people in the producer community who want to make standards so low that even the worst places can pass."

Turkeys

Turkeys are one of the few domesticated animals native to North America. However, present-day turkeys have little resemblance to their wild ancestors. Modern turkeys are bred to gain weight quickly, particularly in the breast. Turkeys are raised much the same way that broiler chickens are raised. At around six weeks of age, the baby birds are moved into growing houses in which they spend the remainder of their lives. Conditions there are crowded, as they are for chickens, and can lead to feather-pecking and cannibalism. Turkeys are slaughtered similarly to chickens at around three to six months of age. Figure 4.13 shows that U.S. turkey production peaked in the late 1990s to more than 300 million turkeys per year and then began to decline. Approximately 250 million turkeys were produced in 2005.

Ducks and Geese

Domestic ducks and geese are raised for their meat, eggs, and feathers. Most ducks are raised indoors, similarly to chickens, and are fed fortified corn and soybeans. Geese are raised in covered enclosures for the first six weeks of their lives and then allowed to forage for grass in fields. Most ducks are raised in Wisconsin and Indiana, whereas most geese are raised in California and South Dakota. Federal law prohibits the use of hormones in duck and goose production. Furthermore, the USDA's Food Safety and Inspection Service reports in the fact sheet "Turkey . . . from Farm to Freezer" (October 2001, http://www.fsis.usda.gov/Fact_Sheets/turkey_from_farm_to_freezer/index.asp) that antibiotics are not routinely given to the birds, but may be used to cure illnesses. However, a withdrawal period of several days is required before the birds can be slaughtered. Ducks and geese are slaughtered with electrocution baths followed by throat slitting.

Duck and geese products are mostly sold in specialty markets. The tongues and feet of the animals are considered a delicacy in parts of Asia (particularly Hong Kong) and are also sold in Asian-American markets. High-value products from ducks and geese include down feathers, smoked meat products, liver pâté (paste), and foie gras (pronounced *fwah grah*, meaning "fat liver" in French).

FOIE GRAS CONTROVERSY. Foie gras is obtained by force-feeding male ducks and geese a rich mixture containing corn, fat, salt, and water over a short amount of time. This regimen causes the birds' livers to become fatty and hugely swollen, six to ten times their normal size.

The feeding process, called gavage, is usually started two to four weeks before slaughter. It is accomplished using an electronic pump that forces food through a twelve- to sixteen-inch tube that is placed down the bird's throat. The birds are force-fed several times a day and held in cramped cages or pens so that they cannot move. This prevents them from losing weight during the fattening process.

FIGURE 4.13

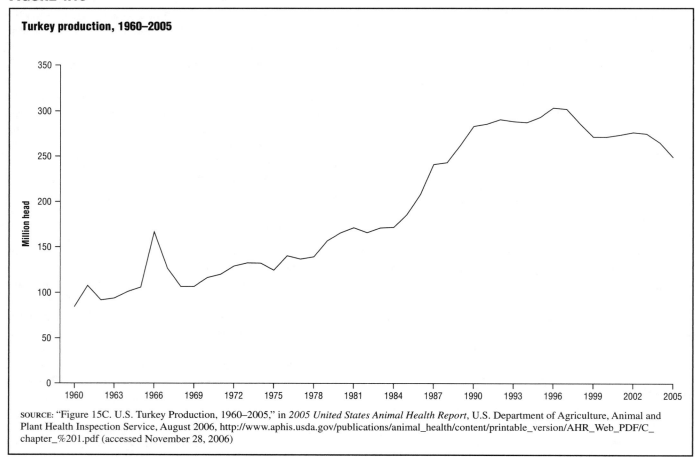

Turkey production, 1960–2005

SOURCE: "Figure 15C. U.S. Turkey Production, 1960–2005," in *2005 United States Animal Health Report*, U.S. Department of Agriculture, Animal and Plant Health Inspection Service, August 2006, http://www.aphis.usda.gov/publications/animal_health/content/printable_version/AHR_Web_PDF/C_chapter_%201.pdf (accessed November 28, 2006)

Animal welfarists are highly critical of gavage. The HSUS states that the birds suffer pain from swollen abdomens and lesions in their throats. It also says that autopsies conducted on dead birds subjected to gavage show severe liver, heart, and esophagus disorders.

Foie gras is a gourmet delicacy that is expensive, selling for up to $45 per pound. It is available at upscale restaurants and specialty stores. Most foie gras comes from France. As of 2007, there were only two commercial producers of foie gras in the United States, and both used duck livers. One producer is located in the Hudson Valley of New York and the other in the Sonoma Valley of California. The producers defend the use of the gavage process, saying that it does not gag the birds because they do not chew their food anyway.

In 2004 California Governor Arnold Schwarzenegger signed a bill into law that will ban by 2012 the force feeding of ducks and geese to produce foie gras and ban the sale of the product in California. In 2006 the Chicago City Council passed an ordinance banning the sale of foie gras within the city limits. According to the animal welfare organization Farm Sanctuary (October 12, 2006, http://www.nofoiegras.org/FGlaws.htm), foie gras has also been banned in Israel and many European countries.

HOGS AND PIGS

Hogs and pigs are domesticated swine. A pig is a young swine that is not yet sexually mature. A young female hog is called a gilt. A female adult hog is called a sow. The generic term *hog* is generally used to refer to all hogs. Hogs are curious and intelligent animals, supposedly smarter than dogs. They have sensitive noses, which they use to root around the ground for their food and explore their surroundings. Pregnant sows like to build nests of grass. Under natural conditions sows give birth to (or farrow) a litter of piglets twice per year. Each litter averages eight piglets that suckle for about three months. The normal life expectancy of a hog is twelve to fifteen years.

Modern Hog Industry

Hogs have been popular farm animals for centuries. In *1990–1995 Changes in U.S. Swine Management Practices* (October 1997, http://www.aphis.usda.gov/vs/ceah/ncahs/nahms/swine/swine95/sw95Pt3.pdf), the Animal and Plant Health Inspection Service (APHIS) reports that the 1850 agricultural census showed an inventory of 30.3 million hogs. This number increased to 62.8 million hogs by 1900. Furthermore, in the information sheet "The USDA's Role in Equine Health Monitoring" (June

FIGURE 4.14

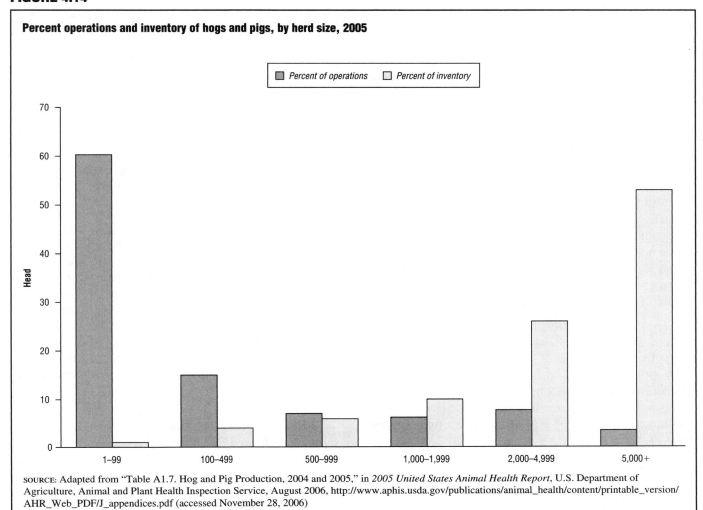

Percent operations and inventory of hogs and pigs, by herd size, 2005

Legend: ■ Percent of operations □ Percent of inventory

Y-axis label: Head

SOURCE: Adapted from "Table A1.7. Hog and Pig Production, 2004 and 2005," in *2005 United States Animal Health Report*, U.S. Department of Agriculture, Animal and Plant Health Inspection Service, August 2006, http://www.aphis.usda.gov/publications/animal_health/content/printable_version/ AHR_Web_PDF/J_appendices.pdf (accessed November 28, 2006)

1996, http://www.aphis.usda.gov/vs/ceah/ncahs/nahms/ equine/equine98/eqrole.pdf), APHIS notes that 76% of U.S. farms produced hogs in 1900. Hogs were favored because hog meat and fat were so versatile. Pork could be canned, smoked, or cured to provide food for long periods of time. Lard—the fat produced from hogs—was widely used as cooking oil and in making candles.

The total U.S. hog inventory in 2005 was 61.4 million. (See Table 4.2.) The total number of hogs on U.S. farms has remained virtually constant for more than a century, although the number of farms raising hogs has declined dramatically. Figure 4.14 shows the breakdown of hog farms and their inventories for 2005. Just over 60% of all hog farms each had less than ninety-nine hogs each. Only 3% of all hog farms were each raising five thousand hogs or more. However, more than half of all hogs in the United States (53%) lived on farms that included at least five thousand hogs each.

The hog industry has undergone tremendous consolidation. Hendrickson and Heffernan report that four companies controlled 49% of all U.S. pork production in 2003: Smithfield Foods, Premium Standard Farms, Seaboard Corporation, and Prestage Farms. The top four companies engaged in pork packing (Smithfield Foods, Tyson Foods Inc., Swift and Company, and Hormel Foods) controlled 64% of the market in 2003. The vast majority of hogs raised in the United States are concentrated on a few massive CAFOs. These facilities not only finish the hogs, as is done in the cattle industry, but also raise them. Major pork producers operate farrowing complexes, nurseries, and growing-feeding units.

The annual per capita consumption of pork products in the United States has changed little over the past century. (See Figure 4.2.) In 1910 annual consumption was 38.2 pounds per person. In 2004 it was 47.8 pounds per person.

Hog-Raising Practices

Confinement buildings for hogs can be hundreds of feet long and contain up to twelve thousand hogs. They typically feature concrete or slatted floors—concrete floors can be easily cleaned and slatted floors allow manure and urine to fall into pits below. Hogs are kept on short tethers or confined in cages and pens to prevent them from getting exercise, which might build muscle instead of fat and toughen the meat. Crowded conditions can lead to aggressive behavior among the hogs, including tail chewing, biting, and fighting. Tail docking and teeth clipping are commonly practiced to help prevent injuries from these behaviors. Antibiotics, hormones, and other drugs are routinely administered to speed growth and prevent deadly diseases.

GESTATION CRATES. Breeding sows are often kept in individual stalls or confined with tethers until they are ready to farrow. Gestation crates, as they are called, are typically around seven feet long and just wide enough for the sow to lie down but not turn around (about two feet). The sow eats, urinates, and defecates where she stands. When she is ready to give birth, the sow may be moved to a farrowing pen in which she and her piglets will be kept tightly confined.

The USDA's National Animal Health Monitoring System (NAHMS) conducts a national swine survey every five to six years. The most recent report, *Swine 2000* (August 2001, http://www.aphis.usda.gov/vs/ceah/ncahs/nahms/swine/index.htm), reports that 83.4% of sows on U.S. farms are farrowed in total confinement facilities, and 81.8% of pigs are raised in total confinement nurseries.

Industry officials defend the use of gestation crates, saying that the crates are necessary to keep aggressive sows from fighting with each other over food. Fighting can cause injuries that lead to miscarried fetuses. Pork producers believe that caged sows receive beneficial individual attention to their health and nutrition needs. The National Pork Producers Council (June 17, 2005, http://www.nppc.org/public_policy/gestation_stalls.html) states that hogs are better off raised indoors because they are protected from "extreme changes in temperature, snow, rain, mud and parasites."

The use of gestation crates has been banned in the United Kingdom and Sweden. The European Union plans to phase out use of the crates by 2013. In 2002 Florida voters passed an amendment to the state constitution to outlaw the use of gestation crates. The move is largely symbolic, as the state is not a major hog producer. Following the vote, the Florida Farm Bureau reported that only two small hog farms in the state used gestation crates, and that one of them had already shut down and the other was phasing out of business. In November 2006 Arizona voters passed a similar measure banning the use of gestation crates for pigs.

OTHER PRACTICES. Generally, week-old pigs are subjected to teeth clipping, tail docking, and ear notching. The males are castrated at this time. These procedures are

done without anesthesia. Once the piglets reach around fifty-five pounds, they are moved to indoor finishing pens. Piglets are raised to slaughter weight, typically 250 pounds, at around four to six months of age. Spent breeding sows are usually slaughtered at around two to three years of age.

According to the NAHMS *Swine 2000* report, nearly 18% of sows and gilts were culled during the first five months of 2000. The primary reasons were age (41.9%), reproductive failure (21.3%), and lameness (16%). Respiratory disease was also a cause of mortality, accounting for 28.9% of nursery deaths and 39.1% of deaths in grower/finisher pigs.

Animal welfarists are critical of hog-raising practices in the United States. They consider the intense confinement too stressful for intelligent and social animals such as hogs. They also condemn early weaning as cruel to sows and piglets. Factory-farmed hogs not only suffer from excessive crowding, stress, and boredom but also experience serious breathing disorders because of high concentrations of ammonia from their waste materials. Critics also say that hogs experience feet and leg deformities from standing on floors made of improper materials.

Hog Slaughter

Hogs are generally killed via electrocution or by stunning followed by bleeding out. Electrocution is accomplished by stunning the hog with a wand with sufficient shock to stop its heart. This is called cardiac arrest stunning and is the technique most large hog slaughter plants use. Hogs can also be given an electrical shock to the head to render them unconscious. Next, the animals are hoisted up by their back feet and bled via a small incision in the chest. Fully electrocuted hogs are also bled out in this manner. The dead hogs are then lowered into vats of scalding water to remove hair. The meat can then be processed.

According to Grandin's instructions for electrical stunning, a hog stunned with sufficient amperage in the correct location will feel no pain. Insufficient amperage and an improper current path will cause the animal pain. Grandin recommends that head-stunned hogs be bled out within thirty seconds of being stunned to prevent them from regaining consciousness.

As noted earlier, between 2001 and 2005 Grandin oversaw audits conducted for restaurants at dozens of beef and pork plants. The most recent audit findings are in Grandin's "2005 Restaurant Animal Welfare Audits of Federally Inspected Beef and Pork Slaughter Plants."

Grandin's audit of pork plants shows some problems. She reports that three out of twenty-eight plants audited had sensible pigs on the bleedline. One of these plants had only one operator responsible for stunning more than one thousand pigs per hour, whereas the more successful plants used two operators for this purpose. Grandin also notes that one plant had a problem with "poor handling with excessive yelling and hitting" by operators. All the plants did receive an acceptable or excellent rating for correct hot wanding procedures.

HORSES

APHIS reports in "The USDA's Role in Equine Health Monitoring" that approximately twenty million horses lived on U.S. farms in 1900. This number declined significantly over the next century. In the *2002 Census of Agriculture*, the USDA notes that in 2002 there were 3.6 million horses living on over 542,000 farms in the United States. The country's total horse inventory could be much higher, because exact inventories are not known for horses kept for racing, breeding, showing, and pleasure purposes.

Horsemeat Controversy

Banning the slaughter of horses for food is the goal of many animal welfare groups. Although horses are not specifically cultivated in the United States for human consumption, there is a growing overseas market for this meat, primarily in Europe and Asia. Horse meat is increasingly popular in these regions because of the scares concerning mad cow disease.

According to APHIS (October 5, 2005, http://www .aphis.usda.gov/vs/nahps/equine/horse_transport/), sixty-three thousand horses were slaughtered in 2003. More than two million horses were slaughtered between 1989 and 2003. APHIS indicates that some of the horses were blind, lame, or old. The horses were sold at auction terminals and transported in trailers to horse slaughter plants in the United States or Canada. There are only three such plants in the United States: two in Texas and one in Illinois. The plant in Illinois burned down in 2002, but reopened in June 2004. Horses slaughtered in the United States are covered by the Humane Methods of Slaughter Act. They must be rendered unconscious before being hoisted onto the bleed rail and cut open. Like cattle, horses are stunned by a shot in the head with a bolt gun.

In November 2005 federal legislation was passed that prohibited for one year the use of federal funds for USDA-conducted ante mortem (predeath) inspections of horses at three U.S. slaughter plants. Animal welfare groups believed that this would effectively end horse slaughtering in the United States. The ban went into effect in March 2006. However, just before its effective date, the horse slaughter industry petitioned the USDA and received permission to conduct privately funded ante mortem inspections at the slaughter plants. Thus, horse slaughtering for human consumption was allowed to continue. According to "HSUS and Others Seek Injunction to Halt USDA in Its Attempt to Buck Congress on Horse Slaughter" (February 22, 2006, http://www.hsus .org/pets/pets_related_news_and_events/usda_threatens _horse_slaughter.html), the HSUS and several animal organizations and legislators were furious by what they saw as USDA circumvention of the intent of the law that was passed.

In September 2006 the U.S. House of Representatives passed the American Horse Slaughter Prevention Act, which would permanently ban the slaughter of horses in the United States for human consumption and the domestic and international transport of horses intended for slaughter. However, the measure was not addressed by the U.S. Senate before it adjourned in late 2006. Vicki Mabrey indicates in "Horse Slaughter Industry May Be on Its Last Legs" (*ABC News*, September 6, 2006) that the opponents of the bill believe it infringes on the private property rights of horse owners. The HSUS advocates humane euthanasia for horses that are severely ill or injured and promotes horse rescue and adoption programs.

FISH

Fish farming, or aquaculture, has been around for at least a millennium. Historians believe that the Chinese practiced aquaculture around the year 900 to raise fish for their emperor's dinner table. China is still a leading producer of farmed fish. Commercial aquaculture is also a big business in the United States. According to Juliet Eilperin, in "Fish Farming's Bounty Isn't without Barbs" (*Washington Post*, January 24, 2005), the U.S. fish farming industry had $1 billion in sales during 2004. Nearly all the rainbow trout and catfish consumed in the United States come from farm operations. Besides freshwater fish, saltwater fish are also raised in farm environments.

Fish farming is accomplished in one of two ways. Producers use netted enclosures in near-offshore ocean waters or they build separate enclosures inland. The second method is considered more environmentally friendly because the farmed fish and their waste are separated from fish living in natural waters. In-ocean farms occasionally lose fish to the surrounding waters, and environmentalists fear that these fish may spread diseases to their wild counterparts. In-ocean farms can also only be used for saltwater species, not freshwater. Fish farms typically keep as many fish as possible in the smallest amount of space possible. These confined operations can cause health problems, particularly sea lice infestation, in the farmed fish.

Several animal welfare groups oppose aquaculture, claiming that farmed fish are subjected to severe overcrowding in water pens contaminated with large amounts of fecal matter.

TABLE 4.6

Production data on miscellaneous livestock, 2002

Commodity	Number of farms	Inventory	Number sold
Milk goats	22,389	290,789	113,654
Angora goats	5,075	300,753	91,037
Meat and other goats	74,980	1,938,924	1,109,619
Mules, burros, donkeys	29,936	105,358	17,385
Mink	310	1,113,941	2,506,819
Rabbits	10,073	405,241	886,841
Ducks	26,140	3,823,629	24,143,066
Geese	17,110	173,000	200,564
Pigeons	4,405	449,255	1,160,364
Pheasants	4,977	2,267,136	7,206,460
Quail	3,742	4,888,196	19,157,803
Emus	5,224	48,221	15,682
Ostriches	1,643	20,560	16,038
Bison	4,132	231,950	57,210
Deer	4,901	286,863	43,526
Elk	2,371	97,901	16,058
Llamas	16,887	144,782	18,653

SOURCE: "Table A1.13. Production Data on Miscellaneous Livestock, 2002," in *2005 United States Animal Health Report*, U.S. Department of Agriculture, Animal and Plant Health Inspection Service, August 2006, http://www.aphis.usda.gov/publications/animal_health/content/printable_version/AHR_Web_PDF/J_appendices.pdf (accessed November 28, 2006)

OTHER FARM ANIMALS

Inventory data for various other farm animals are shown in Table 4.6.

The per capita consumption of lamb and mutton (meat from adult sheep) in the United States decreased from 4.9 pounds per year in 1945 to 0.83 pounds per year in 2004. (See Figure 4.2.) In "Sheep and Wool: Background" (November 14, 2006, http://www.ers.usda.gov/Briefing/Sheep/background.htm), the ERS blames competition from poultry, pork, and beef, and "declining acceptance of lamb" as the reasons for decreased consumption in the United States. According to the National Agricultural Statistics Service's *2005–2006 Statistical Highlights of U.S. Agriculture* (June 29, 2006, http://www.nass.usda.gov/Publications/Statistical_Highlights/2006/stathighnar.htm), there were 6.2 million sheep and lambs on U.S. farms in 2005 and nearly 5.1 million of them were shorn for wool. U.S. wool production was at 37.2 million pounds in 2005 and continues a historical decline. Figure 4.15 shows that U.S. inventories of sheep and lambs have declined dramatically since peaking in 1990 at nearly 11.4 million head.

In *2002 Census of Agriculture* the USDA estimates that in 2002, 4,132 farms had an inventory of 231,950 bison and that 25,340 bison were slaughtered at federally inspected plants. Bison meat is being heavily marketed by the entrepreneur Ted Turner. In 2001 Turner opened a chain of restaurants called Ted's Montana Grills (http://www.tedsmontanagrill.com/) that feature bison meat. He also formed the company U.S. Bison to market the meat to upscale restaurants and consumers. According to the article "To Ranchers, Buffalo Is the Other Red Meat" (*Boston Globe*, June 2003), Turner owns 35,000 bison at his ranches in Montana, New Mexico, and Nebraska.

WELFARE-FRIENDLY FARMING?

The most strict animal rights activists are opposed to the farming of animals to produce products for human consumption and use. They often embrace a vegan lifestyle, in which no animal products are consumed or used. Others are vegetarians. Vegetarians do not eat meat, but may consume secondary products, such as milk or eggs. For example, lacto-vegetarians eat dairy products, whereas ovo-vegetarians eat eggs. Lacto-ovo vegetarians eat both.

Vegans and vegetarians make up a small but increasing minority of the U.S. population. In "How Many Adults Are Vegetarian? The Vegetarian Resource Group Asked in a 2006 National Poll" (*Vegetarian Journal*, July–August 2006), Charles Stahler reports that 2.3% of U.S. adults consider themselves strict vegetarians. Many more people are part-time vegetarians or occasionally eat vegetarian meals. Not all vegetarians embrace their chosen diet for animal rights reasons—many have health, environmental, and/or religious reasons instead of or besides ethical ones.

There is also growing demand in the United States for meat and other products from animals that are raised or slaughtered using more humane methods. Food suppliers are beginning to make changes that represent significant reforms in animal welfare and slaughter. Some of these changes have no doubt been driven by pressure from vocal animal rights groups. For example, PETA has been conducting aggressive publicity and picketing campaigns against major fast-food chains in the United States, and many fast-food chains are implementing more welfare-friendly policies.

Some farmers have initiated reforms on their own. For example, some smaller hog farms are allowing their sows to farrow in straw-filled huts or barns instead of in gestation crates. Welfare-friendly farming is considered part of a larger movement called organic farming. Organic farming of crops involves no use of pesticides or herbicides. This produces a more natural product that many consumers consider healthier and more environmentally friendly. According to the ERS, in "Organic Farming and Marketing" (January 4, 2007, http://www.ers.usda.gov/Briefing/Organic/), organic farming was one of the fastest-growing segments of U.S. agriculture during the 1990s.

Some livestock farmers offer meat and other products from animals cultivated using organic methods. The animals are not given antibiotics or other drugs (except some necessary vaccines) and are housed in more natural conditions than those used in factory farms. The farmers

FIGURE 4.15

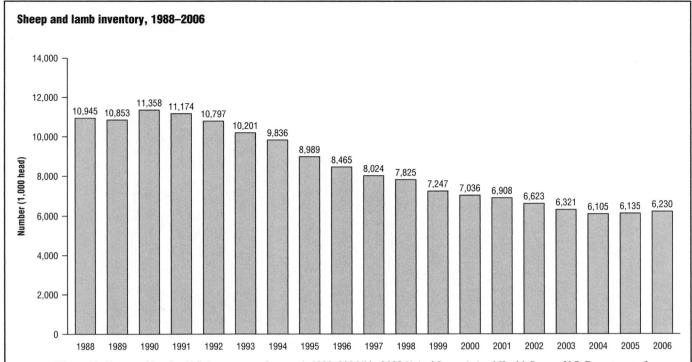

Sheep and lamb inventory, 1988–2006

SOURCE: "Figure 12. Sheep and Lambs: U.S. Inventory on January 1, 1988–2006," in *2005 United States Animal Health Report*, U.S. Department of Agriculture, Animal and Plant Health Inspection Service, August 2006, http://www.aphis.usda.gov/publications/animal_health/content/printable_version/ AHR_Web_PDF/C_chapter_%201.pdf (accessed November 28, 2006)

accommodate the animals' natural nutritional and behavior requirements. For example, ruminating animals are given access to pasture. Figure 4.16 and Figure 4.17 show the dramatic increase in the organic livestock and poultry inventories between 1992 and 2005. Nearly 230,000 organic cows, swine, sheep, and lambs and close to 14.2 million chickens and other poultry were being raised as of 2005. (See Table 4.7.)

Farmers are not allowed to label their products as organic unless they meet specific requirements established by the U.S. government in the National Organic Program. The organic standards govern living conditions, access to the outdoors, feed rations, and health care practices. No growth hormones or genetic engineering are allowed, and the animals are not fed animal byproducts. There are also restrictions on manure management and slaughter procedures. The farmers must provide documentation to the USDA demonstrating that they are following these standards to use the organic label.

Some animal protection groups have implemented their own programs to define and certify welfare-friendly farming operations. In 2000 the American Humane Association (AHA) established the Free Farmed Certification Program. Producers that want to use the label "Free Farmed" pay a fee to the AHA and must meet specific standards for food and water management, living conditions, and transport, handling, and slaughter techniques.

Humane Farm Animal Care (HFAC) is an independent nonprofit organization that administers the "Certified Humane Raised and Handled" program. The HFAC was formed in 2003 by former members of the Free Farmed organization. HFAC programs are funded by various animal welfare organizations, including the HSUS and the American Society for the Prevention of Cruelty to Animals. Products are labeled "Certified Humane" if the producers meet specific criteria for animal care that are enforced through an inspection and verification process.

It has also become common for livestock farmers to market products labeled "all natural," "cage free," "grass fed," "pasture raised," "free range," or "free roaming." Critics say that these labels are marketing ploys and are not clearly defined or verified by regulatory agencies or animal welfare groups. For example, the label "cage free" has no legally enforceable meaning.

The USDA allows producers to label a product as "all natural" as long as it is "minimally processed and contains no artificial ingredients." However, the label can be applied to meat from animals that received antibiotics and other drugs to promote growth. Producers that market free-range or free-roaming chickens are required by the USDA to provide their chickens access to the outside. However, there is no verification process in place to prove this claim. Critics point out that the requirement is

FIGURE 4.16

Certified organic livestock, by animal type, selected years 1992–2005

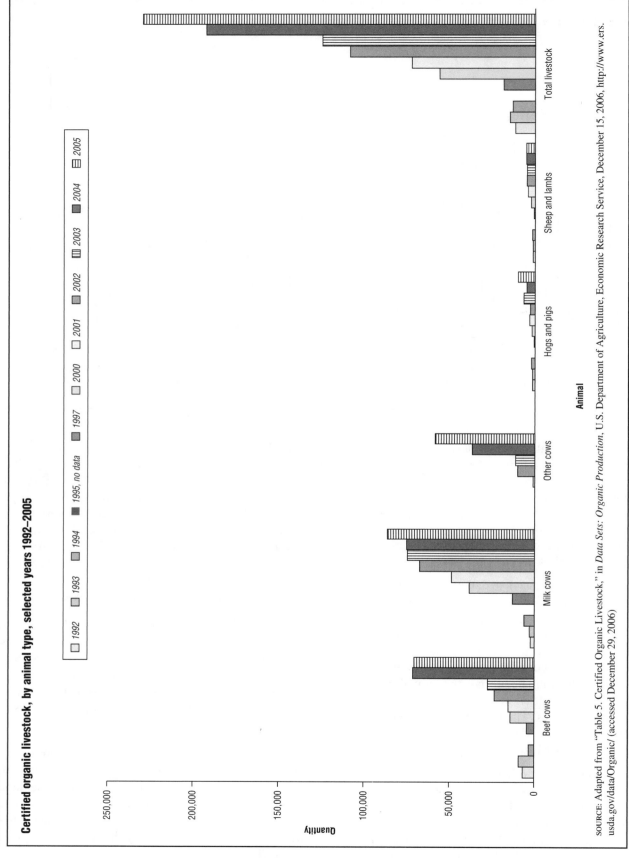

SOURCE: Adapted from "Table 5. Certified Organic Livestock," in *Data Sets: Organic Production*, U.S. Department of Agriculture, Economic Research Service, December 15, 2006, http://www.ers. usda.gov/data/Organic/ (accessed December 29, 2006)

FIGURE 4.17

Certified organic poultry, by type, selected years 1992–2005

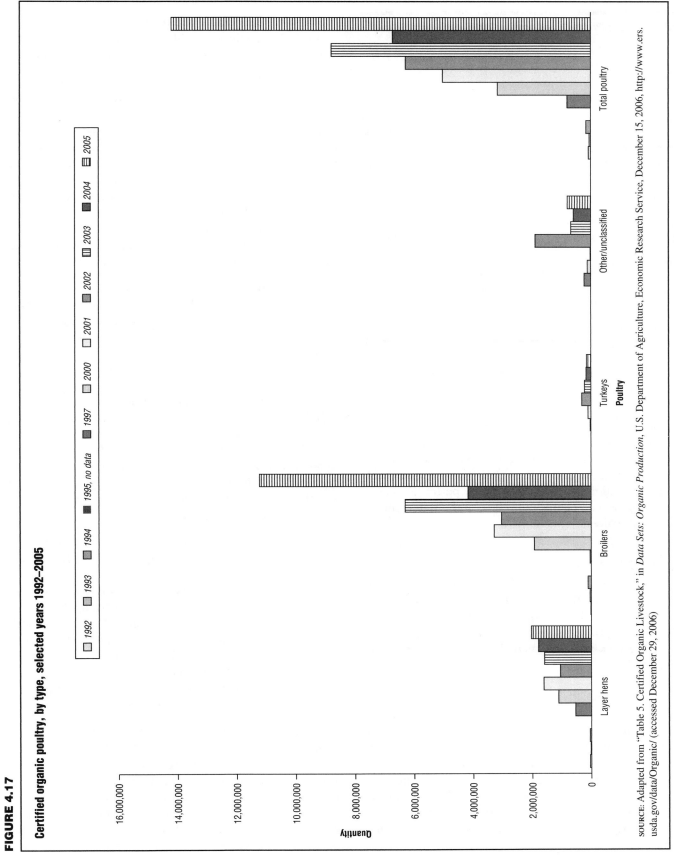

SOURCE: Adapted from "Table 5. Certified Organic Livestock," in *Data Sets: Organic Production*, U.S. Department of Agriculture, Economic Research Service, December 15, 2006, http://www.ers. usda.gov/data/Organic/ (accessed December 29, 2006)

TABLE 4.7

Certified organic livestock and poultry, 2005

Cows, pigs, and sheep

Beef cows	70,219
Milk cows	86,032
Other cows[a]	58,172
Hogs & pigs	10,018
Sheep & lambs	5,347
Total	**229,788**
Chickens and other poultry	
Layer hens	2,031,056
Broilers	11,225,879
Turkeys	144,086
Other/unclassified	792,249
Total	**14,193,270**
Other animals[b]	**15,689**
Grand total	**14,438,747**

[a]Includes unclassified cows and some young stock.
[b]Includes goats, buffalo, bison, rabbits, and other specialties.

SOURCE: Adapted from "Table 5. U.S. Certified Organic Livestock, 2005, by State," in *Data Sets: Organic Production*, U.S. Department of Agriculture, Economic Research Service, December 15, 2006, http://www.ers.usda.gov/Data/Organic/Data/Livestock.xls (accessed December 29, 2006)

satisfied at some chicken houses by including a small door that leads out into a small caged area open to the environment.

The USDA definitions of "free range," "pasture fed," and "free roaming" for nonpoultry animals say that the animals must have been allowed to eat grass and live outdoors during at least part of their lives. Animal welfare groups claim that the USDA rarely performs inspections to verify such claims but relies on the statements of livestock producers.

HUMAN HEALTH ISSUES

Because humans consume so many animal products, there is a correlation between the health of farm animals and human health. Even people who do not have moral or philosophical problems with the treatment or consumption of livestock are concerned about some factory farming methods.

Use of Antibiotics

One of the biggest concerns is the routine administration of low doses of antibiotics to farm animals to prevent them from developing diseases and to cure any that might already have diseases. This is called nontherapeutic, subtherapeutic, or preventive antibiotic use. Many people fear that it could lead to development of antibiotic-resistant diseases in animals and humans. Scientists already know that some bacteria are able to adjust to and tolerate low dosages of weaker antibiotics. Once they achieve this resistance it is much more difficult to kill them and requires increasingly stronger types of antibiotics.

Animal-to-Human Disease Transmission

Another concern related to animal welfare is the fear that U.S. farm animals could transmit diseases to humans, either through live contact or from the consumption of tainted meat products.

Diseases that can be transmitted from animals to humans are called zoonoses. Zoonoses associated with farm animals include anthrax (an infectious disease caused by spore-forming bacterium), brucellosis (a flulike illness transmitted by bacteria), leptospirosis (a bacterial disease that can cause a variety of symptoms in humans), bovine tuberculosis (a respiratory disease), streptococcus suis (a meningitis-like disease mostly associated with pigs), orf (a viral skin disease), and ringworm (a fungal skin disease). Of major concern is a group of diseases called transmissible spongiform encephalopathies (TSEs).

MAD COW DISEASE. One TSE is called bovine spongiform encephalopathy (BSE), commonly known as mad cow disease. BSE is a neurological disease of cattle that is believed to be caused by misshapen protein cells called prions. Prions enter brain cells and disrupt normal cell operation, resulting in severe brain damage and ultimately death. BSE devastated farm animal populations in England during the 1980s and 1990s. Millions of animals were killed because they either had the disease or as a precaution against the disease. Scientists believe that BSE is a fairly new disease that emerged in cattle that had been fed animal byproducts from sheep contaminated with scrapie (another type of spongiform encephalopathies). Byproducts from slaughtered infected cattle were inadvertently fed to healthy cattle, leading to widespread infection.

Medical authorities suspect that humans can contract a similar brain-wasting disease by eating meat from BSE-infected animals. The human disease is called variant Creutzfeldt-Jakob disease (vCJD). This is a new form of an already known disease called Creutzfeldt-Jakob disease (CJD). The causes of classic CJD are not well understood; however, it is extremely rare and has been found mostly in older people. By contrast, most of the victims of vCJD have been in their twenties and are believed to have eaten BSE-tainted beef. CJD and vCJD cause severe brain damage and are ultimately fatal.

In December 2003 the first case of BSE in the United States was confirmed in a downer Holstein cow tested in Washington state. The test results were obtained nearly two weeks after the cow had been slaughtered. All meat products associated with cattle slaughtered as part of the same batch were recalled. However, some of the meat had already been sold and possibly consumed by humans. U.S. authorities believe that the infected cow had been imported from Canada. Federal officials claimed the beef was safe, however, because the parts that carry the infection—brain, spinal cord, and intestines—were removed at the slaughterhouse.

TABLE 4.8

Samples tested for bovine spongiform encephalopathy (BSE), by collection site, June 1, 2004–March 17, 2006

Collection site	Targeted samples	% of total
Slaughter plant*	32,560	5.03
Renderer	356,879	55.16
On-farm	34,464	5.33
Public health lab	191	0.03
Diagnostic lab	2,804	0.43
3D-4D	202,844	31.35
Other	17,303	2.67
Total	**647,045**	**100.00**

*Does not include antemortem condemned animals transported to offsite facilities (3D/4D collection sites) for sampling.

SOURCE: "Table 1. Number of Targeted Samples Tested by Collection Site Type from June 1, 2004, through March 17, 2006," in *Summary of Enhanced BSE Surveillance in the United States*, U.S. Department of Agriculture, Animal and Plant Health Inspection Service, Centers for Epidemiology and Animal Health National Surveillance Unit, April 27, 2006, http://www.aphis.usda.gov/newsroom/hot_issues/bse/downloads/SummaryEnhancedBSE-Surv4-26-06.pdf (accessed December 28, 2006)

Since 1990 the USDA has conducted a BSE surveillance program on U.S. cattle. At first the program concentrated on cattle exhibiting clinical signs of BSE or other neurological disorders. In 1993 testing was extended to downer cattle at slaughterhouses. In 2001 the program was expanded to include cattle that died of unknown causes. These target populations are believed to be the animals in which BSE is most likely to be found if it is present. In June 2004 an "enhanced" surveillance program was begun to test as many cattle as possible considered to be high risk for BSE. Table 4.8 shows the number of samples tested between June 1, 2004, and March 17, 2006. The vast majority of samples were obtained from cattle at rendering facilities and 3D-4D facilities (slaughtering plants that salvage meat unsuitable for human consumption).

FEARS OF AVIAN INFLUENZA. As of 2007 scientists were growing increasingly concerned about the transmission of avian influenza A to humans. Avian influenza A, also known as the bird flu, is a disease that was first detected during the late 1800s. Before the 1990s it was found only in birds and a few species of pigs. In 1997 the first known cases in humans appeared in Hong Kong, causing six deaths. The human outbreak coincided with a severe infection throughout the Hong Kong poultry industry. The World Health Organization reports in "Avian Influenza H5N1 Infection in Humans: Urgent Need to Eliminate the Animal Reservoir—Update 5" (January 22, 2004, http://www.who.int/csr/don/2004_01_22/en/index.html) that an estimated 1.5 million birds—the country's entire flock of poultry—had to be destroyed. Scientists determined that the avian influenza A strain known as H5N1 was capable of mutating rapidly and acquiring genes from viruses infecting other animal species (including humans). An epidemic of mutated H5N1 in humans could be devastating as humans have no natural immunity to the disease. Domestic poultry are believed to be most susceptible to the H5N1 strain.

According to the World Organisation for Animal Health (2007, http://www.oie.int/downld/AVIAN%20INFLUENZA/Graph%20HPAI/graphs%20HPAI%2013_04_2007.pdf), the H5N1 virus was found in poultry in forty countries between the close of 2003 and April 13, 2007. Those countries include China, Hong Kong, Japan, Russia, Thailand, the United Kingdom, and Vietnam, among others. The number of human cases reported to the World Health Organization between 2003 and April 11, 2007, was 291 (2007, http://www.who.int/csr/disease/avian_influenza/country/cases_table_2007_04_11/en/index.html). Of that number, 172 people had died in 12 countries. Concerns about a possible pandemic have prompted U.S. federal, state, and local governments to consider plans to handle an outbreak and to stockpile medical and other emergency supplies. The U.S. Department of Health and Human Services maintains a Web site (http://www.pandemicflu.gov/) that offers the latest information on the situation. On April 17, 2007, the FDA announced that a vaccine to protect humans against the disease was available.

FUR FARMING

Fur farming is a unique agricultural enterprise for two reasons. First, most of the animals involved are wild instead of domesticated. Second, the animals are raised and killed for their pelts only. The most popular fur animal is the mink. According to FurKills.org (2006, http://furkills.org/talking_points.shtml), it takes, on average, about forty mink pelts to produce one fur coat.

Mink are wild animals that are kept in cages on fur farms. They typically breed in the early spring and give birth to litters in late spring. An average litter contains four or five babies, or kits, that are weaned after six to eight weeks. The kits are vaccinated against common diseases. During the late summer and early fall the mink naturally molt (lose their summer fur) and regrow a thick winter coat. The mink are killed in late autumn or early winter. Some are retained for breeding purposes.

According to the *2002 Census of Agriculture*, the USDA reports that there were 310 mink farms in the United States in 2002. Approximately 1.1 million pelts were produced in 2002. The U.S. Fur Commission (2005, http://www.furcommission.com/farming/Graphics/Map05.jpg) notes the top five mink-pelt producing states are Wisconsin, Utah, Minnesota, and Oregon.

The fur industry is harshly criticized by animal rights activists and welfarists, who say that the animals are kept in miserable conditions and in small cages. The HSUS explains that overbreeding by farmers to produce desirable coat colors leads to serious and painful deformities in the animals. Farming and slaughter of fur animals are not regulated by the USDA. The most common killing techniques are gassing, electrocution, and breaking of the animals' necks. Fur farming has been banned in many western European countries.

Animal welfarists and rights activists have conducted antifur campaigns since the 1960s. PETA's "I'd rather go naked than wear fur" campaign was begun in the 1990s and has featured celebrities such as Pamela Anderson and Kim Basinger posing nude. PETA activists also regularly disrupt fashion shows featuring fur-clad models and protest outside stores selling fur. However, fur sales have continued to rise in the United States. According to the Fur Information Council of America (2006, http://www.fur.org/poen_faqs.cfm?sect=fact), fur sales increased from $1 billion in 1991 to $1.8 billion in 2005. Industry analysts indicate that fur demand is driven by weather and economy rather than by animal issues. A Gallup poll conducted in May 2006 found that 62% of those asked believed that the buying and wearing of clothing made of animal fur was morally acceptable. (See Figure 4.18.)

Mink farmers defend their animal husbandry and slaughtering procedures as humane. They argue that mink in the wild rarely live longer than one year and insist that the mink are handled carefully, both for their welfare and to protect their valuable coats from damage. Producers also insist that the mink are killed quickly and humanely using veterinary-approved methods. In "Fur Ethics" (November 2001, http://www.furcommission.com/resource/perspect999 as.htm), Delia Montgomery interviews a veteran mink farmer, who claims that "animals raised for their fur are inherently the best cared for farm animals."

FIGURE 4.18

Public opinion on the morality of buying and wearing clothing made of animal fur, May 2006

NEXT, I'M GOING TO READ YOU A LIST OF ISSUES. REGARDLESS OF WHETHER OR NOT YOU THINK IT SHOULD BE LEGAL, FOR EACH ONE, PLEASE TELL ME WHETHER YOU PERSONALLY BELIEVE THAT IN GENERAL IT IS MORALLY ACCEPTABLE OR MORALLY WRONG. HOW ABOUT … BUYING AND WEARING CLOTHING MADE OF ANIMAL FUR?

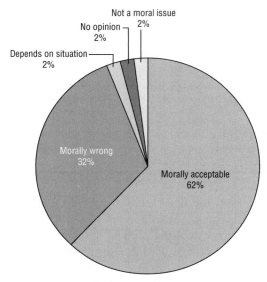

SOURCE: Adapted from *Gallup Poll Social Series: Moral Issues*, The Gallup Organization, May 2006, http://www.galluppoll.com/content/Default.aspx?ci=1681&pg=1&t=EgBIu3wMnGwfz1Z61o1DGiH.1GFUccU9KJfoS%2fG1GD6xxF2x2qNLENH2teq7BVOyIniNuSHpqTLe0Q0FdmvZMBRlNMxSTcvM7Z4C66obCYPsj.lisL-9YTWLGccIA8VrxncH4EdzffG172ZCuEGrNDZrt1S27lJ4 (accessed November 17, 2006) Copyright © 2006 by The Gallup Organization. Reproduced by permission of The Gallup Organization.

CHAPTER 5
RESEARCH ANIMALS

Research animals are animals that humans use solely for scientific and product testing. They are used in medical and veterinary investigations and training; in the testing of drugs, cosmetics, and other consumer products; and in educational programs. The *Scientific American* (August 4, 2004) estimates that as many as one hundred million animals per year (mostly mice and rats) may be used in research, testing, and medical and veterinary training programs in the United States. Millions more research animals are kept as classroom pets or teaching aids to educate children in schools.

Living animals used as specimens to test drugs and products, practice medical and surgical procedures, and investigate diseases and bodily systems are called laboratory animals. Laboratory animals often die from these procedures or are euthanized by researchers after they are no longer needed. The plight of laboratory animals has been a major issue for animal rights advocates since the 1970s.

Increasingly, the use of dead animals to teach dissection skills to children is coming under fire. Dissection is a procedure in which an organism is cut apart for scientific examination. If the organism is alive at the time, the procedure is called vivisection. However, the term "vivisection" has come to be used to refer to all invasive research and testing performed on live animals for scientific purposes.

Live animals are used in modern medical research because some of their bodily systems mimic those of humans. This makes them useful test subjects for drugs, vaccines, and other products intended for humans. They are also useful training tools for doctors, surgeons, and veterinarians who need to practice medical procedures, such as inserting a catheter, administering anesthesia, or performing operations.

People who support the use of animals in research are passionate in their belief that the benefits to people far outweigh the consequences to animals. They point out the important medical and veterinary advances that have resulted. On the contrary, animal rights activists uniformly condemn this use. The most extreme activists have broken into laboratories, released animals, and physically harassed the researchers involved. Animal welfarists work to minimize the pain these animals experience during testing and to improve their living conditions.

The Gallup Organization includes a question about laboratory animals in the morality poll it conducts each year. (See Figure 5.1.) The poll conducted in May 2006 showed that 61% of Americans surveyed find "medical testing on animals" to be morally acceptable, whereas 32% find it morally wrong. Another 5% said the morality depends on the situation, and 2% had no opinion. These numbers were virtually unchanged from those obtained in annual polls conducted since 2001.

Science and Engineering Indicators is a report published by the National Science Board every two years. Each report includes polls and questionnaires conducted on public understanding and attitudes about various topics related to science and engineering. The 2002 report is the most recent of the reports to include public opinion polls on the use of animals in scientific research. Figure 5.2 and Figure 5.3 compare public opinion on the use of mice versus the use of dogs and chimpanzees in medical research that causes pain and injury to the animals but produces new information on human health problems. The results show that 67% of respondents approve of the use of mice in such a manner, whereas only 44% approve of the use of dogs and chimpanzees. This finding is not surprising, as people typically have more charitable feelings toward dogs and chimpanzees than they do toward mice. According to the Humane Society of the United States (HSUS), the National Science Board has found that approval for painful tests on dogs and chimpanzees has generally decreased since

FIGURE 5.1

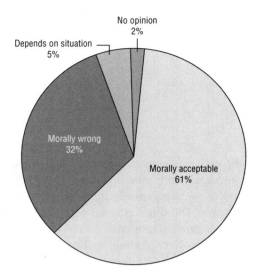

Public opinion on the morality of medical testing on animals, May 2006

NEXT, I'M GOING TO READ YOU A LIST OF ISSUES. REGARDLESS OF WHETHER OR NOT YOU THINK IT SHOULD BE LEGAL, FOR EACH ONE, PLEASE TELL ME WHETHER YOU PERSONALLY BELIEVE THAT IN GENERAL IT IS MORALLY ACCEPTABLE OR MORALLY WRONG. HOW ABOUT... MEDICAL TESTING ON ANIMALS?

No opinion 2%

Depends on situation 5%

Morally wrong 32%

Morally acceptable 61%

SOURCE: Adapted from *Gallup Poll Social Series: Moral Issues*, The Gallup Organization, May 2006, http://www.galluppoll.com/content/Default.aspx?ci=1681&pg=1&t=EgBIu3wMnGwfz1Z61o1DGiH.1GFUccU9KJfoS%2fG1GD6xxF2x2qNLENH2teq7BVOyIniNuSHpqTLe0Q0FdmvZMBRlNMxSTcvM7Z4C66obCYPsj.lisL-9YTWLGccIA8VrxncH4EdzffG172ZCuEGrNDZrt1S27lJ4 (accessed November 17, 2006) Copyright © 2006 by The Gallup Organization. Reproduced by permission of The Gallup Organization.

FIGURE 5.2

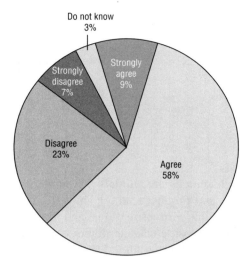

Public opinion on the use of mice in scientific research, 2001

SCIENTISTS SHOULD BE ALLOWED TO DO RESEARCH THAT CAUSES PAIN AND INJURY TO ANIMALS LIKE MICE IF IT PRODUCES NEW INFORMATION ABOUT HUMAN HEALTH PROBLEMS. DO YOU STRONGLY AGREE, AGREE, DISAGREE, OR STRONGLY DISAGREE?

Do not know 3%

Strongly disagree 7%

Strongly agree 9%

Disagree 23%

Agree 58%

SOURCE: Adapted from "Appendix Table 7.26. Public Assessment of Use of Mice in Scientific Research: 2001," in *Science & Engineering Indicators—2002*, National Science Foundation, Division of Science Resources Statistics, 2002, http://www.nsf.gov/statistics/seind02/append/c7/at07-26.pdf (accessed January 9, 2007)

1985, when 63% of those asked expressed approval for it. (See Table 5.1.)

This decrease may be the result in part of the fact that many people react emotionally to the thought of animals in distress. Scientists and researchers—those who work with the animals directly—use clinical terms to describe their work. They refer to laboratory animals as animal models and speak of them as specimens. Antivivisection groups gain support for their views by publicizing the gruesome details of experiments. Photographs of restrained animals with bolts through their brains or sores on their bodies can disturb the public, no matter how scientifically justified the experiments may be.

The modern antivivisection movement began in the nineteenth century. In *Animals' Rights, Considered in Relation to Social Progress* (1894), the humanitarian Henry S. Salt writes that "the practice of vivisection is revolting to the human conscience, even among the ordinary members of a not over-sensitive society." This was only seventy-six years after the publication of Mary Shelley's *Frankenstein; or, The Modern Prometheus* (1818), a story about a scientist who creates a mutant

human from spare parts. The anthropologist Susan Sperling states in *Animal Liberators: Research and Morality* (1988) her beliefs that the antivivisectionists of the nineteenth century and the twenty-first century share a common fear: scientific manipulation of living beings.

HISTORY
Early Times

Vivisection on animals and humans dates back to at least the ancient Greeks and Romans. During the third and second centuries BC human bodies were vivisected and dissected at the medical school in Alexandria, Egypt, by Herophilus and Erasistratus. Historians believe that more than six hundred living criminals were subjected to vivisection. Human dissection and vivisection were generally forbidden throughout the rest of Egypt and in the Roman Empire because of moral concerns.

Galen (circa 130–200 AD) was a Greek physician who moved to Rome and administered to gladiators and emperors. He frequently practiced vivisection on animals, particularly goats, pigs, monkeys, oxen, and dogs. Even though Galen made some important anatomical discoveries, he relied so heavily on animal models that he developed some misconceptions about human anatomy. However, his teachings formed the basis of Western medical science well into the Middle Ages. The Catholic Church frowned on human

FIGURE 5.3

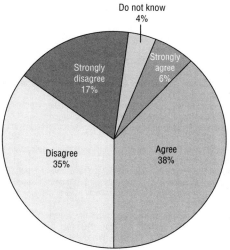

Public opinion on the use of dogs and chimpanzees in scientific research, 2001

SCIENTISTS SHOULD BE ALLOWED TO DO RESEARCH THAT CAUSES PAIN AND INJURY TO ANIMALS LIKE DOGS AND CHIMPANZEES IF IT PRODUCES NEW INFORMATION ABOUT HUMAN HEALTH PROBLEMS. DO YOU STRONGLY AGREE, AGREE, DISAGREE, OR STRONGLY DISAGREE?

- Do not know 4%
- Strongly agree 6%
- Strongly disagree 17%
- Disagree 35%
- Agree 38%

SOURCE: Adapted from "Appendix Table 7.27. Public Assessment of Use of Dogs and Chimpanzees in Scientific Research: 1988–2001," in *Science & Engineering Indicators—2002*, National Science Foundation, Division of Science Resources Statistics, 2002, http://www.nsf.gov/statistics/seind02/append/c7/at07-27.pdf (accessed January 9, 2007)

TABLE 5.1

Public opinion on the use of chimpanzees and dogs in painful and injurious research, selected years 1985–2001

SCIENTISTS SHOULD BE ALLOWED TO DO RESEARCH THAT CAUSES PAIN AND INJURY TO ANIMALS LIKE DOGS AND CHIMPANZEES IF IT PRODUCES NEW INFORMATION.

Year	Supporting/strongly supporting animal research	Opposing/strongly opposing animal research
1985	63	30
1988	53	42
1990	50	44
1992	53	42
1995	50	46
1997	46	51
1999	50	47
2001	44	52

SOURCE: Kathleen M. Conlee and Sarah T. Boysen, "Table 3. Public Opinion on Using Chimpanzees and Dogs in Painful and Injurious Research," in *The State of the Animals III: 2005*, Humane Society of the United States, December 31, 2005, http://www.hsus.org/web-files/PDF/hsp/SOA_3-2005_Chap9.pdf (accessed December 13, 2006)

dissection and vivisection during this period, meaning that only animals were available for anatomical study, though some adventurous souls still used humans in their research.

Few advances in medical science were made until the 1500s, when the Belgian doctor Andreas Vesalius

FIGURE 5.4

Jeremy Bentham. *The Library of Congress.*

challenged many of Galen's ideas. Vesalius began to uncover the mysteries of blood circulation after performing autopsies on human corpses. He also practiced vivisection on animals and wrote about its importance in the study of anatomy. Vesalius was followed by the British physician and anatomist William Harvey. By performing animal vivisection and dissecting the corpses of executed criminals, Harvey discovered the role of the heart in pumping blood throughout the body.

Seventeenth, Eighteenth, and Nineteenth Centuries

In the seventeenth century a new philosophy was introduced by the French philosopher René Descartes. Descartes and his followers believed that animals were unthinking, unfeeling machines. This allowed researchers to perform all manner of experiments on live animals without any moral concerns. In 1764 these practices and ideas were criticized by the French philosopher François-Marie Arouet de Voltaire. Voltaire noted that vivisection uncovered organs of feeling in animals, proving that animals were not machines, but sentient (feeling) beings. Later in the century the British philosopher and political scientist Jeremy Bentham summarized his thoughts on the subject in *An Introduction to the Principles of Morals and Legislation* (1789): "The question is not, Can they reason? Nor, Can they talk? but, Can they suffer?" (See Figure 5.4.)

TABLE 5.2

Major organizations devoted to issues involving animal research, by founding date, 1883–1992

Founding date	Organization	Stated mission
1883	American Anti-Vivisection Society (AAVS)	Devoted to legally and effectively ending the use of animals in science through education, advocacy, and the development of alternative methods to animal use.
1895	New England Anti-Vivisection Society (NEAVS)	Works to expose and replace animal experiments in laboratories and classrooms with ethically and scientifically responsible modern research methods.
1929	National Anti-Vivisection Society (NAVS)	Goals include ending the use of animals in research, product testing, and education; educating the public about the cruelty and waste of vivisection; and encouraging development of non-animal methodologies.
1950	American Association for Laboratory Animal Science (AALAS)	Advances responsible care and use of laboratory animals to benefit people and animals.
1965	American Association for Accreditation of Laboratory Animal Care (AAALAC)	Voluntary accreditation organization founded by veterinary and scientific groups to promote uniform animal-care standards.
1974	Public Responsibility in Medicine and Research (PRIM&R)	Group dedicated to furthering research and promoting ethical ideals within the research community.
1979	National Association for Biomedical Research (NABR)	Provides the collective voice for the scientific community on national policy involving animal use in research, education and product safety testing.
1981	Johns Hopkins University Center for Alternatives to Animal Testing (CAAT)	Funded by the Cosmetics, Toiletry, and Fragrance Association to research alternatives to animal testing.
1981	Michigan Society for Medical Research	Non-profit science education organization that supports biomedical research and the judicious use of animals in research.
1985	Physicians Committee for Responsible Medicine (PCRM)	Advocates alternatives to harming animals for educational or research purposes.
1986	The Scientists Center for Animal Welfare (SCAW)	A non-profit educational association of individuals and institutions involved in research. The group's goal is to promote the welfare of animals used in research, testing, and educational programs.
1991	Americans for Medical Progress (AMP)	Non-profit organization devoted to protecting society's investment in research by promoting public understanding of and support for the appropriate role of animals in biomedical research so that scientists are able to continue their quest for cures and improved methods of treatment for illness, injury and disease.
1991	Ethical Science & Education Coalition (ESEC)	Educational affiliate of the NEAVS that works to protect the rights of students who decide not to dissect or otherwise use animals in a harmful way.
1992	Center for Laboratory Animal Welfare (CLAW)	Affiliated with the Massachusetts SPCA, this organization advocates alternatives to animal testing.

SOURCE: Created by Kim Masters Evans for Thomson Gale

Throughout the eighteenth and nineteenth centuries philosophers debated the moral issues involved in animal vivisection. According to historians, the poor and working-class people of the time opposed animal vivisection because they associated it with the dissection of human corpses. The unclaimed bodies of poor people and criminals were often turned over to medical colleges for dissection. There were also well-publicized cases of grave robbing and body snatching to supply researchers with human corpses. These events horrified the common people and made them suspicious of scientists and doctors engaged in medical research.

The nineteenth century also witnessed organized efforts from animal welfare organizations to achieve legislation against animal cruelty in the United Kingdom and United States. The Cruelty to Animals Act was passed in Britain in 1849 and amended in 1876 to restrict the use of animals in research. In 1875 the Society for the Protection of Animals Liable to Vivisection was founded by Frances Power Cobbe. It was later called the Victorian Street Society. In 1898 Cobbe founded the British Union for the Abolition of Vivisection, an organization that is still active.

Vivisection was also fought by welfarists in the United States. In 1871 Harvard University founded one of the first vivisection laboratories in the country, despite opposition from the Massachusetts Society for the Prevention of Cruelty to Animals. Various antivivisection groups were founded, including the American Anti-Vivisection Society in 1883 and the New England Anti-Vivisection Society (NEAVS) in 1895. (Table 5.2 provides a list of some of the major U.S. organizations involved in advocating or opposing the use of animals in scientific research beginning in 1893.) The new antivivisection groups tried, unsuccessfully, to outlaw the practice of vivisection. Legislation was passed during the 1890s that outlawed repetition of painful animal experiments for the purpose of teaching or demonstrating well-known and accepted facts.

First Half of the Twentieth Century

In December 1903 American writer Mark Twain published the short story "A Dog's Tale" in *Harper's Magazine*. The story was written to protest cruelty to animals and their use in research. It is told from the viewpoint of a dog that lives with the family of a scientist. The dog saves the family's baby from a nursery fire but later sees her own puppy blinded and killed during an experiment performed by the scientist to impress his friends. Although some critics condemned the work as overly sentimental, animal welfarists of the time were pleased that it brought public attention to the issue of animal experimentation.

In 1906 Congress passed the Pure Food and Drug Act (PFDA). The original act did not require any type of testing to ensure that a product was safe or effective. This would change after some tragic events occurred. According to Susan E. Wilson-Sanders of the University of Arizona, in "Mrs. Brown's Sad Story: A History of the Food, Drug, and Cosmetic Act" (September 23, 2005, http://www.ahsc.arizona.edu/uac/notes/classes/Alternmethod/ Fdapap03.htm), many Americans were injured, sickened, or even killed by unsafe potions, "snake oils," and patent medicines sold by entrepreneurs during the early decades of the twentieth century. Some of these products contained incredibly toxic substances, such as dinitrophenol, a compound used to make explosives.

During the 1920s and 1930s hair dyes containing an aniline compound called paraphenylenediamine became popular. Even though it was well known that aniline compounds were harmful to the eyes, a cosmetics company still chose to introduce a brand of mascara called Lash-Lure containing these chemicals. Doctors reported thousands of eye injuries caused by the product, and even a few deaths after patients suffered serious infections. Many states banned the use of aniline dyes in personal-care products. Wilson-Sanders reports that Lash-Lure contained twenty-five to thirty times more aniline than the amount commonly used in hair dyes.

Wilson-Sanders mentions several other popular cosmetic products of the time that caused injury, such as Anti-Mole, Berry's Freckle Ointment, Bleachodent (a teeth whitener), Dr. Dennis's Compound, Koremlu cream, and Dewsberry Hair Tonic. These products contained high concentrations of acids or other toxic chemicals. Whisker dyes marketed to men contained dangerous levels of silver or lead acetate. A popular depilatory (hair removal cream) contained rat poison.

According to Wilson-Sanders, doctors lobbied Congress throughout the 1930s to crack down on dangerous drugs and personal products sold to Americans, but they were opposed by powerful marketing groups. In 1937 nearly one hundred people (mostly children) died after drinking a product called Elixir of Sulfanilamide containing sulfa drugs dissolved in diethylene glycol (antifreeze). The public was outraged and pressured Congress to strengthen the original PFDA and include cosmetics. The Food, Drug, and Cosmetics Act (FDCA) was passed in 1938. It contained a requirement for animal testing.

Wilson-Sanders notes that the first tests were conducted on rats and could last less than one month. The testing requirements were gradually amended to include different species and to last for longer time periods. By 1957 drug testing had to be performed on rats or dogs for up to six months. By the 1980s testing was required to last twelve to eighteen months. Testing on pregnant animals was instituted in the 1960s following the thalidomide tragedy. Thalidomide is a drug that was widely prescribed in Canada and Europe during the late 1950s to treat nausea in pregnant women. More than ten thousand deformed babies resulted. Although the drug had been extensively tested on animals, it had not been tested on pregnant animals. New guidelines for testing the effects of drugs on animal reproduction and fetus development were incorporated into the FDCA.

Second Half of the Twentieth Century

Historians note that the antivivisection movement subsided with the advent of World War I (1914–18) and did not resurge until the 1960s. One of the driving forces behind the movement's rebirth was the story of Pepper, a Dalmatian who disappeared from her family's backyard in Pennsylvania in July 1965. The family tracked the dog to an animal dealer in New York, but he refused to return the dog. The family enlisted the help of the Animal Welfare Institute, the Pennsylvania State Police, and New York Congressman Joseph Resnick, but they were too late. Pepper had been sold to a hospital in New York City that conducted an experiment on her and euthanized her.

The story was widely publicized and led to public outrage. Bills were introduced in the U.S. House of Representatives and the U.S. Senate calling for animal dealers and laboratories to be licensed and inspected by the U.S. Department of Agriculture (USDA) and required to meet certain humane standards of care. During the debate, which took place between 1965 and 1966, Democratic Senator Warren Magnuson of Washington said, "We do not think we can allow the needs of research, great as they may be, to promote either the theft of a child's pet or the growth of unscrupulous animal dealers." The bills were opposed by strong lobbying groups and were in danger of failing, until a story ran in the February 4, 1966, issue of *Life* magazine.

"Concentration Camps for Dogs" was the story of a police raid on a dog dealer's facility in Maryland. The story included horrific photographs of abused dogs kept in filthy cages until they could be sold to research laboratories. According to the article, the dogs were to be sold at auction for thirty cents per pound. Letters flooded politicians' offices, and editorials appeared in major newspapers around the country calling for federal legislation.

A few months later Congress passed the Laboratory Animal Welfare Act of 1966. It called for the licensing of animal dealers and regulation of laboratory animals. The original act applied to dogs, cats, primates, guinea pigs, hamsters, and rabbits. In 1970 the act was renamed the

Animal Welfare Act (AWA) and amended to cover several other warm-blooded animals. A year later the USDA decided to exclude rats, mice, and birds from coverage under the act, arguing that the department did not have the staff needed to regulate the huge numbers of such animals involved. It also noted that most of these small animals were used at research institutions that had other oversight protections in place to regulate their use.

The publication of *Animal Liberation: A New Ethics for Our Treatment of Animals* (1975) by the Australian philosopher Peter Singer brought more coverage to the use of animals in scientific research. The book includes disturbing photographs and descriptions of animals being subjected to all sorts of painful procedures for questionable purposes. Singer argues that the pain and suffering inflicted on the animals is too high a moral price to pay for scientific research.

In 1976 the animal activist Henry Spira led a campaign protesting the American Museum of Natural History's research on the effects of castration and mutilation on cats' sexual behavior. The campaign was hailed as a success by activists after the museum halted the research a year later. Spira then turned his attention to the testing of cosmetics on animals, particularly the Draize eye test, in which chemicals are put into the eyes of restrained animals.

Spira formed a coalition of animal welfare and antivivisection groups to educate the public about animal testing of cosmetics. In full-page advertisements in major newspapers, Spira accused major cosmetics companies of being cruel to animals. Public response was immediate. Several companies, including Revlon and Avon, announced their intention to cease animal testing and find new alternatives. In 1981 the Cosmetics, Toiletries, and Fragrance Association funded the founding of the Center for Alternatives to Animal Testing (CAAT) at Johns Hopkins University in Baltimore, Maryland. By the end of the 1980s Revlon and Avon had ceased animal testing.

In 1985 Congress amended the AWA to require that researchers minimize animal pain and distress whenever possible through use of anesthesia, analgesics (painkillers), and humane euthanasia. New requirements were added regarding the physical and psychological well-being of dogs and primates used in research work. Throughout the 1980s and 1990s animal welfare groups petitioned and sued the USDA to add mice, rats, and birds to the animals covered under the AWA but were unsuccessful. In 1990 AWA coverage was extended to horses and other farm animals.

Scientists engaged in animal research watched with concern as animal welfare and antivivisection groups launched aggressive publicity campaigns against them. In 1979 the National Association for Biomedical

TABLE 5.3

Medical advances achieved through animal research, selected years 1796–2003

Year	Advance (type of animal)
1796	Vaccine for smallpox developed (cow)
1881	Vaccine for anthrax developed (sheep)
1885	Vaccine for rabies developed (dog, rabbit)
1902	Malarial life cycle discovered (pigeon)*
1905	Pathogenesis of tuberculosis discovered (cow, sheep)*
1919	Mechanisms of immunity discovered (guinea pig, horse, rabbit)*
1921	Insulin discovered (dog, fish)*
1928	Pathogenesis of typhus discovered (guinea pig, rat, mouse)*
1929	Vitamins supporting nerve growth discovered (chicken)*
1932	Function of neurons discovered (cat, dog)*
1933	Vaccine for tetanus developed (horse)
1939	Anticoagulants developed (cat)
1942	The Rh factor discovered (monkey)
1943	Vitamin K discovered (rat, dog, chick, mouse)*
1945	Penicillin tested (mouse)*
1954	Polio vaccine developed (mouse, monkey)*
1956	Open heart surgery and cardiac pacemakers developed (dog)
1964	Regulation of cholesterol discovered (rat)*
1968	Rubella vaccine developed (monkey)
1970	Lithium approved (rat, guinea pig)
1973	Animal social and behavior patterns discovered (bee, fish, bird)*
1975	Interaction between tumor viruses and genetic material discovered (monkey, horse, chicken, mouse)*
1982	Treatment for leprosy developed (armadillo)
1984	Monoclonal antibodies developed (mouse)*
1990	Organ transplantation techniques advanced (dog, sheep, cow, pig)*
1992	Laproscopic surgical techniques advanced (pig)
1995	Gene transfer for cystic fibrosis developed (mouse, nonhuman primate)
1997	Prions discovered and characterized (hamster, mouse)*
1998	Nitric oxide as signaling molecule in cardiovascular system discovered (rabbit)*
2000	Brain signal transduction discovered (mouse, rat, sea slug)*
2002	Mechanism of cell death discovered (worm)*
2003	Non-invasive imaging methods (MRI) for medical diagnosis developed (clam, rat)*

*Denotes Nobel Prize-winning work.

SOURCE: "Historically, What Have Been the Tangible Benefits of Animal Research?" in *CDC News: Overview of Animals in Scientific Research Fact Sheet*, U.S. Department of Health and Human Services, Centers for Disease Control and Prevention, November 16, 2006, http://www.cdc.gov/about/news/2006_11/animal_care/factsheet_ar_general.htm (accessed December 28, 2006)

Research (January 21, 2005, http://www.nabr.org/about.html) was founded in Washington, D.C., with the mission of "advocating sound public policy that recognizes the vital role of humane animal use in biomedical research, higher education and product safety testing." In 1981 the Foundation for Biomedical Research and the Michigan Society for Medical Research (MISMR) were founded with similar goals.

These organizations work to counter claims by animal rights activists that animal research and testing are cruel practices with little to no scientific value. Table 5.3 is a listing provided by the Foundation for Biomedical Research of medical advances achieved through animal research. RDS: Understanding Animal Research in Medicine is an organization based in the United Kingdom that represents the interests of British researchers conducting animal research. The RDS (2007, http://www.rds-online.org.uk/pages/page.asp?i_ToolbarID=3&i_PageID=37)

maintains a timeline of the major medical and veterinary breakthroughs of each decade that have been achieved through animal testing.

PEOPLE FOR THE ETHICAL TREATMENT OF ANIMALS (PETA) AND THE SILVER SPRINGS MONKEY CASE. In 1981 a little-known organization called People for the Ethical Treatment of Animals (PETA) gained national prominence through an exposé on paralysis experiments on monkeys at the Institute of Behavioral Research in Silver Springs, Maryland. The research was funded by the National Institutes of Health (NIH) and led by Edward Taub. It involved depriving monkeys of sensory input into their spinal cords to give them denervated arms, or arms in which the nerves were not active. The monkeys gnawed and licked their arms, producing wounds. Taub hired Alex Pacheco to work as a laboratory assistant. Unbeknownst to Taub, Pacheco had cofounded PETA the year before. Pacheco photographed the monkeys, then reported the lab to authorities. A subsequent raid led to the filing of animal cruelty charges against Taub.

The incident came to be known as the Silver Springs Monkey Case. Even though the charges against Taub were eventually dropped, the publicity made PETA famous. The monkeys were confiscated, and Congress forced the NIH to cease the research. This was viewed as a major triumph by people involved in antivivisection and the growing animal rights movement.

The Animal Enterprise Protection Act of 1992 was enacted against "animal enterprise terrorism." The law prohibits "causing physical disruption to the functioning of an animal enterprise." Three types of animal enterprises are defined:

- Commercial or academic enterprises using animals to produce food or fiber or for agriculture, research, or testing

- Zoos, aquariums, circuses, rodeos, and other legal sporting events

- Fairs and similar events designed to advance agricultural arts and sciences

Offenses that can be charged under the act include using the mail to cause physical disruption at animal enterprises and stealing, damaging, or causing the loss of property used by animal enterprises. Property includes animals and records. People who cause or who conspire to cause economic damages more than $10,000 can be fined and/or imprisoned for up to one year. Aggravated offenses include causing serious bodily injury or death to another person during physical disruption to an animal enterprise. These offenses have penalties ranging from ten years to life in prison. The act also states that restitution can be demanded to cover any loss of food production or farm income associated with an offense and the cost of repeating any experiments that were interrupted or ruined.

HUNTINGDON LIFE SCIENCES BECOMES A TARGET. PETA continued to use infiltration and secretly obtained photographs and videotapes to publicize the realities of animal research. In 1996 and 1997 the group conducted an eight-month undercover investigation at a Huntingdon Life Sciences (HLS) facility in New Jersey. The HLS is a major target of antivivisection groups because it is one of the largest contract companies conducting animal research. A PETA member began working at the HLS and secretly collected documents, photographs, and videotapes that PETA used to file a formal complaint against the HLS with the USDA. PETA also released some of the material to the media.

The HLS countersued PETA, claiming that the materials were obtained by illegal means and that PETA had violated the Economic Espionage Act and the Animal Enterprise Protection Act. In December 1997 a mutual settlement was reached in which PETA agreed to turn over all records taken from the HLS and cease trying to infiltrate HLS property for five years, and the HLS agreed to drop its lawsuit against PETA. A gag order was put into place forbidding PETA from publicly discussing information it collected during the case, excluding the information that it had already released to the media.

In 1999 Stop Huntingdon Animal Cruelty (SHAC), a new animal rights group, began using radical and violent means against HLS headquarters in the United Kingdom. Cars were firebombed and company executives were assaulted outside their homes. Several activists were arrested and jailed for violent crimes.

SHAC began targeting companies providing the HLS with services, funding, and equipment. Banks, brokerage houses, and investment companies with ties to the HLS were picketed and flooded with threatening letters, faxes, and e-mails. Employees were harassed and sometimes assaulted. Their homes were vandalized. The intimidation tactics were effective, as many companies decided to sever their business ties with the HLS. By 2002 no commercial bank in the United Kingdom would loan money to the company. According to Alan Cowell, in "Scene Shifts in Fight against British Testing Lab" (*New York Times*, January 22, 2002), the company's stock dropped in value from $3 per share in 1993 to $0.06 a share in 2002, even though the company was making a modest profit.

In 2002 the company moved its stock market listing to the United States. Cowell reports that the HLS was taken over "on paper" by Life Sciences Research, a company set up by the HLS and incorporated in Maryland. This arrangement allows the HLS to take advantage of U.S. privacy laws that protect the identity of certain investors. An American arm of SHAC known as SHAC USA was formed to lead an intimidation campaign against the HLS and companies that do business with it. SHAC USA (October 27, 2006, http://colorado.indymedia.org/newswire/display/7294/index.php) states that the group uses an array of tactics "from protests, to letter writing, to phone blockades, publicity stunts, and direct action." SHAC USA also notes that underground activists associated with the Animal Liberation Front support SHAC USA by conducting "economic sabotage and live liberations from the HLS and the lab's breeders."

SHAC USA lists a number of "direct actions" taken against HLS employees, its suppliers, and customers. During late January and early February 2005 these actions included splattering homes with paint, filling locks with glue, breaking windows, setting off smoke bombs in offices, and harassing company executives on vacation and at church. Activists claim they followed the son of the chief executive officer of one of the HLS's pharmaceutical clients to school and handed out leaflets to the boy's classmates accusing the HLS of torturing animals.

In May 2004 SHAC USA and seven individuals associated with it were indicted in New Jersey under federal charges for violating the Animal Enterprise Protection Act, stalking, and conspiracy to commit terrorism. The case went to trial in February 2006, and the organization and six of the individuals were found guilty. They were sentenced to various prison terms ranging up to six years. SHAC USA officially ceased to exist; however, animal activists developed a new Web site at http://www.shac7.com that publicizes the case and seeks to raise money and moral support for the imprisoned individuals. The Web site summarizes the details of the case and continues to accuse the HLS of abusing animals by "punching 4-month-old beagle puppies in the face, dissecting a live monkey, falsifying scientific data, and violating Good Laboratory Practice laws over 600 times" (November 16, 2006, http://www.shac7.com/hls.htm).

The HLS (2007, http://www.huntingdon.com/index.php?currentNumber=3&currentIsExpanded=0) defends its practices, stating that it is "committed to providing the highest levels of animal husbandry and welfare." It also notes that in 2003 it was accredited by the Association for Assessment and Accreditation of Laboratory Animal Care (AAALAC) and is one of only a few contract research organizations in the world to be accredited. The AAALAC is an independent nonprofit organization founded in 1965 by scientists and veterinarians engaged in animal research. The AAALAC (2007, http://www.aaalac.org/accreditation/benefits.cfm) notes that accreditation "demonstrates a willingness to go above and beyond the minimums required by law. It tells the public that the institution is committed to the responsible care and use of animals in science."

Mainstream antivivisection and welfarist groups condemn the violent tactics used by radical activists and instead wage public relations and political campaigns against the use of research animals.

FEDERAL LEGISLATION AND OVERSIGHT

Facilities that use certain species of live laboratory animals for research purposes must abide by laws and policies governing their use. Even though there are a few state laws that also apply, most of the applicable legislation and oversight is provided by federal agencies.

Animal Welfare Act

Animal Welfare Act (AWA) regulations are enforced by the Animal Care unit of the USDA's Animal and Plant Health Inspection Service (APHIS). The regulations govern the housing and care of the animals and include licensing, registration, veterinary, and record-keeping requirements. Covered facilities must register with the USDA.

The AWA does not apply to cold-blooded animals, rats, mice, or birds. According to the law, these animals do not fall under the definition of *animal*. This condition was made permanent in May 2002 as part of new federal legislation. The AWA does cover dogs, cats, rabbits, primates, guinea pigs, hamsters, marine mammals, and "other warm-blooded animals."

Under the AWA each research facility must have an attending veterinarian who is required to provide adequate veterinary care to the facility's animals. The law defines *adequate veterinary care* as "what is currently the accepted professional practice or treatment for that particular circumstance or condition." Each research facility must have an institutional officer who is responsible for legally committing the facility to meet AWA requirements. This officer or the chief executive officer of the facility must appoint an institutional animal care and use committee (IACUC) to assess the research facility's animal program, buildings, and procedures. The IACUC must include at least three members—a chairperson, a veterinarian, and a person not affiliated with the institute—to represent "general community interests." IACUC members have to be qualified based on their experience and expertise.

The IACUC is responsible for reviewing a research facility's animal use program and inspecting the facilities in which animals are housed and studied. These evaluations must be done at least once every six months. Written reports are required and must be made available to APHIS and to any federal agencies that provide funding to the facility. The IACUC is also responsible for investigating any complaints lodged against the facility regarding the care and use of the animals. This includes complaints from the general public. The IACUC has the power to approve or disapprove proposed animal care and use activities and to ask for modifications in these activities. It can also suspend particular animal activities if it believes they are not being conducted in accordance with its wishes.

Under the AWA any proposed activities must meet certain criteria. Some of the major requirements include:

- Procedures must "avoid or minimize discomfort, distress, and pain to the animals."

- Researchers must consider alternative procedures that will not cause more than momentary or slight pain and provide reasons in cases where alternatives cannot be used.

- Researchers must provide written assurance that the activities "do not unnecessarily duplicate previous experiments."

Any procedures that may cause more than momentary or slight pain or distress require that pain-relieving drugs be administered, unless withholding the drugs is "scientifically justified." Animals cannot be administered paralyzing drugs unless they are also given anesthesia. Those that experience severe or chronic pain or distress that cannot be relieved are required to be painlessly euthanized as soon as possible, unless researchers seek and receive an exemption from the IACUC.

According to APHIS, in September 2006 there were 1,120 registered research facilities in the United States. (See Table 5.4.) California had the most facilities (161), followed by New York (78), Massachusetts (76), Texas (74), and Pennsylvania (62). APHIS (January 24, 2007, http://www.aphis.usda.gov/ac/publications/reports/R_cert _holders.pdf) maintains a list of the research institutions that includes the names and addresses of the facilities, which are mostly colleges and universities, pharmaceutical companies, hospitals, and biotechnology laboratories.

All research facilities are required to comply with AWA regulations. Federal facilities are not required to register with the USDA and are not subject to USDA inspections, though they are required to comply with USDA standards for animal care established under the AWA and must submit annual reports to the USDA regarding their use of regulated laboratory animals. The AWA requires that nonfederal research facilities receive at least one inspection per year to determine compliance with the law.

All registered research facilities must submit annual reports to the USDA listing the number and species of animals used in research, testing, and experimentation and indicating whether pain-relieving drugs were administered.

TABLE 5.4

USDA-licensed research facilities

[As of September 7, 2006]

State	Number
Alabama	11
Alaska	2
Arizona	13
Arkansas	10
California	161
Colorado	25
Connecticut	15
Delaware	6
District of Columbia	6
Florida	23
Georgia	18
Hawaii	2
Idaho	4
Illinois	38
Indiana	24
Iowa	17
Kansas	13
Kentucky	5
Louisiana	11
Maine	9
Maryland	30
Massachusetts	76
Michigan	26
Minnesota	29
Mississippi	5
Missouri	30
Montana	4
Nebraska	12
Nevada	3
New Hampshire	2
New Jersey	36
New Mexico	8
New York	78
North Carolina	27
North Dakota	3
Ohio	42
Oklahoma	15
Oregon	9
Pennsylvania	62
Puerto Rico	6
Rhode Island	6
South Carolina	12
South Dakota	5
Tennessee	17
Texas	74
Utah	9
Vermont	5
Virginia	19
Washington	24
West Virginia	4
Wisconsin	26
Wyoming	3
Total	**1,120**

SOURCE: Adapted from "Research," in *Facility Lists: Research*, U.S. Department of Agriculture, Animal and Plant Health Inspection Service, September 7, 2006, http://www.aphis.usda.gov/ac/publications/reports/ R_cert_holders.txt (accessed December 6, 2006)

If the drugs were not administered for procedures that caused pain or distress, the report must explain why their use would have interfered with the research or experiment.

Health Research Extension Act

In 1985 the Health Research Extension Act (HREA) was passed. This act requires that facilities conducting animal research, training, and testing activities that receive funding from the Public Health Service (PHS) follow an animal welfare policy called the Public Health Service Policy on the Humane Care and Use of Laboratory Animals (PHSP). The PHS includes government agencies such as the Centers for Disease Control and Prevention, the U.S. Food and Drug Administration (FDA), and the NIH. The NIH is the main public source of funding for biomedical research in the United States.

Affected animal research facilities must follow the recommendations given in the PHS's *Guide for the Care and Use of Laboratory Animals* (1996, http://books.nap.edu/readingroom/books/labrats/) regarding housing, cleanliness, husbandry, veterinary care, and use of measures to alleviate pain and distress. The standards are similar to those found in the AWA, but the HREA applies to all vertebrates, including mice, rats, and birds.

The HREA requires facilities to file annual reports that describe their animal care and use programs and how they comply with the AWA and the PHSP. The PHSP is administered by the NIH Office for Protection from Research Risks. Research facilities that receive funding from the NIH must have at least five people on their IACUC. The NIH also reviews planned animal studies to ensure that animal models are appropriate and that no more animals than necessary are used.

Food, Drug, and Cosmetic Act

Another major piece of federal legislation that affects laboratory animals is the Food, Drug, and Cosmetic Act (FDCA). The FDCA defines drugs as follows:

• Articles intended for use in the diagnosis, cure, mitigation, treatment, or prevention of disease

• Articles (other than food) intended to affect the structure or any function of the body of man or other animals

Drugs must receive FDA approval before they can be sold in the United States. Although the FDA does not specify the tests that must be done, the agency does not allow human testing to occur if animal safety testing is considered inadequate or incomplete.

Cosmetics are defined as articles other than soap that are applied to the human body for "cleansing, beautifying, promoting attractiveness, or altering the appearance." Soaps are specifically excluded from the regulatory definition of cosmetics and so do not fall under the FDCA.

Cosmetic products and their ingredients (except for color additives) are not subject to premarket FDA approval. However, it is illegal to distribute cosmetics that contain substances that could harm consumers under normal use. Although animal testing is not required by the law, it is recommended by the FDA to ensure product

safety. Cosmetic products that are not adequately tested for safety must have a warning statement on their front label reading "WARNING—The safety of this product has not been determined."

Some consumer products are considered both a drug and a cosmetic under the law, such as dandruff shampoos, fluoride-containing toothpastes, combination antiperspirants/deodorants, and makeup products or moisturizers that contain sunscreens. These products are subject to provisions of the laws that apply to both drugs and cosmetics.

Other Federal Legislation

The Federal Hazardous Substances Labeling Act was passed in 1960. The Consumer Product Safety Commission administers the law as it applies to household products. This law affects animals because household products (such as cleaners) that contain hazardous chemicals must warn consumers about their potential hazards. A hazardous substance is defined as one that is toxic, corrosive, flammable, or combustible; that is extremely irritating or sensitizing; or that generates pressure through heat, decomposition, or other means. Toxicity tests are required to determine these conditions.

Other laws governing chemicals that must be tested for toxicity include the Toxic Substances Control Act and the Federal Insecticide, Fungicide, and Rodenticide Act. Both of these laws are administered by the Environmental Protection Agency. Animals are commonly used to test the products regulated by all of this legislation.

In 2000 the Chimpanzee Health Improvement, Maintenance, and Protection (CHIMP) Act was passed, calling for the creation of a national sanctuary system for chimpanzees no longer needed in research programs conducted or supported by federal agencies. In 2002 the NIH awarded a contract to Chimp Haven Inc. to establish and operate a sanctuary under the CHIMP Act in Shreveport, Louisiana. Construction began in 2003, and the facility was dedicated in 2004. Table 5.5 shows a timeline compiled by the HSUS of major events in the formation of the national sanctuary system for chimpanzees. Most chimpanzees involved in federal research programs were bred or captured from the wild to be used in hepatitis and acquired immune deficiency syndrome research. (See Figure 5.5 for the percentage breakdown of federal research grants involving chimpanzee research between 2000 and September 2004.) The CHIMP Act is extremely controversial because it allows the animals to be recalled for research purposes if there is a "public health need." Because the act does not call for permanent retirement of chimpanzees, many animal activist groups have called for its repeal.

TABLE 5.5

National chimpanzee sanctuary system timeline of events, April 15, 1999–June 28, 2006

Date	Action
April 15, 1999	A coalition that includes representatives from the research, animal-protection, zoo, and sanctuary communities writes a letter regarding the issue of chimpanzee "retirement" and submits it to U.S. Rep. J.E. Porter (R-IL) and U.S. Sen. A. Specter (R-PA).
November 22, 1999	H.R. 3514, the Chimpanzee Health Improvement, Maintenance, and Protection (CHIMP) Act, is introduced in the U.S. House of Representatives by Rep. J. Greenwood (R-PA). This bill will require the federal government to provide for permanent "retirement" of chimpanzees who are identified as no longer needed for research.
May 18, 2000	The House Committee on Commerce holds a hearing on H.R. 3514. Those presenting testimony include J. Goodall (Jane Goodall Institute), J. Strandberg (NIH), T. Nelson (National Chimpanzee Research Retirement Task Force), and A. Prince (New York Blood Center).
June 14, 2000	S. 2725, the Chimpanzee Health Improvement Maintenance and Protection (CHIMP) Act, is introduced in the U.S. Senate by Sens. R. Smith (R-NH) and R. Durbin (D-IL).
September 20, 2000	S. 2725 gains approval by the Senate Health, Education, Labor, and Pensions Committee.
October 24, 2000	The House passes H.R. 3514 with the Bliley amendments.
December 6, 2000	The Senate passes S. 2725 unanimously.
December 20, 2000	President Clinton signs the CHIMP Act into public law (P.L. 106–551).
April 16, 2001	The National Center for Research Resources (NCRR), part of the National Institutes of Health (NIH), publishes a "source sought" notice to determine whether there is an existing nonprofit that fulfills the requirements of the CHIMP Act and is interested in serving as the "contractor" of the sanctuary system.
September 28, 2001	NIH publishes a request for proposal for an entity to operate and maintain a sanctuary system via the CHIMP Act.
December 20, 2001	The departments of Labor, Education, Health and Human Services and related agencies' 2002 Appropriations Act (H.R. 3061) allocates $5 million to begin construction of the national chimpanzee sanctuary facilities.
January 10, 2002	President G.W. Bush signs H.R. 3061 into public law, including $5 million toward construction of the national sanctuary system.
September 30, 2002	NIH announces the award of a contract to Chimp Haven to establish and operate a chimpanzee sanctuary, pursuant to the CHIMP Act.
May 1, 2003	Chimp Haven, the contractor of the national chimpanzee sanctuary system, breaks ground on its Shreveport, La., facility.
January 11, 2005	NIH publishes a notice of proposed rule making regarding standards of care for chimpanzees held in the national chimpanzee sanctuary system.
June 28, 2006	Chimp Haven receives full accreditation by the Association for Assessment and Accreditation of Laboratory Animal Care International.

SOURCE: Adapted from Kathleen M. Conlee and Sarah T. Boysen, "Table 4. National Chimpanzee Sanctuary System: Timeline of Events," in *The State of the Animals III: 2005*, Humane Society of the United States, December 31, 2005, http://www.hsus.org/web-files/PDF/hsp/SOA_3-2005_Chap9.pdf (accessed December 13, 2006)

FIGURE 5.5

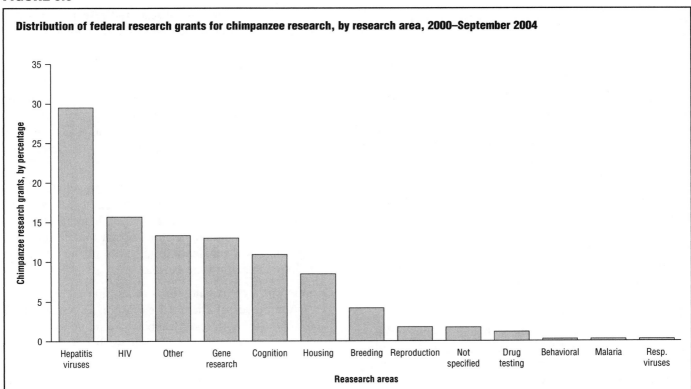

Distribution of federal research grants for chimpanzee research, by research area, 2000–September 2004

SOURCE: Kathleen M. Conlee and Sarah T. Boysen, "Figure 1. Chimpanzee Research Grants, 2000–September 2004," in *The State of the Animals III: 2005*, Humane Society of the United States, December 31, 2005, http://www.hsus.org/web-files/PDF/hsp/SOA_3-2005_Chap9.pdf (accessed December 13, 2006)

LABORATORY ANIMALS AND THEIR USES

Determining the number of animals used for research in the United States is extremely difficult, because rats, mice, birds, and cold-blooded animals are not regulated by the AWA and do not have to be counted. It is widely agreed that rats and mice make up a huge majority of research animals. The National Research Council notes in *National Need and Priorities for Veterinarians in Biomedical Research* (2004) that approximately twenty-three million rats and mice were used in biomedical research during 1998 and that the number was expected to increase by 10% to 20% annually through 2010. If this prediction held true, as many as ninety-nine million rats and mice were needed during 2006 for biomedical research. Some estimates place the total number even higher. In 2002 Jonathan Knight and Alison Abbott estimated in "Mouse Genetics: Full House" (*Nature*, June 20, 2002) that sixty million mice would be needed just to complete the mouse genome (a study of the genetic makeup of the mouse with the function of every gene identified). The *Scientific American* (August 4, 2004) estimates that close to one hundred million mice are "consumed" annually in U.S. laboratories.

As shown in Table 5.6, there were 1,101,958 AWA-registered animals used in live research during fiscal year 2004. California laboratories used the most regulated animals (116,395), followed by Massachusetts (89,031), Pennsylvania (79,273), Ohio (70,245), and New Jersey (65,180). Together, these five states accounted for more than one-third of all regulated research animals.

Figure 5.6 shows the breakdown of regulated research animals by species in 2004. Rabbits made up the largest portion (23%), and guinea pigs made up 22%. Hamsters made up 16% of the total. Pigs, sheep, and other farm animals totaled 10%. Together, dogs, cats, and nonhuman primates constituted 13% of all regulated animals. These species are the ones that arouse the most public concern in the research animal debate. Other covered species constituted 16% of the total.

The total number of regulated research animals used annually over the thirty-two-year period from 1973 to 2004 is shown in Figure 5.7. Over the first twenty years of this period (1973 to 1992), the average was 1.8 million animals per year. For the twelve-year period from 1993 to 2004 the average dropped to 1.3 million per year.

Biomedical Research

The vast majority of research animals are used in biomedical research. Biomedicine is a medical discipline based on principles of the natural sciences, particularly biology and biochemistry.

The NIH maintains the Computer Retrieval of Information on Scientific Projects (CRISP; http://www.crisp.cit.nih.gov/), a database of biomedical research projects that have received funding from federal agencies dating back to 1972. The CRISP database can be searched to find information about the use of animals in federally funded research projects at universities, hospitals, and other research institutions. For example, a search conducted in February 2007 using the search term *dogs* returned 179 projects in which dogs played a role. Information supplied about each project includes the name of the principal investigator, the name and address of the research institution, the starting and ending dates of the project, the federal agency providing funding, and a description of the project.

DRUG TESTING. According to the FDA, in "The Beginnings: Laboratory and Animal Studies" (January 30, 2006, http://www.fda.gov/fdac/special/testtubetopatient/studies.html), drug companies typically test new drugs on at least two different animal species to see if they are affected differently. Animal testing is performed to determine specific characteristics, such as:

- How much of the drug is absorbed into the bloodstream

- Any toxic side effects

- Appropriate dosage levels

- How the drug is metabolized (broken down) by the body

- How quickly the drug is excreted from the body

The results from animal tests tell researchers if and how new drugs should then be tested on humans.

Product Testing

Millions of research animals are used to test products intended for industrial and consumer markets in the United States. Product safety testing exposes animals to chemicals to determine factors such as eye and skin irritancy. Common product safety tests conducted with animals include:

- Acute toxicity tests determine the immediate effects of chemical exposure. The LD-50 test is an example. In this test animals are exposed to chemicals through ingestion, inhalation, or skin contact to determine the concentration necessary to kill 50% of the test group within a specific time period.

- Skin and eye irritancy tests determine the effects on skin and eyes of chemical exposure. One example is the Draize eye test. Rabbits are commonly used because they cannot blink and wash out the chemicals.

- Subchronic and chronic toxicity tests determine the effects of long-term chemical exposure.

- Genetic toxicity tests determine the effects of chemical exposure on reproductive organs.

TABLE 5.6

Animals used at USDA-registered research facilities, by state, fiscal year 2004

[Total reported = 1,101,958]

States	All other covered species	Cats	Dogs	Guinea pigs	Hamsters	Nonhuman primates	Other farm animals	Pig	Rabbits	Sheep	Total by state:
AK	2,112	0	3	0	0	0	0	0	0	0	2,115
AL	682	204	1,043	453	60	991	1,262	624	2,086	62	7,467
AR	303	0	205	142	61	55	0	105	200	0	1,071
AZ	5,614	41	191	108	598	138	82	689	599	31	8,091
CA	13,053	2,116	2,777	31,907	7,556	4,321	6,854	4,151	42,016	1,644	116,395
CO	1,321	308	535	2,796	829	28	152	622	735	385	7,711
CT	1,404	45	336	763	1,357	344	0	387	875	11	5,522
DC	8,592	19	105	547	1,186	402	0	905	820	89	12,665
DE	1,032	595	298	3,795	5,464	—	2,489	3,241	16,020	193	33,127
FL	2,563	637	287	503	194	321	65	1,217	876	247	6,910
GA	16,033	714	1,296	1,461	9,822	3,207	713	885	5,141	40	39,312
HI	22	1	1	0	442	0	0	39	42	0	547
IA	866	1,657	2,355	6,740	39,163	4	1,386	1,028	5,058	882	59,139
ID	129	17	50	16	0	0	19	0	54	3,955	4,240
IL	4,384	709	2,171	5,916	1,100	451	434	1,009	8,931	385	25,490
IN	7,649	600	1,224	1,337	1,862	617	187	368	2,204	146	16,194
KS	7,948	901	1,577	34	423	278	268	3,626	660	48	15,763
KY	379	63	206	468	294	69	16	71	532	0	2,098
LA	165	220	1,045	182	0	2,213	2,223	179	2,614	12	8,853
MA	3,322	230	3,548	28,910	10,264	4,936	1,204	4,337	31,636	644	89,031
MD	12,536	938	1,507	13,074	12,497	5,507	639	2,190	9,015	407	58,310
ME	120	0	0	4	12	0	662	33	216	0	1,047
MI	5,011	402	4,057	12,374	550	1,401	407	1,292	2,513	18	28,025
MN	1,334	1,176	1,918	6,666	673	158	985	3,614	3,807	598	20,929
MO	6,121	1,487	2,195	7,573	8,273	132	214	936	3,857	30	30,818
MS	71	119	303	0	179	88	126	176	163	24	1,249
MT	8	12	0	0	316	9	180	0	198	71	794
NC	4,193	407	1,184	9,151	48	296	286	3,030	4,728	219	23,542
ND	10	52	18	3	3	0	3,891	2,219	366	4,350	10,912
NE	433	1,214	1,024	3,271	38,977	79	269	258	4,478	172	50,175
NH	104	20	1	1	275	13	0	408	79	0	901
NJ	8,102	155	5,409	29,096	5,073	3,758	242	1,064	12,281	0	65,180
NM	220	25	402	225	40	24	0	121	41	0	1,098
NV	1,119	—	149	95	—	—	—	31	210	307	1,911
NY	13,258	2,913	5,724	15,962	13,404	2,700	904	1,774	7,711	403	64,753
OH	5,452	1,105	4,315	27,605	3,016	1,156	397	3,261	23,779	159	70,245
OK	723	131	826	715	110	106	304	56	486	95	3,552
OR	631	49	77	806	432	1,643	65	694	412	297	5,106
PA	5,863	2,113	5,933	14,882	2,566	4,192	1,043	2,551	39,631	499	79,273
PR	15	0	0	0	343	200	0	37	48	0	643
RI	507	27	33	76	127	25	49	217	73	72	1,206
SC	2,090	319	267	346	15	574	48	242	893	0	4,794
SD	107	18	11	10	492	13	538	1	16	90	1,296
TN	1,045	229	1,124	853	797	182	165	1,199	928	1	6,523
TX	13,491	555	1,719	7,157	3,456	5,377	2,474	2,524	14,476	987	52,216

TABLE 5.6

Animals used at USDA-registered research facilities, by state, fiscal year 2004 [CONTINUED]

[Total reported = 1,101,958]

States	All other covered species	Cats	Dogs	Guinea pigs	Hamsters	Nonhuman primates	Other farm animals	Pig	Rabbits	Sheep	Total by state:
UT	1,540	128	319	1,092	1,280	4	30	133	1,018	130	5,674
VA	2,488	175	2,260	1,037	489	1,623	114	1,000	2,990	4	12,180
VT	188	11	22	347	7	0	13	55	124	1,010	1,777
WA	3,725	272	1,017	4,806	215	3,394	332	505	1,982	170	16,418
WI	2,901	448	3,822	730	1,328	3,965	192	1,400	3,653	139	18,578
WV	54	49	26	60	25	4	0	0	284	111	613
WY	279	14	17	9	28	0	33	0	18	81	479
Species total	**171,312**	**23,640**	**64,932**	**244,104**	**175,721**	**54,998**	**31,956**	**54,504**	**261,573**	**19,218**	

SOURCE: "Animals Used in Research," in *Animal Care Reports: Annual Reports of Enforcement by Fiscal Year: 2004*, U.S. Department of Agriculture, Animal and Plant Health Inspection Service, 2004, http://www.aphis.usda.gov/ac/awreports/awreport2004.pdf (accessed November 28, 2006)

FIGURE 5.6

Animals used at all USDA-registered research facilities, fiscal year 2004

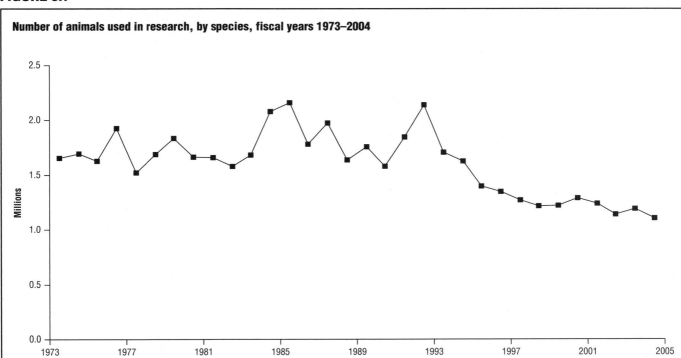

SOURCE: Adapted from "Animals Used in Research," in *Animal Care Reports: Annual Reports of Enforcement by Fiscal Year, 2004*, U.S. Department of Agriculture, Animal and Plant Health Inspection Service, 2004, http://www.aphis.usda.gov/ac/awreports/awreport2004.pdf (accessed November 28, 2006)

- Birth defects tests determine the effects of chemical exposure on offspring.
- Cancer potential tests determine the potential of chemical exposures for causing cancer.

CONSUMER PRODUCTS. Some companies selling consumer products, such as cosmetics and household cleaners, advertise that they do not conduct animal testing on their products or that their products are "cruelty-free." In some cases this statement may be somewhat misleading. For example, according to the CAAT (January 29, 2007, http://altweb.jhsph.edu/faqs.htm#13), such claims can mean various things, including:

- Animal testing has not been performed on the products and/or their ingredients in the previous five years.
- Animal testing was performed on the products and/or ingredients by another company (for example, a supplier).
- Nonanimal testing was performed on finished products made from ingredients already known to be safe because of previous animal testing.

CAAT points out that the vast majority of cosmetic ingredients used by the industry have been tested on animals at some point in time, or are known to be safe based on decades of use. It notes that smaller cosmetics companies tend to produce final products made from

FIGURE 5.7

Number of animals used in research, by species, fiscal years 1973–2004

SOURCE: Adapted from "Number of Animals Used by Research from the First Reporting Year (FY 1973) to the Present," in *Animal Care Reports: Annual Reports of Enforcement by Fiscal Year, 2004*, U.S. Department of Agriculture, Animal and Plant Health Inspection Service, 2004, http://www.aphis.usda.gov/ac/awreports/awreport2004.pdf (accessed November 28, 2006)

purchased ingredients, rather than from ingredients developed in-house. Larger companies that develop new ingredients for cosmetics must use animal testing or viable alternatives to prove that the ingredients are safe for consumer use.

The National Anti-Vivisection Society's *Personal Care for People Who Care* (2005) lists hundreds of companies that produce personal care (for example, bath products, deodorants, and antiperspirants), household (for example, bathroom and kitchen cleaners and furniture polishes), pet care, and cosmetic products and tells whether they do or do not test their products on animals.

In addition, the book identifies companies that do not use any animal-derived ingredients in their products. Other animal rights organizations, such as PETA, maintain similar types of lists. Some provide a seal that compliant companies can use to mark their products for easy identification by shoppers.

In February 2003 the Council of the European Union and the European Parliament approved the Seventh Amendment of Council Directive 76/768/EEC (the Cosmetics Directive). It will place a ban on the testing of cosmetics on animals in Europe in 2009. In addition, in 2009 the sale and import of new cosmetics tested on animals using eleven specific tests will be banned. Another ban will be implemented in 2013 on the sale and import of cosmetics tested on animals for three toxicity tests (assuming that valid alternative tests have been established by that time).

Dissection

Dead animals used for dissection in schools make up a small portion of all research animals. The HSUS states in "Back to School Shouldn't Mean Back to Dissection Says the HSUS" (September 23, 2004, http://www.hsus .org/press_and_publications/press_releases/back_to_school _shouldnt_mean_back_to_dissection_says_the_hsus.html) that an estimated six million animals—mostly frogs, pig fetuses, and cats—are dissected by U.S. schoolchildren each year. Dissection has been considered a staple of biology classes since the 1960s, when the National Science Foundation urged schools to implement a more hands-on science curriculum.

The first legal challenge against school dissection lodged by a student occurred in California in 1987. A high school student sued her school for not allowing her to perform an alternative to dissection. California and Florida became the first states to allow students to opt out of dissection in the mid- to late 1980s. According to "Dissection Laws" (August 30, 2006, http://www.hsus .org/animals_in_research/animals_in_education/dissection _laws.html), the HSUS notes that other states have since followed suit with choice-in-dissection laws or policies:

Illinois, Louisiana, Maine, Maryland, Massachusetts, New Jersey, New Mexico, New York, Oregon, Pennsylvania, Rhode Island, and Virginia.

By the early twenty-first century many students were expressing ethical and moral concerns about the practice of dissection in the classroom. Some school districts now offer students alternatives, such as computer models. The National Science Teachers Association defends dissection as a valuable learning tool for children, but urges teachers to be flexible in offering alternatives.

Surgical/Medical Training and Behavior Research

It is estimated that the use of laboratory animals for surgical/medical training and behavior research makes up only a small part of the number of research animals used. However, this category is one that is particularly criticized by antivivisection groups. In the past, surgeons training to operate on humans and animals almost always practiced on live animals. Many of these surgeries were terminal surgeries, meaning that the animals are not allowed to regain consciousness. The animals are euthanized while they are under the effects of anesthesia.

The Physicians Committee for Responsible Medicine (PCRM) reports in "Alternatives to Animal Labs in Medical Schools" (January 30, 2007, http://www.pcrm .org/resch/anexp/alertliveanimallabs.html) that more than 85% of all U.S. medical schools have eliminated live animal labs to train medical students. Many veterinary schools are limiting the number of terminal surgeries required of their students. Some veterinary schools conduct dissection labs. According to the PCRM, many schools now use animal cadavers donated by people whose pets or livestock have died of natural causes or have been humanely euthanized because of illness or injury.

SOURCES OF RESEARCH ANIMALS

Research animals are obtained by laboratories from animal breeders and brokers licensed by the USDA. These licenses fall into two types:

- Class A—Breeders who sell animals that they have bred and raised on their own premises and who buy animals only to replenish their breeding stock

- Class B—Breeders, dealers, brokers, and operators of auction sales that purchase and/or resell live or dead animals, often obtained from city or county animal shelters

Breeders who sell fewer than twenty-five dogs and/or cats per year that were born and raised on their own premises, for research, teaching, or testing purposes, are exempt.

APHIS (http://www.aphis.usda.gov/ac/publications .html) reports that in September 2006 there were 4,974

Class A breeders and 1,185 Class B breeders/dealers/brokers in the United States. Note that not all these licensees sell animals to research laboratories. Some sell animals to pet stores and other animal enterprises.

Lab animal suppliers advertise their animals in the *Lab Animal Buyer's Guide* (http://guide.labanimal.com/guide/). It lists more than five hundred companies and over eight hundred products and services. Animals available include frogs, toads, salamanders, newts, cats, dogs, ferrets, chickens, ducks, cattle, goats, sheep, swine, rabbits, nonhuman primates (monkeys, chimpanzees, and so on), birds, fish, opossums, woodchucks, exotic animals, invertebrates, and a wide assortment of rodents.

Purpose-Bred Animals

The vast majority of laboratory research animals are purpose-bred, meaning that they are born and raised under controlled conditions and may be genetically manipulated. Purpose-breeding of laboratory animals is becoming more and more common as researchers demand animals with particular genetic makeups. For example, researchers investigating narcolepsy use dogs bred to be born with the condition. Charles River Laboratories in Wilmington, Massachusetts, is a leading breeder and supplier of purpose-bred animals.

Random-Source Animals

Live animals for research can also be purchased from random sources. For example, dogs and cats obtained from animal shelters are considered random-source animals. Researchers acquire these animals from dealers with USDA Class B licenses or directly from shelters. Class B dealers can acquire random-source dogs and cats for resale, but only from the following sources:

- Other USDA licensed dealers

- State-, county-, or city-owned and operated animal pounds or shelters

- Humane groups and contract pounds organized as legal entities under the laws of their state

- People who have bred and raised the animals on their own premises

Class B dealers are prohibited from obtaining dogs and cats from private individuals who did not breed and raise the animal on their own premises.

The rules that Class B dealers must follow when acquiring animals are primarily intended to prevent them from selling pets to research facilities. USDA regulations also require Class B dealers to hold live dogs and cats for specific time periods before reselling them, and the dealers have to keep records, including physical information about each animal (age, color, sex, species, and breed) and the names and addresses of the seller and buyer of each

TABLE 5.7

Holding periods required for dogs and cats held by USDA-licensed "B" dealers

IF the source is	AND the dog/cat's age is	THEN the holding period is
a private pound, contract pound or shelter	any age	10 full days, not including the day of acquisition and the time in transit
a state, city, or county operated pound or shelter	any age	5 full days, not including the day of acquisition and the time in transit
a private individual who bred and raised the dog/cat on his/her premises	< or = 120 days	24 hours, not including the time in transit
a private individual who bred and raised the dog/cat on his/her premises	>120 days	5 full days, not including the day of acquisition and the time in transit
another USDA licensed dealer or exhibitor who has already held the dog/cat for the required holding period	any age	24 hours, not including the time in transit
another USDA licensed dealer or exhibitor who has not held the dog/cat for the required holding period	any age	5 full days, not including the day of acquisition and the time in transit

SOURCE: "Licensed 'B' Dealer," in *Random Source Dog and Cat Dealer Inspection Guide*, U.S. Department of Agriculture, Animal and Plant Health Inspection Service, April 2000, http://www.aphis.usda.gov/ac/dealer/randomsource.pdf (accessed January 3, 2007)

animal. (See Table 5.7.) This gives pet owners a chance to track down lost pets that were sold to Class B dealers by animal shelters. Random-source dealers are listed in the *Lab Animal Buyer's Guide*. Some animal protection groups also maintain lists of Class B dealers they believe sell random-source dogs and cats to laboratories.

Random-source animals are used in research where genetic diversity is important. According to the MISMR, in "The Use of Pound Animals in Biomedical Research" (2006, http://www.mismr.org/educational/pound.html), random-source animals are primarily used in biomedical research on cardiovascular diseases, cancer, diabetes, arthritis, lung disorders, orthopedics, birth defects, hearing loss, and blindness. Dogs are the subject of choice for heart and kidney disease research. Cats are frequently used in research devoted to the central nervous system, strokes, and disorders of the brain, eyes, and ears. The MISMR (2006, http://www.mismr.org/about/) notes that use of these animals in research benefits not only human medicine but also veterinary medicine.

Random-source dogs and cats are far less expensive than those that are purpose-bred. The MISMR reports in "Use of Pound Animals in Biomedical Research" that in 2006 the cost of a shelter dog or cat was $60 to $200, compared with $422 to $580 for a purpose-bred one. It also claims that less than 2% of the ten million animals that reside in shelters each year are used for medical research. The organization claims that these animals would be euthanized in the shelters anyway because of the pet overpopulation problem.

Animal welfare organizations disagree, however, noting that neither municipal animal shelters nor Class B dealers all follow the regulations. Many fail to keep animals for the assigned period, and dealers often do not keep detailed records of the animals they sell. Despite regulations of the industry, lost family pets do periodically become the subjects of experiments when they are not held for the entire waiting period. In addition, there has been much controversy over Class B dealers, some of whom have been known to steal pets from homes and yards. Welfarists and animal rights activists often criticize the NIH for funding research projects that use shelter dogs and cats. The NIH leaves source decisions to individual research institutions. Although some people are pushing for legislation to outlaw the use of shelter animals in medical research, the MISMR argues in "Use of Pound Animals in Biomedical Research" that this would drive up the cost of research and costs to local communities that must house and euthanize unwanted animals. Those involved in the animal welfare and rights movement respond with evidence that more and more animal shelters are adopting a "no-kill" policy—meaning they will euthanize only in cases of severe illness or temperament problems but not because of overpopulation—so shelter animals will not necessarily be euthanized and may instead be adopted.

CLASS B DEALER BUSTED BY THE USDA. In August 2003 federal authorities raided Martin Creek Kennels in Williford, Arkansas, and confiscated more than one hundred dogs and one cat. The facility had a USDA Class B license to purchase and resell animals. The raid resulted from an undercover videotape obtained by the animal protection group Last Chance for Animals. The videotape documented many cases of abuse and neglect at the facility and several incidences of dogs being shot to death and thrown into mass graves. Brenda Shoss reports in "Pet Theft Thugs: They're Real. They're Nearby" (March 24, 2005, http://www.kinshipcircle.org/columns _articles/0052.html) that the kennel purchased stolen pets from bunchers (people who steal pets, pick up strays, and take in dogs and cats given away for free and sell them to Class B dealers). The kennel bought stolen pets for $5 to $30 per animal and sold them using falsified paperwork to research laboratories for $150 to $700 per dog and $50 to $200 per cat.

Shoss notes that the kennel had been in business for sixteen years, and during that time it sold thousands of animals to research laboratories. In February 2005 C. C. Baird, the owner of the kennel, and his family were fined $262,700 by the USDA and had their Class B licenses revoked permanently.

Because of cases such as this, those in the animal rights and welfare community, as well as veterinarians, frequently warn against placing "free to good home"

advertisements, fearing that the animals offered will end up in the hands of bunchers or Class B dealers.

REDUCTION, REFINEMENT, AND REPLACEMENT

In 1959 William Russell and Rex Burch published *Principles of Humane Experimental Technique*, which advocated three principles for the animal research industry: reduction, refinement, and replacement. Russell and Burch called these principles "the three R's for the removal of inhumanity" in the scientific community.

The book was largely ignored until the 1980s, when public protest against the use of animals in laboratory testing became more widespread. Scientists and animal welfare organizations then embraced the three Rs as scientifically reasonable and humane goals for the industry. The three Rs, however, are guiding principles, not legal requirements.

The three Rs are defined as follows:

• Reduction is a goal to reduce the number of animals used in research overall by reducing the number required for individual experiments or areas of study without sacrificing the statistical validity of the results. In other words, researchers are urged to use statistics to determine the minimum number of animals that can be used in an experiment and still provide valid data. Another goal is to reduce the number of procedures that require whole animals. For example, tissues from an animal used in one experiment could be used in other experiments in place of live whole animals.

• Refinement is a goal to refine experimental and care practices to reduce animal suffering and distress and encourage well-being. Such practices include the use of painkillers during and after experiments, the use of humane euthanasia techniques, and improvements in animals' living environments.

• Replacement is a goal to replace live laboratory animals with suitable alternatives (for example, computer simulations) and to replace higher animal species with lower species.

Search for Alternatives to Animal Tests

In 1993 the National Institutes of Health Revitalization Act was passed, requiring formation of an agency to oversee validation of alternatives to toxicological animal testing. The result was the Interagency Coordinating Committee for the Validation of Alternative Methods (ICCVAM) and the National Toxicology Program Interagency Center for the Evaluation of Alternative Toxicological Methods (NICEATM).

The ICCVAM is responsible for establishing validation criteria and for encouraging government agencies

TABLE 5.8

Alternative test methods submitted to the ICCVAM for evaluation

[As of November 30, 2005]

Test method	Toxicity category
Up-and-Down Procedure (UDP)	Acute toxicity
In Vitro Methods for Assessing Acute Systemic Toxicity	
Botulinum Toxin Testing	Biologics and vaccines
Corrositex ® Assay	Dermal corrosivity and irritation
EpiDerm™, Episkin™ and Rat Skin Transcutaneous Electrical Resistance (TER) Assays	
Frog Embryo Teratogenesis Assay—*Xenopus* (FETAX)	Developmental toxicity
In Vitro Endocrine Disruptor Screening Assays	Endocrine disruptor
Murine Local Lymph Node Assay (LLNA)	Immunotoxicity
In Vitro Test Methods for Detecting Ocular Corrosives and Severe Irritants	Ocular toxicity
EpiOcular™ Model	
In Vitro 3T3 NRU Phototoxicity Test Method	Phototoxicity
In Vitro Pyrogenicity Test Methods	Pyrogenicity

Note: ICCVAM is the Interagency Coordinating Committee on the Validation of Alternative Methods, a division of the National Institute of Environmental Health Sciences.

SOURCE: "Test Method Evaluations," in *Activities and Publications: Test Methods,* National Institutes of Health, National Institute of Environmental Health Sciences, The Interagency Coordinating Committee on the Validation of Alternative Methods, November 30, 2005, http://iccvam.niehs.nih.gov/methods/review.htm (accessed December 14, 2006)

TABLE 5.9

Traditional skin corrosivity testing performed on the skin of living animals, by exposure and observation times

Corrosive category (category 1) (applies to authorities not using subcategories)	Potential corrosive subclasses[a] (UN packing group classification[b])	Corrosive in at least 1 of 3 animals	
		Exposure	Observation
Corrosive	Corrosive subcategory 1A (I)	≤3 minutes	≤1 hour
	Corrosive subcategory 1B (II)	>3 minutes/≤1 hour	≤14 days
	Corrosive subcategory 1C (III)	>1 hour/≤4 hours	≤14 days

[a]Classifications designated by the United Nations (UN) Globally Harmonised System for the Classification and Labelling of Chemical Substances and Mixtures (GHS).
[b]Corresponding UN packing group classifications to be used for the transport of dangerous goods.

SOURCE: "Table 1.1. Skin Corrosive Category and Subcategories," in *Recommended Performance Standards for In Vitro Test Methods for Skin Corrosion,* National Institutes of Health, National Institute of Environmental Health Sciences, Interagency Coordinating Committee on the Validation of Alternative Methods (ICCVAM) and the National Toxicology Program (NTP) Interagency Center for the Evaluation of Alternative Toxicological Methods (NICEATM), May 2004, http://iccvam.niehs.nih.gov/methods/ps/ps044510.pdf (accessed January 3, 2007)

that regulate toxicity testing to accept validated methods. The NICEATM facilitates information sharing among all the parties involved.

Table 5.8 lists the alternative test methods that have been submitted to the ICCVAM for review and evaluation. Two of the tests are considered particularly promising: the local lymph node assay (LLNA) and Corrositex. The LLNA is a mouse-based test for determining if new chemicals cause allergic contact dermatitis (skin reactions). The traditional test for this condition used guinea pigs. The LLNA is reported to use fewer animals and cause much less pain and distress than the traditional test. It is also much faster. CAAT reports in "New Alternative Test Should Save Thousands of Guinea Pigs" (January 2000, http://altweb.jhsph.edu/news/2000/20000110.htm) that the LLNA has been accepted by the U.S. Environmental Protection Agency, the FDA, the Occupational Safety and Health Administration, and the Consumer Product Safety Commission as an alternative test method for assessing allergic contact dermatitis.

Corrositex is an in vitro (outside the body) test in which synthetic skin is used to test chemical irritancy. In vitro tests are commonly conducted in test tubes. The traditional test for skin irritancy relied on rabbits and could take several weeks. The new one takes just a few minutes or hours. Corrositex and other in vitro skin corrosion tests could be used to satisfy corrositivity test-

ing required by various agencies. The new tests would replace the current testing protocol in which corrosive substances are placed on the skin of living animals (usually rabbits) for specific lengths of time, as shown in Table 5.9. The extent of tissue damage in the animals is assessed after the exposure time to determine the corrositivity of the chemicals. The ICCVAM notes in *Recommended Performance Standards for In Vitro Test Methods for Skin Corrosion* (May 2004, http://iccvam.niehs.nih.gov/methods/ps/ps044510.pdf) that use of the new tests could "avoid pain and distress that may result from the application of corrosive substances to animals."

Pain and Distress

One of the goals of refinement is to relieve animal pain and distress. APHIS tracks the occurrence of pain and distress in regulated animals, as shown in Table 5.10. These numbers are based on reports by research institutions to APHIS for fiscal year 2004. As shown in Figure 5.8, 56% of the regulated animals experienced no pain or distress, 36% experienced pain or distress but were administered drugs for relief, and 8% suffered pain and distress but were not given drugs for relief. Hamsters and guinea pigs were the species most involved in experiments in which pain and distress were not relieved. More than sixty-seven thousand of them fell into this category during 2004. In addition, nearly twenty-seven hundred dogs, cats, and primates also suffered pain and distress that was not relieved.

Animal welfare groups express doubts about the validity of APHIS pain and distress numbers, saying that these numbers are greatly underreported by research institutions. In 1998 the HSUS launched a Pain and Distress

TABLE 5.10

Animals used in research at facilities registered with the U.S. Department of Agriculture (USDA), by species, and pain/distress and relief measures, fiscal year 2004

	No pain and/or distress—no drugs were needed for relief	Pain and/or distress—drugs were used for relief	Pain and/or distress—no drugs could be used for relief	Total animals used
Rabbits	148,125	106,447	7,001	261,573
Guinea pigs	148,077	72,255	23,772	244,104
Hamsters	82,533	49,889	43,299	175,721
All other covered species	106,471	56,568	8,273	171,312
Dogs	35,338	28,321	1,273	64,932
Non-human primates	27,827	26,131	1,040	54,998
Pigs	17,571	35,521	1,412	54,504
Other farm animals	23,564	8,224	168	31,956
Cats	14,074	9,188	378	23,640
Sheep	11,830	7,256	132	19,218
Total number of animals	**615,410**	**399,800**	**86,748**	**1,101,958**

SOURCE: Adapted from "Animals Used in Research: No Pain and/or Distress—No Drugs Were Needed for Relief (Category C)," "Animals Used in Research: Pain and/or Distress—Drugs Were Used for Relief (Category D)," and "Animals Used in Research: Pain and/or Distress—No Drugs Could Be Used for Relief (Category E)," in *Animal Care Reports: Annual Reports of Enforcement by Fiscal Year, 2004*, U.S. Department of Agriculture, Animal and Plant Health Inspection Service, 2004, http://www.aphis.usda.gov/ac/awreports/awreport2004.pdf (accessed November 28, 2006)

FIGURE 5.8

Pain and/or distress breakdown for animals used in research, fiscal year 2004

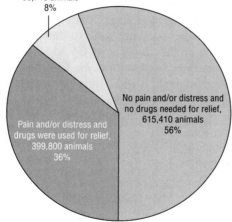

SOURCE: Adapted from "Animals Used in Research: No Pain and/or Distress—No Drugs Were Needed for Relief (Category C)," "Animals Used in Research: Pain and/or Distress—Drugs Were Used for Relief (Category D)," and "Animals Used in Research: Pain and/or Distress—No Drugs Could Be Used for Relief (Category E)," in *Animal Care Reports: Annual Reports of Enforcement by Fiscal Year, 2004*, U.S. Department of Agriculture, Animal and Plant Health Inspection Service, 2004, http://www.aphis.usda.gov/ac/awreports/awreport2004.pdf (accessed November 28, 2006)

The HSUS acknowledges that animal rights advocates want to eliminate animal testing, not reform it. The organization states, "The HSUS would like to see the day when animals are no longer used in harmful research. However, we believe the most urgent public priority is eliminating pain and distress among laboratory animals" (October 26, 2006, http://www.hsus.org/animals_in_research/pain_distress/pain_ distress_campaign/).

Scientists recognize that eliminating pain and distress in laboratory animals is not only humane but also good scientific practice. The animal use policy at Vanderbilt University, for example, acknowledges that experimental results can be compromised by a physical or mental state of distress in the subject and recommends relieving pain and distress in animal subjects.

One concept embraced by the HSUS is the use of humane endpoints. This means that test animals can be humanely euthanized after exhibiting specific symptoms of a disease rather than dying of the disease itself.

GENETIC ENGINEERING

Genetic engineering is the scientific manipulation of genetic material. Animals have been the subject of genetic engineering research and experiments for several decades. Transgenic animals are animals that carry a foreign gene that has been deliberately inserted through genetic engineering. They are widely used in biomedical research and pharmaceutical development. Most of these animals are farm animals. Raising these transgenic animals for the cultivation of pharmaceutical products is known as pharming. For example, scientists have pharmed transgenic sheep and goats that produce foreign proteins in their milk. Production of these proteins could have enormous medical and industrial benefits for humans. As of early 2007, pharmed substances were still

Initiative to focus attention on issues involved in assessing and relieving pain in laboratory animals. The HSUS publishes the quarterly newsletter *Pain and Distress Report* to publicize these issues. The goal of the initiative is to eliminate pain and distress in research animals by 2020.

in the development stage and had not yet been commercialized.

Another growing area of genetic engineering is xenotransplantation. The term *xeno* comes from the Greek word *xenos*, meaning "foreign" or "strange." In xenotransplantation organs from animals are transplanted into humans. Research continues on the genetic engineering of pigs so that they can grow organs that will not be rejected by human bodies. Scientists believe that harvesting organs from transgenic pigs could one day solve the human organ shortage that at present exists, saving millions of human lives. The technology is almost to the point of making this possible. Some people consider this to be medical progress, but others see it as another injustice perpetrated against animals for the sake of humans, noting that there would not be an organ shortage if more people were willing to become organ donors.

Cloning is a form of genetic manipulation in which a later-born genetic twin can be produced. In July 1996 the first mammal cloned from adult cells was born, a product of research at the Roslin Institute in Edinburgh, Scotland. Dolly was cloned from an udder cell taken from a six-year-old sheep. She was a fairly healthy clone and produced six lambs of her own. Before she was euthanized by lethal injection on February 14, 2003, Dolly had been suffering from lung cancer and arthritis. An autopsy (postmortem examination) of Dolly revealed that, other than her cancer and arthritis, she was anatomically like other sheep. (See Figure 5.9.) Between 1996 and 2007 other animals were cloned, including sheep, mice, cows, a gaur (an endangered Asian ox), goats, pigs, rabbits, dogs, and cats. Not all the animals have survived, and most have been born with compromised immunity and genetic disorders. Cloning is still new technology, and the success rate is low.

The company Genetic Savings and Clone financed the first successful cat cloning in 2001. It resulted in a cat that did not exactly duplicate the cat from which it was cloned. The company refined its cloning technique and in December 2004 made its first sale, receiving $50,000 for a cloned kitten named Little Nicky. The kitten was a twin to a Maine Coon cat named Nicky that died during early 2004. In February 2005 the company sold its second cloned cat (Little Gizmo) to an owner whose cat had died in 2004. However, lack of customers forced Genetic Savings and Clone to close at the end of 2006. Another company, ViaGen, banks tissue collected from pets for future cloning. Although ViaGen did not clone pets as of February 2007, it has successfully cloned livestock. The idea of pet cloning becoming commonplace is enormously disturbing to those in the animal rights and welfare movement, who note that the pet overpopulation

FIGURE 5.9

Dolly, the first cloned mammal. *Photograph by Jeff Mitchell. Archive Photos. Reproduced by permission.*

problem in the United States has already meant homelessness for billions of pets.

Besides the pet market, cloning also holds potential in other animal fields. Farmers may be able to vastly increase meat, milk, and egg production by cloning their best-producing animals. The scientific implications of cloning are impressive. It could benefit millions of people. Yet, the ethical questions are troubling to some.

A Gallup poll conducted in May 2006 found that 29% of those asked believed that cloning of animals was morally acceptable. (See Figure 5.10.) Lydia Saad reports in "Cloning Humans Is a Turn Off to Most Americans" (Gallup News Service, May 16, 2002) that in 2002, 38% of respondents favored the cloning of endangered species to keep them from becoming extinct. Only 15% favored the cloning of pets. Therefore, public support does not seem to be fully behind animal cloning, even though the practice proceeds in the laboratory.

FIGURE 5.10

Public opinion on the morality of cloning animals, May 2006

NEXT, I'M GOING TO READ YOU A LIST OF ISSUES. REGARDLESS OF WHETHER
OR NOT YOU THINK IT SHOULD BE LEGAL, FOR EACH ONE, PLEASE TELL ME
WHETHER YOU PERSONALLY BELIEVE THAT IN GENERAL IT IS MORALLY
ACCEPTABLE OR MORALLY WRONG. HOW ABOUT...CLONING ANIMALS?

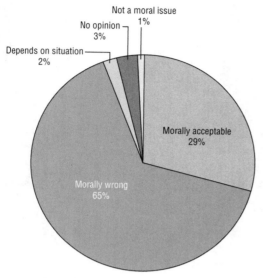

Not a moral issue
1%

No opinion
3%

Depends on situation
2%

Morally acceptable
29%

Morally wrong
65%

SOURCE: Adapted from *Gallup Poll Social Series: Moral Issues*, The
Gallup Organization, May 2006, http://www.galluppoll.com/content/
Default.aspx?ci=1681&pg=1&t=EgBIu3wMnGwfz1Z61o1DGiH.1G
FUccU9KJfoS%2fG1GD6xxF2x2qNLENH2teq7BVOyIniNuSHpq
TLe0Q0FdmvZMBRlNMxSTcvM7Z4C66obCYPsj.lisL-9YTWLGccI
A8VrxncH4EdzffG172ZCuEGrNDZrt1S27lJ4 (accessed November 17,
2006) Copyright © 2006 by The Gallup Organization. Reproduced by
permission of The Gallup Organization.

CHAPTER 6
ANIMALS IN SPORTS

The eleventh edition of *Merriam-Webster's Collegiate Dictionary* (2003) defines a sport as recreation that includes physical activity. Most people would think of a sport as an athletic competition that demonstrates skills such as physical strength, stamina, agility, and speed. Humans recognized centuries ago that many animals possess such skills naturally and could be used in sporting events.

In the United States today the major sports in which animals are involved are horse racing, greyhound racing, sled dog racing, rodeos, and organized animal fighting. Except for animal fighting, all these are considered legitimate sports.

The legitimate sports probably began as friendly competitions between people wanting to show off their animals, but the most popular evolved into businesses in which large amounts of money are involved. Horse racing and greyhound racing are intertwined with the legalized gambling industry. Rodeos and sled dog races largely depend on sponsors. Sponsors are companies that provide financial backing in exchange for being allowed to advertise during an event—for example, by placing advertisements around an arena, in programs, or on uniforms or vehicles. Even animal fighting has become a business of sorts, with profits driven almost entirely by illegal gambling.

In all these sports, skilled animals can be quite profitable for the people who own, train, and manage them. Some animals involved in the sports industry are well cared for during their athletic "careers"; others are horribly abused. Sports animals that are less skilled, injured, past their prime, or unwilling or unable to compete anymore have different prospects. Some retire and live comfortably, whereas others are sold to the slaughterhouse or are killed.

The fate and well-being of animals in sports lie in the hands of humans. To some animal rights activists, this is the root of the problem. They believe that animals should not be used by people for any purpose at all, including sports. Animal welfarists focus their attention on uncovering, publicizing, and outlawing practices in animal sports that they consider harmful to the animals. Animal participation is defended by insiders and fans who feel that their right to enjoy a recreational activity is being threatened by overzealous activists who do not understand the nature of these sports.

ROOTS OF ANIMAL SPORTS

All animal sports have their roots in historical customs: religious rituals; contests staged for audience entertainment; and warfare, hunting, and herding practices. Blood sports, such as animal fighting, may have their roots in animal sacrifice, but were really popularized by the Romans as entertainment. Thousands of wild animals died in Rome's Coliseum while doing battle with each other or with gladiators. These events were often more like slaughters than sports. The animals were usually tortured with hot spikes or even dabbed with burning pitch to make them fight more ferociously and violently.

Blood sports surged in popularity in Europe during the Middle Ages. These included bears, bulls, dogs, and cocks (roosters) fighting with each other in various forums. Baiting involved a large animal, such as a bull or bear, being set upon by a group of dogs. When legislation was passed in England and the United States outlawing bear- and bull-baiting, cockfighting and dogfighting became more popular. These blood sports required less space than baiting and could be conducted without drawing as much public attention.

Horse Racing

Sporting events involving horses have their origins in warfare, hunting, and herding practices, in which fast horses were a necessity. Archaeological records indicate that horse racing occurred in ancient Babylon, Syria, and Egypt. It was an event in the Greek Olympic Games as

TABLE 6.1

Horse sports other than racing and rodeos

Category	Description	Organizations
Cattle events	Cutting or herd work: Rider on horseback selects a single calf from a herd in the arena, guides it into the center of the arena, and then using fast starts and turns, prevents it from escaping back to the herd.	National Reined Cow Horse Association, National Reining Horse Association, National Cutting Horse Association, United States Team Penning Association
	Reining: Rider maneuvers horse through various moves, including figure-eight patterns, 360 degree spins, and sliding stops.	
	Cow work: Rider maneuvers horse to control the movements of a running steer, including herding it back and forth along a fence and circling around an arena.	
	Team penning or sorting: Team of 2 or 3 riders on horseback must cut specifically marked cattle from a herd and herd them to designated areas.	
Dressage	Rider moves horse through a series of carefully choreographed movements and patterns.	United States Dressage Federation
Endurance	Long-distance trail riding conducted over natural terrain.	American Endurance Ride Conference
Eventing or combined training	A three-in-one competition including dressage, cross-country jumping, and show jumping.	Fédération Equestre Internationale
Foxhunting	A sport in which riders and dogs hunt foxes in the countryside.	American Masters of Foxhound Association
Hunter-jumper	Equestrian event in which horses and riders jump over obstacles.	National Hunter and Jumper Association
Polo	Two teams of players riding thoroughbred horses play a game similar to hockey using a small ball and mallets.	United States Polo Association
Polocrosse	Combination of polo and lacrosse in which riders use racquets instead of mallets.	American Polocrosse Association
Ride and tie	Long-distance race in which two people and one horse form a racing team. During a race the people alternate riding the horse and running.	Ride and Tie Association
Steeple chase	Equestrian event in which horses and riders jump over fences.	National Steeplechase Association
Vaulting	Sport in which a rider uses gymnastic moves to vault onto and dismount from moving horse.	American Vaulting Association

SOURCE: Created by Kim Masters Evans for Thomson Gale

early as 664 BC. Selective breeding of horses dates back thousands of years and was practiced by the ancient Arabs and Romans. The Romans held chariot races in huge arenas called hippodromes, the most famous of which was the Circus Maximus.

Horse racing with riders became widespread during the Middle Ages, particularly in England. Knights returning from the Crusades brought back fast Arabian stallions that were bred with sturdy English mares to produce a new line of horses called Thoroughbreds. Thoroughbred racing was popular with the aristocrats and royalty of British society, earning it the title "Sport of Kings." Human dependence on the horse during hunting and herding led to the creation of many other competitions in which horses excelled, such as jumping over obstacles or chasing lost cows. Thus, rodeo sports were born.

Greyhound Racing

Greyhound racing probably began several millennia ago with the Bedouin tribes of Africa and Asia. It was popular with the Egyptian pharaohs and in ancient Greece and Rome. Aristocrats of the Middle Ages used greyhounds to hunt rabbits, deer, and foxes. During the 1500s Queen Elizabeth I is credited with inventing a hunting sport called coursing in which greyhounds were used to pursue hares. Greyhound racing came to be called the "Sport of Queens." It did not become popular in the United States until the 1800s.

SPORTS ANIMALS TODAY

The only animals used in major sports today are domesticated ones: horses, bovines (calves, bulls, and steers), dogs, and cocks.

Horses are the most versatile sporting animal, participating on a large scale in sports besides racing and rodeos. (See Table 6.1.) However, none of these sports are performed by horses alone. All of them include humans, who ride the horses, run alongside them, or are pulled behind in carts.

Although bovines are not nearly as glamorous as horses, they still play a major role in two organized sports: bullfighting and rodeos. Bullfighting has a long and illustrious past, but it has never caught on in North America. It is extremely popular in Spain and Portugal, some Latin American countries (Mexico, Peru, Colombia, Venezuela, and Ecuador), southern France, and the African island of Pemba. In Portugal the bull is not killed in the ring but may be slaughtered afterward.

Rodeos have a much shorter history. They evolved in North America to show off the work done by ranch hands and cowboys during the 1800s to herd and control cattle. Besides their dependence on bovines, bullfighting and rodeos are unique among sports for another reason. They are the only major animal sports in which humans compete against (or kill) animals.

Dogs participate on a large scale in three sports: sled dog racing, greyhound racing, and organized fighting. These sports differ widely in their legitimacy. Sled dog racing evolved as a sport to show off the skills of hardy dogs that have been pulling sleds in snowbound regions for centuries. By contrast, greyhound racing began as a competition between fast and graceful dogs but evolved into a gambling pastime. Organized dogfighting is illegal in every state. Despite its illegitimacy, or maybe because of it, dogfighting continues to be popular. Its roots lie in the blood sports enjoyed by the ancient Romans at the Coliseum.

All three of these dog sports are largely breed-specific: Malamutes (named for the Malemiut Inupiat tribe) and Siberian huskies compete in sled races, greyhounds in track racing, and pit bulls in fighting. Only sled dog racing pairs humans and dogs during the sporting event. Greyhound racing and dogfighting are dog-only competitions.

There are also a variety of new amateur sporting events that are emerging for dogs. Agility-based competitions, such as catching Frisbees and traversing obstacles, are growing in popularity. One of the newest dog sports is called fly ball. This is a relay event in which teams of dogs compete against each other to jump over hurdles and race to retrieve a ball. In 2000 the International Federation of Cynological Sports (IFCS) was formed in Europe to unite organizations holding dog sports in various countries around the world. (Cynology is the scientific study of canines.) The IFCS is working to bring dog sports, such as those involving agility, to the Olympic Games.

A cock is the adult male of the domestic fowl (*Gallus gallus*), also known as a rooster. Cocks participate in only one organized sport: cockfighting. Cockfighting is illegal in most states and is considered a blood sport because the roosters that participate are frequently killed or mutilated during the fight.

MAJOR ANIMAL SPORTS AND THEIR CONTROVERSIES

Animal sports enthusiasts argue that the animals are doing what they do naturally. Horses and greyhounds love to run, cocks naturally fight with each other in the barnyard, wild dogs fight over who will lead the pack, and unbroken livestock naturally try to buck off a rider. People involved in legitimate animal sports argue that the animals are well cared for because their welfare is crucial to the success of the sport and the people involved. In other words, they say it makes no sense for the owner or manager of a sports animal to mistreat that animal and perhaps lose money as a result. They also insist that safeguards are in place to ensure that animals are not mistreated during a sporting event and receive proper medical care if they are injured.

Critics counter by explaining that animal sports are not sports at all, but performances forced out of animals that have no choice in the matter. They believe that sports animals are not behaving naturally but doing things that they are either trained to do or have been bred over many generations to do. Because so much money is involved in animal sports, animal welfare and rights advocates say greed and financial advancement are the main motivators behind animal sports. General problems with animal sports revolve around four main issues:

- Overbreeding of the animals
- Mistreatment during training, performances, and the off-season
- Lack of veterinary care
- The ways in which unwanted sports animals are destroyed

Horse Racing

Thoroughbred horse racing is the king of animal sports in the United States. It is a multibillion-dollar industry involving people who breed, manage, train, own, and ride the horses, and the people who own and manage racetracks. Indirectly, the industry provides income to feed and equipment suppliers, veterinarians, and other support personnel. The industry is also a source of income for those state governments that allow gambling at racetracks and/or off-track betting locations.

THE RACES. The Jockey Club reports in "Thoroughbred Racing and Breeding Worldwide" (October 2, 2006, http://www.jockeyclub.com/factbook.asp?section=17) that in 2005 there were 52,257 Thoroughbred horse races in the United States. The total purse, or amount won by the owners of the winning horses, for all races was nearly $1.1 billion. As shown in Figure 6.1, the number of Thoroughbred races held each year has generally declined since 1995. Purses increased through the late 1990s as gambling increased in popularity around the country and by 2001 leveled off at just under $1.1 billion per year. (See Figure 6.2.)

As of 2007 there were about 130 Thoroughbred racetracks in the United States (http://www.trackinfo.com/index2.html). Some racetracks are only open seasonally, whereas those in warm climates are open year round. Racetracks vary in size and in ownership; some are government owned, and some are owned by private and public companies.

The three most prestigious Thoroughbred races in the United States are the Kentucky Derby at the Churchill Downs track in Kentucky, the Preakness Stakes at Pimlico in Maryland, and the Belmont Stakes at Belmont Park in New York. The races are held over a five-week period during May and June of each year. A horse that wins all three races in one year is said to have won the "Triple Crown." Only eleven horses have ever captured the Triple Crown—most recently, a horse named Affirmed in 1978.

WELFARE OF RACING HORSES. The racehorse industry prides itself on the enormous investments it has made in horse health issues. Millions of dollars have been spent on veterinarian research concerning the injuries and illnesses that affect racehorses. The Grayson-Jockey Club Research Foundation is the leading private source of funding for research into horse health issues. The foundation, which dates back to 1940, is operated by the Jockey Club,

FIGURE 6.1

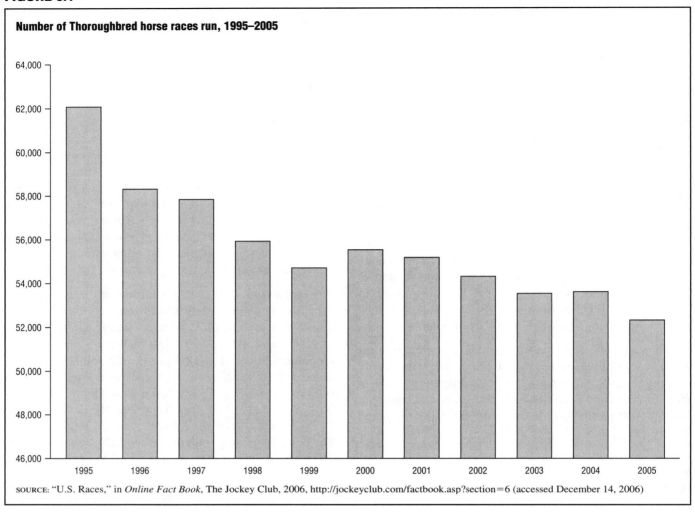

Number of Thoroughbred horse races run, 1995–2005

SOURCE: "U.S. Races," in *Online Fact Book*, The Jockey Club, 2006, http://jockeyclub.com/factbook.asp?section=6 (accessed December 14, 2006)

though it accepts donations from private individuals, Thoroughbred clubs, racetracks, and other organizations. In 2006 it allocated more than $957,000 to universities conducting equine research projects and has contributed more than $13 million since 1983 (2007, http://www.grayson-jockeyclub.org/default.asp). The foundation receives financial support from donations and from special racing events staged by horse racetracks. During 2006 the foundation funded research in a variety of illnesses and injuries found in horses.

Most animal welfare groups are opposed to horse racing and contend that racehorses are treated as investments rather than as living beings. Specifically, they offer the following reasons for opposing the sport:

- Thoroughbred racehorses have been inbred to the point that their bodies are too heavy for their slender, fragile legs.

- Broodmares are forced to come into season too often and at unnatural times to lengthen the potential training season for their offspring.

- Racehorses are drugged when they have injuries or illnesses (such as hairline fractures) so that they can still compete.

- Track surfaces are too hard.

- The racing season is too long.

- Horses are run too young, risking damage to bones that are not fully mature.

- The industry is regulated by state governments that have a vested interest in making the industry profitable, not in safeguarding animal welfare.

- Racehorses suffer injuries and deaths during training and races.

As shown in Table 6.2, there were 320 racehorse fatalities in California alone between 2004 and 2005. In addition, the California Horse Racing Board reports in the *Thirty-Fifth Annual Report of the California Horse Racing Board: A Summary of Fiscal Year 2004–2005 Racing in California* (2006, http://www.chrb.ca.gov/annual_reports/2005_annual_report.pdf) that 514 racing-related

FIGURE 6.2

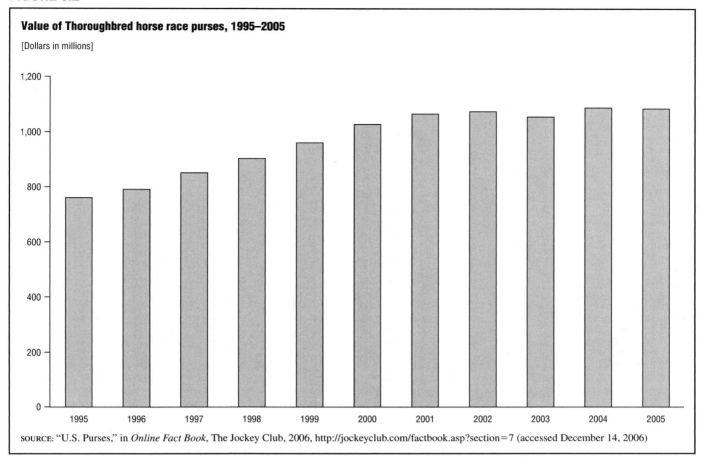

Value of Thoroughbred horse race purses, 1995–2005

[Dollars in millions]

SOURCE: "U.S. Purses," in *Online Fact Book*, The Jockey Club, 2006, http://jockeyclub.com/factbook.asp?section=7 (accessed December 14, 2006)

injuries to horses were reported in California for this same time period, most of them to Thoroughbreds.

The slaughter of racehorses is a particularly controversial topic. Ray Paulick reports in "Death of a Derby Winner: Slaughterhouse Likely Fate for Ferdinand" (*Blood-Horse Magazine*, July 25, 2003) that Ferdinand, the winner of the 1986 Kentucky Derby, was possibly slaughtered for meat in Japan. Demand for horse meat has skyrocketed in parts of Asia and Europe. Horses intended for human consumption cannot be injected with drugs, either as painkillers or as a humane method of euthanization. By contrast, horses sold to rendering plants can be given drugs for pain in transit and can be euthanized by lethal injection. Horses sold for horse meat are given no painkillers in transit, and when they reach the slaughterhouse, they are knocked unconscious, then have their throats cut (in the same way that cattle are slaughtered).

The U.S. Department of Agriculture's (USDA) Animal and Plant Health Inspection Service notes in *Horse Transport Yearly Report* (2006, http://www.aphis.usda.gov/vs/nahps/equine/horse_transport/yearly-rpt.html) that in 2004, 58,736 horses were slaughtered in the United States for human consumption overseas. It is unknown how many of these horses came from the racing industry. Animal welfare groups allege that many injured racehorses are

not humanely euthanized but are shipped off to slaughter without being given painkillers. Besides the three horse meat slaughterhouses in the United States (two in Texas and one in Illinois), there are several in Mexico and Canada. Welfarists complain that racehorses going to meat slaughterhouses travel for many hours in cramped carriers with no food or water.

In 1996 Congress passed the Commercial Transportation of Equines for Slaughter Act, but the regulations enforcing the act were not published until December 2001. According to the Humane Society of the United States (HSUS), in "Get the Facts on Horse Slaughter" (2007, http://www.hsus.org/pets/issues_affecting_our_pets/equine_protection/get_the_facts_on_horse_slaughter.html), the new rules allow the horses to be transported for up to twenty-eight hours without water, food, or rest.

RETIRED RACING HORSE ADOPTION. There are several organizations around the country that rescue retired racehorses and either adopt them out or provide lifetime sanctuary and care for them. Two of the largest are the Thoroughbred Retirement Fund (TRF) and the New Vocations Racehorse Adoption Program.

The TRF is a nonprofit organization founded in 1982 by Monique S. Koehler. Since 1986 it has placed thousands

TABLE 6.2

Racehorse fatalities in California, 2004–05

Associations		Breed of horse						Occurred during		
Thoroughbred	TB	QH	APP	AR	ST	P	Race	Train[a]	Other[a]
Los Angeles Turf Club	44	—	—	—	—	—	19	16	9
Churchill Downs Operating Co.	33	—	—	—	—	—	13	17	3
Del Mar Thoroughbred Club	17	—	—	—	—	—	7	7	3
Oak Tree Racing Assn.	24	—	—	—	—	—	10	9	5
Churchill Downs Fall Operating Co.	23	—	—	—	—	—	11	9	3
Bay Meadows Operating Co.	31	—	—	—	—	—	16	7	8
Bay Meadows Operating Co. (Fall)	11	—	—	—	—	—	6	2	3
Pacific Racing Assn.	23	—	—	—	—	—	13	7	3
Pacific Racing Assn.	14	—	—	—	—	—	9	2	3
Harness									
Capitol Racing LLC	—	—	—	—	6	—	1	1	4
Calif. Expo & State Fair[b]	—	—	—	—	—	—	—	—	—
Sacramento Harness Assn.[b]	—	—	—	—	—	—	—	—	—
Quarter horse	—	—	—	—	—	—	—	—	—
Los Alamitos	—	—	—	—	—	—	—	—	—
Quarter Horse Racing Assn.	9	35	1	3	—	2	29	10	11
Fairs									
Stockton (San Joaquin County Fair)	4	—	—	—	—	—	3	1	—
Pleasanton (Alameda County Fair)	4	—	—	—	—	—	2	2	—
Vallejo (Solano County Fair)	8	—	—	—	—	—	1	4	3
Santa Rosa (Sonoma County Fair)	7	—	—	—	—	—	3	1	3
San Mateo (San Mateo County Fair)		1	—	—	—	—	—	—	1
Ferndale (Humboldt County Fair)	1	—	—	—	—	—	1	—	—
Pomona (Los Angeles County Fair)	14	—	—	—	—	—	6	4	4
Fresno (Fresno District Fair)	5	—	—	—	—	—	4	—	1
Totals[c]	**272**	**36**	**1**	**3**	**6**	**2**	**154**	**99**	**67**

TB=Thoroughbreds
QH=Quarter horses
ST=Standardbreds
APP=Appaloosas
AR=Arabians
P=Paint
[a]Training and other fatalities include fatalities that occurred at auxiliary training facilities.
[b]No fatalities reported.
[c]Per breed and circumstance; total fatalities = 320.

SOURCE: "Racehorse Fatalities," in *Thirty-Fifth Annual Report of the California Horse Racing Board: A Summary of Fiscal Year 2004–2005 Racing in California*, California Horse Racing Board, 2006, http://www.chrb.ca.gov/annual_reports/2005_annual_report.pdf (accessed December 14, 2006)

of horses in adoptive homes, at horse sanctuaries, or in therapeutic programs for mentally and physically challenged people. The TRF also partners with several prison facilities around the country to operate work programs in which inmates feed and care for retired racehorses at stables built at the prisons. The article "TRF Caring for Record Number of Retired Horses" (*Renews*, Winter 2005) notes that the TRF took in 168 new horses in the fall of 2004, bringing its total to 903. Most of the new horses came from small racetracks in the Northeast and Midwest that closed after the racing season. The TRF purchased the horses to keep them from going to slaughterhouses. Many of the racehorses rescued by the TRF come from miserable conditions and suffer because of serious neglect and untreated medical conditions.

The New Vocations Racehorse Adoption Program adopts out retired racehorses (Thoroughbred and standardbred) at two facilities in Ohio. The group placed more than three hundred horses during 2006 (January 24, 2007, http://www.horseadoption.com/). The organization notes that most of the horses it has placed over the years had suffered injuries during their racing careers and required rehabilitation before placement. In addition, adopted racehorses must undergo training to be acceptable pleasure-riding horses. The program has strict requirements for people considering adoption and charges an adoption fee of several hundred dollars per horse, depending on its age and physical condition. Horses that are old and/or unrideable are sometimes adopted out for free.

Greyhound Racing

Greyhounds were brought to the United States during the late 1800s to help control the jackrabbit population on farms in the Midwest. Eventually, local farmers began holding races. Early races were held using a live rabbit to lure the dogs to race. In about 1912 Owen Patrick Smith invented a mechanical lure for this purpose. The first circular greyhound track opened in Emeryville, California, in 1919.

THE SPORT. In 2006 there were thirty-nine greyhound racetracks operating around the country. (See Table 6.3.)

TABLE 6.3

Number of greyhound racetracks, by participating state, September 2006

State	Number
Alabama	3
Arizona	2
Arkansas	1
Colorado	2
Florida	15
Iowa	2
Kansas	2
Massachusetts	2
New Hampshire	3
Rhode Island	1
Texas	3
West Virginia	2
Wisconsin	1

SOURCE: Adapted from "Racing States and the Number of Racetracks in Each," in *U.S. Greyhound Racing Fact Sheet*, Greyhound Network News and the Greyhound Protection League, September 2006, http://www.greyhounds.org/gpl/contents/PDFs/One_Page_Fact_Sheet_Sept%202006.pdf (accessed December 14, 2006)

Greyhound racing is most prevalent in Florida, where there are fifteen tracks, the most of any state. The Florida Department of Business and Professional Regulation, Division of Pari-Mutuel Wagering reports in *2005/2006 Permitholder Activity Report* (2006, http://www.state.fl.us/dbpr/pmw/statistics/2005_06/ytd_2005_06.pdf) that $477 million was wagered at the state's greyhound tracks during the fiscal years 2005 and 2006.

According to "Greyhound Racing Facts" (2007, http://www.hsus.org/pets/issues_affecting_our_pets/running_for_their_lives_the_realities_of_greyhound_racing/greyhound_racing_facts.html), the HSUS reports that revenue from greyhound racing declined by 45% in the 1990s, leading to closure or cessation of live racing at many tracks around the country. In addition, seven states specifically banned live greyhound racing during the 1990s: Idaho, Maine, North Carolina, Nevada, Vermont, Virginia, and Washington.

Three major organizations manage greyhound racing in the United States: the National Greyhound Association (NGA), the American Greyhound Track Operators Association (AGTOA), and the American Greyhound Council (AGC; a joint effort of the NGA and AGTOA). The NGA represents greyhound owners and is the official registry for racing greyhounds. All greyhounds that race on U.S. tracks must first be registered with the NGA. The AGTOA represents greyhound track operators. The AGC manages the industry's animal welfare programs, including farm inspections and adoptions.

The AGC (2006, http://www.agcouncil.com/racing.cfm?page=3) estimates that greyhound breeding farms and racing kennels pump approximately $96 million every year into local economies through the purchasing of goods and services.

WELFARE OF RACING GREYHOUNDS. The HSUS and other animal welfare organizations are strongly opposed to greyhound racing for the following reasons:

- It is not governed by the Animal Welfare Act (AWA) under the USDA as are other commercial animal enterprises, such as zoos and circuses.

- The industry severely overbreeds greyhounds in the hopes of producing winners, leading to the destruction of thousands of puppies each year.

- A racing greyhound's career is typically over at the age of four, well below its average life span of twelve years, meaning that thousands of adult dogs are also destroyed each year when they are no longer useful.

The AGC states that it has adopted standard guidelines for the care of greyhounds and the maintenance of kennel facilities based on the veterinary textbook *The Care of the Racing Greyhound* (2006). All the nation's greyhound breeding farms and kennels are subject to unannounced inspections to verify that they are complying with the industry's animal welfare guidelines. Violators can be expelled from the sport.

The AGC (2006, http://www.agcouncil.com/adoption.cfm?page=2) claims that greyhound tracks contribute about $2 million each year to local greyhound adoption programs and that twenty thousand dogs were adopted in 2005. The organization insists that more than 90% of all registered greyhounds are retired to farms for breeding purposes or adopted out as pets.

Animal welfare groups claim that thousands of adult greyhounds are destroyed each year by the racing industry. The Greyhound Protection League claims that 11,936 greyhounds were culled (killed) in 2005 alone. (See Table 6.4—note that some of these numbers are calculated from estimates.) The league believes that 606,633 greyhound puppies and adult dogs have been killed by the industry between 1986 and 2005.

MASS KILLING. David M. Halbfinger reports in "Dismal End for Race Dogs, Alabama Authorities Say" (*New York Times*, May 23, 2002) that in May 2002 Robert Leroy Rhodes was arrested and charged with felony animal cruelty after the remains of more than two thousand greyhounds were found on his property in Baldwin County, Alabama. The man, who worked as a security guard at the Pensacola Greyhound Park in Florida, claimed that the track paid him $10 a piece to shoot the dogs and dispose of their carcasses on his eighteen-acre farm. He admitted to performing the service for forty years at the request of race dog owners. Authorities report that autopsies indicate some of the dogs were not killed instantly and therefore suffered before they died. It is a felony in Alabama to torture an animal. Racetrack officials denied involvement in the case and fired Rhodes

TABLE 6.4

Estimated number of greyhounds bred, adopted, retained, and killed, 1986–2005

Year	Number of litters born (NGA)	Estimated number born	Dogs individually registered to race (NGA)	Farm puppies culled before racing	Estimated greyhounds adopted[b]	Estimated dogs retained for breeding	Racing dogs killed	Total killed
2005	4,300	28,036	26,207	1,829	14,600	1,500	10,107	11,936
2004	4,977	32,450	26,262	6,187	14,500	1,600	10,162	16,349
2003	5,171	33,714	26,277	7,437	14,500	1,800	9,977	17,414
2002	5,205	33,936	27,142	6,794	14,000	1,800	13,142	19,936
2001	5,015	32,698	26,797	5,901	13,000	1,800	11,997	17,898
2000	5,234	34,126	26,464	7,662	13,000	2,000	11,464	19,126
1999	5,266	34,334	27,059	7,275	13,000	2,000	12,059	19,334
1998	5,034	32,822	26,036	6,786	13,000	2,000	11,036	17,822
1997	5,192	33,852	28,025	5,827	12,500	2,000	13,525	19,352
1996	5,438	35,456	28,877	6,579	12,000	2,000	13,977	21,456
1995	5,749	37,483	31,688	5,795	10,000	2,100	19,588	25,383
1994	6,232	40,633	34,746	5,887	8,500	2,200	24,046	29,933
1993	6,805	44,369	39,139	5,230	6,000	2,500	30,639	35,869
1992	7,690	50,139	38,023	12,116	3,000	2,500	32,523	44,639
1991	8,049	52,479	38,430	14,049	1,000	3,500	33,930	47,979
1990	9,473	61,764	38,615	23,149	650	3,200	34,765	57,914
1989	7,690	50,139	38,443	11,696	450	3,000	34,993	46,689
1988	7,979	52,023	37,784	14,239	300	2,750	34,734	48,973
1987	7,638	49,800	33,021	16,779	200	2,500	30,321	47,100
1986	6,688	43,606	30,219	13,387	75	2,000	28,144	41,531
Total[a]	124,825	813,859	629,254	184,604	164,275	44,750	421,129	606,633

Notes:
Litters: As reported by the National Greyhound Association (NGA), the U.S. registry organization.
Total born: Derived by multiplying the total number of litters by an average of 6.52 pups per litter.
Individuals registered to race: As reported by the NGA in the *The Greyhound Review*, the official industry publication. Each owner pays an additional fee to the NGA to have a dog individually registered.
Culled: This column shows the total number of young dogs that disappear annually between birth and individual registration at 18 months of age. Few pups or young dogs are ever delivered to rescue groups.
Organized, large-scale adoption efforts did not take place until the mid 1990's. During the late 1980's it is estimated that only a few hundred dogs made it into adoptive homes nationwide. During the previous 50 years of dog racing, all greyhounds that were not used for breeding were routinely destroyed.
[a]To arrive at an estimated eighteen-year total of greyhounds killed, one must also subtract the number of dogs still in racing system (approximately 38,000), the number of puppies/youngsters currently at farms (approximately 26,000) and the breeding stock required to produce thousands of litters a year (about 500 males and 3,000 females).
[b]A liberal estimate of figures from those in the adoption community.

SOURCE: Adapted from "U.S. Racing Greyhound Breeding Statistics and Analysis of the Annual Numbers of Dogs Killed from 1986–2005," in *Know the Facts about Greyhound Racing*, Greyhound Protection League, 2006, http://www.greyhounds.org/gpl/contents/PDFs/Know_The_Facts_Sept06.pdf (accessed December 14, 2006)

along with several other security guards and a kennel operator.

Alabama authorities eventually charged four greyhound owners and trainers under the state's animal cruelty law based on statements from Rhodes and Clarence Ray Patterson, a kennel owner at the Pensacola Greyhound Track. At an April 2004 hearing, the Baldwin County sheriff testified that Rhodes, who died in 2003, had admitted killing between two thousand and three thousand greyhounds that were too sick or old to race. Florida investigators testified that Florida kennel owners and trainers paid Rhodes to shoot unwanted greyhounds because it was cheaper than having the animals humanely euthanized by a veterinarian. However, in 2005 the defendants' lawyers succeeded in having the case dropped after arguing that insufficient evidence existed and that the deceased Rhodes could not be cross-examined.

CONCERNS ABOUT DRUGGING. Alan Snel reports in "Drugs Taint Integrity of Greyhound Races" (*Tampa Tribune*, May 3, 2004) that forty-four racing greyhounds in Florida tested positive for cocaine following their races

during fiscal year 2003. In total, Snel notes, 119 greyhounds had tested positive for cocaine since 2001. Owners of greyhounds testing positive were forced to forfeit their winnings, but there was no recourse for bettors who had wagered on greyhounds that might have won if the drugged dogs had been disqualified. Drug test results are not obtained until several weeks after a race has run. Rapid-screening tests that could provide results at the race track are considered too expensive by the greyhound racing industry.

Snel questions why state officials did not investigate how the drugs had gotten into the dogs' systems. The president of the National Greyhound Association suggested that the cause could be trace amounts of cocaine on the hands of trainers or other people touching the dogs. State officials denied that trainers were purposely drugging greyhounds to influence race outcomes.

In "Gaming Industry Bets on Davis—and Crist" (*Miami Herald*, September 24, 2006), Mary Ellen Klas reports that Florida greyhound racing tracks had contributed hundreds of thousands of dollars to the campaign funds of the gubernatorial candidates Charlie Crist (Republican) and Jim Davis (Democrat). Both candidates had indicated a willingness to expand gambling activities at existing racetracks in the state—a move staunchly opposed by the outgoing Governor Jeb Bush. According to Klas, the greyhound industry is especially keen to install video lottery terminals at the racetracks that would allow gamblers to compete against one another to win money. In November 2006 Crist won the election and assumed office in January 2007.

Sled Dog Racing

The sport of sled dog racing is small but extremely popular throughout Alaska, Canada, and parts of northern Europe. In North America the sport traces its origins to Native Americans, who for centuries have used hardy dogs bred for cold weather to pull their sleds. Typical draft animals, such as horses and oxen, were unsuitable for this purpose because of their weight and food requirements.

IDITAROD. The most famous sled dog race is called the Iditarod. It is held in Alaska in early March of each year and includes dozens of teams competing for thousands of dollars in prize money. In general, the race covers roughly 1,150 miles (from Anchorage to Nome, Alaska) and is completed in anywhere from eight to sixteen days. The speed record (set in 2002) is eight days, twenty-two hours, and forty-six minutes. Just over $750,000 in prize money was awarded to winning racers for the 2005 Iditarod (February 2, 2007, http://www.iditarod .com/learn/2006results.html).

Mushers (human sled drivers) are allowed to start the Iditarod with up to sixteen dogs. A typical team includes fifteen dogs, one of which is the leader. The others are arranged in pairs behind the lead dog. The pair closest to the sled carries the heaviest load among the dogs. No dog substitutions are allowed during the race. If one or more dogs drop out for any reason, they cannot be replaced. The remainder carry the load. The dogs wear booties on their paws to help protect against cuts and abrasions.

The Iditarod includes about twenty-four checkpoints along the way. Each team is required to take three breaks during the race: one twenty-four-hour break and two eight-hour breaks. Mushers leave dogs that are sick, tired, or injured at one of the checkpoints for transport back to the starting point. According to race officials, each checkpoint has a veterinarian available.

Hazards of the race include the weather conditions, wildlife, and unpredictable terrain. Temperatures can drop to as low as −40° F during the race. However, unusually warm temperatures (up to 50° F) are also a problem as they can contribute to heat stress in the dogs and cause spoilage of dog food stored along the route.

The Iditarod received little media attention outside of Alaska until 1985, when a woman (Libby Riddles) won the race for the first time. Another woman, Susan Butcher, won the Iditarod four times between 1986 and 1990. The resulting publicity not only boosted the profile of the race but also brought more scrutiny and criticism from animal welfare organizations.

WELFARE OF SLED DOGS. The HSUS opposes the Iditarod Trail Sled Dog Race, arguing that the sled dogs are forced to run "too far and too fast" in brutal weather and racing conditions. Critics point out that the pressure to run the Iditarod faster every year pushes the dogs beyond their limits.

In addition, the HSUS lists in "Facts about the Iditarod" (2007, http://www.hsus.org/pets/issues_affecting _our_pets/facts_about_the_iditarod.html) the following problems:

- The race experiences dog deaths and injuries almost every year.

- At least 120 sled dogs are known to have died during the race since its inception, including fifteen to nineteen dogs in the first race alone. Two dogs died in 2001, one dog died in 2002, and one dog died in 2003. Dogs have died from heart and other organ failures because of overexertion, pneumonia, and injuries, including being strangled in towlines (the ropes that stretch from the dogs' harnesses to the sled) and rammed by sleds.

- At least three mushers have been disqualified from races for beating or kicking dogs or forcing dogs to run through dangerously deep slush. Two of the dogs in these cases died.

- Race dogs have suffered heat stress, dehydration, diarrhea, pulled tendons, and cut paws because of their participation in the Iditarod.

- Sled dog breeders kill puppies that are unable or unwilling to become good racers.

The HSUS also notes that most sled dogs are confined to short tethers in large dog yards when they are not racing. Tethering as a means of primary confinement is not permitted by the USDA for its licensed dog breeders and is opposed by the HSUS.

Iditarod mushers and supporters acknowledge that the race is grueling and can be dangerous, but they believe that sufficient rules and safeguards are in place to protect the dogs from injury and abuse. Many people involved in the sport believe that the dangers and wildness of the race enhance its allure.

The Sled Dog Action Coalition (SDAC) is another organization opposed to the Iditarod. Founded in 1999 by

a former schoolteacher, the SDAC (2006, http://
www.helpsleddogs.org/remarks.htm) lists hundreds of
quotes from newspaper reporters, mushers, and other
sources regarding abuses and mishaps that take place
during racing and training. The SDAC calls for specific
reforms to be made in race procedures to ensure the
safety of the sled dogs.

Rodeos

The word *rodeo* comes from the Spanish word
rodear, meaning "to surround." Originally, a rodeo was
a roundup of cattle that happened once or twice per year.
Open-range grazing was common in western North
America during the 1800s, and cowboys were hired to
round up the cattle and herd them to market. Following
these cattle drives, as they were called, the cowboys
would often congregate and hold informal contests to
show off their skills at riding and roping.

THE RODEO BUSINESS. Rodeos now take place all
over North America, even in big cities. They are seen
by their fans as wholesome family entertainment that
glorifies the rugged and hardworking cowboys of the
Old West.

Animal welfare groups estimate that several thousand
rodeos take place each year. Professional rodeo stars
travel from event to event and compete for millions of
dollars in prize money. Most big-money rodeos in the
United States are sponsored by the Professional Rodeo
and Cowboy Association (PRCA). Besides professional
rodeos, the organization also sponsors amateur rodeo
events for children and youth.

The animals used in rodeos include horses, bulls,
steers (male cattle that have been castrated before reach-
ing sexual maturity), and calves. Typical rodeo events
include bareback bull riding, saddle bronc riding (in
which a bucking horse, or bronco, is ridden), bareback
horse riding, steer wrestling, calf and steer roping, and
barrel racing (in which riders guide their horses around
barrels positioned around an arena).

WELFARE OF RODEO ANIMALS. The PRCA defends
the treatment of animals used in rodeos it sponsors,
claiming that it has an extensive animal welfare program that governs the care and handling of rodeo animals and requires that a veterinarian be on-site during a
rodeo. The PRCA posts an undated booklet on its Web
site that it says includes "current" information on injury statistics compiled by on-site veterinarians at PRCA rodeos.
As of May 2007 "Animal Welfare: The Care and Treatment of Professional Rodeo Livestock" (http://prorodeo
.org/pdfs/AnimalWelfare.pdf) notes that out of 60,971 animal exposures there were only twenty-seven animal injuries. No information is provided on the rodeo events or
dates associated with these statistics.

Animal welfare organizations are opposed to rodeos.
They argue that rodeos are not representative of Old West
ranching ways but are businesses that use animals as
pieces of athletic equipment. They say that most injured
rodeo animals are not humanely euthanized but are sent
to slaughterhouses without receiving veterinary attention
or painkillers. They also point out that today's rodeo
animals are not naturally wild and unbroken as they
might have been when rodeos first started in the 1800s
but are relatively tame animals that must be physically
provoked into displaying wild behavior. This is particularly true for the bucking animals.

Rodeo opponents say that bucking is unnatural
behavior provoked in rodeo animals by tormenting them
with painful straps and spurs. They also claim that bucking animals are sometimes poked with cattle prods or
sharp sticks or rubbed with caustic ointments right before
they are released from their chutes to incite more frenzied
bucking action during the ride.

The PRCA notes that bucking horses do wear flank
straps that encourage them to kick their legs high in the air.
However, the PRCA requires that the flank strap be lined
with fleece or neoprene and placed loosely around the
horses. The animal rights group People for the Ethical
Treatment of Animals (PETA) says on its antirodeo Web
site (http://bucktherodeo.com/) the straps are cinched
tightly around the animals' sensitive abdomen and groin
areas, causing the animals to buck to try to throw off the
painful devices. The PRCA denies that the straps are pulled
tight, arguing that a tight strap would actually restrict a
horse's movement and not permit it to jump into the air.

Riders in several rodeo events wear and use spurs.
The PRCA requires that the spur points be dull and that
the wheel-like rowels on the spurs be able to roll along
the animal's hide, rather than be locked. The organization
contends that this prevents any injury to the animal from
spurring. Riders who violate these rules or injure an
animal are subject to disqualification. PETA argues that
even dull spurs are painful because they are kicked into
the animals' sides. It compares being poked by a dull
spur to being hit by a hammer.

Cockfighting

Cockfighting is performed by cocks outfitted with
sharp spikes called gaffs on their legs. Two cocks are
thrown into a pit together, where they fight to the death.
Cockfighting was banned by most states during the
1800s. As of 2006, it was illegal in forty-eight states.
(See Table 6.5.) It was a felony in thirty-three states and a
misdemeanor offense in seventeen others. States differ in
their treatment of cockfight spectators and those caught
in possession of birds for fighting.

Because cockfighting is still legal in Louisiana and
New Mexico and in Mexico and many Asian countries,

TABLE 6.5

Laws and loopholes regarding cockfighting, by state, November 2006

State	Cockfighting: on the law books	Cockfighting: a felony or a misdemeanor	Loophole: possession of cocks for fighting	Loophole: being a spectator at a cockfight	Loophole: possession of implements
Alabama	Code of Ala. § 13A-12-4	Misdemeanor	Legal	Legal	Legal
Alaska	Alaska Stat. § 11.61.145	Felony	Felony	Misdemeanor[h]	Legal
Arizona	A.R.S. § 13-2910.03, A.R.S. § 13-2910.04	Felony	Felony	Misdemeanor	Legal
Arkansas	§ 5-62-101	Misdemeanor[b]	Legal	Legal	Legal
California	Cal Pen Code § 597b Cal Pen Code § 597j Cal Pen Code § 597c Cal Pen Code § 597i	Felony[c]	Misdemeanor	Misdemeanor	Misdemeanor
Colorado	C.R.S. 18-9-204	Felony	Felony	Felony	Felony
Connecticut	Conn. Gen. Stat. § 53-247i	Felony	Felony	Felony	Legal
Delaware	11 Del. C. § 1326	Felony	Felony	Misdemeanor	Legal
Florida	Fla. Stat. § 828.122	Felony	Felony	Felony	Felony
Georgia	O.C.G.A. § 16-12-4	Felony[d]	Legal	Legal	Legal
Hawaii	HRS § 711-1109	Misdemeanor	Legal	Legal	Legal
Idaho	Idaho Code § 25-3506	Misdemeanor	Legal	Misdemeanor	Legal
Illinois	510 ILCS 70/4.01	Felony[e]	Felony[e]	Misdemeanor	Misdemeanor
Indiana	Burns Ind. Code Ann. § 35-46-3-9, Burns Ind. Code Ann. § 35-46-3-8, Burns Ind. Code Ann. § 35-46-3-10, Burns Ind. Code Ann. § 35-46-3-8.5	Felony	Misdemeanor	Misdemeanor	Misdemeanor
Iowa	Iowa Code § 717D.2, Iowa Code § 717D.4	Felony	Felony	Misdemeanor	Felony
Kansas	K.S.A. § 21-4319	Misdemeanor	Legal	Misdemeanor	Legal
Kentucky	KRS § 525.130	Misdemeanor	Legal	Misdemeanor	Legal
Louisiana		Legal[f]	Legal	Legal	Legal
Maine[a]	17 M.R.S. § 1033	Felony	Felony	Misdemeanor	Legal
Maryland	Md. CRIMINAL LAW Code Ann. § 10-608, Md. CRIMINAL LAW Code Ann. § 10-605	Felony	Felony	Misdemeanor	Felony
Massachusetts	ALM GL ch. 272, § 94, ALM GL ch. 272, § 95	Felony	Felony	Misdemeanor	Legal
Michigan	MCLS § 750.49	Felony	Felony	Felony	Felony
Minnesota	Minn. Stat. § 343.31	Felony	Felony	Misdemeanor	Legal
Mississippi	Miss. Code Ann. § 97-41-11	Misdemeanor	Legal	Legal	Legal
Missouri	§ 578.173 R.S.Mo.	Felony	Legal	Misdemeanor	Misdemeanor
Montana	Mont. Code Anno., § 45-8-210	Felony	Felony	Legal	Legal
Nebraska	R.R.S. Neb. § 28-1005	Felony	Felony	Felony	Legal
Nevada	Nev. Rev. Stat. Ann. § 574.070	Felony[e]	Legal	Felony[e]	Legal
New Hampshire	RSA § 644:8-a	Felony	Felony	Felony	Legal
New Jersey[a]	N.J. Stat. § 4:22-24, N.J. Stat. § 4:22-26	Felony	Felony	Felony	Legal
New Mexico		Legal[g]	Legal	Legal	Legal
New York	NY CLS Agr & M § 351	Felony	Misdemeanor	Misdemeanor	Legal
North Carolina	N.C. Gen. Stat. § 14-362	Felony	Legal	Felony	Legal
North Dakota	N.D. Cent. Code, § 36-21.1-07	Felony	Felony	Misdemeanor	Legal
Ohio	ORC Ann. 959.15, ORC Ann. 959.99	Misdemeanor	Misdemeanor	Misdemeanor	Legal
Oklahoma	21 Okl. St. § 1692.2, 21 Okl. St. § 1692.5, 21 Okl. St. § 1692.6 21 Okl. St. § 1692.3,	Felony	Felony	Misdemeanor	Felony
Oregon	ORS § 167.428, ORS § 167.431	Felony	Felony	Misdemeanor	Misdemeanor[j]
Pennsylvania	18 Pa.C.S. § 5511	Felony	Felony	Felony	Legal
Rhode Island	R.I. Gen. Laws § 4-1-9, R.I. Gen. Laws § 4-1-10, R.I. Gen. Laws § 4-1-11	Felony	Felony	Felony	Legal
South Carolina	S.C. Code Ann. § 16-17-650	Misdemeanor	Legal	Misdemeanor	Legal
South Dakota	§ 40-1-9	Misdemeanor	Legal	Misdemeanor	Legal
Tennessee	Tenn. Code Ann. § 39-14-203	Misdemeanor	Misdemeanor	Misdemeanor	Legal
Texas	Tex. Penal Code § 42.09	Felony	Legal	Legal	Legal
Utah	Utah Code Ann. § 76-9-301 Utah Code Ann. § 76-9-301.5	Misdemeanor	Legal	Misdemeanor	Legal
Vermont	13 V.S.A. § 352, 13 V.S.A. § 353	Felony	Felony	Felony	Legal
Virginia	Va. Code Ann. § 3.1-796.125	Misdemeanor	Legal	Misdemeanor[i]	Legal
Washington	Rev. Code Wash. (ARCW) § 16.52.117	Felony	Felony	Felony	Legal
West Virginia	W. Va. Code § 61-8-19a, W. Va. Code § 61-8-19, W. Va. Code § 61-8-19b	Misdemeanor	Misdemeanor	Misdemeanor	Legal

there is a commercial breeding industry in the United States. However, the AWA prohibits the interstate transport of birds for cockfighting into states with laws against cockfighting. As of 2005, the act also prohibited the transport of fighting gamecocks into or out of states where cockfighting is still legal and banned the exporting of fighting gamecocks to foreign countries.

In May 2004 the Louisiana House Agriculture Committee voted to defeat a bill that would have banned

TABLE 6.5

Laws and loopholes regarding cockfighting, by state, November 2006 [CONTINUED]

State	Cockfighting: on the law books	Cockfighting: a felony or a misdemeanor	Loophole: possession of cocks for fighting	Loophole: being a spectator at a cockfight	Loophole: possession of implements
Wisconsin	Wis. Stat. § 951.08, Wis. Stat. § 951.18	Felony	Felony	Misdemeanor	Legal
Wyoming	wyo.stat. § 6-3-203				
	48 Illegal	33 Felony	25 Felony	12 Felony	6 Felony
	2 Legal	16 Misdemeanor	7 Misdemeanor	29 Misdemeanor	5 Misdemeanor
		2 legal	18 Legal	9 Legal	39 Legal
Washington DC	§ 22-1015	Felony	Felony	Misdemeanor	Legal
American Samoa	Legal	Legal	Legal	Legal	Legal
Guam	Legal	Legal	Legal	Legal	Legal
Puerto Rico	Legal	Legal	Legal	Legal	Legal
Virgin Islands	Legal	Legal	Legal	Legal	Legal

[a]These states do not use the terms "felony" or "misdemeanor", but rather have felony and misdemeanor equivalent penalties.
[b]While it is not specifically prohibited by state law, cockfighting can be prosecuted under the general anti-cruelty statute.
[c]A second or subsequent offense can be a felony. Felony charges may also be leveled against persons responsible for the mutilation of birds.
[d]While it is not specifically prohibited by state law, cockfighting can be prosecuted under the general anti-cruelty statute which includes felony level provisions.
[e]A repeat offense can trigger felony prosecution.
[f]Cockfighting is legal under state law but has been prohibited in 9 Louisiana parishes [*Orleans, Saint Bernard, Jefferson, East Baton Rouge, Lafayette, Beauregard, Plaquemines, Caddo, and Calcasieu*].
[g]Cockfighting is legal under state law but has been prohibited in 13 New Mexico counties [*Bernadillo, Cibola, Colfax, Doña Ana, Grant, Los Alamos, McKinley, Rio Arriba, Sandoval, San Juan, San Miguel, Santa Fe, Taos*] and 28 municipalities [*Albuquerque, Aztec, Belen, Bernalillo, Bosque Farms, Clayton, Corrales, Deming, Espanola, Eunice, Ft. Sumner, Gallup, Grants, Hobbs, Las Cruces, Las Vegas, Lordsburg, Los Lunas, Los Ranchos de Alb, Raton, Rio Rancho, Ruidoso, Santa Fe, Silver City, Taos, Truth or Consequences, Tucumcari, Williamsburg*]
[h]First offense is a violation, second offense is a misdemeanor.
[i]Being a spectator is illegal only when an admission fee is paid.
[j]Cockfighting and dogfighting paraphernalia illegal.

SOURCE: "Cockfighting: State Laws," in *Humane Society of the United States Fact Sheet*, Humane Society of the United States, November 2006, http://files.hsus.org/web-files/PDF/cockfighting_statelaws.pdf (accessed December 14, 2006)

---

cockfighting in the state. A majority of the commissioners felt that cockfighting was of cultural and economic importance to Louisiana.

According to Drew Jubera, in "The Fight of Its Life" (*Atlanta Journal and Constitution*, March 9, 2003), the Louisiana cockfighting industry generates millions of dollars in revenue. The state has more than seventy cockfighting pits that draw spectators from across the country. The larger pits can seat hundreds of people and charge gamecock owners as much as $1,000 to participate in a fight. Winners can earn $50,000 in these matches. Superior gamecocks sell for up to $300 each.

Jubera interviewed people involved in cockfighting to find out why they participated in it. Most said that they admired the natural fighting talents of cocks. Although they admitted that cockfighting was violent, they did not think that it was cruel to the birds. One breeder insisted that it would be crueler to keep the birds from fighting, because they love fighting so much.

In April 2006 the HSUS filed a legal petition demanding that the U.S. Postal Service discontinue delivery of two magazines—*The Gamecock* and *The Feathered Warrior*. The HSUS claims that the magazines promote cockfighting activities by listing schedules of cockfighting events and including advertising for gamecocks and implements used in cockfighting. Both magazines are published in Arkansas. The petition was filed under provisions of the AWA that prohibit the use of the U.S. mail for promoting animal fighting. In February 2007 the HSUS filed a lawsuit against Amazon.com for carrying the two magazines.

Dogfighting

Dogfighting is widely considered to be one of the most horrific forms of animal abuse—by members of animal welfare groups, criminal justice representatives, and law enforcement officials. In the United States dogfighting is an illegal, multimillion-dollar gambling industry, often associated with gangs, auto theft, arms smuggling, money laundering, and drug trafficking. Dogs most often used in dogfighting are pit bulls, which are not considered a specific breed but are rather a mix of breeds, the most predominant being the American Staffordshire terrier. Because pit bulls are extremely loyal to their owners and have powerful, muscular bodies and strong jaws, they can be bred and trained to exhibit aggressive behavior toward other dogs, although all pit bulls are not necessarily aggressive by nature. Fights typically go on for hours, sometimes to the death. Generally, a fight goes on until a dog gives up or an owner concedes defeat. Dogs that survive the fights frequently die hours or days later because of shock, blood loss, or infection. Bets placed in the range of $10,000 to $50,000 are typical during a dogfight.

Fighting dogs are judged on their gameness, which is determined by a dog's willingness and eagerness to fight and its reluctance to yield or back down during the fight. Selective breeding and grueling, cruel training methods are used to enhance gameness. Fighting dogs are usually drugged with steroids and other stimulants to enhance their aggression.

The article "They Don't Eat Quiche, But They Like Dogfighting" (*WAGER: Weekly Addiction Gambling Education Report*, December 13, 2000) discusses research findings on the cultural aspects of dogfighting in the southern United States. Researchers interviewed thirty-one men involved in dogfighting in Louisiana and Mississippi. They found that dogfighting was closely associated with the men's need to assert their masculinity. A "game" dog brought the owner status and prestige among other dog owners. Any dog showing cowardice or a willingness to quit reflected poorly on its owner's masculinity and was killed.

Fighting dogs are often trained on treadmills or devices called catmills. A catmill holds an animal, such as a cat, rabbit, or small dog, just out of reach of the training dog while it runs. Police report that these bait animals are often pets stolen from local neighborhoods and are usually killed during the training. Mild-tempered pit bulls that show no fighting inclinations are also used as bait dogs. Maryann Mott reports in "U.S. Dog-Fighting Rings Stealing Pets for 'Bait'" (*National Geographic News*, February 18, 2004) that pet theft by dogfighting rings was on the rise in the United States.

Dogfighting is illegal in all fifty states. (See Table 6.6.) It is a felony in forty-eight states and a misdemeanor in two others. Even being a spectator at a dogfight is a felony in some states. Possession of a dog for fighting is illegal in forty-seven states.

Animal welfare groups and police departments across the United States want to strengthen state and federal laws to make possession of a fighting dog a felony in every state. They also ask major newspapers not to accept advertisements selling dogs that use descriptive words such as *game dog* or *game bred*, as these terms imply that the dog is intended for fighting. The HSUS asks people to notify the organization whenever such ads appear in their local newspapers.

The article "Police Seize 36 Pit Bulls in Dog-Fighting Bust" (*Charlotte Observer*, January 22, 2007) provides an estimate from the North Carolina program manager for the HSUS that as many as fifty thousand people around the United States were dog fighters. In "Blood Sport: A Dramatic Rise in Illegal Dogfighting Overwhelms Authorities and Strikes Fear in Some Neighborhoods" (*Columbus Dispatch*, May 5, 2002), Kathy Lynn Gray reports that incidents increased by approximately 300% between 1992 and 2002. Law enforcement and animal control officers across the country report huge increases in the number of pit bulls they have confiscated in recent years. One county in Ohio seized nearly two thousand pit bulls in 2002. More than half of the dogs showed injuries or scars typical of fighting dogs.

The article "Dogs' Blood Brings Big Bucks" (ABCNews.com, January 28, 2003) reports on the growing concern of police in dealing with organized dogfights. The report describes a raid at a Columbus, Ohio, auto body shop in which forty people were arrested and nearly $25,000 in cash was confiscated, along with some handguns and drugs. The spectators had come from as far away as Alabama to see the fight. Police believe that dogfighting has changed from a small-time rural activity to a well-organized business that advertises over the Internet. They are increasingly concerned about the number of drug dealers and gang members they see involved in dogfighting and the large amounts of money that are bet.

The HSUS reports in "Busts Rout Out Dogfighters in Texas and Florida" (January 14, 2005, http://www.hsus.org/hsus_field/animal_fighting_the_final_round/busts_rout_out_dogfighters_in_texas_and_florida.html) that in January 2005 Texas authorities uncovered the largest dogfighting event in state history. A raid in Bexar County resulted in the arrest of more than twenty-five people and seizure of ninety pit bulls. Texas authorities received tips about the dogfight from the HSUS. HSUS activists monitor Web sites and magazines devoted to game dogs and alert police when they believe a dogfight is going to take place.

In 2006 the HSUS successfully convinced many national retailers to stop selling the DVD *Hood Fights, Vol. 2: The Art of the Pit*, which allegedly shows violent and bloody scenes from staged pit bull fights. According to "'Hood Fights II' Down for the Count" (July 7, 2006, http://www.hsus.org/hsus_field/animal_fighting_the_final_round/recent_activities/hood_fights_ii_pulled.html), the HSUS notes that major companies including Circuit City, Best Buy, and Netflix dropped the DVDs after learning that the videos may violate federal law. The Punishing Depictions of Animal Cruelty law prohibits the "depiction of animal cruelty with the intention of placing that depiction in interstate or foreign commerce for commercial gain." The HSUS notes that it has contacted legal authorities in Texas, the state where the DVD was produced, about prosecuting the producers under federal law.

Federal Legislation against Animal Fighting

In late 2006 Congress considered, but did not act on, legislation that would strengthen existing animal fighting laws. The Animal Fighting Prohibition Enforcement Act (H.R. 817) would make it a federal felony to move fighting animals across state lines to engage in fights, as well as increase the exhibition or sponsoring of such fights from a misdemeanor to a felony if the animals were transported across state lines. The law would also prohibit selling, transporting, buying, or delivery of any instrument (such as knives and blades) used in cockfighting across state or international borders.

TABLE 6.6

Summary of dog fighting laws, by state, 2004

State	Dogfighting: on the law books	Dogfighting: a felony or a misdemeanor	Loophole: possession of dogs for fighting	Loophole: being a spectator at a dogfight
Alabama	§ 3-1-29	Felony	Felony	Felony
Alaska	§ 11.61.145	Felony	Felony	Misdemeanor
Arizona	§13-2910.01 to 02	Felony	Felony	Felony
Arkansas	§ 5-62-120	Felony	Felony	Misdemeanor
California	§ 597.5	Felony	Felony	Misdemeanor
Colorado	§ 18-9-204	Felony	Felony	Felony
Connecticut	§ 53-247	Felony	Felony	Felony
Delaware	§ 1326	Felony	Felony	Misdemeanor
Florida	§ 828.122	Felony	Felony	Felony
Georgia	§ 16-12-37	Felony	Legal	Legal
Hawaii	§ 711-1109.3	Felony	Felony	Legal
Idaho	§ 25-3507	Misdemeanor	Legal	Misdemeanor
Illinois	510 ILCS 5/26-5	Felony	Felony	Misdemeanor
Indiana	§ 35-46-3-4 to 9.5	Felony	Misdemeanor	Misdemeanor
Iowa	§ 717D.1 to 6	Felony	Felony	Misdemeanor
Kansas	§ 21-4315	Felony	Felony	Misdemeanor
Kentucky	§ 525.125 to 130	Felony	Felony	Misdemeanor
Louisiana	14:102.5	Felony	Felony	Misdemeanor
Maine[a]	17 MRS §1033	Felony	Felony	Misdemeanor
Maryland	Art. 27 § 59	Felony	Felony	Misdemeanor
Massachusetts	Ch. 272 § 94 to 95	Felony	Felony	Misdemeanor
Michigan	§ 28.244	Felony	Felony	Felony
Minnesota	§ 343.31	Felony	Felony	Misdemeanor
Mississippi	§ 97-41-19	Felony	Felony	Felony
Missouri	§ 578.025	Felony	Felony	Misdemeanor
Montana	§ 45-8-210	Felony	Felony	Felony
Nebraska	§ 28-1005	Felony	Felony	Felony
Nevada	§ 574.070	Felony	Legal	Felony[b]
New Hampshire	§ 644:8-a	Felony	Felony	Felony
New Jersey[a]	§ 4:22-24	Felony	Felony	Felony
New Mexico	§ 30-18-9	Felony	Felony	Felony
New York	Agr & M § 351	Felony	Misdemeanor	Misdemeanor
North Carolina	§ 14-362.2	Felony	Felony	Felony
North Dakota	§ 36-21.1-07	Felony	Felony	Misdemeanor
Ohio	§ 955.15 to 16	Felony	Felony	Felony
Oklahoma	21 § 1694 to 1699.1	Felony	Felony	Misdemeanor
Oregon	§ 167.365	Felony	Felony	Felony
Pennsylvania	18 Pa.C.S. § 5511	Felony	Felony	Felony
Rhode Island	§ 4-1-9 to 13	Felony	Felony	Felony
South Carolina	§ 16-27-10 to 80	Felony	Felony	Felony[b]
South Dakota	§ 40-1-9 to 10.1	Felony	Felony	Misdemeanor
Tennessee	§ 39-14-203	Felony	Felony	Misdemeanor
Texas	§ 42.10	Felony	Misdemeanor	Misdemeanor
Utah	§ 76-9-301.1	Felony	Felony	Misdemeanor
Vermont	13 VSA § 352	Felony	Felony	Felony
Virginia	§ 3.1-796.124	Felony	Felony	Misdemeanor
Washington	§ 16.52.117	Felony	Misdemeanor	Misdemeanor
West Virginia	§ 61-8-19 to 19a	Felony	Misdemeanor	Misdemeanor
Wisconsin	§ 951.08	Felony	Felony	Misdemeanor
Wyoming	§ 6-3-203	Misdemeanor	Misdemeanor	Misdemeanor
	50 Illegal	48 Felony	41 Felony	20 Felony
	0 Legal	2 Misdemeanor	6 Misdemeanor	28 Misdemeanor
			3 Legal	2 Legal
Washington, DC	Ch. 106	Felony	Felony	Misdemeanor
American Samoa	Legal	Legal	Legal	Legal
Guam	§ 34205	Violation	Legal	Legal
Puerto Rico	15 LPRA § 235	Felony	Legal	Misdemeanor
Virgin Islands	19 VIC § 2613a	Felony	Felony	Felony

[a]These states do not have felony or misdemeanor offenses per se, but rather have felony and misdemeanor equivalent penalties.
[b]A repeated offense can trigger a felony prosecution.

SOURCE: "Dogfighting: State Laws," in *Dogfighting: State Laws*, Humane Society of the United States, April 2004, http://files.hsus.org/web-files/PDF/dogfighting_statelaws.pdf (accessed January 3, 2007)

CHAPTER 7
ENTERTAINMENT ANIMALS

Entertainment animals are those that perform or are displayed publicly to amuse people. These animals appear in circuses, carnivals, animal shows and exhibits, amusement and wildlife theme parks, aquariums, zoos, museums, fairs, and motion pictures and television programs. Although these venues are diverse, they all have one thing in common: They use animals for human purposes. Many of these purposes are purely recreational. Others combine recreation with educational goals, such as teaching the public about the conservation and preservation of endangered species. In either case, the animals are a source of income for their owners.

Entertainment animals include both wild and domesticated types. Wild exotic animals such as elephants, lions, and tigers are the most popular. They are objects of curiosity because people do not encounter them in their daily lives. The word *exotic* means "foreign" or "not native" but also suggests an air of mystery and danger that is alluring to people, who will often pay to see exotic animals living in cages. By contrast, domestic animals must do something to make money, because most people will not pay to see ordinary dogs and cats lying around. They might, however, pay to see them jump through fiery hoops or walk on their hind legs pushing baby carriages. They will pay even more to see wild animals do such things.

This unnatural basis of the exotic animal business is what makes it unacceptable to animal rights groups. They believe that wild animals should live in the wild, unaffected by human interference, and not be forced to do things that do not come naturally to them. Animal welfarists fear that exotic animals are not housed, trained, and cared for in a humane manner, particularly at circuses, carnivals, and roadside zoos and parks. The animals at these venues frequently are treated poorly, living in deplorable conditions without access to veterinary care. Performing animals must be trained to be entertainers, and many trainers use cruel and abusive methods.

Animal rights advocates feel that even nonperforming captive wild animals live unnatural existences. They are either removed from their natural habitats or born into captivity. Some people argue that this is beneficial to the animals and the perpetuation of their species. Animals in the wild face many dangers, including natural predators, starvation, hunters, and poachers. Their natural habitats in many parts of the world are shrinking as human development takes up more and more space.

Some exotic animals live longer in captivity than they would in the wild, and some species might die out completely if humans did not capture specimens of them to preserve. Large zoos often do this kind of work, and they may also take in exotic animals that have been surrendered by or rescued from smaller, less capable zoos and parks. However, even these large zoos are in the entertainment business, earning money by displaying captive animals to the public. Does the end justify the means? This is one of the fundamental questions in the debate over animals in entertainment.

HISTORY

The use of animals for entertainment dates back thousands of years. Even ancient civilizations were fascinated by exotic animals. Archaeological evidence shows that lions were kept in cages in Macedonia as far back as 2,000 BC. Egyptian, Chinese, Babylonian, Assyrian, and Roman rulers also collected wild animals, as did the Abbasid princes of Arabia. Ancient collections often included elephants, bears, giraffes, and big cats. Historians believe that wild animals were kept and shown off by rulers as a symbol of power and wealth.

Wild-animal performances were perfected in the traveling menageries, circuses, and sideshows of the 1800s. Most acts of the time focused on the ferocity of the animals and the bravery of the trainer. Lions were trained to roar and swat at the trainers, who fended them off with whips and chairs. These daring acts thrilled audiences, but the training methods used could be brutal. Trainers had to establish absolute dominance over their animals to prevent them from actually attacking. Animals were usually beaten, starved, and sometimes even had their teeth pulled to render them less dangerous.

In the nineteenth century horses, dogs, and other domesticated animals performed in variety shows throughout Europe and the United States. Near the end of the century, animal acts were incorporated into a new form of American entertainment: vaudeville. Vaudeville shows consisted of short theatrical acts performed on stage. They usually included jugglers, singers, dancers, magicians, comedians, and performing animals. Vaudeville remained popular until about 1920, when it was overshadowed by radio and motion pictures. These new entertainment media also featured animal acts.

The movie and television industry became major media outlets for animal entertainment during the latter part of the twentieth century. Circuses and other traditional shows featuring live wild animal acts faded in popularity as they competed with new venues, such as theme parks and aquariums with exotic animals. In 1964 the first Sea World marine park opened in San Diego, California. The San Diego Zoo's Wild Animal Park was established in 1969. Busch Gardens of Florida began in the late 1950s as a beer-tasting factory open to the public. Over the following two decades the company added elaborate bird and animal acts and amusement park rides to create a theme park. During the late 1990s Sea World and Walt Disney World both added massive animal theme parks to their existing attractions.

Exotic animal acts evolved during the twentieth century. These shows are often marketed as a chance for people to get closer to nature and to help protect endangered species. Tourists pay to swim with captive dolphins at beach resorts. Sea World in Orlando, Florida, advertises "amazing animal encounters" for its guests with orcas, dolphins, sea lions, and stingrays.

U.S. LEGISLATION AND REGULATION

Performing animals in the United States had little legal protection until 1970, when the Animal Welfare Act (AWA) was amended to include animals exhibited to the public. Regulation and enforcement of the act is handled by the U.S. Department of Agriculture's (USDA) Animal and Plant Health Inspection Service (APHIS). Animal exhibitors that show animals for compensation and either obtain or dispose of animals in commercial transactions must be licensed. Exhibitors that do not receive compensation and do not buy, sell, or transport animals only need to register.

Licensing is required for:

- Zoos (except those operated by the federal government)

- Exhibits, shows, and acts that feature captive marine mammals (dolphins, porpoises, whales, polar bears, sea otters, seals, walruses, and other mammals with fins or flippers)

- Tourist attractions exhibiting animals, such as roadside zoos

- Carnivals and circuses

- Promotional exhibits in which regulated animals are used to promote or advertise goods and services

- Owners who exhibit animals doing tricks or otherwise performing for a live audience or on tape

Exemptions from the license requirement are granted for pet and horse shows, rodeos, hunting events, exhibits of farm animals at agricultural events, private collectors who do not publicly show or sell animals, enterprises that keep animals in a wild state (such as game and hunting preserves), and exhibits that feature animals not covered by the AWA—mainly birds, reptiles, and fish.

Under the AWA licensed exhibitors must provide "adequate care and treatment in the areas of housing, handling, transportation, sanitation, nutrition, water, general husbandry, veterinary care, and protection from extreme weather and temperatures." The exhibitors are required to keep records detailing the veterinary care that the animals receive. As shown in Table 7.1, there were 2,647 licensed exhibitors and seventeen registered exhibitors operating in 2006. California has the most licensed animal acts (255), followed by Florida (251), Texas (240), Illinois (131), and Pennsylvania (124).

Regulations are also designed to ensure public safety. Dangerous animals can be publicly exhibited only under the direct control of an experienced trainer. There are time limits for exhibits, and the animals have to be fed and watered and handled in a humane manner that prevents unnecessary stress or discomfort. Physical abuse and withholding food are not permissible training methods. Traveling exhibits have to submit their performance schedules to APHIS before each tour. Exhibitors that violate standards are subject to warnings and civil actions such as license suspensions or fines.

Criticisms of the AWA and APHIS

The AWA regulations are criticized by animal welfarists as being minimal standards that provide little protection and are poorly enforced. Penalties for violating the AWA are civil, not criminal. The USDA reports that it conducted 3,577 inspections of animal exhibits in 2004. (See Table 1.6 in Chapter 1.)

TABLE 7.1

Number of USDA-licensed and registered animal exhibits, by state, September 2006

State	Licensed exhibits		Registered exhibits	
	Number	Percentage of total	Number	Percentage of total
Alaska	11	0.4%	0	0%
Alabama	38	1%	0	0%
Arkansas	23	0.9%	0	0%
Arizona	21	0.8%	0	0%
California	255	9.6%	0	0%
Colorado	29	1.1%	0	0%
Connecticut	47	1.8%	0	0%
District of Columbia	0	0%	0	0%
Delaware	2	0.1%	0	0%
Florida	251	9.5%	1	5.9%
Georgia	83	3.1%	2	11.8%
Guam	3	0.1%	0	0%
Hawaii	12	0.5%	0	0%
Iowa	43	1.6%	0	0%
Idaho	15	0.6%	0	0%
Illinois	131	4.9%	2	12%
Indiana	61	2.3%	0	0%
Kansas	27	1.0%	0	0%
Kentucky	22	0.8%	1	5.9%
Louisiana	25	0.9%	0	0%
Massachusetts	48	1.8%	0	0%
Maryland	30	1.1%	0	0%
Maine	7	0.3%	0	0%
Michigan	117	4.4%	4	24%
Minnesota	68	2.6%	2	12%
Missouri	79	3.0%	0	0%
Mississippi	15	0.6%	0	0%
Montana	18	0.7%	0	0%
North Carolina	74	2.8%	0	0%
North Dakota	14	0.5%	0	0%
Nebraska	12	0.5%	0	0%
New Hampshire	16	0.6%	0	0%
New Jersey	45	1.7%	0	0%
New Mexico	15	1%	0	0%
Nevada	38	1.4%	0	0%
New York	121	4.6%	0	0%
Ohio	70	2.6%	3	17.6%
Oklahoma	30	1.1%	0	0%
Oregon	41	1.5%	0	0%
Pennsylvania	124	4.7%	0	0%
Puerto Rico	4	0.2%	0	0%
Rhode Island	5	0.2%	0	0%
South Carolina	50	1.9%	0	0%
South Dakota	19	0.7%	0	0%
Tennessee	38	1.4%	0	0%
Texas	240	9.1%	0	0%
Utah	14	0.5%	0	0%
Virginia	59	2.2%	1	5.9%
Vermont	4	0.2%	0	0%
Washington	32	1.2%	0	0%
Wisconsin	90	3.4%	1	5.9%
West Virginia	10	0.4%	0	0%
Wyoming	1	0.04%	0	0%
Totals	**2,647**		**17**	

SOURCE: Adapted from "Exhibitors," in *Facility Lists: Exhibitors*, U.S. Department of Agriculture, Animal and Plant Health Inspection Service, September 7, 2006, http://www.aphis.usda.gov/ac/publications/reports/C_cert_holders.txt (accessed December 15, 2006) and "Registered Exhibitors," in *Facility Lists: Registered Exhibitors*, U.S. Department of Agriculture, Animal and Plant Health Inspection Service, September 7, 2006, http://www.aphis.usda.gov/ac/publications/reports/E_cert_holders.txt (accessed December 15, 2006)

Entertainment animals are often protected by state and local anticruelty laws, but the Humane Society of the United States (HSUS) claims that some states exempt USDA-licensed animal acts (particularly circuses) from meeting anticruelty standards. Animal rights groups also say that the USDA refuses to allow its inspectors to testify in criminal cruelty cases. Some local governments forbid or tightly regulate animal acts.

The HSUS advocates one of two legislative approaches at the local level:

- A ban on any mental and physical harassment of wild animals for the purpose of entertainment and a ban on their use in unnatural behaviors (such as jumping through hoops, wrestling with people, and so on)

- A ban on the use of all wild animals for entertainment unless regulations are in place to ensure their safety and that of the public

CIRCUSES

Circuses have used performing animals, mostly horses, elephants, lions, tigers, bears, and monkeys, for centuries. Animal rights and welfare groups are critical of circuses that feature animals. They say that the animals are treated poorly and spend long hours in small cages or chained to the ground. The HSUS (2007, http://www.hsus.org/wildlife/issues_facing_wildlife/circuses/circus_myths.html) makes the following claims against circuses:

- Many circus animals are not owned by the circuses but are leased from exotic animal dealers under seasonal contracts.

- Circuses do not provide proper veterinary care for the animals they own or lease.

- Circus animals spend too much time in transport in trucks and railcars that are not air conditioned or heated.

- Traveling circus animals are often deprived of food and water for long periods.

- Circus training methods include beatings and food deprivation.

Major animal welfare and rights groups, such as the HSUS and People for the Ethical Treatment of Animals (PETA), advocate animal-free circuses. PETA's anti-circus Web site (2006, http://www.circuses.com/attacks-ele03.asp) lists hundreds of captive animal attacks it says have occurred since 1990. PETA claims that these rampages result from the animals' rebelling against years of abuse and deprivation. The HSUS also maintains a list of animal incidents (escapes, attacks, and alleged abuse cases) associated with circuses and other animal entertainment acts. Table 7.2 lists those that occurred since 2000. The most widely publicized was the 2003 attack of Las Vegas showman Roy Horn of the Siegfried and Roy act. Horn was critically injured after being attacked in the neck by one of the show's tigers during a live performance.

TABLE 7.2

Humane Society accounts of violent events involving circus animals, 2000–04

Date	Location	Entertainment venue	Incident
5/31/2004	San Francisco	Six Flags Marine World	Elephant trainer gored, in critical condition
3/8/2004	Illinois	Hawthorn Corporation	Elephant owners found in violation of Animal Welfare Act (AWA)
12/22/2003	United Kingdom	Bobby Roberts Circus	Elephant escapes ring and roams residential area before being recaptured
12/2/2003	Moscow	Children's theater group	Bear kills trainer during feeding
11/27/2003	Ecuador	Circus	Police shoot and kill two escaped lions that attacked a child
11/23/2003	Illinois	Performing animal firm	United States Department of Agriculture (USDA) confiscates an elephant with a serious illness
10/3/2003	Las Vegas	Siegfried & Roy casino act	Tiger mauls performer, in critical condition
6/9/2003	Brownsville, TX	Traveling circus	Two zebras escape and roam highway. Zebras and bystander injured.
5/5/2003	Orlando, FL	Gatorland	Handler attacked by alligator, receives lacerations to face
4/29/2003	Columbus, OH	Ringling Bros & Barnum Bailey Circus	Handler bitten by alligator on hand
4/25/2003	Russia	Circus	Animal trainer killed by lions
Spring 2003	Russia	Circus	12-year-old girl killed by runaway circus lion
4/21/2003	Spain	International Circus	Tiger bites arm off man who reaches into cage
4/7/2003	Indonesia	Circus	Elephant kills trainer
3/21/2003	Lincoln, NE	Shriners Circus	Pony escapes and runs down street before being recaptured
2/3/2003	Jacksonville, FL	Universoul Circus	Tiger escapes cage and roams before being recaptured
8/22/2002	Virginia	Sterling and Reid Circus	Animal handlers arrested for animal cruelty
8/10/2002	Rhinebeck, NY	Carson and Barnes Circus	Truck carrying elephants overturns on highway
July 2002	Canada	Shriners Circus	Three elephants deported from Canada for possibly carrying tuberculosis
8/10/2001	Australia	Lennon's Circus	Lion tamer attacked by 3 lions, receives severe lacerations
5/23/2001	Mexico	Hermanos Rodriguez Ayala Circus	Two lions escaped and roamed around town before being recaptured
8/17/2001	Spain	Circus	Three lions and one tiger escape and kill several circus animals
3/25/2001	Chicago, IL	Shrine Circus	Onlooker files complaint about elephant being beaten with hook
3/25/2001	Allentown, PA	Royal Palace Circus of Sarasota	Snake charmer bitten in abdomen by cobra
3/21/2001	Moscow	Durov's Little Corner	Trainer crushed to death in elephant's pen
12/29/2000	Germany	Circus	Tiger escapes cage and roams onto nearby road causing 12 mile traffic jam
12/15/2000	India	Circus	Performer mauled to death by three tigers during performance
11/4/2000	Germany	Circus	Liger (mix of tiger and lion) critically wounds 5-year-old girl
8/4/2000	Brazil	Circus	Six lions escape from cage and roam town before being killed by police
4/24/2000	Thailand	Suan Nongnuch Animal Park	Elephant kills woman and seriously injures 2 other spectators
4/20/2000	Yucca Valley, CA	Culpepper and Merriweather Circus	Elephant and three horses escape. Elephant injures person.
4/3/2000	Brazil	Circus	Five lions kill and eat six-year-old boy. Lions had not been fed for 5 days.
4/2/2000	Baton Rouge, LA	Sterling and Reid Circus	Bear falls out of truck on highway
3/7/2000	Poland	Circus	Three tigers escape and roam town. Police kill 1 tiger and 1 bystander.
2/4/2000	Tampa, FL	Ramos Family	Elephant who had killed trainer found dead
2/3/2000	Deland, FL	Clyde Beatty-Cole Bros	USDA inspector finds many scars and health problems on two elephants
1/23/2000	Tampa, FL	Ramos Family	Elephant tramples keeper to death
1/8/2000	India	Elephant parade	One man killed and several spectators injured by elephant stampede

SOURCE: Adapted from text in *Circus Incidents: Attacks, Abuse, and Property Damage*, Humane Society of the United States, June 2004, http://www.hsus.org/web-files/PDF/2004_HSUS_Circus_Incidents.pdf (accessed January 3, 2007)

Elephants

Elephants are particularly difficult to keep in confinement because of their immense size. Welfarists claim that many circus elephants are mistreated, malnourished, and sick with tuberculosis. A common tool for training elephants is called an ankus or bullhook, a long rod with a sharp hook on the end. Critics charge that elephant trainers beat the animals with the rod and poke the hook into tender areas of the elephant's hide behind its ears.

PETA (February 2005, http://www.circuses.com/savelota.asp) describes the life of a circus elephant named Lota. She lived at the Milwaukee Zoo from 1954 until 1990, when she was acquired by the Hawthorn Corporation, a company that trains exotic animals and leases them to circuses. PETA claims that Hawthorn handlers beat Lota and that she suffered from malnutrition and tuberculosis. The company has been criticized by animal welfare groups for years for its problems.

The HSUS reports in "USDA Seizes the Moment, Orders Hawthorn to Give Up 16 Elephants" (March 25,

2004, http://www.hsus.org/wildlife/wildlife_news/) that in April 2003 the Hawthorn Corporation was charged by the USDA for violations of the AWA. Later that year the USDA confiscated a fifty-eight-year-old elephant named Delhi from the company and sent it to the Elephant Sanctuary in Hohenwald, Tennessee. In March 2004 Hawthorn owner John Cuneo admitted to committing at least nineteen violations of the AWA and agreed to relinquish ownership of all sixteen of his elephants by August 2004 to settle the USDA lawsuit. He was assessed a $200,000 civil penalty. In July 2004 Cuneo filed court motions seeking to vacate the consent order against him. A long series of legal maneuvers began that extended well beyond the original August 2004 deadline for relinquishing the elephants.

In *Hawthorn Elephant Update* (February 14, 2006, http://www.aphis.usda.gov/ac/stakeholder/stakeholder4.pdf), APHIS notes that two of the elephants (Tess and Sue) subsequently died in Hawthorn facilities. In late 2004 two more elephants (Lota and Misty) went to live at the

Elephant Sanctuary. Lota died there in February 2005 after a long battle with tuberculosis. Two other elephants were placed with other facilities approved by the USDA. In January 2006 eight more Hawthorn elephants were sent to the Elephant Sanctuary. And, more than a year later, Jeff Long reports in "Owner Finds Home for Last 2 Elephants" (*Chicago Tribune*, February 27, 2007) that Pat Derby, co-founder of the Performing Animal Welfare Society (PAWS), agreed to admit the remaining two Hawthorn elephants (Nicholas and Gypsy) to PAWS's San Andreas sanctuary in California.

In 2002 the animal rights group In Defense of Animals (IDA) sponsored speaking engagements around the country for a former circus animal trainer, who described beatings administered to elephants with bullhooks. He claimed that brutal training methods are routinely used at the Clyde Beatty-Cole Brothers Circus and Ringling Brothers and Barnum and Bailey Circus. The IDA also obtained video footage of what it says are abusive training methods being practiced on circus animals.

The Ringling Brothers and Barnum and Bailey Circus defends its elephant training and breeding programs. The circus, which is owned by Feld Entertainment, operates an animal retirement facility and the Center of Elephant Conservation (CEC) in Florida. The CEC was founded in 1995 to conserve, study, and breed Asian elephants. According to company officials (2006, http://www.ringling.com/cec/), the CEC is a five-million-dollar, two hundred-acre facility dedicated to preserving the species, of which only thirty-five thousand are left in the wild. The CEC is not open to the public but admits researchers, conservationists, and academicians by arrangement. Feld Entertainment (2006, http://www.ringling.com/cec/apr2005birth.aspx) boasts that the CEC is "home to the world's largest and most genetically diverse Asian elephant population in the Western hemisphere." According to the CEC, its latest calf, Irvin, was born in June 2005.

Animal rights groups contend that breeding elephants to work in the circus is not really conservation. They believe that wild animals should live undisturbed in their natural environments and that resources should be focused on protecting and expanding natural habitats. They do not generally advocate the use of captivity as a conservation tool.

MOVIES AND TELEVISION

Animals have been performing in movies and television shows ever since those media were invented. (See Figure 7.1.) Rin Tin Tin was a famous war dog that starred in silent movies during the 1920s. The story of another dog, Lassie, appeared in book form in 1940, in a movie in 1943, and on television in 1954. The original television show ran for seventeen years. Another dog gained fame in the title role of the move *Benji* in 1974.

Popular animal movies of the 1980s included *White Fang* and *Turner and Hooch*.

The orca Keiko became famous because of the 1993 movie *Free Willy*. In the movie Keiko portrayed a whale liberated from captivity with the help of a boy. JoBeth McDaniel, in "Won't Somebody Please Save This Whale?" (*Life*, November 1993), described the irony of the poor conditions in which Keiko lived in a Mexican amusement park. In response, the Free Willy Foundation raised millions of dollars to have Keiko moved in 1996 to an aquarium in Oregon. (See Figure 7.2.) There he gained weight and recuperated from various health ailments. In 1998 Keiko was flown to Iceland to live in a bay pen in his native waters. His handlers tried to teach Keiko skills he would need in the wild, such as catching live fish on his own. In 2002 Keiko was released. But he did not join an ocean pod of whales as was hoped. Instead, he took refuge in a calm bay in Norway and remained semidependent on humans for food until his death in 2003 from pneumonia.

During the 1990s animal stories in the media became so popular that an entire cable television network was devoted to them. Animal Planet was launched in 1996 as a project of Discovery Communications. It broadcasts such popular shows as *Animal Cops*, *Animal Precinct*, *The Crocodile Hunter*, *The Jeff Corwin Experience*, *The Planet's Funniest Animals*, and *Wild Rescues*.

Animal Precinct is a reality show that goes on patrol with New York City's Humane Law Enforcement (HLE) agents. These agents are empowered to respond to cruelty complaints, perform investigations, and arrest people for crimes against animals. They were granted this power in 1866 when the American Society for the Prevention of Cruelty to Animals established its original charter with the state of New York. *Animal Cops* is a similar series based on the work of the Detroit-based Michigan Humane Society. Due to the popularity of such shows, additional programs were created in Houston, Miami, and San Francisco. Since their inception, these shows have gained an enormous fan base, and the agents and officers featured have earned celebrity status because of their work.

American Humane Association Monitors Animal Welfare

During the filming of the 1939 movie *Jesse James*, a horse was killed when it was forced to jump off a cliff for a scene. Public complaints led to the formation of the film-monitoring unit of the American Humane Association (AHA). The AHA opened an office in Los Angeles in 1940.

In 1980 the AHA was awarded a contract with the Screen Actors Guild (SAG) to monitor the safety and welfare of animals appearing in movies and television shows featuring SAG performers filmed in the United States. The Producer-Screen Actors Guild Codified Basic

FIGURE 7.1

The cast members Tommy Norden, Brian Kelly, and Luke Halpin with the dolphin star Bebe, who played Flipper on the 1960s television show of the same name. *AP/Wide World Photos/NBC. Reproduced by permission.*

Agreement of 1998 includes a provision that producers must notify the AHA before using animals on a set and provide AHA representatives with access to the set while animals are being filmed. This applies to movies, television shows, commercials, and music videos that include SAG performers.

The AHA reviews scripts and works with animal trainers and production staff to ensure that animals are not harmed during filming. The AHA monitors hundreds of productions each year in the United States. The AHA's contractual authority does not extend beyond the United States. However, producers sometimes invite the AHA to oversee animal filming at foreign locations. The AHA has no oversight authority on non-SAG productions, such as reality shows and documentaries. The AHA has pub-

licly criticized the television shows *Survivor* and *Fear Factor* for incidents in which animals were killed or injured by the shows' contestants.

The AHA guidelines are laid out in the document *American Humane Association Guidelines for the Safe Use of Animals in Filmed Media* (October 2005, http://www .americanhumane.org/site/DocServer/LA_Guidelines_Web2 .pdf ?docID=1821). The guidelines cover what filmmakers and crew should do before and during production to ensure animal safety. The AHA rates movies based on their adherence to these guidelines. Ratings for nearly two thousand movies are provided on the AHA Web site (2007, http://www.ahafilm.info/movies/movieratings.phtml).

The AHA Web site also describes in detail how particular animal scenes were filmed in dozens of movies.

FIGURE 7.2

Keiko at the Oregon Coast Aquarium, Newport, Oregon, 1997. *CORBIS/Kevin Schafer. Reproduced by permission.*

Usage of deceptive camera angles, body doubles, fake blood, computer graphics, and other tricks is described.

Ralph Frammolino and James Bates, in "Questions Raised about Group That Watches Out for Animals in Movies" (*Los Angeles Times*, February 9, 2001), are critical of the AHA's role in overseeing animal filming. They claim that the AHA provides too little oversight and is reluctant to criticize the major movie studios, which fund its work. The AHA's budget comes from a fund that is overseen by producers and the SAG.

ZOOS

The word *zoo* is short for "zoological garden." The term, taken from the Greek word *zoion*, meaning "animal," first came into English usage in the mid-1800s. The London Zoological Society established a garden around 1828 to display its collection of wild animals. At first the garden was private, accessible only to members who paid a subscription fee. The society wanted to distinguish itself from the common animal exhibits of the time, but the need for funds drove the society to open the garden to the public in 1846. The new zoo was hugely popular, receiving more than one hundred thousand visitors during its first year. The royal menagerie at the Tower of London was closed around this time and its animals were presented to the zoo.

In 1874 the first American zoo opened to the public in Philadelphia. It featured animals from around the world, as well as elaborate gardens, architecture, and art. Early zoos kept wild animals in cages, but during the mid-1800s the German exhibitor Carl Hagenbeck Jr. advocated the use of natural settings for zoo animals. In 1907 he opened a zoo in which the animals were exhibited on artificial islands that resembled their natural habitats. He felt that this approach was better for both the animals and the spectators. Even though few other zookeepers adopted his ideas at the time, they were one of the hallmarks of a top zoo by the end of the twentieth century.

Accredited Zoos

In 1924 the American Association of Zoological Parks and Aquariums was founded. Today it is called the Association of Zoos and Aquariums (AZA). It is a nonprofit organization that works to advance conservation, education, science, and recreation at zoos and aquariums. According to its Web site (2007, http://www.aza.org/AboutAZA/), the AZA is "dedicated to the advancement of accredited zoos and aquariums in the areas of animal care, wildlife conservation, education and science." Zoos and aquariums that meet AZA's professional standards can be accredited by the organization. In 2007 there were more than two hundred AZA-accredited zoos and aquariums, located mostly in North America, housing more than seven hundred thousand animals.

In "The Collective Impact of AZA-Accredited Zoos and Aquariums" (August 2006, http://www.aza.org/AboutAZA/Documents/CollImpact.pdf), the AZA notes that accredited zoos and aquariums provide the following services yearly:

- Receive 143 million visitors (more than attend major league football, basketball, and baseball games combined)

- Receive over $100 million in financial support and millions of volunteer work hours from patrons

- Dedicate $83 million to educational programs

- Educate more than forty-five million people each year

- Participate in more than seventeen hundred conservation projects all over the world

- Employ over thirty-three thousand workers

The AZA also works to ensure the long-term breeding and conservation of a variety of species. As of 2006, 149 species of mammals, birds, reptiles, amphibians, fish, and invertebrates were protected under its Species Survival Plan.

The zoos accredited by the AZA in the United States are generally well respected by the public and even by many animal welfarists. For example, the HSUS acknowledges that large zoos educate the public about wildlife and help conserve, preserve, and restore endangered species. However, this does not spare accredited zoos from some criticisms.

In "Cruel and Usual" (*U.S. News and World Report*, August 5, 2002), Michael Satchell examines the animal disposal practices of some major U.S. zoos. Satchell tracked down a dozen primates, birds, and other exotic animals that had left the prestigious Rosamond Gifford Zoo in Syracuse, New York, for a menagerie in Texas. He found the animals living in filthy cages alongside an interstate highway amid trash and weeds. The menagerie had gone out of business.

Anne Baker, the executive director of the Rosamond Gifford Zoo, which is accredited by the AZA, said she had relied on references and information supplied by the Texas facility to make her decision. Satchell, however, points out that if the director had checked with the USDA she would have found that unfavorable inspection reports had been issued for the menagerie.

The AZA's code of ethics requires accredited institutions to acquire animals from and dispose of animals to other AZA institutions or to non-AZA members with "the expertise, records management capabilities, financial stability, and facilities required to properly care for and maintain the animals" (2007, http://www.aza.org/AboutAZA/ADPolicy/). Satchell claims that this procedure is often violated by AZA zoos that "loan" or "donate" unwanted animals to unaccredited roadside zoos and animal parks. These facilities are frequently substandard and provide poor care. Satchell quotes an HSUS spokesperson as saying that the practice is "the dirty little secret" of the respectable zoos.

Satchell bases his accusations on a review of database records from the International Species Information System, which is used by major zoos to track animal transfers, and from interviews with government, zoo, and animal rights personnel. Satchell concludes that large zoos in New York, California, Hawaii, Tennessee, Georgia, Colorado, Arizona, Alabama, Missouri, and Washington, D.C., have transferred unwanted animals to substandard facilities and to dealers with alleged links to the exotic animal trade.

Unaccredited Zoos

According to the AZA (2007, http://www.aza.org/Accreditation/AccreditationIntro/), it accredits only 10% of U.S. zoos. As such, there are thousands of unaccredited small "roadside zoos," petting zoos, animal parks, and similar exhibits that display animals to the public. The HSUS says that these small zoos often barely meet minimal federal standards for animal care. Most of these facilities include exotic animals, such as lions and tigers. Many are run by entrepreneurs with little experience in the proper care of exotic animals and with limited financial resources. Some call themselves animal preserves and achieve tax-exempt status so that they can solicit donations for their "conservation" work.

All licensed animal exhibits are subject to USDA inspection, but animal welfare groups claim that poorly run facilities often receive bad inspection reports for years and are still not closed down. A case in point is the Gentry Wild Wilderness Safari in Gentry, Arkansas. Robin Mero describes in "Wilmoth Settles" (*Morning News*, June 28, 2002) the park's questionable past.

According to Mero, the owner of the two-hundred-acre drive-through park was ticketed and fined numerous times for animal violations since 1988. In 1995 he paid an $8,000 civil penalty in an out-of-court settlement as a result of charges based on violations from 1992 to 1994. USDA inspections conducted in 1999–2000 resulted in a host of new charges that the facility violated AWA requirements for proper veterinary care, recordkeeping, housekeeping, and housing of its animals. This resulted in a $10,000 civil penalty that was also settled out of court. Half of the penalty is a fine. The other half must be spent upgrading the facility and training employees. According to Tracy M. Neal Park, in "Owners Deny Negligence in Chimp Incident" (*Benton County Daily Record*, February 23, 2005), the park was sued by a worker who claimed that two of her fingers were bitten off by a chimpanzee in the park in October 2004.

In "USDA Files Complaint against Zoo" (*St. Louis Post-Dispatch*, February 2, 2005), Brad Urban reports on alleged problems at the Wesa-A-Geh-Ya Zoo in Warren County, Missouri. The zoo houses many wild animals, including big cats, wolves, and a bear. According to Urban, the USDA alleges that the park has committed "numerous violations" of the AWA, including "repeated instances" in which the facility failed to meet minimum standards of veterinary care. The violations were noted during eleven inspections that occurred between July 2001 and October 2003. Most of the violations involved housing and veterinary care for the zoo's lions and tigers.

Another roadside zoo in legal trouble was located in Colton, California. Tiger Rescue was a nonprofit sanctuary for big cats maintained on property near the residence of its owners, John Weinhart and Marla Smith. In "Neglecting over 90 Tigers, 58 Cubs Found Stuffed into Freezer" (April 22, 2003, http://www.pet-abuse.com/cases/1275/), the HSUS reports that in 2003 authorities found the corpses of more than ninety tigers (fifty-eight of which were tiger cubs) when they raided the property. In 2005 Weinhart was found guilty of fifty-six felony counts that included animal cruelty and child endangerment (Weinhart's child lived at the residence). Smith, the other owner, pleaded guilty in return for a shortened sentence.

ANIMAL THEME PARKS

Animal theme parks are large tourist attractions that combine elements of zoos (or aquariums) and amusement parks to entertain the public. According to the National Amusement Park Historical Association, theme parks have their origins in the "pleasure gardens" of medieval Europe. These gardens featured live entertainment, games, and other forms of recreation. Although their popularity faded in Europe, pleasure gardens evolved into amusement parks in the United States and were widely popular by the end of the 1800s.

The first oceanarium (a large saltwater aquarium) in the United States is thought to be Marine Studios of Florida. Later named Marineland, the oceanarium opened in June 1938 and received twenty thousand visitors its first day. Its popularity led to the opening of a similar facility, Marineland of the Pacific, in southern California in 1954. These oceanariums were more like amusement parks than traditional educational aquariums. They relied on performing dolphins, pilot whales, seals, and sea lions to entertain crowds.

In 1963 came the release of the popular movie *Flipper*, about a dolphin who befriends a young boy. It became a hit television show a year later. (See Figure 7.1.) Public demand for performing dolphins and other sea creatures skyrocketed. In 1964 George Millay developed a marine life park called Sea World in San Diego, California, and in 1965 Sea World acquired Shamu, a female orca captured from the wild.

Shamu was one of many orcas captured during the early 1960s for use in the entertainment industry. According to *Frontline* in *A Whale of a Business* (November 1997, http://www.pbs.org/wgbh/pages/frontline/shows/whales/), the first captive orca had been collected for Marineland of the Pacific in 1961. The animal lived for only one day. She repeatedly smashed herself against the walls of her tank until she died. *Frontline* lists 133 known orcas captured between 1961 and 1997, along with their life spans in captivity. Many lived only for a few months, whereas the average life span for an orca in the wild is thirty to fifty years. *Frontline* estimates that 102 of the 133 captive orcas have died.

The original Shamu survived for six years. In the intervening years Sea World has continued to acquire orcas and call at least one of them by the stage name Shamu for performance purposes. Eventually, the company trademarked the name.

During the 1970s and 1980s Sea World marine parks opened in Ohio, Florida, and Texas. In 1989 they were purchased by Anheuser-Busch, which already operated Busch Gardens, a popular park in Florida featuring bird acts, animal shows, and amusement park rides. In 2000 the company opened another theme park, also in Florida, named Discovery Cove, where visitors can experience wildlife up close and swim with dolphins and stingrays. The stingers are cut off of the stingrays to make them harmless to people. An aviary includes hundreds of exotic birds that people can hand feed. According to company officials (December 8, 2006, http://www.orlandowelcomecenter.com/discovery-cove-environment.htm), the Sea World marine parks, Busch Gardens, and Discovery Cove are home to more than sixty thousand animals. The officials note that "these animals serve as ambassadors for their species by helping to entertain, educate and inspire millions of people."

Many animal welfare and rights groups are critical of the Anheuser-Busch theme parks and Disney's Animal Kingdom, an attraction opened at Walt Disney World in Florida in 1998. PETA (2006, http://www.helpinganimals.com/travel_feat_deadlydest.asp) refers to these parks as "deadly destinations" and notes that hundreds of animals have died at these facilities because of improper care.

PETA argues that living conditions are not healthy for the animals in captivity and disputes claims by the owner companies of animal parks that they further conservation efforts. The Animal Rights Foundation of Florida states in "Disney's Animal Kingdom" (August 16, 2006, http://animalrightsflorida.org/Disney.html) that "Disney bulldozed tens of thousands of acres of wildlife habitat in the central Florida flatlands, killing native gopher tortoises and other animals" to build its Animal Kingdom, a park for imported wild animals.

The HSUS focuses its efforts on eliminating dolphin petting pools at animal theme parks. These are areas of shallow water around which visitors can gather and touch and feed dolphins. In the report *Biting the Hand That Feeds: The Case against Dolphin Petting Pools* (Spring 2003, http://www.hsus.org/marine_mammals/what_are_the_issues/marine_mammals_in_captivity/), the HSUS notes that animal theme parks are increasingly offering such opportunities for the public to experience physical contact with wild animals and marine life via feeding, petting, and swimming programs. The HSUS provides a number of arguments against holding cetaceans (dolphins, whales, porpoises, and so on) in captivity to entertain humans and particularly against using them in petting pools. HSUS field investigations conducted between 1996 and 2003 reveal that visitors to petting pools are not properly supervised by theme park staff and expose themselves and the animals to various health and safety hazards. The HSUS also notes that many of the dolphins in petting pools appear obese and show signs of injury from aggressive competition over food. Allowing the public to feed captive dolphins also sets a dangerous precedent, the HSUS believes, given that the government actively discourages people from feeding wild dolphins under the Marine Mammal Protection Act. Finally, the HSUS disputes the claim by the theme park industry that petting pools are educational, noting that "hand-feeding dead fish to obese dolphins in a cramped, overcrowded and featureless tank of chemically treated water provides visitors with scant insight into normal dolphin behavior in the natural environment."

CHAPTER 8
SERVICE ANIMALS

Service animals are those that work for humans doing particular tasks. These tasks may be as mundane as pulling plows or as sophisticated as finding underwater mines. Throughout history, animals have helped humans hunt wildlife, herd livestock, guard people and property, and wage warfare. Animals are also trained for more humanitarian causes, such as rescuing the lost and providing aid and comfort to people with certain physical and psychological needs.

Whatever the task may be, the common factor is that service animals help humans with their needs and desires. Some people see this as a clever use of resources. Many believe it is a mutually beneficial bond, but others see it as a form of slavery. Some animal rights activists believe that animals should not be used for any purpose by humans. Even though they rarely speak out against uses that the public views as benevolent, they are extremely critical of military uses of animals because the animals are exposed to great danger. This is also true for animals doing some police and rescue jobs.

Welfarists are also concerned that working animals should be trained and treated with care. Animal groups recommend that only positive reinforcement be used when service animals are trained. They also point out that service animals should be carefully screened to ensure that they are a good match with their potential human partners. Finally, they remind people that the needs of service and assistance animals must be considered along with the needs of the people being served. In general, however, welfarists tend to support programs that train service and therapeutic animals because so many of these programs rescue homeless animals from shelters.

HISTORY

The first service animals were probably dogs domesticated from wolves around 13,000 BC. Humans learned to use the natural instincts and skills of the dogs to help them chase down and capture prey. As other animals were domesticated over the next ten thousand years, they, too, became useful for doing tasks.

All ancient cultures put animals to work. Societies dependent on hunting used dogs to help them and enlisted more exotic species, such as mongooses and birds of prey. Agricultural societies used cats to protect the grain supplies and dogs to protect and herd livestock. Oxen, donkeys, camels, horses, mules, and other beasts of burden pulled plows in the fields, carried loads on their backs, and pulled carts to market. Sheep and pigs were led across fields at planting time to step on seeds and push them into the ground. Sheep were also used to trample on grain to thresh it after it was harvested.

As civilizations grew, they developed public services and engaged in commerce and warfare with each other. This meant that animals had to travel well. Horses became important as a means of transportation and in delivering mail. The military use of animals has a long history. Many horses, camels, and even elephants were ridden into battle by soldiers and died along with them. Armies used beasts of burden to haul their ammunition and supplies. Some smaller animals also had military uses. For example, carrier pigeons and dogs made effective battlefield messengers.

Valuable Traits Encouraged

The role of service animals in hunting, agriculture, transportation, and warfare changed little over thousands of years. Breeding was manipulated to produce strains that served particular purposes. This was especially true for horses and dogs.

Horses reached their heyday in the Old West of the nineteenth century. The Pony Express is a famous example of their historical importance. This mail delivery system operated from April 1860 to November 1861 between St. Joseph, Missouri, and San Francisco, California, a distance of more than nineteen hundred miles.

European colonists brought dogs with them to North America and found that Native Americans were already using them for hunting, sentry duty, and sled pulling and as pack animals. Eventually, the colonists used trained dogs to attack Native Americans in battle.

Changing Roles

In the United States, service animals continued in their traditional roles until the late 1800s. Then the urbanization and innovations of the Industrial Revolution slowly eliminated the need for many of them. Motorized vehicles took over nearly all the work formerly done by horses and beasts of burden in transportation, warfare, and agriculture. Over the next century many people turned to electronics instead of dogs to guard their property and to chemicals instead of cats to kill rodents. Some vital tasks previously performed by working animals have become activities of sport and recreation—for example, hunting and herding with dogs and using horses to pull carriages.

The use of animals (particularly dogs) in military and public service, however, continues to grow. In addition, animals serve as aides and provide companionship and therapy to people with specific physical and mental needs.

HUNTING
Early Times

Hunting was the first task in which animals were put into service to humans. Prehistoric hunters took advantage of the natural instincts and skills of carnivorous (meat-eating) animals, such as dogs, which had been domesticated from wolves. The hunters trained the dogs to accompany them on hunts and turn over any captured prey. Prehistoric cave paintings show humans and dogs cooperating to pursue and capture large prey.

Falconry

Falconry is thought to date back to around 2,000 BC in China. It is a form of hunting conducted with the use of trained birds of prey, such as falcons, hawks, owls, or eagles. These birds are also called raptors. Falconry was particularly important in the Middle East and is discussed at length in the Koran, the holy book of Islam. It became popular among European nobility during the Crusades and was fashionable until the invention of firearms.

Falconry is still practiced today as a sport in the United States. (See Figure 8.1.) According to the California Hawking Club (January 20, 2007, http://www .calhawkingclub.org/apprentice/default.htm), in 2006 there were approximately seven thousand licensed falconers in the United States. Falconry has strict licensing require-

FIGURE 8.1

A falconer holds a peregrine falcon wearing a hood and jesses. *Photograph by Robert J. Huffman. Field Mark Publications. Reproduced by permission.*

ments because it uses wild birds that are protected species. Animals commonly hunted using falconry are rabbits, squirrels, pigeons, quail, and waterfowl.

Dogs

Dogs have historically been used in hunting. In the United States, dogs are used to hunt upland game birds and waterfowl, such as pheasant, quail, partridge, ducks, and pigeons. Dogs are also used to hunt squirrels, bears, raccoons, mountain lions, foxes, and other prey. The primary dog breeds used in hunting are beagles, spaniels, griffons, retrievers, setters, pointers, and hounds. Dogs that hunt mostly by scent are called scent hounds, and dogs that hunt mostly by sight are called sight hounds. Hunting dogs perform a variety of tasks, including tracking prey, pointing prey out to the hunter, and retrieving downed prey after it is shot.

CONTROVERSIES OVER USING HUNTING DOGS. Hunting with dogs has become a controversial issue in some areas where it is common. In "Hunters Howling" (*Atlanta Journal and Constitution*, April 13, 2003), Stacy Shelton reports on increasing conflicts in southern Georgia between hunters using dogs and landowners. Dog running, as it is called, is a long-standing tradition in rural areas of the state. Landowners accused hunters of letting their dogs trespass onto private property during deer-hunting season (mid-October to mid-January). Hunters said that property owners were being unreasonable and had killed at least one hunting dog. The landowners claimed that hunters had threatened them and told them that they should fence their property if they did not want hunting dogs on it.

In July 2003 the Georgia legislature passed a bill that severely restricts the hunting of deer with dogs in the state. It can only be conducted on large pieces of property of at least one thousand acres. The owners or lessees of the property must obtain a permit from the state before allowing a hunt. All hunters have to label their dogs and vehicles with the permit number. In this way, trespassers can be easily identified and reported to authorities. Some companies that own huge tracts of land in southern Georgia, such as the International Paper Company, have decided not to allow hunting with dogs on their property anymore.

One particularly controversial form of hunting conducted with the help of dogs and horses is foxhunting. Hunters on horseback pursue foxes across the countryside using packs of hounds. Though foxhunting has been practiced in the United Kingdom for hundreds of years, animal welfare groups have been trying to get it outlawed since the 1940s because they consider it cruel to the foxes. In February 2002 Scotland passed a bill outlawing mounted hunting with dogs. After much political maneuvering, a similar bill was passed in England and Wales that went into effect in February 2005. The debate over the bill in the United Kingdom was generally divided between social classes, with upper-class landowners opposing it. Foxhunting has traditionally been a sport of the wealthy in the United Kingdom, including members of the royal family. The most prestigious foxhunting club in the country is operated by the Duke of Beaufort and dates back to the 1700s. According to Jill Lawless, in "Fox-Hunt Ban Has Fur Flying among Britons" (Associated Press, February 20, 2005), the Duke's club staged a mock foxhunt after the law went into effect as a form of social protest. Four people not part of the club were arrested for using dogs to hunt hares (rabbits). The new law bans the hunting of any mammal with the use of dogs.

In "Americans Going to Dogs" (*International Herald Tribune*, February 10, 2005), Brian Knowlton reports that there are 169 recognized foxhunts each year in the United States. This number has reportedly grown over the last decade as foxhunting becomes more popular in the country. A spokesperson for People for the Ethical Treatment of Animals (PETA) said, "I can't think of a more cruel way for an animal to die: to be pursued to the point of exhaustion, then ripped apart." The foxhunters at Elkridge-Hartford, a private hunting club in rural Maryland, defend their sport as a conservation measure for foxes. Club members own thousands of acres of undeveloped property around the area. A club official noted, "There wouldn't be all the fox we chase if it wasn't for foxhunting."

GUARD DUTY

Animals have been used to guard people and property from various threats for tens of thousands of years. Prehistoric humans were the first to figure out that dogs could warn them of the approach of wild animals. The ancient Greeks and Romans used dogs to guard their towns and military fortresses.

Guard duty encompasses several tasks performed by animals. One is to alert humans to danger. Another is to provide physical protection from danger. Many animals can provide alerts but not protection. For example, canaries were once used in mines to warn miners that dangerous gases were present. Because canaries are sensitive to small dosages of these gases, their deaths gave the miners time to leave dangerous areas before they, too, were overcome. This was not a trained or voluntary response by the canaries. By contrast, dogs can alert people to an approaching predator and defend them against it.

Dogs are still the most popular type of guarding animals. Besides their traditional guard duties, dogs are increasingly used to warn humans about impending natural phenomena, such as earthquakes. For years, researchers have been studying claims that dogs can somehow sense when an earthquake is about to happen. The speculation is that dogs may hear rumbling noises or sense vibrations occurring deep within the earth that precede actual ground movement.

Guarding Livestock

Historically, the best guards for livestock (cows, sheep, goats, and so on) have been dogs. Guard dogs protect livestock from common predators, such as coyotes, mountain lions, bears, and wild dogs. This is one job that dogs continue to do regularly.

Livestock guard dogs do not herd the animals and have been bred not to chase or harm them. Llamas and donkeys are also used as guard animals by some sheep producers in the western United States. In "Guard Llamas Keep Sheep Safe from Coyotes" (*National Geographic News*, June 10, 2003), Cameron Walker reports that llamas have natural aggressive tendencies toward canines, such as coyotes. Llamas that spot a predator near their sheep will strike defensive postures, sound alarm cries, and run toward the predator while kicking at the air. Sheep farmers in western states have found that llamas are even more effective guards than dogs. Llamas and donkeys are both naturally protective of sheep and aggressive toward coyotes and wild dogs. However, they are afraid of mountain lions and bears. Their main advantages are that they live longer and are less prone to accidents than guard dogs. Donkeys are also used in the Alps to guard sheep.

Guarding Territory and People

Dogs are also the most popular animal used for guarding territory and people. This job requires large breeds that are strong, protective, and territorial. The breeds most often used for this work are Doberman pinschers, rottweilers, komondors, German shepherds, and chows.

Guard dogs are not the same as watchdogs. Watchdogs bark when a stranger approaches them or their territory. Even small dogs, such as Chihuahuas, make good watchdogs. Guard dogs are intended to scare away and even attack intruders. Many guard dogs are employed by security companies. They work with handlers and human guards to patrol sites or protect individuals. Other guard dogs work without human accompaniment. They are placed on commercial and industrial properties, such as junkyards, at night.

Animal welfarists are highly critical of the use of unaccompanied guard dogs at commercial and industrial sites. They claim that these working dogs are given a minimum amount of food, water, and veterinary care, are kept in isolation in dangerous environments, and are treated cruelly to instill aggressive behavior.

Megan Metzelaar describes in "Guard Dog Update" (*ActionLine*, Winter 2002–2003) the hardships endured by some New Jersey guard dogs. According to Metzelaar, many guard dogs are leased from security companies. They are rotated around to different properties so that the dogs will not become accustomed to and possibly friendly with people in that area. The constant uncertainty makes the dogs feel vulnerable and insecure, which makes them even more aggressive. Critics say that the constant movement also makes it difficult for concerned people to monitor the condition of the dogs and report abuse and neglect to authorities.

MANUAL LABOR

Manual labor is work that requires physical skill and energy. The ancient Egyptians were one of the first great civilizations to put animals to work. They used a variety of animals for transportation and as beasts of burden or pack animals, mainly donkeys, oxen, camels, horses, and hinnies. (A hinny has a horse for a father and a donkey for a mother.) These animals were also used to pull plows in the fields and to thresh grain in mills. During the Middle Ages humans developed effective animal control devices such as stirrups, collars, and shoes that allowed animals to work even harder.

In the United States, mechanized equipment has replaced most of the work done by beasts of burden. Draft horses and mules are still used by a few farmers, particularly those in communities that use traditional farming techniques, such as the Amish.

Nearly all developing countries rely heavily on draft animals for agricultural work. (See Figure 8.2.) According to the Centre for Tropical Veterinary Medicine (February 1, 2005, http://www.vet.ed.ac.uk/ctvm/Research/DAPR/DAPR%20Background.htm), draft animals provide much-needed power for farming work and transportation in many tropical and subtropical countries. The most commonly used animals are cattle, buffalo, donkeys, and horses.

In the United States, some tasks historically performed by animals have become activities of leisure. For example, entrepreneurs in many large cities offer carriage rides to tourists. Animal welfarists are critical of these ventures, saying that carriage horses are forced to work under hazardous conditions on city streets crowded with traffic and often do not receive proper housing and care.

In "Carriage Horses: Cruelty Is the Name of the Trade" (2006, http://www.equineadvocates.com/carriage.html), the horse protection group Equine Advocates lists tragedies involving carriage horses that occurred between 1994 and 2000. Several horses have been hit by cars and at least one was electrocuted. The group says that horse-drawn carriage rides have been banned in several major cities for humane reasons.

In her book *The Horse: The Most Abused Domestic Animal* (1997), the animal welfarist Greta Bunting lists a host of problems associated with commercial carriage horses:

- The horses work long hours and are exposed to bad weather, dangerous traffic, and exhaust fumes.

- The horses are not fed and watered as often as they should be by their operators to cut down on "messes" on the streets.

- The horses experience many leg and hoof problems from walking repeatedly on asphalt and concrete surfaces.

- Some of the horses do not receive proper veterinary care.

- Retired carriage horses are often sent to the slaughterhouse.

FIGURE 8.2

A Sri Lankan farmer uses oxen to plow a rice paddy. © *Tim Page/Corbis. Reproduced by permission.*

LAW ENFORCEMENT

Law enforcement agencies around the world use animals (mostly dogs and horses) to help them perform security work. Dogs are, by far, the most common animals used.

Dogs

Many dogs are used by U.S. law enforcement agencies at the local and national levels to perform important tasks. These agencies include police and sheriff departments, arson investigators, the Federal Bureau of Investigation, the U.S. Department of Customs, the U.S. Department of Agriculture (USDA), the U.S. Department of Corrections, and the Drug Enforcement Agency.

The dogs are specially trained to work with officers during searches and arrests and to sniff out illegal substances. Dogs have incredibly sensitive noses. Their sense of smell is several thousand times better than that of humans. Dogs can smell tiny quantities of substances and can distinguish particular scents with amazing accuracy. This natural ability has proven to be an extremely useful tool in law enforcement applications.

The use of dogs by local police dates back to nineteenth-century Europe. British policemen on patrol often took their pet dogs with them as they walked the streets. Many police stations had mascot dogs just for this purpose. The successful use of dogs by military units during World War I (1914–18) brought added attention to the use of dogs in police work. During the 1930s British police departments set up official programs for the training and use of police dogs.

In 1907 the New York City Police Department incorporated police dogs into its work. However, the value of dogs for this work was not immediately recognized in the United States. They were used by only a dozen police forces through the early 1950s. Police dogs were sometimes used for intimidation purposes during the civil rights protests of the 1960s.

Many fire departments use dogs as part of their arson investigation teams. Arson dogs are specially trained to sniff for the presence of accelerants, such as gasoline, at sites where arson is suspected. Because of their incredible sense of smell, arson dogs can detect tiny amounts of accelerants lingering on surfaces inside buildings and vehicles or on people's clothes. The dogs indicate a find by either sitting or attempting to gain eye contact with their handlers. Because arsonists often hang around the scene of the crime, arson dogs are discreetly led through crowds gathered to watch fires to sniff for the presence of accelerants on people's clothing or belongings. Any suspicious finds are subjected to detailed laboratory testing.

Federal agencies that guard U.S. borders have used dogs since the 1970s. In 1970 the U.S. Customs Service began using dogs to sniff out narcotics being smuggled into the country at major border crossings. The U.S. Immigration and Naturalization Service (INS) also used dogs to help intercept illegal aliens and prevent smuggling. The USDA's Animal Plant Health Inspection Service employed dogs at international airports and border crossings to sniff people's luggage for banned plant and animal products. People sometimes try to sneak in items that may pose a disease threat to U.S. crops and animals. By 2001 dozens of dogs were part of the USDA's Beagle Brigade.

In 2003 these agencies were grouped together into the Department of Homeland Security. The canine resources of the individual agencies were combined into a new agency called U.S. Customs and Border Protection (CBP). The CBP reports in "CBP Canine Team Again Takes 'Paws to Recognize'" (*U.S. Customs and Border Protection Today*, September–October 2005) that in 2005 it had more than twelve hundred canine teams in operation. Many are stationed at airports, seaports, and border crossings around the country. Drug-sniffing dogs are also sometimes used in schools.

Horses

Horses have been used in law enforcement work for centuries. They were the fastest and surest form of transportation for officers for many years. Even after cars became common, many law enforcement agencies continued to use mounted patrols. According to MountedPolice .com (August 30, 2006), there are hundreds of jurisdictions around the United States that use horse-mounted officers.

Mounted units are popular in both rural and metropolitan areas. According to the United Mounted Peace Officers of Texas (August 15, 2006, http://www.tumpot .org/552.html), Texas authorities use 102 mounted units for patrols around the state. They are particularly useful in backcountry areas on dirt roads and rugged terrain. Several large U.S. police departments use mounted patrols for crowd control and to provide greater visibility of officers on the streets.

Mounted units are not without controversy. There have been injuries to horses, police, and members of the public. Because mounted units often perform crowd control during protests and demonstrations, the horses and the riders are exposed to people who may be angry and confrontational. There are reports of police horses being pelted with marbles and even garbage. Protesters claim that police often charge their horses into crowds, knocking over and injuring people.

Walking for many hours on city streets under stressful conditions is not easy on the horses. A few instances are reported each year of police horses throwing off or kicking their riders.

SEARCH, RESCUE, AND RECOVERY

Search and rescue (SAR) and body recovery work are performed by a variety of public service agencies in conjunction with private organizations. Some SAR units utilize dogs to help find missing humans, rescue people in danger, and recover bodies after disasters strike. Animals that assist in SAR work are generally considered valuable and noble by modern societies.

According to the National Association for Search and Rescue (2007, http://www.nasar.org/nasar/sar_dog_fact _sheet.php), there were over 150 SAR dog units across the country in 2006. The breeds most often used for this work are German shepherds, Dobermans, rottweilers, golden retrievers, giant schnauzers, and Labrador retrievers.

One of the most remarkable displays of SAR dogs in action occurred after the September 11, 2001 (9/11), terrorist attacks on the United States. More than 350 dogs scoured the rubble of the World Trade Center in New York City, along with their human trainers, looking for survivors and corpses. These dogs were from all over the United States and from foreign countries. The work was difficult. SAR dogs suffered from paw cuts and burns, dehydration, burning eyes, and psychological stress. Some handlers reported that their dogs became depressed after not finding any live victims and could not eat or sleep normally. Campaigns were begun to collect donated booties and other items needed by the SAR dogs who participated in helping during the 9/11 aftermath, and donations poured in from around the world.

HUMANITARIAN MINE DETECTION

Since World War II trained dogs have been used in military applications to detect land mines on the battlefield. In 1988 the United Nations called on the international community to devote resources to humanitarian demining—detecting and removing mines left over from numerous civil and regional conflicts around the world. A collaboration of governments, nongovernmental organizations (NGOs), and commercial enterprises has resulted to tackle the problem. The organization Adopt-a-Minefield (2007, http://www.landmines.org/crisis/) estimates that seventy to eighty million land mines remain in the ground in dozens of countries. Furthermore, exploding land mines kill as many as twenty thousand civilians each year.

According to the Geneva Centre for Humanitarian Demining (2002, http://www.gichd.ch/fileadmin/pdf/about_gichd/brochures/brochure_2002_e.pdf), since 1989 more than seven hundred dogs have been used in humanitarian demining operations in nearly twenty-three countries. Dogs' excellent sense of smell is particularly effective for detecting mines made up of nonmetal components. These mines are not detectable using metal detecting equipment.

In the early 1990s Bart Weetjens seized on the idea of training rats to detect underground mines. He began the NGO Anti-Persoonsmijnen Ontmijnende Product Ontwikkeling (APOPO; Anti-Personnel Mines Demining Product Development). APOPO collected Gambian giant pouched rats from Africa and trained them to detect mines while wearing harnesses controlled by human handlers. Rich Cookson reports in "A Nose for Danger" (*The Independent*, March 10, 2005) that the rats are highly intelligent, easily tamed, and have good senses of smell. Their light weight (typically less than six pounds) makes them far less likely than dogs to detonate buried mines. In 2000 APOPO began field-testing the rats in African countries plagued by mine problems. In "No Wizards, Just Patient Teachers" (*Journal of Mine Action*, August 2006, http://maic.jmu.edu/JOURNAL/10.1/personal/weetjens/weetjens.htm), Bart Weetjens and Jina Kim note that since 2003 the demining rats have been used in actual minefields throughout Africa.

MEDICAL SERVICE

Animals that provide for the physical and mental well-being of humans are perhaps the most admired of all working animals. They guide, aid, assist, and comfort people with all kinds of physical and mental disabilities, impairments, and problems.

Aiding the Physically Impaired

Many people troubled with physical impairments rely on trained dogs to improve their quality of life. According to Assistance Dogs International Inc. (2003, http://www.adionline.org/), a coalition of nonprofit organizations that train and place assistance dogs, assistance animals fall into three broad categories:

- Guide animals for the blind and visually impaired

- Hearing animals for the deaf and hearing impaired

- Assistance animals for those with other physical disabilities

HELP FOR THE BLIND OR VISUALLY IMPAIRED. Guide dogs have been trained to assist blind people for nearly two centuries. Figure 8.3 shows a guide dog at work with its owner. According to the Seeing Eye (2006, http://www.seeingeye.org/AboutUs.asp?sc=fq#2t), guide dogs

FIGURE 8.3

A golden retriever guides a visually impaired woman across the street. *Photograph by Peter Skinner/Science Source/Photo Researchers Inc. Reproduced by permission.*

for the blind typically work for seven to eight years and are then adopted as pets by their owners or others.

Guide Dog Users Inc. (GDUI) is an affiliate of the American Council of the Blind. The organization reports increasing problems with attacks on guide dogs by aggressive dogs while walking on city streets. It wants state laws enacted that will protect blind people and their guide dogs from any harassment or obstruction. In *A State Legislator's Handbook on Guide Dog Protection* (December 2001, http://www.gdui.org/handbook.html), the GDUI describes attacks on guide dogs and their devastating physical, emotional, and financial consequences. The GDUI estimates that it costs up to $60,000 to properly train a guide dog team.

HELP FOR THE DEAF OR HEARING IMPAIRED. Hearing dogs are specially trained to alert their deaf or hard-of-hearing owners to particular noises, such as a doorbell, knock at the door, oven timer, crying baby, alarm clock, or smoke alarm. When the dogs hear these noises, they make physical contact with their owners and lead them to the source of the noise.

HELP FOR OTHER PHYSICAL CONDITIONS. Service dogs do a variety of tasks for people with debilitating conditions, such as paralysis, lameness, epilepsy, or Parkinson's disease. The dogs are trained to pick up dropped items, fetch objects (such as a phone), pull wheelchairs, open and close doors, turn light switches on and off, and perform other tasks as needed. They can even assist people who are unsteady on their feet by providing a means of support and balance. Some service dogs are trained to summon help if their partner needs it.

"Seizure alert dogs" are trained to identify signs—generally undetectable to humans—that their human companion is going to have a seizure. Some dogs have demonstrated an ability to predict when a person is going to have a seizure up to an hour before it happens. No one knows exactly how these dogs know when a person is going to have a seizure, but some scientists speculate that the dogs may be aware of certain physical or behavioral changes such as dilated pupils or slight changes in skin color or facial expressions that occur. The dog may be trained to remain with the person throughout the seizure, sometimes lying on top of the person to steady him or her and prevent injury, and helping him or her up afterward.

NOT ALL CASES ARE SUCCESSFUL. Although the vast majority of service animals are greatly appreciated for their work, there have been cases of abuse. In February 2002 a blind man in Pennsylvania was charged with brutally killing his guide dog, Inky. The man allegedly went into a rage while intoxicated and kicked the dog to death. He was sentenced to up to twenty-three months in prison and ordered to pay $1,000 to a guide dog association. Animal welfarists use the case to point out that service animals and their human partners must be carefully screened and monitored to ensure that a good match is made and that the animals will be cared for properly.

One controversial issue associated with guide dogs is the use of breeding programs to produce them. Many organizations and training schools rescue dogs from pounds and animal shelters. This provides good homes for dogs that might otherwise be euthanized. Animal welfarists are critical of schools that breed their own dogs because there are already so many unwanted dogs in the country.

Mental and Physical Therapy

Another medical service that animals provide is therapeutic rather than utilitarian. Therapy animals provide emotional support or assist in rehabilitation activities. For example, therapy animals can comfort people undergoing psychological counseling. Many organizations working with abused children use therapy dogs in their programs. Petting and hugging the dogs relaxes the children and allows them to open up to counselors. Similar programs are used to calm children suffering from autism.

Therapy dogs also visit hospitals, orphanages, and nursing homes to cheer people who may be lonely or depressed. Only gentle and social dogs with good dispositions are used in this work. They must go through rigorous training and receive Canine Good Citizenship certification. The human participants are screened beforehand to ensure that they like animals and find them comforting.

Medical Detection

The idea of using animals in medical detection received credibility following the publication of Hywel Williams and A. Pembroke's article "Sniffer Dogs in the Melanoma Clinic" (*Lancet*, April 1, 1989). Williams and Pembroke describe a patient who had sought medical help about a worrisome mole on her leg. The woman reported that her dog constantly sniffed at the mole and seemed interested in it. Doctors discovered that the mole was cancerous and removed it. Similar stories have been reported by other dermatologists. Doctors speculate that dogs may be able to smell some unique scent emitted by cancerous skin cells.

Carolyn M. Willis et al. performed a study to test the ability of six dogs to detect by smell the presence of cancerous cells in urine samples and reported their findings in "Olfactory Detection of Human Bladder Cancer by Dogs: Proof of Principle Study" (*British Medical Journal*, September 25, 2004). The dogs were tested with urine from healthy people, people diagnosed with bladder cancer, and people diagnosed with other illnesses. As a group, the dogs successfully identified cancerous urine 41% of the time. This is well above the 14% success rate Willis et al. expected from chance alone. The two best performing dogs were cocker spaniels. They were correct 56% of the time.

Michael McCulloch et al. report in "Diagnostic Accuracy of Canine Scent Detection in Early- and Late-Stage Lung and Breast Cancers" (*Integrative Cancer Therapies*, March 2006) the results of a study in which they trained five dogs to identify breath samples from cancer patients. McCulloch et al. found that the dogs correctly detected 99% of the samples from lung cancer patients and 88% from breast cancer patients. The dogs made incorrect detections in 1% of lung cancer patients and in 2% of breast cancer patients. It is believed that the dogs are able to detect trace amounts of chemicals not ordinarily present in the breath of healthy people.

MILITARY SERVICE

Of all the service and assistance animals in use, animals used by the military are the most controversial. To animal welfarists and animal rights activists, the use of animals by the military can be extremely disturbing. These animals are often put into tremendous danger, and many of them die during their service. On the contrary, members of

FIGURE 8.4

A relief of a Greek horse-drawn chariot. © *Ganni Dagli Orti/Corbis.*

the military say that service animals have saved many human lives in battle. They argue that animal deaths in war are regrettable but permissible if human lives are saved. Animal rights activists and welfarists argue that animals involved in warfare do not know what they are fighting for or against and have poor chances of surviving.

Although some animal work is classified, it is known that the U.S. military has used horses, pigeons, dogs, chickens, dolphins, beluga whales, sea lions, and other marine mammals during combat. Besides horses, many of these animals are still used in modern warfare.

History

Humans have used animals in military roles for at least thirty-five hundred years. Sometime before 1500 BC, the Mesopotamians used horses to pull their chariots during battle. (See Figure 8.4.)

Elephants were used in warfare as early as 1100 BC. Roman armies assembled entire formations of attack dogs for battle. Dogs were also used in military campaigns by Attila the Hun (406–453). Cavalry units in which warriors fought while riding horses date back to around 800 to 700

BC. In the 1500s European soldiers began using heavy artillery and cannons that were pulled by teams of horses. War dogs were used for guard and messenger duty.

According to *Wild Horses: An American Romance* (July 19, 2001, http://net.unl.edu/artsFeat/wildhorses/), most of the six million horses that served the U.S. military in World War I were killed. The deaths of millions of other horses in military service to other countries severely depleted the world's horse population. World War I was the last war in which horses played a major role in combat. By 1942 all U.S. cavalry units were disbanded or mechanized.

Coincidentally, this was the same year that dogs were first officially inducted into the U.S. Army. A group called Dogs for Defense asked Americans to donate dogs to the army. Dogs were trained for guard and police duty, to pull sleds, to carry packs and messages, to help reconnaissance patrols find hidden enemy soldiers, and to help the medical corps find and rescue wounded soldiers.

Following World War II the surviving dogs were returned to their owners. This was not the case in later wars. Military officials were afraid of a trained military dog attacking someone in civilian life. It became common practice to euthanize unusable and retired war dogs or leave them behind on the battlefield. Animal welfarists and soldiers were strongly against this policy, particularly after the Vietnam War (1954–75).

Military historians estimate that war dogs saved thousands of U.S. soldiers from death or injury during the Vietnam War. Approximately four thousand service dogs guarded troops, alerted them to booby traps, and pulled the wounded to safety. The U.S. War Dog Association (2006, http://www.uswardogs.org/id31.html) lists the names of nearly three hundred dogs that were killed in action during the war. Most service dogs that survived the war were left behind in Vietnam when U.S. troops pulled out. The fate of these dogs is unknown. Many veterans, including the Vietnam Dog Handlers Association, are lobbying for a national memorial to be built in Washington, D.C., to honor the service of war dogs. According to Scott Schonauer in "New Law Allows Adoption of Military Dogs" (*Stars and Stripes*, November 26, 2000), thirty thousand dogs have served in the U.S. military since World War II.

In November 2000 President Bill Clinton signed a new law into effect that allows retired military dogs to be adopted rather than euthanized. New owners have to agree not to hold the government responsible for any injuries or damages caused by former military dogs. Because of their extensive training, the dogs are expected to be useful in law enforcement and rescue work. In December 2005 President George W. Bush signed legislation allowing the military to adopt out active-duty military dogs to their handlers under certain circumstances. The new law resulted after a U.S. Air Force sergeant and her bomb-sniffing dog were injured in Iraq by an improvised explosive device (IED). C. Todd Lopez reports in "Sergeant Thanks Congress for Helping Keep Her Team Together" (February 1, 2006, http://www.af.mil/news/story.asp?storyID=123015993) that Sergeant Jamie Dana was critically injured, while her dog, Rex, suffered minor injuries. As she began to recover, Dana asked the military for permission to adopt Rex. At first, her request was denied, because the adoption law only applied to retired dogs, and Rex still had many years of service left. Widespread media attention and the support of powerful legislators in the U.S. Senate and U.S. House of Representatives helped push through legislation that allows active-duty military dogs to be adopted out at the military's discretion. In January 2006 Dana officially adopted Rex.

Current Uses

According to Donna Miles in "Military Working Dogs Protect Forces, Bases during Terror War" (September 3, 2004, http://www.defenselink.mil/news/Sep2004/n09032004_2004090306.html), as of September 2004 about twenty-three hundred dogs were working as sentries, detecting land mines and bombs, and performing search, rescue, and recovery tasks for the U.S. military. Many were stationed in Afghanistan or Iraq to deal with ongoing military conflicts in those countries. Military dogs are trained at the Military Working Dog Center at Lackland Air Force Base in San Antonio, Texas. The most common breeds used are German shepherds, Dutch shepherds, and Belgian Malinois (a variety of Belgian shepherd). The military conducts its own breeding program and purchases suitable dogs from other breeders. Most dogs have a military career of around ten years and are then retired from the service.

Hundreds of animals were used by the U.S. military during the 2003 invasion of Iraq, including dogs, dolphins, pigeons, and chickens. The use of animals was criticized by animal rights and welfare groups, including PETA, the HSUS, and the United Poultry Concerns. In "War: Tell Congress to Leave the Animals Out of It!" (April 2003, http://www.peta.org/Automation/AlertItem.asp?id=686), PETA states that "these animals never enlisted, they know nothing of Iraq or Saddam Hussein, and they probably won't survive." Other activists have accused the military of wasting animals needlessly when sophisticated equipment could be used instead.

The military dogs in Iraq help perform various tasks, including guard duty, bomb detection, scouting, and even apprehending enemy soldiers. The HSUS donated $9,000 to buy thirty cooling vests for K-9 dogs in battle with the U.S. Marines in Iraq. The vests wrap around the dogs' midsections and have pockets for inserts that remain cool for hours. The HSUS was worried that the dogs would suffer from hot desert temperatures (as high as 120° F) during the summer months. Birds were deployed in Iraq as early-warning alerts in the event of a chemical or biological attack. However, their use is not considered a success. Nearly every chicken died after only days in the desert because of heat, stress, illness, or injury. Some may have been killed and eaten by hungry U.S. troops. The chickens were replaced with nearly two hundred pigeons, but these birds, too, died in large numbers.

More successful was the use of some specially trained dolphins. U.S. forces used two bottle-nosed Atlantic dolphins named Makai and Tacoma to seek out underwater mines along the Iraqi coast. The dolphins were trained to find the mines without detonating them and then alert handlers to their presence.

Frontline reported on the U.S. Navy's historical use of dolphins and other marine mammals in *A Whale of a Business* (November 1997, http://www.pbs.org/wgbh/pages/frontline/shows/whales/). The navy began its Marine Mammal Program in 1960. Marine mammals were trained to perform tasks such as filming objects underwater, retrieving and delivering equipment, and guarding vessels against enemy divers. They were used during the Vietnam War and later in the Persian Gulf during the 1980s.

Dolphins are trained to detect enemy divers and attach restraining devices to them so they can be apprehended by human handlers. These devices include a line with a buoy that floats to the surface. Sea lions are trained to actually pursue any fleeing divers who go ashore. Mine-hunting dolphins identify and mark mines so that they can be decommissioned or later exploded safely. In 2007 the U.S. Navy announced plans to use dolphins and sea lions to patrol the waters off a naval base near Seattle, Washington. The marine animals are trained to detect and catch potential terrorists attacking from the water.

Stray Animals Offer Comfort during War

Besides the dogs in official U.S. military service, soldiers stationed around the world often befriend stray dogs and cats in other countries. Soldiers report that these dogs and cats provide them with much-needed comfort and companionship during military conflicts. Many military personnel serving in Iraq found that they wanted to adopt the strays they had grown to love. According to Ron Harris, in "Dogs of War Win U.S. Hearts" (*St. Louis Post-Dispatch*, February 6, 2004), Laura Salter, the director of the World Society for the Protection of Animals, said, "We get three to six calls or e-mails a week from soldiers, fathers, mothers, wives, and siblings trying to find out how to get a dog from Iraq to the United States."

Because only military animals are allowed to fly on Department of Defense planes, the soldiers must find alternative means of transporting their adopted friends back to the United States. Flying an animal across international borders and dealing with bureaucratic issues can cost as much as $2,000, so international animal welfare groups and military support organizations have joined together to raise money and attract volunteers to transport these animals to their new homes.

Adopting a pet while on a tour of duty is, however, strictly against U.S. military rules. Under General Order 1A, soldiers may receive a reduction in rank or a court-martial if they are caught with a pet while in active service overseas. According to the armed forces, this is due largely to the threat of disease from strays in foreign countries. According to Dru Sefton, in "Despite Military Rules, War Zone Pets Make It to States" (Newhouse News Service, February 23, 2005), the U.S. Air Force reported in early 2005 that fifty-three people were treated for rabies after coming into contact with an infected stray at Bagram Air Base in Afghanistan.

Sefton notes that Bonnie Buckley—who founded Military Mascots, a nonprofit group devoted to assisting military personnel send their adopted pets home and mailing pet food to bases in Iraq and Afghanistan—acknowledges that she helps service people undermine their superior officers. She also maintains that the group will not bring a pet to the United States unless a specific family intends to take it in. Animal welfare groups are ambivalent about the practice, reminding those in the military that there are millions of homeless pets already in the United States in need of adoption.

CHAPTER 9
PETS

Pets are animals that humans keep for pleasure rather than utility. Their value is mostly emotional. They help to fulfill human desires for companionship, affection, entertainment, and ownership. Historians are not sure when humans first started keeping animals as pets. Keeping an animal for pleasure rather than for food or work was possible only for people who were well off and had the resources to feed extra mouths. For centuries pet ownership was mostly limited to the upper classes of society—royalty, aristocrats, and landowners. The modern age of pet keeping began in the mid-1800s, when a thriving middle class emerged in society. This was the first time that many people had the time and money to keep animals solely for companionship and pleasure. Owning pets eventually became more and more popular.

The American Pet Products Manufacturers Association (APPMA) was founded in 1958 and is the nation's leading pet industry trade group. More than nine hundred companies were members of the association as of 2007. Every two years the APPMA releases data on pet ownership. According to the *2005–2006 National Pet Owners Survey* (2006, http://www.appma.org/press_industrytrends .asp), nearly 359 million animals are kept as pets in the United States. Freshwater fish, cats, and dogs are the most popular. Other common pets include horses, rabbits, livestock, pigeons and poultry, guinea pigs, turtles, snakes, ferrets, gerbils, lizards, and miscellaneous reptiles and rodents. Sixty-three percent of U.S. households had a pet, up from 56% in 1988. Nearly half owned more than one pet. The APPMA estimates that U.S. pet owners spent $38.4 billion in 2006 on pet supplies, equipment, and services. This is more than double the $17 billion spent in 1994.

The Gallup Organization conducted a poll in December 2006 to learn more about Americans and their pets. Gallup found that 60% of the people polled had at least one pet. A breakdown of ownership by pet type is shown in Figure 9.1. A breakdown by owner demographics is included in Table 9.1. White people, people between the ages of eighteen and forty-nine, and people living in the South or West were found to be the most likely pet owners. Some respondents had multiple pets of different species. For example, the poll notes that 17% reported having both a cat and a dog. Just over half of cat owners (51%) reported having multiple cats in their household, whereas 41% of dog owners said they had more than one dog.

Pets have a unique status. Legally, they are considered personal property. This offers them some protection under the law, as damaging someone else's property is a crime. From a psychological standpoint some pets enjoy a higher value and are considered members of the family, almost like children. In October 2006 the federal government acknowledged this bond with passage of the Pets Evacuation and Transportation Standards Act. The act requires that federal, state, and local emergency preparedness officials include pets and service animals (such as seeing-eye dogs) in their plans for evacuating and sheltering people during disasters. The law was spurred by events following Hurricane Katrina along the Gulf Coast during 2005. Many distressed pet owners were forced to leave their animals behind when they were evacuated. Others refused to leave without their pets, putting themselves in great danger.

It surprises many pet owners to learn that some animal rights groups are opposed to the idea of keeping pets. Pet ownership is a thorny issue in the animal rights debate. Some activists believe that any use of any animal for any human purpose is wrong. However, when it comes to pets, many consider this stance too radical. A great number of those who work to improve animal welfare are pet owners. Most animal rights groups and animal welfarists focus their attention on particular pet problems, such as neglect, abuse, and overpopulation. They are particularly critical of breeders and pet stores

FIGURE 9.1

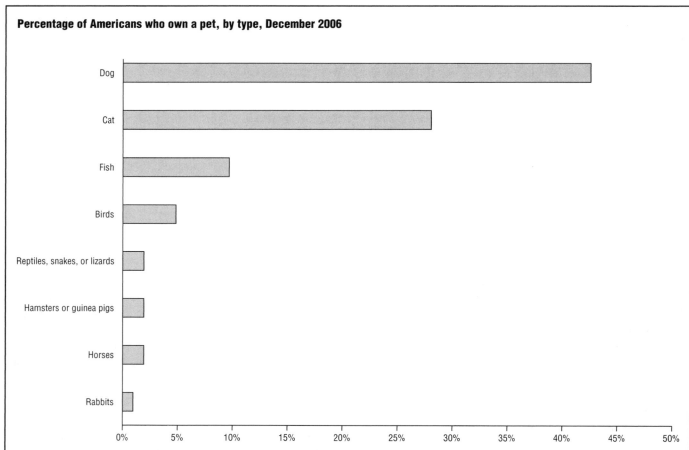

Percentage of Americans who own a pet, by type, December 2006

SOURCE: Adapted from text in Frank Newport, Jeffrey M. Jones, Lydia Saad, and Joseph Carroll, *Americans and Their Pets*, The Gallup Organization, December 21, 2006, http://www.galluppoll.com/content/Default.aspx?ci=25969&t=C4beVokGrmzlhI0.Hd57excCoq7XlxsimrtmY2DBFNcG8AtIS7%2fV0lszxB-PeuGqr-OS0rTDI5CP2lkviyHf4ICOjy1L%2fUH-%2fFBjUMMC1hLmGF6Dx0SNAswJrjMuRlBs9-wJRR8lAdoUc0s3BNJAnCpQzO8qM57LZJFhKguV4%2fga (accessed December 29, 2006) Copyright © 2006 by The Gallup Organization. Reproduced by permission of The Gallup Organization.

TABLE 9.1

Pet ownership, by demographic group, December 2006

	Total pet owner %	Own dog %	Own cat %
18- to 49-year-olds	68	50	35
50- to 64-year-olds	57	43	29
65 years and older	43	33	17
East	51	35	29
Midwest	58	46	24
South	61	49	27
West	68	47	41
Whites	63	46	33
Non-whites	49	38	17

SOURCE: Frank Newport, Jeffrey M. Jones, Lydia Saad, and Joseph Carroll, "Pet Ownership by Groups," in *Americans and Their Pets*, The Gallup Organization, December 21, 2006, http://www.galluppoll.com/content/Default.aspx?ci=25969&t=C4beVokGrmzlhI0.Hd57excCoq7Xlxsimrtm Y2DBFNcG8AtIS7%2fV0lszxB-PeuGqr-OS0rTDI5CP2lkviyHf4ICOjy1L% 2fUH-%2fFBjUMMC1hLmGF6Dx0SNAswJrjMuRlBs9-wJRR8lAdoUc0s3 BNJAnCpQzO8qM57LZJFhK guV4%2fga (accessed December 29, 2006). Copyright © 2006 by The Gallup Organization. Reproduced by permission of The Gallup Organization.

that sell pets to the public. The keeping of wild animals as pets is condemned by all major organizations working for animal rights and welfare.

Some groups state that people keep pets for the wrong reasons. They argue that some people get pets to compensate for their inability to engage in healthy social contact with other people. Pets may be a crutch or a time-filler to these people. Others rely on pets to build their egos or make them feel good about themselves in some way. The ability to control another living being can be a powerful motivator. Some people see pets as disposable items to be kept as long as they are useful or fun, and discarded when they are not. Many people think that taking care of a pet is educational for children because it teaches them responsibility and respect for other living creatures. Some people believe that keeping a pet has a spiritual basis and that it brings them closer to nature.

The common thread in all these reasons is that they focus on the needs and wants of the pet owner rather than the pet. Some people feel this is only fair, as it is the pet owner who provides food, shelter, and care. Should people be allowed to keep animals as pets as long they take care of them? There is a movement by some humane organizations to refer to pets as companion animals and to owners as guardians. These terms demonstrate the desire of these groups to elevate pets from property status to wards or dependents.

SHELTERS, POUNDS, AND EUTHANASIA

Despite the popularity of pets, every year millions of them wind up in public and private shelters. The vast majority are cats and dogs. They are either turned in by owners who no longer want them or are picked up as strays. Some are lost pets that can be reunited with their owners, but many are homeless animals with no place to go. In "HSUS Pet Overpopulation Estimates" (October 12, 2006, http://www.hsus.org/pets/issues_affecting_our _pets/pet_overpopulation_and_ownership_statistics/hsus _pet_overpopulation_estimates.html), the HSUS estimates that U.S. shelters receive six to eight million cats and dogs each year. Approximately half of these animals are euthanized (killed). The remainder are adopted or reclaimed by owners.

History

According to the HSUS, the first public pounds were constructed during the 1700s to impound stray livestock. As American society changed from rural to urban, these facilities switched their focus to stray dogs and became dog pounds. Rabies was a serious public health threat well into the twentieth century, with thousands of cases reported each year. The vast majority of cases were contracted by people from domestic dogs, so animal control departments operated dog pounds as part of public health and safety programs. Their mission was to protect people rather than to ensure the welfare of the dogs.

Following World War II (1939–45), rabies vaccinations for dogs became mandatory in the United States. This program, combined with effective stray dog control, dramatically reduced the occurrence of rabies in dogs. Pounds continued to pick up stray dogs (and cats by this time) but mostly to control aggressive and nuisance animals and "clean the streets" than as rabies protection. Pounds also became centralized facilities for people to get rid of unwanted pets.

Dog pounds came to be called animal shelters. They held stray animals for a few days (if there was room) to see if their owners would reclaim them. If not, unwanted strays and pets were sold to research laboratories or given to anyone who wanted them. Unclaimed and unplaced animals were killed using whatever means were available. Public animal shelters received little funding from

TABLE 9.2

Shelter euthanasia of owned animals, selected years 1973–2000

Year	Total owned dogs and cats	Euthanized	Approximate % of owned animals euthanized
1973	65 million	13.5 million	21.0
1982	92 million	8–10 million	10.0
1992	110 million	5–6 million	5.5
2000	120 million	4–6 million	4.5

SOURCE: Deborah J. Salem and Andrew N. Rowan, "Table 1. Shelter Euthanasia of Owned Animals," in *The State of the Animals: 2001*, Humane Society of the United States, 2001

local governments, and humane treatment and euthanasia were not a priority in most jurisdictions.

This began to change as the animal welfare movement gained momentum during the 1960s and 1970s. Shelters came under increasing pressure to focus on welfare issues besides public health and nuisance concerns. Some municipal governments began contracting their shelter operations to nonprofit animal welfare organizations, such as local humane societies and rescue groups. These organizations held fund-raisers and were able to secure private donations to help shelters operate. However, most shelters continued to euthanize large numbers of animals as the homeless animal population surged out of control.

Euthanasia

The word *euthanasia* comes from a Greek term meaning "good death." During the 1800s it was first used to describe mercy killing conducted with the approval of the law. In the twentieth century euthanasia of shelter animals was conducted on a massive scale. However, euthanasia rates have been generally declining since the late twentieth century. The HSUS reports that the number of euthanized cats and dogs has dropped considerably in the United States, from about 13.5 million deaths per year in 1973 to four to six million deaths in 2000, whereas over the same period the total number of cats and dogs has nearly doubled. (See Table 9.2.)

Animal People is an animal organization that issues the monthly publication *Animal People News*. Each year in its July–August edition the newspaper compiles data collected over the three previous fiscal years on the number of animals killed in shelters in selected representative cities and states around the country. These data are used to estimate national shelter killing rates. In 2006 *Animal People News* (http://www.animalpeoplenews.org/ 06/7-8/7.06.swf) estimated that 4.4 million shelter animals were euthanized in the United States. Figure 9.2 compares this estimate with estimates from previous years dating back to 1970.

FIGURE 9.2

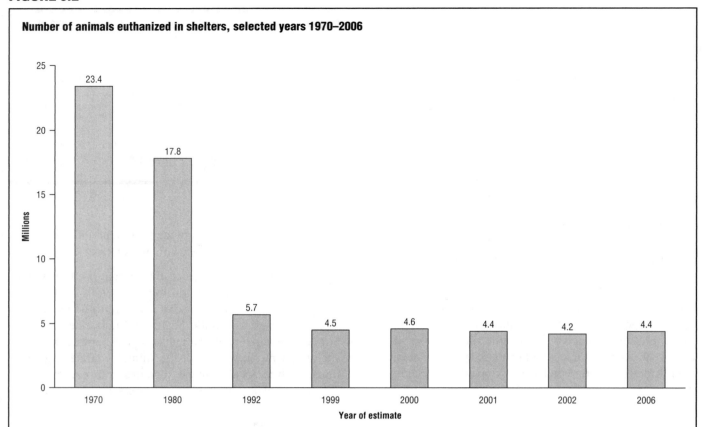

Number of animals euthanized in shelters, selected years 1970–2006

SOURCE: Adapted from Merritt Clifton, "Latest Data Shows Shelter Killing Down to 4.2 Million/Year," in *Animal People News*, Animal People, Inc., July/August 2003, http://www.animalpeoplenews.org/03/7.8/latestShelterKilling78.03.html and "Gains Against Shelter Killing Come Hard in the Gulf States, West & Midwest," in *Animal People News*, Animal People, Inc., July/August 2006, http://www.animalpeoplenews.org/06/7-8/7.06.swf (accessed January 3, 2007)

According to Animal People, there are regional differences in shelter killing rates. In general, shelters located in the Northeast have the lowest euthanasia rates, whereas shelters in the Southeast have the highest rates. This is attributed to several factors, including the weather, the availability of low-cost spay-neuter programs, and animal control policies. The cold winters in the Northeast lower the fertility rates of cats and dogs and claim the lives of stray animals so that fewer end up in shelters. Animal welfare organizations are much more predominant in the Northeast and provide low-cost spay-neuter programs that help control populations of unwanted animals. Many northeastern municipalities charge pet owners licensing fees with higher amounts for unfixed animals. This is far less common in the South.

Euthanasia Methods

Although the public assumes that animals euthanized at shelters are killed by lethal injection, this is not always true. The American Veterinary Medical Association (AVMA) maintains a list of approved euthanasia methods for various types of animals. In *Guidelines for Humane Euthanasia of Animals* (2000, http://www.avma.org/disaster/responseguide/F_euthanasia.pdf), the AVMA states, "Euthanasia techniques should result in rapid loss of consciousness followed by cardiac or respiratory arrest and the ultimate loss of brain function. In addition, the technique should minimize distress and anxiety experienced by the animal prior to loss of consciousness." However, the AVMA admits that "the absence of pain and distress cannot always be achieved."

Acceptable euthanasia methods for cats and dogs include intravenous injection of barbiturates (such as sodium pentobarbital or secobarbital) or potassium chloride/anesthetic, or gassing the animals with inhalant anesthetics (such as ether), carbon dioxide, or carbon monoxide gas. In addition, gassing with nitrogen or argon is considered acceptable with some reservations on cats and dogs, as are the use of electrocution and penetrating captive bolts (bolts shot at point-blank range from a gun into the animal's skull, which if shot at the proper location destroy enough brain tissue to kill the animal instantly) on dogs only. Each of the methods, along with its advantages and disadvantages, is described in the *2000 Report of the AVMA Panel on Euthanasia* (March 1, 2001, http://www.avma.org/issues/animal_welfare/euthanasia.pdf).

The report notes that injection of barbiturates intravenously (within a vein) is the preferred method of euthanasia for horses, dogs, cats, and other small animals. Advantages include rapid and smooth action, minimal physical distress to the animal if the procedure is performed correctly, and relatively low cost compared with other options. The main disadvantages are that each animal must be personally restrained for the procedure, and personnel must be properly trained in giving injections. Also, barbiturates are federally controlled substances that can be purchased only using a U.S. Drug Enforcement Administration registration and order form. Their use is controlled by state law, and there are specific record-keeping requirements that must be met.

In *The Humane Society of the United States Euthanasia Training Manual* (2002), the HSUS recommends injection of sodium pentobarbital as the preferred euthanasia method for companion animals. Intravenous injection is the recommended route of delivery, but intraperitoneal (within the peritoneal cavity in the abdomen) injection is considered acceptable for cats, kittens, and puppies in which intravenous injections cannot be administered easily. Intracardiac injection (within the heart) is considered acceptable only if the animal is already unconscious. Intrahepatic injection (within the liver) is not considered acceptable because of lack of scientific study on the procedure. The HSUS recommends that euthanasia of each animal be carried out by two people—one to hold the animal and one to administer the injection. Both the AVMA and the HSUS stress that shelter personnel performing euthanasia must be well trained.

Lethal injection is a hands-on procedure in which animals and personnel come into close physical contact. When shelters began practicing humane euthanasia, it was thought that a hands-off approach would be easier for the workers performing euthanasia. Gas chambers were common because the euthanizer could perform the procedure from outside the chamber by opening a valve or flipping a switch.

Many shelters still use gassing to euthanize unwanted animals. Although the use of poisonous gases is considered acceptable by the AVMA, the organization notes that "any gas that is inhaled must reach a certain concentration in the alveoli before it can be effective; therefore, euthanasia with any of these agents takes some time." Animal welfarists roundly condemn gassing as a means of euthanasia. In 1998 California passed a law prohibiting the use of carbon monoxide chambers for euthanizing shelter animals.

Animal shelter workers have an incredibly stressful and emotionally demanding job. Many get into the line of work because they care about animals but become frustrated by the public's seeming lack of concern for the tragic fate of many millions of unwanted pets. Most humane organizations believe that the solution to the euthanization problem lies in aggressive sterilization campaigns, better education of pet owners, and successful adoption programs.

Spaying and Neutering

Overpopulation of cats and dogs is a tremendous problem. It is aggravated by the fact that these animals reproduce at high rates. Experts generally agree that massive and sustained birth control methods must be implemented on cat and dog populations to bring the problem under control. Surgical sterilization of female animals is called spaying, or removal of the ovaries, fallopian tubes, and uterus. Male animals are neutered or castrated by having their testicles removed. Pet owners commonly refer to these sterilization procedures as fixing or altering an animal. Increasingly, animal groups use the term *neuter* to refer to sterilization of either males or females.

Veterinarians have been promoting spaying and neutering of pets for several decades. According to the animal organization SPAY USA (2007, http://www.spayusa.org/main_directory/02-facts_and_education/benefits_sn.asp), sterilization has many medical, behavioral, and social benefits, including:

- Female pets do not go into heat (have fertile cycles) during which scents are emitted that attract male animals. Sterilization eliminates the problems associated with male animals that gather and often fight over females in heat.

- Sterilization usually stops male cats (toms) from marking their territory by spraying strong-smelling urine.

- Sterilization makes pets more likely to stay at home than wander.

- Sterilized females cannot develop ovarian or uterine infections and are less likely to develop mammary cancer.

- Sterilized males usually become less aggressive.

- Sterilization helps reduce the number of stray and unwanted animals in the community. This is advantageous for public health and safety reasons and reduces the enormous cost to taxpayers and private agencies of capturing, impounding, and destroying millions of unwanted animals each year.

Some pet owners are resistant to spaying and neutering their pets. Their reasons can include one or more of the following common myths:

- Surgery costs too much or is too painful for the pet.

- Having a litter can be good for the pet and educational for children.

- Fixed animals get fat and lazy.

- Backyard breeding is a fun hobby that brings in extra money.

- Male animals do not need to be fixed because they do not have litters.

- Neutering male dogs robs them of their masculinity and makes them less protective as guard dogs.

- Sterilization is unnatural.

Many states and municipalities actively encourage spaying and neutering of pets as a means to reduce overpopulation. Those with licensing programs usually charge pet owners a lower registration fee if their pets are sterilized. A number of states also sell special license plates that benefit spay/neuter programs.

Increasingly, animal shelters spay and neuter cats and dogs before adoption or require new owners to do so within a certain time period after adoption. In 1998 California passed a law that requires preadoption sterilization of cats and dogs. The San Francisco Society for the Prevention of Cruelty to Animals (SPCA) was one of the first humane groups in the United States to offer low-cost and early spay/neuter surgery.

Low-cost clinics are often run by humane organizations. They operate under nonprofit status, which allows them to save on overhead and tax costs. They offer discounted rates either to the general public or to those people who have adopted an animal from their shelter. The rates can be substantially lower than those charged by veterinarians in private practice. Such clinics are not without controversy. Some veterinarians complain that the clinics have an unfair advantage because of their nonprofit status. A few states have passed laws that prohibit veterinarians associated with nonprofit groups from operating low-cost spay/neuter clinics. Advocates of the clinics insist that they provide a much-needed service and help reduce animal overpopulation.

In the past veterinarians recommended sterilization for cats and dogs around six months of age. During the mid-1990s many humane organizations began advocating early spay/neuter (ESN) programs. Most clinics practicing ESN will perform the surgery on kittens and puppies at least eight weeks old. Shelters flooded with kittens and puppies have heartily embraced the practice because it allows them to sterilize young animals before they are adopted. Some veterinarians are worried about the long-term effects of ESN surgery on the animals' young bones and express concern that it could cause abnormalities in skeletal growth. However, as of 2007 no definitive scientific studies had proven this. Veterinarians report that kittens and puppies that undergo ESN recover from the surgery much quicker than their older counterparts.

In April 2003 the U.S. Food and Drug Administration (FDA) approved use of the drug Neutersol (zinc gluco-

nate neutralized by arginine) for chemical sterilization of three- to ten-month-old puppies. The drug is injected into the testicles and works by stopping the production of sperm. It does not eliminate the hormone testosterone, as traditional neutering does. This may be a drawback, as testosterone is considered a major factor in behavior problems seen in unaltered dogs. According to the press release "First Neutering Drug for Puppies Gains FDA Approval" (May 23, 2003, http://www.prweb.com/releases/2003/5/prweb66823.htm), Neutersol is 99.6% effective, and the injection does not require that the puppy be put under general anesthesia. The FDA recommends that puppies be sedated before the injection to eliminate movement and to help with any pain. Neutersol is expected to be used mostly at animal shelters that wish to sterilize dogs before adoption but do not have ready access to a surgical clinic.

No-Kill Shelters

Some animal welfarists and members of the public criticize shelters for using euthanasia at all. They believe that every animal that enters a shelter deserves the opportunity to be adopted no matter how long it takes. Critics say that this viewpoint is unrealistic. They point out that some animals are too aggressive, injured, or sick to be adopted. There is no practical alternative but to euthanize them. Also, some pet owners rely on shelters rather than private veterinarians to euthanize their sick and elderly pets.

During the 1990s the concept of no-kill shelters became popular. The name implies that no animals are ever euthanized in these shelters—an idea that appeals to many people. In reality, most no-kill shelters still euthanize animals that are unadoptable because of illness or temperament. Some traditional shelters (or open-admission shelters, as they are called) do not like the use of the term "no-kill." They feel it can be misleading and accuse some organizations of using the term just to gain financial support and political favor. Welfare organizations argue among themselves about the exact definition of no-kill and which animals are adoptable.

The truth is that all shelters (public and private) operate with limited space, personnel, and financial budgets. The people who run them must make life-and-death decisions about the animals that enter the facilities. These decisions are based on moral, political, social, and financial considerations. In "No-Kill Movement: No-Kill Legislation" (January 19, 2007, http://www.maddiesfund.org/nokill/nokill_legis_hayden.html#bryant), Taimie Bryant argues that traditional shelters are reluctant to give up the use of euthanasia, seeing it as a necessary evil and an issue that pits themselves, performers of a public service, against a public that refuses to spay and neuter its pets. By contrast, shelters feel euthanasia is the most compassionate option, though not at all a desirable one. In "Seven Basic

Policies for Every Animal Shelter" (*Animal Sheltering*, January–February 1996), the HSUS notes, "Euthanasia of shelter animals to make room for others is a tragic necessity that prevents animal suffering."

Even though many people and organizations wish that euthanasia was not necessary, they also recognize some of the practical drawbacks of the no-kill idea. Nancy Lawson and Carrie Allen, in "What Would It Take?" (*Animal Sheltering*, January–February 2002), describe how the no-kill idea became an advertising and fund-raising slogan for some animal organizations that use it to set themselves apart from traditional shelters.

Popularization of the no-kill idea is generally credited to Richard Avanzino, the president of the San Francisco SPCA from 1976 to 1999. During this period the city achieved the lowest euthanasia rate of any urban city in the nation. The San Francisco SPCA started adoption, spay/neuter, and animal management programs that became models for every other welfare organization. In 1992 Avanzino spoke at an HSUS workshop in Las Vegas on the no-kill movement. He advocated no-kill as a concept and a mission for welfarists, not as a weapon to use against traditional shelters in fund-raising campaigns.

Lawson and Allen also address the difficulties that some organizations encounter when they try to become no-kill shelters. In 1995 the Humane Society of Gallatin Valley in Bozeman, Montana, decided to institute a no-euthanasia policy. However, as the only shelter in the city it also decided to continue accepting any animal that was relinquished. The shelter soon became overwhelmed, and animal welfare suffered. Ganay Johnson, the shelter director, reported that "animals who came in 'adoptable' quickly became unadoptable in a crowded environment that wore on their temperaments and made them sick."

The same problem led some organizations to limit their shelter admissions. Critics state that such shelters do not really serve their communities by accepting only the "cute and cuddly" and turning away difficult-to-adopt animals. This practice is seen as self-serving. It allows these shelters to practice a true no-kill policy but burdens neighboring shelters with the animals they turn away. Yet, the opposite policy can be just as troublesome. Lawson and Allen cite well-meaning shelter groups that refuse to euthanize any animals, even typically unadoptable animals such as aggressive dogs. These animals take up cage space and resources that can be devoted to animals with a reasonable chance of being adopted. Deciding which course of action is better is difficult to make.

The no-kill label is a powerful public relations tool. Many people prefer to donate money to an organization or shelter that advertises itself as no-kill, but no-kill does not necessarily mean no-euthanasia. It also does not guarantee that the animals are being properly cared for and kept in clean, uncrowded, disease-free conditions. Critics state that some people who want to warehouse or hoard animals adopt the label to raise funds. Others may begin with the best intentions and quickly become overwhelmed by the number of animals with severe physical and emotional problems requiring extensive surgery and/or rehabilitation.

Several major cities are already operating or working toward no-kill status. In 1994 the San Francisco SPCA formed an adoption pact with city animal control officials to become the first U.S. city with a no-kill policy. Shelters in Miami, Florida; Richmond, Virginia; and Austin, Texas, have followed suit.

Some organizations and shelters that follow the no-kill philosophy downplay use of the label to describe themselves. For example, the Best Friends Animal Sanctuary was founded in 1984 and is the largest animal sanctuary in the United States. Funded by private donations and located on three thousand acres near Kanab, Utah, in 2007 the sanctuary housed roughly fifteen hundred animals. Most were cats and dogs. The remainder included horses, burros, birds, rabbits, goats, livestock, and other animals. Best Friends takes in animals from all over the country and occasionally from other countries. Some come from shelters where they were considered unadoptable and were going to be euthanized. They may be old, crippled, or sick with chronic illnesses, or may have been traumatized by abuse or neglect. In exchange for taking these animals, the sanctuary asks many of the shelters to take back adoptable animals from Best Friends.

According to Best Friends (2005, http://www.bestfriends .org/aboutus/faq.cfm), many of the animals that come into the sanctuary are readily adoptable or become so following rehabilitation. Others are kept permanently at the sanctuary. Michael Mountain, the founder of Best Friends, is a solid supporter of the no-kill policy. The sanctuary defines no-kill as: "'No-kill' means that animals are not destroyed except in cases of terminal and painful illness, when compassion demands euthanasia because there is no reasonable alternative." As of 2007 Best Friends did not display a no-kill label on its Web site. Instead, it used the slogan "No More Homeless Pets."

Another major organization that supports the no-kill idea is Maddie's Fund. It was founded in 1999 by the billionaire Dave Duffield and his wife, Cheryl, and named after their beloved miniature schnauzer Maddie, who died of cancer in 1997. Maddie's Fund is a pet rescue foundation that advocates a community approach in which animal control agencies, shelters, humane organizations, and private-practice veterinarians work together to achieve no-kill status. Table 9.3 shows the top ten reasons given by Maddie's Fund for a shelter to consider implementing a no-kill policy. Maddie's Fund

TABLE 9.3

Ten reasons Maddie's Fund recommends shelters join the no-kill movement

1. Boosts adoptions.
2. Attracts and retains more volunteers.
3. Improves staff morale.
4. Generates greater community support.
5. Creates better alignment with charitable mission.
6. Enhances image.
7. Increases management skills.
8. Generates more funding.
9. Expands organizational options.
10. Establishes eligibility for Maddie's Fund grant.

SOURCE: "Ten Reasons to Consider No-Kill," in *Maddie's Fund: No-Kill Movement*, Maddie's Fund—The Pet Rescue Foundation, 2005, http://www.maddiesfund.org/nokill/build_reasons.html (accessed January 3, 2007)

provides grants to community coalitions, veterinary medical associations, and colleges of veterinary medicine for programs that advance the no-kill goal.

In February 2005 Maddie's Fund pledged $15.5 million to help New York City achieve no-kill status. In 2003 officials in New York City announced plans to convert all the city's shelters to no-kill by 2008. The effort is being spearheaded by the Mayor's Alliance—a coalition of dozens of animal welfare groups. Experts believe that the program has an excellent chance of success because the Mayor's Alliance is a neutral party rather than a particular animal group with its own agenda. Animal welfare organizations in the city do not have a history of working well together on common goals. The program will increase public awareness about adoptions and spay/neuter programs at the shelters. A new agreement was reached on how the city's animal control operations will coordinate with rescue groups and shelters to reach the no-kill goal.

Owner Turn-ins

In "Human and Animal Factors Related to Relinquishment of Dogs and Cats in 12 Selected Animal Shelters in the United States" (*Journal of Applied Animal Welfare Science*, July 1998), M. D. Salman et al. survey twelve shelters around the country to find out why cat and dog owners are turning in their pets. (Salman is affiliated with the College of Veterinary Medicine and Biomedical Sciences at Colorado State University.) In general, Salman et al. find that the owners had unrealistic expectations for their pets and lacked the knowledge or will to work out problems that arose. Moving was the number one reason given by owners relinquishing their dogs to the shelters. However, Salman et al. find upon interviewing these owners that there were deeper issues involved, mainly behavior problems. In other words, owners who were moving decided to give up their dogs rather than take them along, because the dogs were

unruly. Salman et al. indicate that if the dogs were better behaved, they might have been kept and taken along to the new residence. Similar findings have been reported by humane organizations investigating dog turn-ins at other shelters.

Many organizations believe that shelters need to place greater emphasis on behavior problems. Some shelters now offer training classes to new dog owners or have volunteers work with shelter dogs on basic obedience lessons. It is hoped that this will reduce the number of shelter-adopted dogs that are later relinquished. Breeders and veterinarians are being urged to encourage new dog owners to enroll in obedience classes or seek help from professional trainers. All people involved in reducing pet overpopulation agree that pet owners need to be better educated about the responsibilities and issues involved in raising pets.

Pound Seizure

Following World War II the use of animals in laboratory testing and experimentation increased greatly. Researchers turned to pounds and shelters for a quick and cheap supply of unwanted animals. Many states passed laws that required publicly operated shelters to turn over animals to institutions that requested them, a practice called pound seizure. Animal welfarists were disturbed by this development and blamed the National Society for Medical Research (now the National Association for Biomedical Research) for pushing pound seizure legislation. Many welfare organizations contracted with their local municipalities to privatize shelter operations so that their shelter would not be subject to the laws.

In 1990 the Animal Welfare Act (AWA) was amended to set a minimum holding period of five days for shelter animals before release to research institutions. This holding period is designed to provide a window of opportunity for owners to find their missing pets or for the animals to be adopted by new owners. The AWA also includes record-keeping requirements for dealers who sell shelter animals to research institutions.

Animal rights activists and welfarists universally condemn pound seizure. In "Ban Pound Seizure" (November 15, 2006, http://www.aavs.org/campaign02.html), the American Anti-Vivisection Society notes that three states—Utah, Oklahoma, and Minnesota—still require publicly funded shelters to provide cats and dogs for research purposes. Most states legally allow pound seizure or do not address the issue. In some states the decision is left up to local government authorities. A few states require owners giving up animals to indicate whether or not they give permission for release to research institutions. The AAVS (2007, http://www.banpoundseizure.org/yourstate.shtml) provides a state-by -state listing of laws regarding pound seizure.

According to In Defense of Animals (IDA; June 7, 2006, http://www.idausa.org/facts/poundseizure.html), thirteen states have outlawed pound seizure: Connecticut, Delaware, Hawaii, Maine, Maryland, Massachusetts, New Hampshire, New Jersey, New York, Pennsylvania, Rhode Island, Vermont, and West Virginia. The IDA claims that some cash-strapped shelters engage in pound seizure illegally to raise funds. There are also accusations that shelters hide some animals from public view during the required five-day holding period and then sell them to dealers or research facilities. The IDA suggests that pound seizure puts all pets in a community at greater risk of being stolen.

The Michigan Society for Medical Research (MSMR) says that Massachusetts alone prohibits the use of pound-seizure animals in medical research and that the other twelve states listed by the IDA specifically prohibit the use of pound-seizure animals obtained from in-state shelters. In other words, these twelve states do permit the use of pound-seizure animals obtained from out-of-state shelters. This means that forty-nine states allow pound seizure in some form.

Those who support pound seizure argue that animals that are going to be euthanized by shelters anyway should be used in research. They feel the benefits to humans outweigh animal welfare concerns. Welfarists fear that pets turned over to laboratories will suffer from poor care and die slow, painful deaths as the subjects of medical experiments. They believe that euthanasia at the shelter is preferable to this alternative.

The Physician's Committee for Responsible Medicine (PCRM), a nonprofit organization concerned with medical issues, advocates alternatives to animal experimentation for educational and research purposes. In "Pound Seizure" (2001, http://www.pcrm.org/resch/anexp/pound_seizure.html), Neal D. Barnard, the president of the PCRM, explains that research institutions prefer test animals that are relatively calm, well socialized, and easy to handle. However, these types of animals are also the most likely to be adopted from shelters. Therefore, Barnard disputes the claim that pound seizure is justified because the animals involved would be euthanized anyway.

PUREBRED DOG INDUSTRY

Many animal welfare groups blame dog overpopulation in part on the purebred dog industry. Purebred dogs are those that have been bred from members of a recognized breed over many generations. This ensures that certain appearance and behavior traits are maintained within a breed. Breeding of this type has been practiced for centuries. It was popularized during the Middle Ages by European monks who earned money by breeding dogs with particular traits for aristocrats and members of royalty. It resulted in breeds that were notable for a specific

TABLE 9.4

Terminology used in purebred industry

Breed standard	Set of detailed guidelines established to define the particular characteristics of a breed
Conformation points	Specific criteria within the breed standard (e.g., fur color, shape of paws, size, etc.)
Consanguineous	Descended from the same ancestor
Dam	Mother dog
Fault	A characteristic of a purebred dog that doesn't meet a conformation point
Inbreeding	Breeding of immediate relatives (e.g., brother with sister, father with daughter, etc.)
Linebreeding	Breeding of close relatives (e.g., aunt with nephew, grandfather with granddaughter, cousin with cousin, etc.) or of animals with many common ancestors
Outcrossing	Breeding two dogs from different lines
Pedigree	A listing of ancestors; the family tree
Sire	Father dog
True to type	Showing desired breed characteristics. Also desired characteristics are so ingrained that offspring can be certain to have them also.
Type	Overall appearance including characteristics important to the breed standard
Typey	An adjective used to describe a dog that seems to capture the essence of the breed or closely meets the breed standard
Whelped	Born

SOURCE: Created by Kim Masters Evans for Thomson Gale, 2005

task, such as hunting wildfowl, or had desirable features in their size, shape, fur, ears, and so forth.

Maintaining desirable qualities in a bloodline requires careful choice of mating partners. For example, an excellent hunting dog mated with a poor hunting dog will likely produce offspring that are not good hunters, and so the desirable qualities would be lost. Mating together two excellent hunting dogs will greatly increase the likelihood that the offspring will also be great hunters. This makes them much more valuable. Purebred enthusiasts are passionate about protecting certain qualities within a breed, and reputable breeders work to ensure that breed characteristics are maintained and that purebred puppies are placed in good homes.

The HSUS, in "Get the Facts on Puppy Mills" (2007, http://www.hsus.org/pets/issues_affecting_our_pets/get_the_facts_on_puppy_mills/), estimates that up to five hundred thousand purebred puppies are sold either in pet stores or directly by breeders each year. Purebred puppies and dogs can sell for hundreds or even thousands of dollars. Demand for purebred puppies and dogs has resulted in a multibillion-dollar industry based on breeding, showing, selling, and registering these dogs. Some common terms used in the purebred dog industry are defined in Table 9.4.

Registration, Pedigree, and Papers

The American Kennel Club (AKC) was formed in 1884. It is the largest nonprofit organization in the United States that registers purebred dogs. The second-largest registry is maintained by the United Kennel Club (UKC), which was founded in 1898. These are the two most respected purebred registries in the United States. For a fee they provide registration certificates or "papers" showing that dogs are recognized as belonging to a particular breed. These papers provide a written record of a particular dog's ancestry. Typical registration fees range from $15 to $45. As of 2007 the AKC recognized more than 150 dog breeds and the UKC recognized more than 300 breeds. Each organization is supported by hundreds of local and regional kennel and breed clubs around the country.

The registration papers for purebred dogs are based on information supplied by breeders who are members of their respective clubs. Breeders can register litters born to registered purebred dogs. The registration papers are then turned over to the puppies' new owners. Each owner chooses a unique name for a registered dog that cannot be repeated. Owners can also request a copy of a pedigree (a family tree) for their registered dogs that goes back several generations. The AKC's *Annual Report 2005* (May 4, 2006, http://www.akc.org/about/annual_report/2005/integrity.html) reports that the club registered 920,804 individual dogs and 421,128 litters in that year. According to the AKC, the dog breeds with the most registrations in 2005 were Labrador retrievers, golden retrievers, Yorkshire terriers, German shepherds, and beagles.

Purebreds and Genetic Problems

Dogs as a species are prone to genetic diseases. Jonathan Amos states in "Pedigree Dog Health to be Probed" (BBC News, January 22, 2004) that "dogs are plagued by the greatest number of documented, naturally occurring genetic disorders of any non-human species." There are approximately four hundred inherited disorders associated with dogs. As long as the breeding population remains large, the chances of passing along a genetic disorder are small. This is because the dog blueprint is based on around thirty thousand genes.

Individual genes determine characteristics of a particular dog, such as hair color. Some genes can also carry the triggers for serious diseases and disorders. Two dogs can carry genes with these dangerous triggers but not suffer from the diseases themselves because the genes are recessive rather than dominant in their genetic makeup. However, if these two dogs mate with each other, there is a good chance that some of their puppies will inherit the problem genes from both parents and develop the disorder. At the very least, most of the puppies will inherit the recessive problem gene and later pass it along to their offspring.

In purebred dogs this inheritance problem is extremely aggravated because closely related dogs are bred with one another. This significantly raises the chances that problem genes will be passed on from parents to offspring.

Amos notes that common genetic diseases within specific breeds include heart disease in boxers, bleeding problems in Dobermans, lymphomas in pointers, hip dysplasia in Labrador retrievers, and eye problems in Irish setters.

In 1966 a group of veterinarians teamed with representatives from the Golden Retriever Club of America and the German Shepherd Club of America to found the Orthopedic Foundation for Animals (OFA). The OFA maintains a database of specific genetic disorders in individual purebred dogs. This information allows conscientious breeders to make informed decisions about which dogs should be mated. The OFA encourages breeders to submit health information for many generations so that trends in inheritance can be deduced. The OFA also issues health ratings for dogs in its database to provide potential consumers with important information. For example, the OFA can certify the condition of hips and elbows in particular dogs. This information can be included with the registration papers issued by the AKC. Another certifying organization is the Canine Eye Registration Foundation (CERF). CERF maintains a database on eye health and can certify that a particular purebred dog's eyes are free of genetic disorders.

Experts advise consumers buying a purebred dog to seek dogs whose hips and elbows have been certified "Excellent" or "Good" by the OFA and whose eyes have been certified by CERF to be free of genetic abnormalities. The same conditions should be met in the parents of purebred puppies that consumers consider buying.

Papers Do Not Guarantee Quality or Health

Neither the AKC nor the UKC guarantees the quality or health of a purebred dog. The AKC (2007, http://www.akc.org/reg/about.cfm) makes the following warning: "There is a widely held belief that 'AKC' or 'AKC papers' guarantee the quality of a dog. This is not the case. AKC is a registry body. A registration certificate identifies the dog as the offspring of a known sire [father] and dam [mother], born on a known date. It in no way indicates the quality or state of health of the dog."

The AKC and UKC simply track ancestry records based on the information they are given by breeders. It is an honor system. Unscrupulous breeders can provide false information and register dogs that are not really purebreds, but mixes (or mutts). Such breeders can also purposely breed dogs with known genetic disorders just to achieve a look that is popular with purebred buyers.

During the late 1990s the AKC began random DNA testing to ensure that breeders were supplying accurate information about the purebred dogs they registered. The AKC

(2007, http://www.akc.org/dna/dna_update.cfm) notes that in 2006, 95.5% of the litters tested had correct parentage. This value was up from 89% in 1998.

Purebred Dog Competitions

The AKC and UKC hold thousands of competitions each year in which registered dogs can compete. Some of these events are called dog shows or conformation shows and are designed to show off dogs that exemplify breed standards. These are basically beauty contests in which the focus is on distinctive features that characterize particular breeds. Other competitions highlight skills in hunting, agility, or obedience.

Purebred Registries Compete

The AKC and UKC are recognized as reputable purebred registries in the United States. In addition, some breed clubs maintain well-respected registries—for example, the Australian Shepherd Club of America. However, a number of other registries exist that may operate for dubious purposes. Dog enthusiasts state that unscrupulous registries make money by issuing papers indiscriminately to dogs that are not even purebreds or for dogs that are not from recognized breeds. This allows breeders to sell the dogs for high prices to unsuspecting consumers. Many of these unscrupulous registries are believed to have been started by breeders who have been kicked out of the AKC or UKC for rules violations.

Alternative registries often allow crossbreeds to be registered. These are puppies resulting from mating two desirable breeds together. Usually, the parents are AKC or UKC registered. However, the puppies cannot be registered by these agencies. Crossbreeds are popular with some consumers because they are novel. Examples include:

• Schoodle—mix of schnauzer and poodle

• Labradoodle—mix of Labrador retriever and poodle

• Cockapoo or Spoodle—mix of cocker spaniel and poodle

• Yorkiepoo—mix of Yorkshire terrier and poodle

• Goldendoodle—mix of golden retriever and poodle

• Bug—mix of beagle and pug

Puppy Mills

Puppy mills are facilities that breed puppies in inferior conditions and sell them in commercial markets. The HSUS states in "Get the Facts on Puppy Mills" that puppy mills do not provide adequate veterinary care, food, shelter, and socialization for their puppies. According to the HSUS, thousands of puppy mills existed in the United States as of 2007. Animal welfare groups maintain that puppy mills cause suffering of mother dogs and puppies. Female dogs are bred too often and destroyed when they quit producing puppies. The puppies are often transported over long distances in cramped cages and frequently suffer from debilitating conditions and diseases.

All dog breeders meeting certain criteria must be licensed by the Animal and Plant Health Inspection Service (APHIS) of the U.S. Department of Agriculture (USDA). These licenses fall into two types:

• Class A—Breeders who sell animals that they have bred and raised on their own premises. People with three or fewer breeding females who sell offspring for pets or exhibition are exempt. People who sell animals directly to owners are exempt.

• Class B—People who purchase and resell animals, including dealers, brokers, and auction house operators. Retail pet stores selling nondangerous "pet-type" animals are exempt.

Table 9.5 shows the number of Class A and B licenses by state as of September 2006. The states with the most Class A licenses were Missouri (1,609), Oklahoma (672), Iowa (448), Kansas (434), and Arkansas (379). Together, these five states accounted for 71% of all Class A licenses. The vast majority of the licensed breeders in these states raise puppies for the purebred market. Breeders and brokers sell purebred puppies to pet stores, who in turn sell them to the public. Annual APHIS license fees for Class A and B licenses are listed in Table 9.6. A $10 application fee is required for first-time applicants.

Puppy farming is big business in the Midwest. It was encouraged by the government following World War II as a way for rural people to make more income. Many traditional farmers switched from raising pigs to raising puppies when market conditions were favorable. This was particularly true in Missouri.

MISSOURI: "THE PUPPY PIPELINE." As shown in Table 9.5, Missouri leads the nation in APHIS Class A and B licenses. The state accounts for 32% of all Class A licenses and 14% of all Class B licenses. It is widely agreed that Missouri is the nation's top source for purebred puppies. In December 2003 the radio station KMOX of St. Louis aired the award-winning series *Missouri: The Puppy Pipeline* by Megan Lynch. According to Lynch, the state had an estimated one thousand licensed puppy breeding facilities in 2003, far more than any other state. Experts estimated that as many as one thousand additional unlicensed puppy farms were operating illegally. The state is home to the Hunte Corporation, the world's largest distributor of puppies to pet stores. In 2003 puppy breeding was an estimated $2-billion-a-year business in Missouri. Lynch reviewed the history of the puppy farming industry in the state and reported on problems revealed by state auditors.

TABLE 9.5

Number of licenses granted to Class A breeders and Class B dealers, by state, September 2006

State	Class A breeders		Class B dealers	
	Number	Percentage of total	Number	Percentage of total
Alaska	None	Not applicable	0	Not applicable
Alabama	15	0.3%	10	1%
Arkansas	379	8%	34	3%
Arizona	7	0.1%	2	0.2%
California	20	0.4%	26	2%
Colorado	10	0.2%	13	1%
Connecticut	1	0.02%	6	1%
District of Columbia	None	Not applicable	0	Not applicable
Delaware	None	Not applicable	4	0.3%
Florida	34	0.7%	87	7%
Georgia	29	0.6%	11	1%
Guam	None	Not applicable	0	Not applicable
Hawaii	None	Not applicable	0	Not applicable
Iowa	448	9%	67	6%
Idaho	7	0.1%	1	0.1%
Illinois	53	1.1%	43	4%
Indiana	79	1.6%	26	2%
Kansas	434	9%	61	5%
Kentucky	8	0.2%	4	0.3%
Louisiana	12	0.2%	10	1%
Massachusetts	8	0.2%	12	1%
Maryland	3	0.1%	12	1%
Maine	1	0.02%	2	0.2%
Michigan	25	0.5%	30	3%
Minnesota	86	1.7%	40	3%
Missouri	1,609	32%	165	14%
Mississippi	7	0.1%	2	0.2%
Montana	8	0.2%	2	0.2%
North Carolina	11	0.2%	35	3%
North Dakota	20	0.4%	5	0.4%
Nebraska	170	3.4%	12	1%
New Hampshire	2	0.04%	0	Not applicable
New Jersey	4	0.1%	12	1%
New Mexico	2	0.04%	4	0.3%
Nevada	3	0.1%	7	1%
New York	50	1.0%	33	3%
Ohio	187	3.8%	34	3%
Oklahoma	672	13.5%	58	5%
Oregon	23	0.5%	21	2%
Pennsylvania	185	3.7%	51	4%
Puerto Rico	None	Not applicable	0	Not applicable
Rhode Island	None	Not applicable	3	0.3%
South Carolina	1	0.0%	10	1%
South Dakota	114	2%	16	1%
Tennessee	15	0.3%	19	2%
Texas	134	3%	112	9%
Utah	1	0.02%	7	1%
Virginia	16	0.3%	15	1%
Vermont	None	Not applicable	1	0.1%
Washington	12	0.2%	12	1%
Wisconsin	64	1%	40	3%
West Virginia	None	Not applicable	7	1%
Wyoming	5	0.1%	1	0.1%
Totals	**4,974**		**1,185**	

SOURCE: Adapted from "Breeders," in *Facility Lists: Breeders*, U.S. Department of Agriculture, Animal and Plant Health Inspection Service, September 7, 2006, http://www.aphis.usda.gov/ac/publications/reports/A_cert_holders.txt (accessed December 18, 2006) and "Dealers" in *Facility Lists: Dealers*, U.S. Department of Agriculture, Animal and Plant Health Inspection Service, September 7, 2006, http://www.aphis.usda.gov/ac/publications/reports/B_cert_holders.txt (accessed December 18, 2006)

In 1992 the Missouri legislature passed the Animal Care Facilities Act to establish minimum standards for businesses, shelters, and pounds dealing with cats and dogs. The Missouri Department of Agriculture (MDA) oversees the program, with regulations largely identical to USDA regulations for animal facilities. In *Audit of Animal Care Facilities Inspection Program* (February 15, 2001, http://www.auditor.mo.gov/press/2001-09.pdf), Claire McCaskill of the state auditor office was highly critical of the MDA's oversight of the state's puppy breeding industry. McCaskill stated that MDA facility inspections were "spotty" and resulted in few sanctions against violators. Problems were also cited with apparent conflict of interest, because the program coordinator and one of the inspectors were former commercial dog breeders and still involved in the breeding business. McCaskill concluded, "Commercial dog breeders

TABLE 9.6

USDA license fees for dealers, brokers, and operators of auction sales

Over	But not over	Initial license fee	Annual or changed class of license fee
$0	$500	$30	$40
500	2,000	60	70
2,000	10,000	120	130
10,000	25,000	225	235
25,000	50,000	350	360
50,000	100,000	475	485
100,000	—	750	760

SOURCE: "Table 1. Dealers, Brokers, and Operators of an Auction Sale—Class "A" and "B" License," in *Federal Register*, vol. 69, no. 134, July 14, 2004, http://www.aphis.usda.gov/ac/kitchensink.pdf (accessed December 15, 2006)

have no incentive to comply with Missouri laws, leaving canines at risk for substandard care."

Lynch found that the MDA inspection organization was changed as a result of McCaskill's unfavorable audit. Lynch interviewed the MDA's new director, who instituted standardized procedures that inspectors followed, including a checklist to use during inspections. However, a spokeswoman for the Missouri Alliance for Animal Legislation said that the MDA's improvements were "on paper only" and did not actually bring about change in the industry. She also criticized the MDA's policy of letting breeders with problems make improvements rather than face administrative hearings for noncompliance. The MDA noted that its policy saves time and money.

In *Follow-Up Review of Animal Care Facilities Inspection Program* (December 16, 2004, http://www.auditor.mo.gov/press/2004-91.pdf), a follow-up report on MDA's oversight of puppy farms, McCaskill notes that "most" of the problems cited in the 2001 audit had not been corrected. The problem areas McCaskill cites are as follows:

- Inspectors do not always observe all violations or record all the violations they observe.

- Some inspectors do not believe it is necessary to report all violations or conduct a complete annual inspection.

- Some facilities with chronic poor performance are never penalized.

- State inspectors are duplicating federal inspection efforts.

- Inspections are not conducted annually at every facility as required by law.

- The MDA is reluctant to use the administrative hearing process or confiscate animals from repeat viola-

tors. For example, one facility had been cited for eighty-three recurring violations since December 2000 but had never been penalized.

- Fines for violations are rarely assessed. Those fines that have been assessed are never collected.

- Poor record keeping makes it difficult to determine which facilities have paid their licensing fees.

- The MDA's nine inspectors are so overburdened with other tasks that they do not have time to conduct their inspection duties properly.

- The MDA allows unlicensed operators to continue to operate and sell dogs in violation of state regulations.

McCaskill warns, "These problems have eroded the integrity of the inspection program which is designed to help ensure canines are safely and humanely treated." Auditors accompanying MDA inspectors observed unsanitary and unsafe conditions at some puppy farms. A listing of the most serious problems is provided in Table 9.7. In addition, McCaskill mentions many problems with record keeping, both by inspectors and facility operators.

Aggie M. Opgenorth reports in "Largest Animal Rescue in Tennessee County History Saves 250 Dogs" (Portland Independent Media Center, October 29, 2006) that Tennessee authorities conducted a raid in October 2006 on a Sumner County puppy mill housing more than three hundred dogs. Authorities were tipped off about the situation by a neighbor who took undercover video of the deplorable conditions at the farm. Irene Meuser, the farm owner, had been breeding small dog breeds, such as dachshunds and Pomeranians, and keeping them in crowded, dirty cages in buildings on her property. One official reported, "The stench was so powerful that some deputies had to rush outside to vomit." Investigators found several dead dogs on the property. All the rescued dogs had health problems. More than one hundred humane and rescue organizations banded together to obtain vet care for the animals and have them all spayed and neutered before adoption. All the rescued dogs were placed with new owners.

According to the Animal Legal Defense Fund in "Happy Tails: Caring Prosecutor, Community Shut Down Puppy Mill" (November 28, 2006, http://www.aldf.org/news/details.php?id=201), Meuser pleaded guilty to four counts of animal cruelty. Opgenorth notes that Meuser received $5,000 of the adoption fees collected when the dogs were adopted out. Authorities defended the payment, saying it helped facilitate a deal in which Meuser agreed to plead guilty and relinquish custody of the animals immediately. Otherwise, they would have been held indefinitely as evidence during trial. Furthermore, Opgenorth mentions that Meuser had more than 280 cats and small dogs confiscated in 1996 in a similar case.

TABLE 9.7

Violations observed by Missouri auditors at puppy breeding facilities, 2004

Inspection type	Violations observed by auditor at puppy breeding facilities	Response of inspector
Pre-licensing	Cages with inadequate flooring	Did not observe
	Accumulated fecal material	Did not observe
	Multiple shelters in poor condition	Did not observe
	Improper food storage	Did not observe
	Operator selling puppies prior to obtaining license	Observed, but did not report, told operator "you really shouldn't be doing that"
Annual	Pens with large amounts of fecal accumulation	Observed, but did not report
	Housing facility that did not protect dogs from weather	Observed, but did not report, decided to revisit facility before winter to ensure building was completed
Annual	A piece of unsecured metal covering a drain channel inside the outdoor runs	Did not observe
Pre-licensing	No veterinary care available	Gave applicant up to 30 days to correct, but did not reinspect for 138 days
	Fecal accumulation under and in pens	
	Dirty water or no water in bowls	
Re-inspection of above facility	Fecal accumulation under and in pens	Gave applicant time to correct
	Dirty water or no water	
	Pens with no shelter or shade	
	No food or moldy food in feed bowls	
	Dogs with skin problems	
	A puppy that had been dead for several days in pen	
	28 new violations	
Re-inspection of above facility	14 violations still existing from previous inspections, plus 7 new violations	Gave applicant time to correct
Re-inspection of above facility	15 violations still existing from previous inspections, plus 11 new violations	Gave applicant time to correct

SOURCE: Adapted from text in *Follow-Up Review of Animal Care Facilities Inspection Program*, Office of the Missouri State Auditor, December 16, 2004, http://www.auditor.mo.gov/press/2004-91.pdf (accessed January 3, 2007)

TABLE 9.8

Tips from the Humane Society on picking a good dog breeder

A GOOD DOG BREEDER ...

Keeps her dogs in the home and as part of the family—not outside in kennel runs.
Has dogs who appear happy and healthy, are excited to meet new people, and don't shy away from visitors.
Shows you where the dogs spend most of their time—an area that is clean and well maintained.
Encourages you to spend time with the puppy's parents—at a minimum, the pup's mother—when you visit.
Breeds only one or two types of dogs, and is knowledgeable about what are called "breed standards" (the desired characteristics of the breed in areas such as size, proportion, coat, color, and temperament).
Has a strong relationship with a local veterinarian and shows you records of veterinary visits for the puppies. Explains the puppies' medical history and what vaccinations your new puppy will need.
Is well versed in the potential genetic problems inherent in the breed—there are specific genetic concerns for every breed—and explains to you what those concerns are. The breeder should have had the puppy's parents tested (and should have the results from the parents' parents) to ensure they are free of those defects, and she should be able to provide you with documentation for all testing she has done through organizations such as the Orthopedic Foundation for Animals (OFA).
Gives you guidance on caring and training for your puppy and is available for assistance after you take your puppy home.
Provides references of other families who have purchased puppies from her.
Feeds high quality "premium" brand food.
Doesn't always have puppies available but rather will keep a list of interested people for the next available litter.
Actively competes with her dogs in conformation trials (which judge how closely dogs match their "breed standard"), obedience trials (which judge how well dogs perform specific sets of tasks on command), or tracking and agility trials. Good breeders will also work with local, state, and national clubs that specialize in their specific breed.
Encourages multiple visits and wants your entire family to meet the puppy before you take your puppy home.
Provides you with a written contract and health guarantee and allows plenty of time for you to read it thoroughly. The breeder should *not* require that you use a specific veterinarian.

SOURCE: "How to Identify a Good Dog Breeder—Tips from the Humane Society of the United States," in *How to Find a Good Dog Breeder*, Humane Society of the United States, 2005, http://files.hsus.org/web-files/PDF/ good_breeder_checklist.pdf (accessed January 3, 2007)

BUYER BEWARE. In response to negative publicity about puppy mills, several states have passed lemon laws to protect consumers who buy puppies at pet stores. Such laws typically enable consumers to be reimbursed by pet stores that sell them puppies that turn out to be in poor health. The HSUS hopes that such laws motivate pet stores to pressure breeders to improve the conditions in which puppies are raised. Table 9.8 shows HSUS tips on how consumers can identify a good dog breeder.

Headquartered in Goodman, Missouri, Hunte Corporation is the nation's largest supplier of purebred puppies to pet stores and ships them internationally, primarily to Canada, Japan, Mexico, and Spain. During her December

2003 investigation, Lynch interviewed the chief veterinarian for Hunte Corporation. According to the veterinarian, the company holds breeders and pet stores to high standards and uses state-of-the-art transport vehicles to ship puppies. Incoming puppies are subjected to a veterinary exam and checked against breed standards. Hunte also says it tracks sires and dams with a database to screen out genetic problems. The company's puppies come with a three-year guarantee for the absence of hereditary and genetic disorders.

Kim Townsend operates the anti-puppy mill organization Nopuppymills.com. She also offers information to people who are thinking about purchasing or have purchased a puppy from a pet store. Consumers who purchase pet store puppies can determine where the puppies came from by researching the supplier (breeder) and distributor (broker) numbers that should appear on the paperwork supplied by the store. These seven-digit alphanumeric codes are APHIS registration numbers (e.g., 43-A-0123 or 43-B-4444).

Consumers are urged to contact APHIS and ask for copies of federal inspection reports conducted on the breeder and broker of any puppy they purchase. Backyard breeders and hobby breeders do not have to register with APHIS. Townsend claims to maintain a database of information on thousands of private breeders and brokers that people can research.

Dog enthusiasts encourage consumers to buy only from reputable local breeders and to ask to see the sire and dam of the puppy they are interested in purchasing. A personal visit ensures the consumer that the breeder is operating a clean and well-kept business with healthy, well-adjusted dogs.

ORGANIZATIONS RESPOND. All major animal welfare organizations are opposed to commercial puppy breeding because of the severe pet overpopulation problem. They do not believe that puppies should be commercially bred because millions of unwanted puppies and dogs are euthanized at shelters every year. In "HSUS Pet Overpopulation Estimates," HSUS estimates that approximately 25% of the dogs that wind up in shelters are purebred. Purebred dogs can generally be identified by their coloring, fur, and characteristic appearance.

The AKC does not support random large-scale breeding of dogs for commercial purposes. The organization conducts inspections of breeders who use the AKC registry and of breeders, retail pet shops, and brokers who conduct twenty-five or more registration transactions per year or breed seven or more litters of puppies per year.

FERAL CATS

Feral cats are cats that have reverted to a semiwild state because of lack of human contact and socialization. They avoid humans and often live in large groups called colonies. They may be born into this condition or adjust to it after being stray, lost, or abandoned for a long time. Feral cats are often confused with strays, but there is a difference. Stray cats generally appear scruffy and unclean because they do not groom themselves. They are used to human care and suffer from stress and hunger without it. Feral cats are adjusted to a wild manner of living. If a natural food source is prevalent, they survive fairly well.

The problem is that they also reproduce well. Many animal welfare groups advocate a trap-neuter-return (TNR) management plan for feral colonies. In these programs feral cats are humanely trapped, vaccinated, sterilized, and returned to their colonies. In most cases volunteers feed the colonies and conduct TNR activities. Kittens and any particularly tame adult cats go into adoption programs. In general, it is difficult to turn a truly feral cat into a pet. Where it is possible, it requires a great deal of time and effort. Most welfarists believe that their time is better spent sterilizing the cats than trying to tame them.

Alley Cat Allies was founded in 1990 in Washington, D.C., to provide information on feral and stray cats. Many animal control departments try to control feral cat colonies by capturing and euthanizing the cats. According to Alley Cat Allies (September 22, 2006, http://www.alleycat.org/visitor.html#1), the TNR approach is much more effective and less costly. Colonies of feral cats that are not sterilized and managed will continue to breed and expand, allowing in more cats with which to breed. Unneutered males (toms) spread disease—including feline leukemia and feline immunodeficiency virus—by fighting with each other over females and territory. Feline leukemia is a particularly contagious, fatal disease that feral cats may spread to people's pet cats that go outdoors. Feral cat experts point out, however, that incidences of these diseases are no higher in the feral cat population than in the domestic cat population. By contrast, a feral colony that has been managed through TNR will eventually shrink in number through natural causes of death. Established sterilized colonies will not allow new cats in because they are not needed for breeding, nor will they produce any new kittens.

Feral cats are enormously controversial in the United States. Alley Cat Allies estimates that there were "tens of millions" of feral cats in the United States in 2006. Many people consider them to be a nuisance and blame them for killing birds and other wildlife. Supporters of TNR, however, dispute the numbers of birds killed cited by groups that favor widespread capture and killing of the cats. The hunting of feral (also called free-roaming) cats is legal in South Dakota and Minnesota.

FIGURE 9.3

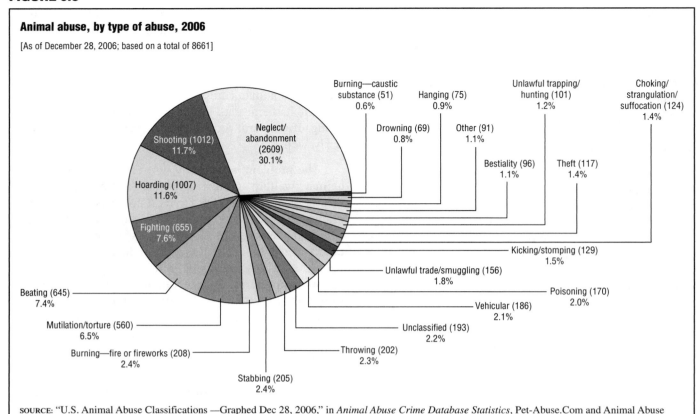

Animal abuse, by type of abuse, 2006

[As of December 28, 2006; based on a total of 8661]

SOURCE: "U.S. Animal Abuse Classifications —Graphed Dec 28, 2006," in *Animal Abuse Crime Database Statistics*, Pet-Abuse.Com and Animal Abuse Registry Database Administration System (AARDAS), December 28, 2006, http://www.pet-abuse.com/pages/cruelty_database/statistics/classifications.php (accessed December 28, 2006)

PET ABUSE AND NEGLECT

Tracking animal abuse cases is difficult because there is no government database of all cases. In 2001 Alison Gianotto of California began an online database of abuse cases—Pet-abuse.com—after her cat was stolen and set on fire. As of December 28, 2006, the database listed information on more than eighty-six hundred cases in the United States. Figure 9.3 shows a breakdown of the cases by abuse type. The largest number of cases involve neglect or abandonment (30.1%), followed by shooting (11.7%), hoarding (11.6%; see below for a discussion of hoarding), fighting (7.6%), and beating (7.4%). Table 9.9 shows the most common types of animals victimized in the animal cruelty cases documented by Pet-abuse.com. Dogs (excluding pit bull breeds) and cats are the most common victims noted.

Data in the database can be searched by state, date, perpetrator name, type of animal, type of abuse, or sex of perpetrator. Photographs are included for some cases. Each case description includes media and/or law enforcement or court references so that information can be verified.

Pet-abuse.com includes data on animal cruelty cases in which there is also documented neglect of a child or elderly person in the household. As shown in Figure 9.4,

more than half of the hoarding cases in the database and one-third of the cases involving animal neglect and/or abandonment were associated with child/elder neglect as of December 2006.

The HSUS compiles statistics on high-profile abuse cases based on media reports. Its most recent report is *First Strike Campaign 2003 Report of Animal Cruelty Cases* (2003, http://files.hsus.org/web-files/PDF/2003Ani malCrueltyRprt.pdf). The report covers 2003 and presents data related to 1,373 cases involving 1,682 perpetrators. Just over half (57%) of the cases involved intentional cruelty, and 43% involved extreme animal neglect.

The HSUS defines abuse (or cruelty) as purposefully depriving an animal of food, water, shelter, socialization, or veterinary care or maliciously torturing, maiming, mutilating, or killing an animal. These are considered intentional acts that give the abuser pleasure. Neglect is not considered to be intentional, but it results in an animal not receiving proper shelter, food, water, attention, grooming, or veterinary care.

As shown in Table 9.10, companion animals were the victims in 71% of the cruelty cases examined by the HSUS in 2003. This percentage is down slightly from

TABLE 9.9

Animal cruelty cases, by animal type, 2006

Animal type	Number of cases
Bird (other farmed)	74
Bird (pet)	208
Bird (wildlife)	193
Captive exotic	163
Cat	1,850
Chicken	374
Cow	207
Deer	70
Dog (non pit-bull)	4,301
Dog (pit-bull)	964
Goat	180
Horse	803
Marine animal (pet)	43
Marine animal (wild)	15
Opossum	23
Other companion animal	25
Other farm animal	91
Other wildlife	120
Pig	145
Rabbit (pet)	202
Rabbit (wild)	28
Raccoon	44
Reptile	158
Rodent/small mammal (pet)	178
Sheep	75
Squirrel	22

SOURCE: Adapted from "Most Common Animals in Animal Cruelty Cases—Graphed Dec 28, 2006," in *Animal Abuse Crime Database Statistics*, Pet-Abuse.Com and Animal Abuse Registry Database Administration System (AARDAS), December 28, 2006, http://www.pet-abuse.com/pages/cruelty_database/statistics/animals_by_cruelty_type.php (accessed December 28, 2006)

FIGURE 9.4

Animal cruelty cases in which documented child/elder abuse also occurred, 2006

[As of December 28, 2006; based on total of 170]

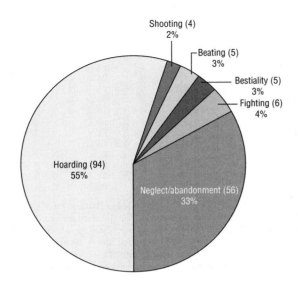

SOURCE: "U.S. Cruelty Types in Cases with Documented Child/Elder Neglect—Graphed Dec 28, 2006," in *Animal Abuse Crime Database Statistics*, Pet-Abuse.Com and Animal Abuse Registry Database Administration System (AARDAS), December 28, 2006, http://www.pet-abuse.com/pages/cruelty_database/statistics/other_neglect_occurring.php (accessed December 28, 2006)

the previous three years. More than half of the animals involved in these cases each year either died from the abuse or had to be euthanized.

Table 9.11 shows that shooting, animal fighting, torturing, beating, and mutilation were the most common violent offenses committed against animals. Overall, the HSUS notes that males were responsible for 92% of the cruelty cases. Adults (aged twenty and up) accounted for 77% of the cruelty cases, whereas teenagers aged thirteen to nineteen accounted for 22% and children aged seven to twelve accounted for 1%. Cruelty cases involving dogs outnumbered those involving cats by a margin of two to one. The HSUS believes that dog cases are more likely to be reported to authorities.

The HSUS statistics show that 15% of the intentional animal cruelty cases also involved some form of concurrent family violence—for example, child or spousal abuse. Authorities have long known about the link between animal abuse and family violence. The American Humane Association (AHA) was founded in 1877 as a collection of organizations working against child and animal abuse. It now operates the National Resource Center on the Link between Violence to People and Animals. The AHA works to strengthen animal abuse laws and, in cases where children abuse animals, to advocate early intervention to prevent the violence from escalating. According to the AHA (2007, http://www.amer

TABLE 9.10

Breakdown of animal abuse victims, by type of animal, 2000–03

Animal type	Percentage of cruelty cases for 2003	2002	2001	2000
Companion animals	71%	76%	74%	76%
Farm animals	18%	15%	14%	12%
Wildlife	4%	5%	6%	7%
Exotic animals	2%	2%	2%	Unknown
Multiple types	5%	2%	4%	5%

SOURCE: "The Following Is a Percentage Breakdown of Animal Abuse Victims for 2003 As Well As a Comparison to 2000, 2001, and 2002," in *The Humane Society of the United States (HSUS) First Strike® Campaign: 2003 Report of Animal Cruelty Cases*, Humane Society of the United States, 2004, http://files.hsus.org/web-files/PDF/2003AnimalCrueltyRprt.pdf (accessed January 11, 2006)

icanhumane.org/site/PageServer?pagename=lk_home), a large majority of families being treated for child abuse incidents also report instances of animal abuse.

Animal Hoarding

Another form of animal abuse is called animal hoarding. Animal hoarders collect large numbers of pets and do not provide proper care for them. Most hoarders start out with good intentions, taking in a few strays to care

TABLE 9.11

Breakdown of common violent offenses committed against animals, 2003

Common offenses	Percent of violent cases	Percent of cases involving males	Percent of cases involving females
Shooting	17%	94%	6%
Animal fighting	17%	93%	7%
Torturing	11%	95%	5%
Beating	11%	97%	3%
Mutilation	10%	95%	5%
Throwing	7%	94%	6%
Burning	6%	91%	9%
Poisoning	4%	100%	0%
Stabbing	3%	78%	22%
Kicking	3%	93%	7%
Dragging	3%	85%	15%
Suffocating	1%	89%	11%
Drowning	1%	89%	11%
Animal sexual abuse	1%	88%	12%
Hanging	1%	83%	17%
Run over with vehicle	1%	100%	0%

SOURCE: Adapted from "The Following Table Is a Breakdown of Common Violent Offenses Perpetrated on Animals," in *The Humane Society of the United States (HSUS) First Strike® Campaign: 2003 Report of Animal Cruelty Cases*, Humane Society of the United States, 2004, http://files.hsus .org/web-files/PDF/2003AnimalCrueltyRprt.pdf (accessed January 11, 2006)

for, but the situation can quickly grow out of control as the animals breed or the person takes in more and more animals. The animals are often kept inside the home and allowed to urinate and defecate there. Hoarders are oblivious to the negative effects of their actions on their pets and even on themselves. They see themselves as animal rescuers. Most will not admit that the severe overcrowding is unsanitary and unhealthy for the animals.

The Hoarding of Animals Research Consortium was founded in 1997 by Gary Patronek to study the hoarding problem and work to increase awareness among mental health and social service workers. The group believes that hoarding is a pathological problem. Some psychiatric experts suspect that it is a psychological disorder similar to obsessive-compulsive behavior.

According to "Lawmakers Tackle Animal Hoarding" (*JAVMA News*, May 1, 2003), in January 2003 authorities discovered the worst case of animal hoarding in U.S. history. An elderly couple living in rural Malheur County, Oregon, was found to have 562 dogs in and around their home. The dogs were scattered around the property, with some living inside the home, some in pens, and some in abandoned cars. Many of the dogs were sick and malnourished. Approximately 130 had to be euthanized. The remaining dogs were distributed among various shelters and rescue groups in the area. The couple was charged with criminal neglect, animal neglect, and criminal mischief. Authorities discovered that they had been charged with similar offenses in 1996 related to the keeping of hundreds of animals at their previous residence in Idaho.

In 2001 Illinois became the first state to pass legislation dealing specifically with animal hoarding as a

crime separate from animal cruelty or neglect. The Illinois law is considered by some animal activists to be model legislation for other states because it recognizes that hoarding may be a mental health problem and recommends psychiatric treatment for offenders.

EXOTIC PETS

The word *exotic* means "foreign" or "not native," but when the word is used to describe pets, it refers to wild animals that are not normally considered pets. These include lions, tigers, wolves, bears, primates, certain rodents and reptiles, and many other species. Exotic pets appeal to people because they are different and, in some cases, dangerous and threatening to others.

Many people feel they have the right to keep any animal as long as they provide proper care for it. Critics say that exotic animals belong in their natural habitats and not in cages, where they can suffer from abuse, neglect, and boredom. Welfarists believe that even well-treated exotic pets should not be kept in captivity because it violates their wild nature. Law enforcement and animal control officers point out that exotic pets pose a health hazard to people because their temperaments can be unpredictable.

Some people think it is wrong to keep wild animals in captivity, even those born in captivity. Exotic breeders argue that an animal born and raised in a cage does not miss the wild because the animal has never experienced it. Critics do not agree with this argument. They believe that captive-born wild animals retain the natural urges and instincts of their species.

Exotic pets are offered for sale in pet stores, on the Internet, at auctions, and in trade publications, such as the *Animal Finder's Guide* (2007, http://www.animalfinders guide.com/). The National Alternative Pet Association (NAPA) provides a list of breeders, dealers, and shops that specialize in exotic pets. The association also provides information and Internet links for a variety of clubs and organizations for exotic pet owners. NAPA complains that people with exotic pets suffer from discrimination and have difficulties finding food, supplies, veterinarians, shelters, and rescue groups for their animals. Zoos are often unwilling to provide needed information and will not take unwanted exotic pets.

Exotic pets are banned or regulated in many states. Table 9.12 was compiled by the Animal Protection Institute in 2006. At that time sixteen states banned private ownership of big cats, wolves, bears, reptiles, and most primates; ten states had partial bans; fourteen states required private owners to obtain a license or permit; and thirteen had little to no oversight of private ownership of exotic pets.

TABLE 9.12

Summary of state laws relating to private possession of exotic animals

State	Category	Animals prohibited
Alabama	N	Fish from the genus Clarias; fish from the genus Serrasalmus; black carp; any species of mongoose, any member of the family Cervidae (deer, elk, moose, caribou), species of coyote, fox, raccoon, skunk, wild rodents or wild turkey
Alaska	B	
Arizona	L	All species of Carnivora (canines, felines, excluding domestic); orangutans, chimpanzees, gorillas, alligators, crocodiles, cobras, vipers
Arkansas	B*	It is unlawful to possess 6 or more bobcat, coyote, deer, gray fox, red fox, opossum, quail, rabbit, raccoon and squirrel
California	B	Primates; Marsupialia; Insectivora (shrews); Chiroptera (bats); Carnivora (non-domestic dog and cats); Proboscidea (elephants); Perissodactyla (zebras, horses, rhinos); Reptilia (crocodiles, cobras, coral snakes, pit vipers, snapping turtles, alligators)
Colorado	B	Sugar gliders, wallabies, wallaroos, kangaroos
Connecticut	B*	The Felidae family (lion, leopard, cheetah, jaguar, ocelot, jaguarundi cat, puma, lynx, and bobcat); the Canidae family (wolf and coyote); the Ursidae family (black bear, grizzly bear, and brown bear); and venomous reptiles, alligators, crocodiles
Delaware	L	
Florida	B* & L	Chimpanzees, gorillas, orangutans, baboons, leopards, jaguars, tigers, lions, bears, elephants, crocodiles,
Georgia	B	Marsupialia (kangaroos); Primates (chimpanzees, gorillas, macaques); Carnivora (canines, felines); Proboscidea (elephants); Crocodylia (crocodiles, alligators, cobras, all poisonous rear-fanged species)
Hawaii	B	Non-Human Primates, Felidae family (lion, leopard, cheetah,); the Canidae family (wolf and coyote); and the Ursidae family (black bear, grizzly bear, and brown bear)
Idaho	N	
Illinois	B*	Lion, tiger, leopard, ocelot, jaguar, cheetah, margay, mountain lion, lynx, bobcat, jaguarundi, bear, hyena, wolf, coyote, or any poisonous life-threatening reptile
Indiana	L	Lions, tigers, jaguars, cougars, panthers, cheetahs, wolves, coyotes, jackals, hyenas, bears, venomous reptiles, alligators, crocodiles, gorillas, bonobos, orangutans, Burmese pythons, reticulated pythons, green and yellow anacondas
Iowa	O	
Kansas	B*	Lion, tiger, leopard, jaguar, cheetah, mountain lion, hybrid of a large cat, bear, or venomous snake
Kentucky	B	
Louisiana	B*	Bears, cougars, or non-human primates
Maine	L	
Maryland	B	Foxes, skunks, raccoons, all species of bears, alligators, crocodiles, all species of wild cats, wolves, nonhuman primates, various venomous reptiles
Massachusetts	B	
Michigan	B* & N	
Minnesota	B*	All members of the Felidae family (except domestic cats); all bears; and all non-human primates
Mississippi	L	Orangutans, chimpanzees, gorillas, macaques, mandrills, baboons, wolves, bears, hyenas, lions tigers, jaguars, leopards, elephants
Missouri	N	Lion, tiger, leopard, ocelot, jaguar, cheetah, margay, mountain lion, Canada lynx, bobcat, jaguarundi, hyena, wolf, coyote, or any deadly, dangerous, or poisonous reptile
Montana	L & N	Cougars, lions, tigers, jaguars, leopards, pumas, cheetahs, ocelots, and hybrids of those large cats that are kept in captivity for use other than public exhibition
Nebraska	B*	Wolf, skunk, or any member of the Felidae (cats, except domesticated) and Ursidae (bear) families
Nevada	N	Alligators, crocodiles, coyotes, foxes, raccoons
New Hampshire	B	Felines, bears, wolves, poisonous reptiles, and non-human primates, unless they are exhibitors
New Jersey	B	Primates; Carnivora (nondomestic dogs and cats, bears); Saura (venomous gila monsters); Serpentes (venomous coral snakes, cobras, vipers, pit vipers); Crocodilia (alligators, crocodiles, gavials); Psittaciformes (ring-necked and monk parakeets); and Rodentia (prairie dogs, ground squirrels)
New Mexico	B	Non-domesticated felines, primates, crocodiles, alligators, and wolves
New York	B	All members of the Felidae family (except domestic cats); all members of the Canidae family (except domestic dogs); all bears; all non-human primates, venomous reptiles, and crocodiles
North Carolina	N	
North Dakota	L	Bears, wolves, wolf hybrids, primates, all non-domesticated cats except Canadian lynx, and bobcat
Ohio	N	
Oklahoma	L	
Oregon	L	Lion, tiger, leopard, cheetah, ocelot, monkey, ape, gorilla, or other non-human primate, wolf or canine not indigenous to Oregon, and bear (except black bear)
Pennsylvania	L	All bears, coyotes, lions, tigers, leopards, jaguars, cheetahs, cougars, wolves, and any crossbreed of these animals, which have similar characteristics in appearance or features
Rhode Island	L	
South Carolina	N	Cervidae, Suidae, Tayassuidae (peccaries), Bovidae (bison, mountain goat, mountain sheep), coyotes, bears, turkeys, and furbearers
South Dakota	L	
Tennessee	B	Primates (gorillas, orangutans, chimpanzees, gibbons, siamangs, mandrills, drills, baboons, Gelada baboons only); Carnivores (all wolves, all bears, lions, tigers, leopards, jaguars, cheetahs, cougars); Proboscidea (all elephants); Perissodactyla (all rhinoceroses); Artiodactyla (all hippos and African buffalos); Crocodylia (crocodiles and alligators); Serpentes (all poisonous snakes); and Amphibians (all poisonous species)
Texas	L	
Utah	B	Ursidae (bears), Canidae (all species), Felidae (all species except domesticated cats), Mustelidae (all species), non-human primates, and certain species of reptiles
Vermont	B	Large felines, bears, wolves, poisonous reptiles, and non-human primates

NAPA (September 2, 2006, http://www.altpet.net/) complains that "even though many exotic pet species have been bred in captivity for a long time now, the laws still treat them like second class pets in some areas." The organization believes that a few bad incidents involving exotic pets have been blown out of proportion and that exotic pet owners are unfairly blamed for declining populations of endangered species. NAPA insists that captive breeding is the only chance for some species. It claims that many public shelters and wildlife rescue groups give

TABLE 9.12

State	Category	Animals prohibited
Virginia	B*	Bears, wolves, coyotes, weasels, badgers, hyenas, all species of non-domesticated cats, alligators, and crocodiles
Washington	N	
West Virginia	O	
Wisconsin	O	
Wyoming	B	Antelope, bighorn sheep, deer, elk, moose or mountain goat, black bear, grizzly bear or mountain lion

Notes:
B=Ban on private ownership of exotic animals—non-domesticated felines, wolves, bears, reptiles, non-human primates.
B*=Partial ban on private ownership of exotic animals—allows ownership of some exotic animals but precludes ownership of the animals listed.
L=Requires the "owner" of the exotic animal to obtain a license or permit or to register the animal with state or local authorities to privately possess the animal (excludes states only requiring import permits).
N=The state does not require the "owner" to obtain a license or permit to possess the animal within the state, but may regulate some aspect thereof (i.e. entry permit, veterinary certificate, etc.).
O=No statute or regulation governing this issue.

SOURCE: Adapted from "Summary of State Laws Relating to Private Possession of Exotic Animals," in *Take Action: Legislation—What's the Law?* Animal Protection Institute, 2006, http://api4animals.org/ (accessed December 28, 2006)

preference to zoos and will euthanize exotic animals instead of allowing private individuals to take them.

All major animal rights and welfare groups oppose the keeping of exotic pets, expressing concern about degradation of natural populations and the care that captive animals receive. Wildlife collectors are blamed for harming sensitive habitats and killing nontarget animals. Animal rights activists and welfarists tend to be opposed to the removal of wild animals from their natural habitats for any purpose. Besides the obvious dangers to the animals, removal can have devastating consequences on the natural habitats of the animals left behind.

Exotic animals kept as pets can suffer from poor nutrition and care at the hands of inexperienced and uninformed owners. The animals may be subjected to painful procedures such as wing clipping, defanging, and declawing. Welfarists believe that only accredited zoos and sanctuaries should care for wild animals kept in captivity. This ensures the proper care for the animals and protects the public safety.

Tigers

While testifying before the U.S. House of Representatives' Subcommittee on Fisheries Conservation, Wildlife, and Oceans, Eric Miller (June 12, 2003, http://www.aza.org/RC/Documents/TestimonyCaptiveWildlifeSafetyAct.pdf), the director of the St. Louis Zoological Park, stated there are between five thousand and ten thousand pet tigers in the United States and that this number exceeds the number of wild tigers living throughout Asia. Wild tigers are an endangered species, and private ownership of them is prohibited by the Endangered Species Act. However, ownership of a captive-born endangered animal is legal in many states.

Accredited zoos have been collecting wild tigers for decades. Many of these tigers were bred in captivity to produce popular zoo babies to bring in crowds. This resulted in an oversupply of adult tigers, many of which wound up in private hands. Pet owners, breeders, circuses, and roadside zoos have interbred different varieties of these animals, resulting in a large population of generic (not purebred) tigers.

Accredited zoos work to preserve endangered tiger species through selective breeding programs. Only purebred tigers with traceable ancestries are used. Generic tigers, or mutts, as they are called, have no value to these programs. Welfarists state that pet tigers are often kept chained or confined in small enclosures and may be beaten into submission.

PET STORES

The APPMA reports in the *2005–2006 National Pet Owners Survey* that Americans spent $24.5 billion on pet food, supplies, and medicine in 2006. Another $1.8 billion was spent purchasing pets. Animal rights groups and many welfare organizations are critical of pet stores that sell animals, particularly those that sell puppies (because of concerns about puppy mills) and exotic animals. The two largest companies in the pet supply industry are PetSmart and PETCO Animal Supplies.

PetSmart has never sold cats and dogs. Instead, it allows local animal shelters and rescue groups to set up adoption centers in its stores to adopt these animals directly to the public. The company does sell small animals (such as gerbils and hamsters), reptiles, fish, and birds. This has drawn criticism from animal rights groups such as People for the Ethical Treatment of Animals (PETA). PETA (2007, http://www.peta.com/feat-petsmart.asp) claims that small animals in PetSmart stores suffer during their captivity and do not receive proper care.

HEALTH AND SAFETY ISSUES

Veterinary Care

Increasing pet ownership has resulted in greater demand for veterinary care. The AVMA represents the interests of more than seventy-four thousand veterinarians. According to the AVMA's *U.S. Pet Ownership and Demographics Sourcebook* (2002), dog owners were far more likely to visit the vet in 2002 than cat owners. Only 25% of cat owners visited the vet at least once per year, compared with 83% of dog owners. Nearly half of cats and dogs were more than six years old. This percentage is up significantly from the 1987 census, indicating that pets are living longer lives. The AVMA credits better living conditions, health care, and nutrition as reasons for pets' growing life spans. Also, statistics indicate that more people are adopting older pets than ever before. In the *2005–2006 National Pet Owners Survey*, the APPMA estimates that pet owners spent $9.4 billion in 2006 on veterinary services.

Risks to People

The largest health risks to people from pets are zoonoses and animal bites. Zoonoses are diseases that can be passed from animals to humans. Scientists report that there are more than 250 distinct zoonoses that have been documented in medical literature. Zoonoses can occur in domesticated and wild animals. However, zoonoses in livestock, cats, and dogs are well known, heavily researched, and largely controlled through vaccination programs. Diseases passed to humans from most other animals, particularly exotic pets, are a different matter. Little is known about them, and they are more difficult to control.

In May 2003 an outbreak of monkeypox in the Midwest captured widespread media attention. Monkeypox is a disease that is related to smallpox but not nearly as lethal. Scientists believe that several people caught monkeypox from pet prairie dogs, which in turn had caught the disease from infected Gambian rats. The import of all African rats was subsequently banned by the U.S. Department of Health and Human Services. Health experts fear that other zoonoses not previously seen in the United States will emerge unless the trade in wild and exotic pets is curtailed.

In "Hedgehog Zoonoses" (*Emerging Infectious Diseases*, January 2005), Patricia Y. Riley and Bruno B. Chomel of the University of California-Davis solidify these concerns by stating, "Overall, ownership of exotic pets should not be encouraged because exotic animals and wildlife do not usually make good pets and can transmit zoonotic agents."

SALMONELLOSIS. The Centers for Disease Control and Prevention (CDC), in "Reptile-Associated Salmonellosis—Selected States, 1998–2002" (*Morbidity and Mortality Weekly Report*, December 12, 2003), comments on a study that reviewed historical data related to hundreds of case reports of salmonella infections recorded in medical literature. Salmonellosis, an infection caused by the bacteria *Salmonella*, can cause diarrhea, fever, and abdominal cramps in patients for several days. Although it does not generally require hospitalization, it can be quite serious for patients with weak immune systems, children, and the elderly. The infection is caused by eating contaminated food or through direct or indirect contact with reptiles and amphibians, such as lizards, snakes, turtles, frogs, and newts. Salmonellae occur naturally in the gastrointestinal tracts of these animals. The CDC concludes that approximately 5% of the cases were zoonotic. Extrapolating on a national basis means that approximately seventy-four thousand of the people contracting salmonellosis each year are infected by reptiles and amphibians.

DOG BITES. Determining the number of dog bites and related injuries that occur in the United States is extremely difficult because there is no nationwide tracking system. The most recent comprehensive and published data were collected in 1994 and are summarized in the CDC report "Nonfatal Dog Bite—Related Injuries Treated in Hospital Emergency Departments—United States, 2001" (*Morbidity and Mortality Weekly Report*, July 4, 2003). The report notes that in 1994 approximately 4.7 million Americans were bitten by dogs. More than half of the victims were children. Nearly eight hundred thousand people sought medical attention for dog bites. The number of these victims treated at hospital emergency rooms was 333,700. Approximately 6,000 of these patients required hospitalization. The remainder were treated and released.

The same report describes a CDC analysis of dog bite injury data collected in 2001 from 66 emergency rooms around the country. Based on these limited data the CDC estimates that approximately 368,000 people required treatment for dog bite injuries at U.S. emergency rooms during 2001. Children under the age of fourteen accounted for an estimated 42% of the cases. The data collected in 2001 indicate that dog bites occurred mostly during the warm months, primarily during July. Although nearly half of all injuries were to the arms and hands, children were most likely to be bitten in the head or neck. Puncture and laceration wounds were the most common types of injuries.

Although this report does not note the breeds of dogs associated with the bite injuries, breed information has been collected by the CDC for fatal injuries from dog bites. After examining the records for 304 fatalities because of dog bites from 1979 to 1996, the CDC concludes in "Dog-Bite-Related Fatalities—United States, 1995–1996" (*Morbidity and Mortality Weekly Report*,

May 30, 1997) that the dog breed (or primary cross breed) could be identified in 199 of the cases. Pit bulls were blamed for seventy of the attacks; rottweilers accounted for thirty-two fatalities; German shepherds caused thirty deaths; huskies were associated with another twenty fatalities; and wolf hybrids were blamed for fourteen deaths. Other breeds identified with fatal dog attacks included Alaskan malamutes, Doberman pinschers, chows, Great Danes, St. Bernards, and Akitas. The CDC notes that unaltered dogs (particularly males) were more likely to bite than spayed/neutered dogs.

Public fears about aggressive dogs have led some jurisdictions around the country to ban particular dog breeds. In "Breed-Specific Bans Spark Constitutional Dogfight" (*National Geographic News*, June 17, 2004), Maryann Mott reports that around two hundred cities and towns have restricted or prohibited ownership of certain breeds. The most frequently targeted breeds (or breed mixes) are pit bulls, rottweilers, Dobermans, German shepherds, chows, Akitas, and Great Danes. Mott notes that bans are often passed after fatal dog attacks occur. Some jurisdictions ban breeds outright, whereas others require owners to carry liability insurance or muzzle their animals in public.

Many animal protection organizations and industry groups, including the AKC and the American Society for the Prevention of Cruelty to Animals, are opposed to breed-specific legislation. They believe that irresponsible breeders and pet owners should be targeted instead, particularly those who train dogs to be aggressive or refuse to keep their dogs fenced or on leashes. Better enforcement of existing animal control legislation is seen as a more effective measure than breed-specific bans. Mott mentions an Ohio law that was passed in 1987 that deems pit bulls to be "vicious" dogs but does not ban them. Owners are required to carry $100,000 liability insurance policies and properly confine and control their dogs at all times.

IMPORTANT NAMES AND ADDRESSES

American Anti-Vivisection Society
801 Old York Rd., #204
Jenkintown, PA 19046
(215) 887-0816
URL: http://www.aavs.org/

American Humane Association
63 Inverness Dr. E
Englewood, CO 80112
(303) 792-9900
FAX: (303) 792-5333
URL: http://www.americanhumane.org/

American Meat Institute
1150 Connecticut Ave. NW, Twelfth Floor
Washington, DC 20036
(202) 587-4200
FAX: (202) 587-4300
URL: http://www.meatami.com/

American Pet Products Manufacturers Association
255 Glenville Rd.
Greenwich, CT 06831
(203) 532-0000
1-800-452-1225
FAX: (203) 532-0551
URL: http://www.appma.org/

American Rescue Dog Association
PO Box 613
Bristow, VA 20136
E-mail: information@ardainc.org
URL: http://www.ardainc.org/

American Society for the Prevention of Cruelty to Animals
(212) 876-7700
E-mail: humane1@aspca.org
URL: http://www.aspca.org/

American Veterinary Medical Association
1931 N. Meacham Rd., Ste. 100
Schaumburg, IL 60173
(847) 925-8070
FAX: (847) 925-1329
E-mail: avmainfo@avma.org
URL: http://www.avma.org/

Animal and Plant Health Inspection Service
U.S. Department of Agriculture
4700 River Rd.
Riverdale, MD 20737
URL: http://www.aphis.usda.gov/

Animal Concerns
EnvironLink Network
PO Box 8102
Pittsburgh, PA 15217
E-mail: support@animalconcerns.org
URL: http://www.animalconcerns.org/

Animal Legal Defense Fund
170 E. Cotati Ave.
Cotati, CA 94931
(707) 795-2533
FAX: (707) 795-7270
E-mail: info@aldf.org
URL: http://www.aldf.org/

Animal People
PO Box 960
Clinton, WA 98236
(360) 579-2505
FAX: (360) 579-2575
E-mail: anpeople@whidbey.com
URL: http://www.animalpeoplenews.org/

Animal Protection Institute
1122 S St.
Sacramento, CA 95814
(916) 447-3085
FAX: (916) 447-3070
E-mail: info@api4animals.org
URL: http://www.api4animals.org/

Animal Welfare Information Center
National Agricultural Library
10301 Baltimore Ave., Room 410
Beltsville, MD 20705
(301) 504-6212
FAX: (301) 504-7125
E-mail: awic@nal.usda.gov
URL: http://www.nal.usda.gov/awic/

Animal Welfare Institute
PO Box 3650
Washington, DC 20027
(703) 836-4300
FAX: (703) 836-0400
E-mail: awi@awionline.org
URL: http://www.awionline.org/

Animals Voice
1354 E. Ave., #R-252
Chico, CA 95926
1-800-828-6423
E-mail: veda@animalsvoice.com
URL: http://www.animalsvoice.com/

Association of Veterinarians for Animal Rights
PO Box 208
Davis, CA 95617-0208
(530) 759-8106
FAX: (530) 759-8116
E-mail: info@avar.org
URL: http://AVAR.org/

Association of Zoos and Aquariums
8403 Colesville Rd., Ste. 710
Silver Spring, MD 20910-3314
(301) 562-0777
FAX: (301) 562-0888
E-mail: G.e.n.e.r.a.l.I.n.q.u.i.r.y.@aza.org
URL: http://www.aza.org/

Best Friends Animal Society
5001 Angel Canyon Rd.
Kanab, UT 84741-5000
(435) 644-2001
E-mail: info@bestfriends.org
URL: http://www.bestfriends.org/

Centers for Disease Control and Prevention
1600 Clifton Rd.
Atlanta, GA 30333
(404) 639-3311
1-800-311-3435
URL: http://www.cdc.gov/

Compassion Over Killing
PO Box 9773
Washington, DC 20016
(301) 891-2458
E-mail: info@cok.net
URL: http://www.cok.net/

Defenders of Wildlife
1130 Seventeenth St. NW
Washington, DC 20036
1-800-385-9712
E-mail: defenders@mail.defenders.org
URL: http://www.defenders.org/

Delta Society
875 124th Ave. NE, Ste. 101
Bellevue, WA 98005-2531
(425) 679-5500
FAX: (425) 679-5539
E-mail: info@deltasociety.org
URL: http://www.deltasociety.org/

Economic Research Service
1800 M St. NW
Washington, DC 20036-5831
(202) 694-5050
1-800-999-6779
E-mail: InfoCenter@ers.usda.gov
URL: http://www.ers.usda.gov/

Farm Animal Reform Movement
10101 Ashburton
Bethesda, MD 20817
1-888-ASK-FARM
E-mail: info@farmusa.org
URL: http://www.farmusa.org/

Farm Sanctuary
PO Box 150
Watkins Glen, NY 14891
(607) 583-2225
FAX: (607) 583-2041
E-mail: info@farmsanctuary.org
URL: http://www.farmsanctuary.org/

Friends of Animals
777 Post Rd., Ste. 205
Darien, CT 06820
(203) 656-1522
FAX: (203) 656-0267
E-mail: info@friendsofanimals.org
URL: http://www.friendsofanimals.org/

Friends of Fur
PO Box 13
Powassan, Ontario
Canada P0H 1Z0
URL: http://www.friends-of-fur.org/

Fund for Animals
200 W. Fifty-Seventh St.
New York, NY 10019
1-888-405-3863
E-mail: info@fundforanimals.org
URL: http://www.fundforanimals.org/

GREY2K USA Education Fund
PO Box 440142
Somerville, MA 02144

(617) 666-3526
1-866-2GREY2K
FAX: (617) 666-3568
E-mail: info@grey2kusaedu.org
URL: http://www.grey2kusaedu.org/

Greyhound Protection League
PO Box 669
Penn Valley, CA 95946
1-800-446-8637
URL: http://www.greyhounds.org/

Guide Dog Users Inc.
14311 Astrodome Dr.
Silver Spring, MD 20906
(301) 598-5771
1-888-858-1008
FAX: (301) 871-7591
URL: http://www.gdui.org/

Guide Horse Foundation
PO Box 511
Kittrell, NC 27544
(252) 433-8448
E-mail: info@guidehorse.com
URL: http://www.guidehorse.org/

Humane Farming Association
PO Box 3577
San Rafael, CA 94912
(415) 771-CALF
FAX: (415) 485-0106
E-mail: hfa@hfa.org
URL: http://www.hfa.org/

Humane Society of the United States
2100 L St. NW
Washington, DC 20037
(202) 452-1100
URL: http://www.hsus.org/

In Defense of Animals
3010 Kerner Blvd.
San Rafael, CA 94901
(415) 388-9641
FAX: (415) 388-0388
E-mail: ida@idausa.org
URL: http://www.idausa.org/

International Association of Assistance Dog Partners
38691 Filly Dr.
Sterling Heights, MI 48310
(586) 826-3938
E-mail: iaadp@aol.com
URL: http://www.iaadp.org/

International Fund for Animal Welfare
411 Main St.
PO Box 193
Yarmouth Port, MA 02675
(508) 744-2000
1-800-932-4329
FAX: (508) 744-2009
E-mail: info@ifaw.org
URL: http://www.ifaw.org/

International Institute for Animal Law
30 N. LaSalle St., Ste. 2900
Chicago, IL 60602
(312) 917-8850
FAX: (312) 263-5013
E-mail: iial@animallawintl.org
URL: http://www.animallawintl.org/

International Professional Rodeo Association
130 E. Yavapai St.
Wickenburg, AZ 85390
(928) 684-5000
FAX: (928) 543-2006
E-mail: info@iprarodeo.com
URL: http://www.iprarodeo.com/

International Sled Dog Racing Association
E-mail: dsteele@brainerd.net
URL: http://www.isdra.org/

Jane Goodall Institute
4245 N. Fairfax Dr., Ste. 600
Arlington, VA 22203
(703) 682-9220
FAX: (703) 682-9312
E-mail: webmaster@janegoodall.org
URL: http://www.janegoodall.org/

Jockey Club
40 E. Fifty-Second St.
New York, NY 10022
(212) 371-5970
FAX: (212) 371-6123
URL: http://jockeyclub.com/

Johns Hopkins University Center for Alternatives to Animal Testing
111 Market Place, Ste. 840
Baltimore, MD 21202-6709
(410) 223-1692
FAX: (410) 223-1603
E-mail: caat@jhsph.edu
URL: http://caat.jhsph.edu/

Last Chance for Animals
8033 Sunset Blvd., #835
Los Angeles, CA 90046
(310) 271-6096
FAX: (310) 271-1890
URL: http://www.lcanimal.org/

Maddie's Fund
2223 Santa Clara Ave., Ste. B
Alameda, CA 94501-4416
(510) 337-8989
FAX: (510) 337-8988
E-mail: info@maddiesfund.org
URL: http://www.maddiesfund.org/

Michigan Society for Medical Research
PO Box 3237
Ann Arbor, MI 48106-3237
(734) 763-8029
FAX: (734) 930-1568
E-mail: mismr@umich.edu
URL: http://www.mismr.org/

National Agricultural Statistics Service
U.S. Department of Agriculture
1400 Independence Ave. SW
Washington, DC 20250
1-800-727-9540
E-mail: nass@nass.usda.gov
URL: http://www.nass.usda.gov/

National Animal Interest Alliance
PO Box 66579
Portland, OR 97266
(503) 761-1139
E-mail: naia@naiaonline.org
URL: http://www.naiaonline.org/

National Association for Biomedical
Research
818 Connecticut Ave. NW, Ste. 900
Washington, DC 20006
(202) 857-0540
FAX: (202) 659-1902
E-mail: info@nabr.org
URL: http://www.nabr.org/

National Association for Search and
Rescue
PO Box 232020
Centreville, VA 20120-2020
(703) 222-6277
1-877-893-0702
FAX: (703) 222-6277
E-mail: info@nasar.org
URL: http://www.nasar.org/

National Chicken Council
1015 Fifteenth St. NW, Ste. 930
Washington, DC 20005-2622
(202) 296-2622
FAX: (202) 293-4005
E-mail: ncc@chickenusa.org
URL: http://www.nationalchickencouncil.com/

National Greyhound Association
PO Box 543
Abilene, KS 67410
(785) 263-4660
E-mail: nga@ngagreyhounds.com
URL: http://www.ngagreyhounds.com/

National Institute for Animal Agriculture
1910 Lyda Ave.
Bowling Green, KY 42104-5809
(270) 782-9798
FAX: (270) 782-0188
E-mail: NIAA@animalagriculture.org
URL: http://www.animalagriculture.org/

National Pork Producers Council
10664 Justin Dr.
Urbandale, IA 50322
(515) 278-8012
FAX: (515) 278-8011
URL: http://www.nppc.org/

National Trappers Association
524 Fifth St.
Bedford, IN 47421-2247
(812) 277-9670

FAX: (812) 277-9672
E-mail: ntaheadquarters@nationaltrappers.com
URL: http://www.nationaltrappers.com/

National Wildlife Federation
11100 Wildlife Center Dr.
Reston, VA 20190-5362
1-800-822-9919
URL: http://www.nwf.org/

New England Anti-Vivisection Society
333 Washington St., Ste. 850
Boston, MA 02190
1-800-822-9919
URL: http://www.neavs.org/

North American Riding for the
Handicapped Association
PO Box 33150
Denver, CO 80233
1-800-369-7433
FAX: (303) 252-4610
URL: http://www.narha.org/

Outdoor Amusement Business
Association
1035 S. Semoran Blvd., Ste. 1045A
Winter Park, FL 32792
(407) 681-9444
1-800-517-OABA
FAX: (407) 681-9445
URL: http://www.oaba.org/

People for the Ethical Treatment of
Animals
501 Front St.
Norfolk, VA 23510
(757) 622-7382
URL: http://www.peta.org/

Performing Animal Welfare Society
PO Box 849
Galt, CA 95632
(209) 745-2606
FAX: (209) 745-1809
E-mail: info@pawsweb.org
URL: http://www.pawsweb.org/

Pet-Abuse.Com
PO Box 5
Southfields, NY 10975
1-888-523-PETS
E-mail: info@pet-abuse.com
URL: http://www.pet-abuse.com/

Professional Rodeo Cowboys
Association
101 Pro Rodeo Dr.
Colorado Springs, CO 80919
(719) 528-4794
URL: http://www.prorodeo.org/

Scientists Center for Animal Welfare
7833 Walker Dr., Ste. 410
Greenbelt, MD 20770
(301) 345-3500
FAX: (301) 345-3503

E-mail: info@scaw.com
URL: http://www.scaw.com/

Showing Animals Respect
and Kindness
PO Box 28
Geneva, IL 60134
(630) 557-0176
FAX: (630) 557-0178
URL: http://www.sharkonline.org/

Sled Dog Action Coalition
PO Box 562061
Miami, FL 33256
E-mail: SledDogAC@aol.com
URL: http://www.helpsleddogs.org/

Society and Animals Forum
PO Box 1297
Washington Grove, MD 20880-1297
(301) 963-4751
E-mail: kshapiro@societyandanimalsforum.org
URL: http://www.psyeta.org/

Society for Animal Protective
Legislation
PO Box 3719
Washington, DC 20027
(703) 836-4300
E-mail: sapl@saplonline.org
URL: http://www.saplonline.org/

Spay/USA
2261 Broadridge Ave.
Stratford, CT 06614
URL: http://www.spayusa.org/

Therapy Dogs International
88 Bartley Rd.
Flanders, NJ 07836
(973) 252-9800
FAX: (973) 252-7171
E-mail: tdi@gti.net
URL: http://www.tdi-dog.org/

TRAFFIC North America
1250 Twenty-Fourth St. NW
Washington, DC 20037
(202) 293-4800
FAX: (202) 775-8287
E-mail: tna@wwfus.org
URL: http://www.traffic.org/

United Gamefowl Breeders
Association
PO Box 98
Albany, OH 45710
(740) 698-0841
FAX: (740) 698-9992
E-mail: sandy.johnson14@verizon.net
URL: http://www.pitmaster.com/ugba/

United Poultry Concerns
PO Box 150
Machipongo, VA 23405-0150
(757) 678-7875
FAX: (757) 678-5070

E-mail: info@upc-online.org
URL: http://www.upc-online.org/

U.S. Bureau of Land Management
Office of Public Affairs
1849 C St., Room 406-LS
Washington, DC 20240
(202) 452-5125
FAX: (202) 452-5124
E-mail: woinfo@blm.gov
URL: http://www.blm.gov/

U.S. Fish and Wildlife Service
U.S. Department of Interior
1849 C St. NW
Washington, DC 20242
1-800-344-WILD
URL: http://www.fws.gov/

U.S. Police Canine Association
PO Box 80
Springboro, OH 45066
1-800-531-1614
URL: http://www.uspcak9.com/

U.S. Poultry and Egg
Association
1530 Cooledge Rd.
Tucker, GA 30084-7303
(770) 493-9401
FAX: (770) 493-9257
URL: http://www.poultryegg.org/

U.S. Sportsmen's Alliance
801 Kingsmill Pkwy.
Columbus, OH 43229
(614) 888-4868

FAX: (614) 888-0326
E-mail: info@ussportsmen.org
URL: http://www.wlfa.org/

Veal Farm
Veal Issue Management
PO Box 900
Antioch, IL 60002
(847) 395-4832
E-mail: info@vealfarm.com
URL: http://www.vealfarm.com/

Wildlife Society
5410 Grosvenor Lane
Bethesda, MD 20814-2144
(301) 897-9770
FAX: (301) 530-2471
URL: http://www.wildlife.org/

RESOURCES

Several resources useful to this book were published by agencies of the U.S. Department of Agriculture, including the Economic Research Service, National Agricultural Statistics Service, Animal and Plant Health Inspection Service, and Food Safety and Inspection Service. Other federal agencies providing information were the U.S. Fish and Wildlife Service, U.S. Customs and Border Protection, Centers for Disease Control and Prevention, National Science Board, National Institutes of Health, U.S. Food and Drug Administration, U.S. Forest Service, National Park Service, Bureau of Land Management, National Marine Fisheries Service, and U.S. Department of Labor.

The U.S. Government Accountability Office (GAO) is the investigative arm of Congress. One GAO publication used for this book was *Wildlife Services Program: Information on Activities to Manage Wildlife Damage* (November 2001).

State agencies and educational institutions providing information included Alberta Farm Animal Care (Canada), American Academy of Child and Adolescent Psychiatry, California Horse Racing Board, Cambridge University Veterinary School, Colorado State University, Georgia Department of Natural Resources, Massachusetts Institute of Technology, McCormick Library of Special Collections, Office of the Statue Auditor of Missouri, Oregon State University, Smithsonian Institution, the State University of New Jersey Rutgers Cooperative Extension, Tufts University School of Veterinary Medicine, University of Arizona, University of Nebraska—Lincoln, University of Saskatchewan College of Agriculture, University of South Carolina, and the Virginia Cooperative Extension. The University of New Mexico School of Law, Center for Wildlife Law, and Michigan State University Animal Legal and Historical Center were invaluable resources for legal documents.

Information on animal industries and businesses was obtained from associations including the American Greyhound Council, American Kennel Club, American Meat Institute, American Pet Products Manufacturers Association, American Veal Association, Association of Zoos and Aquariums, Food Marketing Institute, Fur Industry Council of America, International Sled Dog Racing Association, International Whaling Commission, National Council of Chain Restaurants, National Pork Producers Council, National Renderers Association, National Turkey Federation, Outdoor Amusement Business Association, Pet Industry Joint Advisory Council, Jockey Club, U.S. Fur Commission, and U.S. Trotting Association.

The Web sites of the Ringling Brothers and Barnum and Bailey Circus, Hanneford Family Circus, and Florida Canine Academy were informative. Temple Grandin's Web site (http://www.grandin.com/) was particularly useful as a resource on animal husbandry and slaughtering in the modern agriculture industry.

Organizations involved in animal issues that provided helpful statistics and information include the American Prosecutors Research Institute, American Veterinary Medical Association, Arkonline.com, Assistance Dogs International, Foundation for Biomedical Research, Michigan Society for Medical Research, Minnesota Foundation for Responsible Animal Care, MountedPolice.com, National Alternative Pet Association, National Association for Search and Rescue, Physician's Committee for Responsible Medicine, RDS: Understanding Animal Research in Medicine, U.S. Police Canine Association, U.S. Sportsmen's Alliance, and U.S. War Dog Association. The following resources describe a variety of issues that also affect animals: *The Ecologist* magazine, Monterey Bay Aquarium, Sierra Club, *Society and Animals: Journal of Human-Animal Studies*, Union of Concerned Scientists, United Egg Producers, and *Vegetarian Journal*.

Historical articles and exhibits that proved useful were provided by the Web sites of the Agropolis Museum (France), Brooklyn College at City University of New York, Cairo Museum, Carnegie Museum of Natural History, Chicago Historical Society, Cleveland Museum of

Art, Cleveland Museum of Natural History, Dickinson College, Kashmiri Overseas Association, Liverpool John Moores University, Minnesota State University, San Jose State University, Art Institute of Chicago, Institute of Human Origins, U.S. Armor Association, University College (Canada), University of Michigan, University of Newcastle, Museum of Antiquities (UK), and Jacques Maritain Center at the University of Notre Dame.

A wealth of information was obtained from groups devoted to the causes of animal protection, welfare, and rights. These include Alley Cat Allies, American Humane Association, Animal Legal Defense Fund, Animal News Center, Animal People, Animal Protection Institute, Animal Rescue Foundation, Animal Welfare Institute, Association of Veterinarians for Animal Rights, Best Friends Animal Sanctuary, Blue Horse Charities, Defenders of Wildlife, Doris Day Animal League, Farm Sanctuary, Friends of Animals, Fund for Animals, Greyhound Protection League, Humane Society of the United States, In Defense of Animals, Last Chance for Animals, Maddie's Fund, National Anti-Vivisection Society, New England Anti-Vivisection Society, NoPuppyMills.com, People for the Ethical Treatment of Animals, Petabuse .com, Society and Animals Forum, Showing Animals Respect and Kindness, Sled Dog Action Coalition, Elephant Sanctuary, and United Poultry Concerns.

Animal rights activists and opponents have written some important books that were valuable resources for this work. They include *Beast and Man: The Roots of Human Nature* (1978) and *Animals and Why They Matter* (1983) by Mary Midgley, *Animal Liberation: A New Ethics for Our Treatment of Animals* (1975) by Peter Singer, *Animals, Property, and the Law* (1995) by Gary L. Francione, *Putting Humans First: Why We Are Nature's Favorite* (2004) by Tibor R. Machan, *The Animal Rights Debate* (2001) by Carl Cohen and Tom Regan, *The Case for Animal Rights* (1983) by Tom Regan, *Interests and Rights: The Case against Animals* (1980) and *Rights, Killing, and Suffering: Moral Vegetarianism and Applied Ethics* (1983) by Raymond G. Frey, *The Animals Issue: Moral Theory in Practice* (1992) by Peter Carruthers, *Speciesism* (2004) by Joan Dunayer, *The Animal Rights Crusade: The Growth of a Moral Protest* (1992) by James M. Jasper and Dorothy Nelkin, and *Animal Liberators: Research and Morality* (1988) by Susan Sperling.

The following news organizations and outlets were useful for providing timely stories related to animals: ABC News, *ActionLine*, *Animal Law Section*, *Animal People News*, Animal Planet, *Animal Sheltering*, Associated Press, *Atlanta Journal and Constitution*, BBC News, *Benton County Daily Record*, *Blood-Horse Magazine*, *Boston Globe*, *British Medical Journal*, *Charlotte Observer*, *Columbus Dispatch*, Discovery Communications, *Emerging Infectious Diseases*, *Ethics and Animals*, *International Herald Tribune*, *JAVMA News*, *Journal of Applied Animal Welfare Science*, *Journal of Wildlife Management*, KMOX Radio (St. Louis), *Lancet*, *Los Angeles Times*, *Miami Herald*, *Morbidity and Mortality Weekly Report*, *Morning News*, *National Geographic News*, *Nature*, *New England Journal of Medicine*, *New York Times*, *Oregonian*, *Renews*, *Sacramento Bee*, *Scientific American*, *St. Louis Post-Dispatch*, *Tampa Tribune*, Time.com, *USA Today*, *U.S. News & World Report*, *WAGER: Weekly Addiction Gambling Education Report*, *Washington Post*, and *Washington Times*. The *Frontline* documentary *A Whale of a Business* (November 1997) was very helpful. The Gallup Organization supplied polling results on animal issues.

INDEX

DATE DUE

AUG 11 2009		
NOV 19 2009		
DEC 20 2010		
APR 26 2012		
DEC 05 2012		